# THE ANUNNAKI GUIDEBOOK

## The Sumerian gods are the Greek gods

WILLIAM A. HINSON

# THE ANUNNAKI GUIDEBOOK

## The Sumerian gods are the Greek gods

**The Anunnaki Guidebook**



Researched and Compiled by William A. Hinson

Dedicated to the memory

of the man who started it all

**ZECHARIA SITCHIN**

# CONTENTS

# INTRODUCTION

The *Sumerian King List* allegedly recorded all the rulers of Earth over 400,000 years who were said to be gods, demigods, or immortals . . . or one soul playing all the roles.

In *Sumerian Mythology* the Anunnaki were a pantheon of good and evil gods and goddesses (duality) who came to Earth to create the human race. According to some resources, these gods came from Nibiru - 'Planet of the Crossing.' The Assyrians and Babylonians called the planet 'Marduk', after their chief god. The Sumerians believed one year on the planet Nibiru, called a sar, was equivalent in time to 3,600 Earth years. The Anunnaki therefore had lifespans that were 120 sars which is 120 x 3,600 or 432,000 years. According to the *Sumerian King List* - 120 sars had passed from the time the Anunnaki arrived on Earth to the time of the Great Flood.

According to *Ancient Alien Theory,* the Anunnaki, and other alien groups, came to Earth and seeded the human race in many variations. This research was lead by Zecharah Sitchin and Erich von Däniken among others, you can see much of their research on the *History Channel Series - Ancient Aliens* – which is also found on YouTube.

This physical evidence of ancient astronauts can be found throughout our planet, leading one to conclude that different races visited here at different periods in Earth's history, or the same aliens return and set up various civilizations in which they could inhabit and experience.

In the first large civilization on earth, ancient Mesopotamia, we must first look at the Sumerian and Akkadian mythologies. The Sumerians were the first civilization on our planet to put their stories down in writing, and the first to establish the names and histories of their many gods. The Sumerian gods include the following examples: Enki, the god of water and wisdom; Ninhursag, the earth mother; Dumuzi, the shepherd; Inanna, the goddess of love and war; Ereshkigal, the goddess of the underworld . . . and the list goes on. The Akkadian civilization which replaced the Sumerian civilization, changed the name of the original gods.

The Babylonians replaced the Akkadian civilization and changed the stories around. The Babylonians believed in a male dominated society, they were the first to introduce the concepts of good and evil. The snake became a symbol of evil, women became chaos, and daemons (the intermediaries) became the modern demons. Some of the Babylonian gods included: Ishtar, the goddess of love and war; Ea, the god of wisdom; Nintu (Mami, Belet-Ili), the mother of gods; Tammuz, the shepherd; Irkalla, the goddess of the underworld. Do you see some similarities?

The Egyptian gods and goddesses: Osiris, the god of the dead, ruler of the underworld; Sekhmet, god of war; and Hathor, goddess of love.

In the Greek myths, the gods and goddesses are similar with the others. Ares, the god of war; Aphrodite, the goddess of love; Athena, the goddess of wisdom; Hades, the god of the underworld.

If you read these mythologies in chronological order (from Sumerian gods, to Akkadian gods, to Babylonian gods, to Egyptian gods, to Greek gods and to Roman gods), you will find that the names and point of view changes, but their attributes are virtually identical. However, the Sumerians were more nature-based, they did not have the concepts of good and evil. By the time we get to the Babylonians, their stories are more masculine in nature. You will find words in their stories that you will not find in the Sumerian stories. The Babylonians introduced the concept of good and evil, their women had to ask permission, they had no voice. These stories suggest that their society would control nature.

This is the same concept in Greek and Egyptian mythologies, they were also more society based rather than Nature based.

It is the author's conclusion, that these early Sumerian gods (the Anunnaki) were the same gods of later civilizations. Many of their characteristics match or are very similar to the gods of later civilizations or cultures. The early Greeks themselves even stated that their gods came from the Mediterranean area via Crete. In this my latest work I have provided a list of these gods in a guidebook, which will help the reader better understand the similar or different attributes these gods had through many civilizations and cultures.

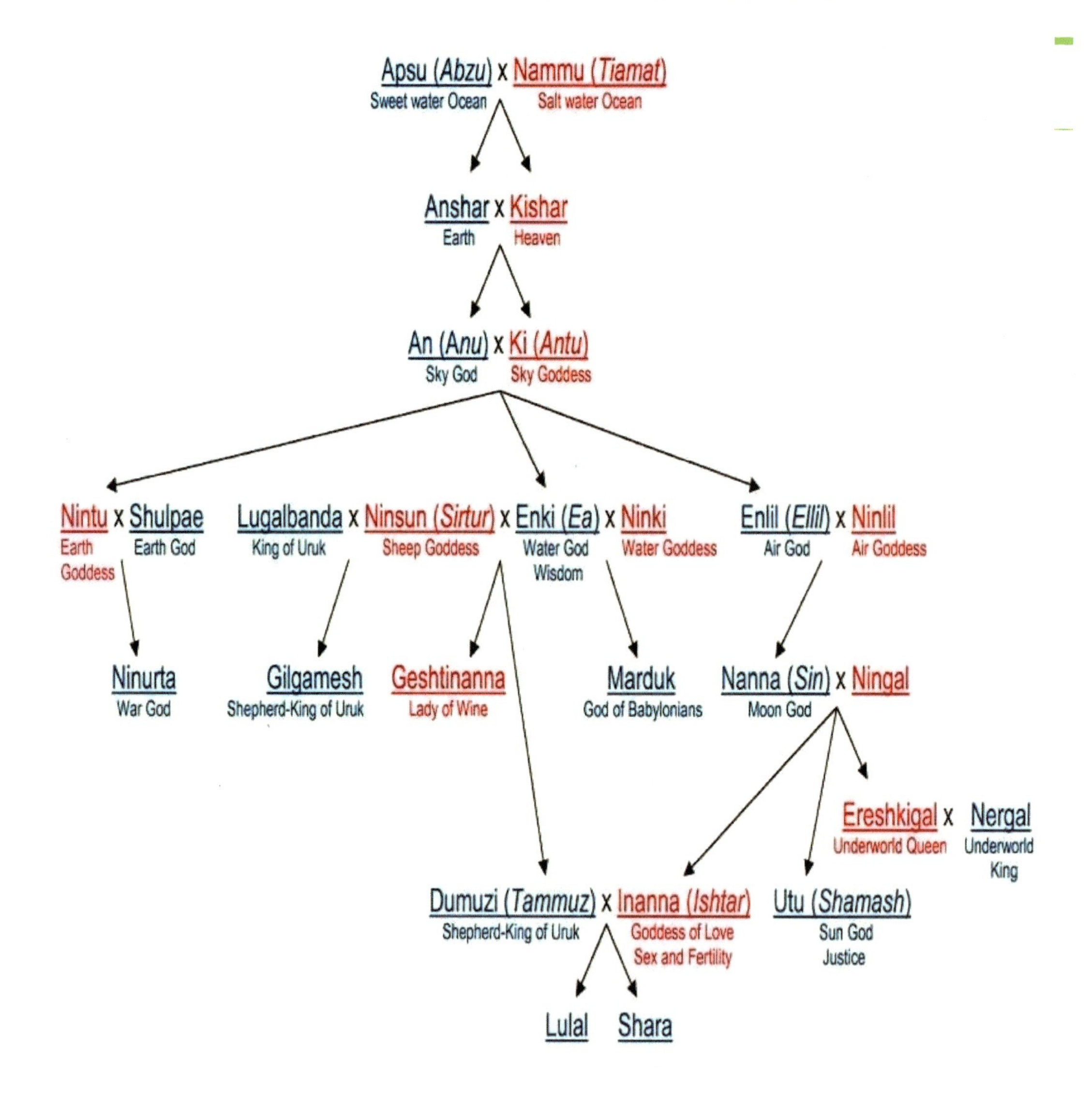


## Aba.el (Abel)

Hevel by the Sumerians. Aba or Atab by the Akkadians. Abel or Abael by the Hebrews. Adapa (adam) and Khawa (Eve) mated and bore twin sons, whom they name Qayin (Kain) and Hevel (Abel). Kain through the guidance of NIN.UR.TA, was instructed in the sowing and reaping of the grains the Nephilim gave to Adapa. His brother Abael through the guidance of MAR.DUK, was instructed in the birthing and raising of animals. After a time, and following the growing of crops by Kain and the raising of sheep by

Abael, they and the products of their labor were presented to EN.LIL and EN.KI. Both earthling sons were praised by EN.LIL, but only Abael received praise from EN.KI. Abael boasted of EN.KI's praise to Kain, and it angered Kain. Eventually the anger grew so deeply in Kain, and he raised a stone and brought it crashing down on the head of his brother, Abael. The life-essence of Abael flowed from his body. When EN.KI was told of what had happened, and of the death of his son, MAR.DUK's apprentice, EN.KI became very enraged, and cursed Kain.

Brought before a council of the *Seven Who Judge,* it was urged by MAR.DUK that Kain be put to death. But EN.KI argued, successfully that he should simply be exiled from the edin. To put him to death would eliminate one avenue for additional earthling procreation and increase. EN.KI's suggestion of exile was agreed upon by the *Seven Who Judge,* and therefore, Kain was allowed to remain alive, but to be forever banished from the Edin. As a sign for all who later would encounter Kain or his descendants, his life-essence was altered so that he would never be capable of growing a beard upon his face.

## Abraham (Abram)

Abram, Abraham, Avram or Ibrahim, son of Terah (Tara) and Amthelo. Abraham the well known founder of the Jewish people.

*The Book of Jasher,* Chapter 7:50-51 - And Terah took a wife and her name was Amthelo the daughter of Cornebo; and the wife of Terah conceived and bare him a son in those days. Terah was seventy years old when he begat him, and Terah called the name of his son that was born to him Abram, because the king had raised him in those days, and dignified him above all his princes that were with him.

Terah took Abram his son and Lot his grandson, the son of Harran, and Sarai his daughter-in-law the wife of Abram his son; and they left and went forth from Ur of the Chaldees to go to the land of Canaan. Near the city of Haran, there was a place that bore Terah's name, known to the Assyrians as Turahi, and to the Akkadians as Turahu.

Terah was an Oracle Priest, one assigned to approaching the "Stone that Whispers" to hear the deity's words and communicate them to the lay hierarchy. It was a function assumed in later times by the Israelite High Priest, who alone was allowed to enter the Holy of Holies, approach the Dvir ("Speaker"), and "hear the voice (of the Lord) speak unto him from off the overlay which is upon the Ark of the Covenant, from between the two Cherubim." During the Israelite Exodus, at Mount Sinai the Lord proclaimed that his covenant with the descendants of Abraham meant that "ye shall be unto me a kingdom of priest." It was a statement that reflected the status of Abraham's own descent: a royal priesthood.

Abraham worshipped El Shaddai (El Elyon) *Genesis* 14:17-24. There exists from Babylonia an early clay tablet that bears the name of a man called Abi-ramu, and the name is rendered as Abarama in the Eblaite tablets. Another bears the name of Sarai, but whether these were the Abram and Sari of the Genesis record or not, we have no way of knowing. Josephus quotes the Babylonian historian Berosus, as saying, "In the tenth generation after the Flood, there was a man among the Chaldeans who was righteous and great..." Josephus regarded this remark as a direct reference to Abraham, even though Berosus did not actually name him. Abraham was, however, named by Hecataeus and by Nicolaus of Damascus.

*The Book of Jasher,* Chapter 8:1-4 - And it was in the night that Abram was born, that all the servants of Terah, and all the wise men of Nimrod, and his conjurors came and ate and drank in the house of Terah, and they rejoiced with him on that night. And when all the wise men and conjurors went out from the house of Terah, they lifted up their eyes toward heaven that night to look at the stars, and they saw, and behold one very large star came from the east and ran in the heavens, and he swallowed up the four stars from the four sides of the heavens. And all the wise men of the king and his conjurors were astonished at the sight, and the sages understood this matter, and they knew its import. And they said to each other, this only betokens the child that has been born to Terah this night, who will grow up and be fruitful, and multiply, and possess all the earth, he and his children for ever, and he and his seed will slay great kings, and inherit their lands.

*The Book of Jasher,* Chapter 8: 10-11 - And when thy servants went out from the house of Terah, to go to our respective homes to abide there for the night, we lifted up our eyes to heaven, and we saw a great star coming from the east, and the same star ran with great speed, and swallowed up four great stars, from the four sides of the heavens. And thy servants were astonished at the sight which we saw, and were greatly terrified, and we made our judgement upon the sight, and knew by our wisdom the proper interpretation thereof, that this thing applies to the child that is born to Terah, who will grow up and multiply greatly, and become powerful, and kill all the kings of the earth, and inherit all their lands, he and his seed forever.

*The Book of Judith* 3:6-9 - This people (Hyksos-Habiru-Hebrons-Hebrews) are descended of the Chaldeans: and they sojourned heretofore in Mesopotamia, because they would not follow the gods of their fathers, which were in the land of Chaldea. For they left the way of their ancestors, and worshipped the God of heaven, the God (Enlil) whom they knew: so they cast them out from the face of their gods, and they fled into Mesopotamia, and sojourned there many days. Then their God commanded them to depart from the place where they sojourned, and to go into the land of Canaan: where they dwelt.

According to the Biblical narrative, Jehovah encouraged Abraham to leave Ur and settle in Haran-a caravan center in northeastern Mesopotamia. From there, Jehovah told Abraham to lead his tribe on a migration towards Egypt. So the Hebrews made their way through Canaan towards the Nile River. Starvation finally forced the tribe to enter the Egyptian region of

Goshen where the Hebrews at first lived well under the pharaoh, but upon the coming of a new king to the Egyptian throne, the Hebrews were forced into slavery.

The Bible states that after four hundred years of slavery in Egypt, the Hebrews were led on an exodus out of Egypt by Moses under the watchful eye of Jehovah.

*The Spear of Destiny,* by Trevor Ravenscroft, cr1973, p.286 - The Jasper Vessel was contained within the bowl of a large Silver Chalice, which was reputed to have been handed by the mysterious figure of Melchizedek to Abraham, the Founder of the Jewish Race. It later came into the hands of Joseph of Arimathea in whose Upper Room the Last Supper took place.

*The Cup of Destiny,* by Trevor Ravenscroft, cr1982, p.153 - This cup is first mentioned in the Old Testament when Melchizedek serves the sacraments of bread and wine to Abraham. Melchizedek, the high priest of the sun oracle situated on Mount Zion, presents the cup to Abraham when he makes the prophecy regarding the future destiny of the Israelites. 'Thy seed shall be numbered according to thc stars.' Thus we see that the cup was associated from the very beginning with the star wisdom which is later characteristic of the quest for the Grail. The Old Testament is a most profound work in which the seed of Abraham is governed by the stars to create a body which shall be a vessel for the Messiah.

## ABAROS (Armaros)

ABAROS, ARMAROS, ARMERS, ARMEN, PHARMAROS, AREAROS was one of the “fallen angels” as listed in *Enoch I.* Armaros taught "the resolving of enchantments," and in Chapter 8:4, "the solution of sorcery."

## ABBADONA (Satanon)

ABBADONA or SATANON, a “fallen angel”, a seraph, at one time the chosen companion of the faithful human female Abdiel. (See En.ki/Poseidon)

## ABGAL (Triton)

ABGAL is the name of a group of water creatures in the mythology of the ancient Sumerians in lower Mesopotamia. The seven spirits in the group are also known as APKALLU or AMPHITRITES. Portrayed as part man/woman and part fish, the Abgal are protective guardians of the realm. They derive from the earlier Apsu or Abzu in the entourage of Enki, the god of wisdom. Their role was that of tutor to the nation, teaching the sciences and arts while fasting during the day, then returning to the waters at nightfall.

TRITON the son of Poseidon (Enki) and Amphitrite. The TRITONS were Mermen of the Mediterranean, with fish-like tails, scales on the body, sharp fish teeth, and webbed fingers with long claws. They could change the tail to legs and walk on land. Their father was a peaceful, helpful deity who assisted sailors in trouble and caused the seas to calm by blowing on his conch shell. His sons, however, were carousers in seaports, causing all kinds of trouble. It was the duty of the Tritons to harness dolphins to Oceanus' chariot and blow conch horns as they swarmed before the Lord of the Ocean.

The original Triton was said to have been female, but most images from ancient times are those of a male. The Tritons are the sons of Poseidon/Neptune and Amphitrite and are described as having humanoid bodies covered in fishes' scales with tails like those of a dolphin. Their heads have matted green or yellow hair, with gills behind their pointed ears, and their wide mouths have huge, fang-like teeth. They are the escorts of the Nereid sea nymphs and the attendants of the sea deities. They precede the sea god.

MERMEN is the male counterpart of the sea-dwelling being known as the mermaid. Like her, he appears in the form of a human above the waist with green hair and beard, but below the waist is the tail of a large fish. The Mermen have a reputation for more terrifying behavior than even the mermaids and can be held responsible for violent storms and sinking ships. They are also thought in British legends to be aggressive toward the mermaids and even devour their own offspring, whereas in the Scandinavian legends the Havmand is more benign. The traditions of Mermen may have been derived from the Abgal of ancient Sumer. The image of the Merman has become familiar in the heraldic repertoire of Europe.

MERMAIDS or MEREMAIDENS is the name of a female water being in the form of a beautiful young woman from the head to the waist, the rest of her body being like the tail of a huge fish. Mermaids have been part of folklore and mythology of maritime and freshwater cultures since ancient times. The derivation of the English name means both "sea" and "lake" maiden, however there are many different regional names in the British Isles, such as the Ben Varrey, Ceasg, Clytie, Gwenhidwy, Liban, Mari Morgan, Merrow, Roane, and Selkie.

The Mermaids are often seen sitting on rocks holding a mirror and combing their long hair whilst singing and enticing curious sailors to come closer to the dangerous rocks. It is this singing that allies them to the Sirens, luring sailors to their doom. Even the ancient accounts, as well as the more modern ones, mention the appearance of these supernaturals in conjunction with misfortune and disaster, although occasionally they can be benevolent. In regional tales from Scotland, Wales, and Cornwall in England, when rescued they have given humans the knowledge of herbal cures for fatal sickness, other rich gifts, and warnings of storms. They may marry with humans, their offspring having webbed feet and fingers, but they usually return to their watery world, where their consorts are called mermen.

During the medieval period in Europe the Mermaid was considered to be an agent of the devil and a symbol of deceit. She was often depicted on church furniture holding a fish, which symbolized the entrapment of the soul of the Christian drawn to sin by charms and flattery. In later periods through to today, the image of the Mermaid is frequently to be seen in the coats of arms of Europe and is part of the repertoire of heraldry.

There is a rich tradition of folktales and songs about Mermaids from other cultures all around the world, such as the Bonito Maidens of the Solomon Islands; the Saivo-Neita and Havfrue of Scandinavia; the Näkinneito of Finland and the Näkineiu of Estonia; the Imanja and Jamaína from Brazil; La Sirena from Spain; the Halfway People of the Micmac of Canada; the Margygr of Greenland; and the Ningyo from Japan.

## ABIGAIL (Rhode)

ABIGAIL by the Sumerians, daughter of Enki (Poseidon) and Amphitrite. RHODE was the daughter of Poseidon (Enki) and Amphitrite. Abigail/Rhode was one of the NEREIDES (or Nereids) were fifty Haliad Nymphs or goddesses of the sea. They were the patrons of sailors and fishermen, who came to the aid of men in distress, and goddesses who had in their care the sea's rich bounty. Individually they also represented various facets of the sea, from salty brine, to foam, sand, rocky shores, waves and currents, in addition to the various skills possessed by seamen. The Nereides dwelt with their elderly father Nereus in a silvery cavern at the bottom of the Aegean Sea. The Nereid Thetis was their unofficial leader, and Amphitrite was the queen of the sea. Together with the Tritones they formed the retinue of Poseidon.

The Nereides were depicted in ancient art as beautiful young maidens, sometimes running with small dolphins or fish in their hands, or else riding on the back of dolphins, hippokampoi (fish-tailed horses) and other sea creatures.

## Adamu (Adam)

Adamu the "Lulus" or "slaves to the gods" by the Sumerians. Amelu or "worker" by the Hebrews (*Genesis* 2:5 and 3:19). The first Man or Adamites were not created from nothing, instead the Anunnaki took a being that was already on the earth who had come about by way of the process of evolution. This being was "Genus Homo" or Ape-man/Ape-woman. Binding upon it the image-the inner genetic makeup - of the Anunnaki themselves. They upgraded *Genus Homo* and 'jumped the gun" on evolution and brought man - *Homo Sapiens* - into existence. This is way scientist can not explain why *Homo Sapiens* has only been around for 49,000 years. We, *Homo Sapiens* were not a process of evolution but a solution to a problem as mentioned in *Genesis* 2:5 ". . . And there was no man "to till the ground . . ." The word being used in Hebrew for man is Adam pronounced "Aw Dawm". This Adam was not a single person but rather what are called Adamah "Those who are of the ground" - a tribe of human beings called Adamites as found in *Genesis* 5:2 "Male and Female created he them, and blessed them and called their name Adam, in the day when they were created." Thus this quote is referring to the primitive workers "Lulu Amelu" that were created to take over the mining on Qi (Earth). The chief scientist Enqi (Enki) and the chief medical officer Ninti (Ninmah) of the Anunnaki used genetic manipulation and In-vitro fertilization, which is fertilization of a biological entity or process developed or maintained in a controlled, non-living environment, as a laboratory vessel; or in glass tubes as depicted on the seal of an ancient Sumerian cylinder. This was done in a laboratory called Shimti meaning "House where the wind of life is breathed in".

In Enki's plan for creating the human race. Translation of the original Sumerian texts. Nintu (Ninmah) and Enki plan the creation of the human race (*Isaiah:* 178-220); Enki, rather than Anu, is speaking at this time. In those versions, Enki reveals his plan for creating the human race.

In this version, he is probably speaking when the story resumes: "While Nintu the birth-goddess is present, let the birth goddess create the offspring . . . let man bear the labor-basket of the gods." They called the goddess and asked her, the midwife of the gods, wise Mami (Ninmah): "You are the birthgoddess, creatress of man. Create lullu-man, let him bear the yoke. the work of Enlil; let man carry the labor-basket of the gods." Nintu opened her mouth and said to the great gods, 'It is not properly mine to do these things. He is the one who purifies all; let him give me the clay, and I will do it." Enki opened his mouth and said to the great gods: "At the new moon, the seventh day, and the full moon, I will set up a purifying bath.

Let them slaughter one god. Let the gods be purified by immersion. With his flesh and blood let Nintu mix the clay. God and man let them be inseparably mixed in the clay; till the end of time let us hear the 'drum.' Let there be spirit from the god's flesh; let her proclaim 'alive' as its sign; for the sake of never forgetting, let there be spirit."

In the assembly, "Aye," answered the great gods, the administrators of destiny. At the new moon, the seventh day, and the full moon, he set up a purifying bath. We-ila, who had rationality . . . slaughtered in the assembly. With his flesh and blood Nintu mixed the clay. Till the end of days they heard the drum. From the flesh of the god there was spirit. She proclaimed "alive" as its sign. For the sake of not-forgetting there was a spirit. After she had mixed the clay, she called the Anunnaki, the great gods.

The Igigi, the great gods, cast their spittle on the clay. Mami opened her mouth and said to the great gods, "You commanded me a task-I have completed it. You slaughtered a god together with his rationality. I have removed your heavy labor, have placed your labor-basket on man. You raised a cry for mankind; I have loosened your yoke, have established freedom.

They heard this speech of hers; they ran around and kissed her feet. "Formerly we called you 'Mami.' Now, may 'Mistress of all the gods' be your name. They entered the house of destiny, Prince La and wise Mami. With the birth goddesses assembled, he trod the clay in her presence. She recited the incantation again and again. Ea, seated before her, prompted her.

When she finished her incantation, she nipped off fourteen pieces of clay. Seven pieces to the right, seven to the left, she placed. Between them she placed the brick. 260-276

There is a gap in the text here. From an Assyrian version we learn that fourteen birth goddesses shape the clay. They make seven males and seven females and align them in pairs. The birth goddesses were assembled; Nintu was seated. She counted the months. At the destined (moment), they called the tenth month. The tenth month came. The end of the period opened the womb. Her face was beaming, joyful. Her head covered, she performed the midwifery. She girded her loins; she made the blessing. She patterned the flour and laid down the brick (baby). "I have created, my hands have done it. Let the midwife rejoice in the prostitute's house; where the pregnant woman gives birth, the mother of the baby severs herself. Let the brick be laid down for nine days that Nintu the midwife be honored.

Let them continually call Mami their . . . praise the birth goddess, praise Kesh. When the bed is laid let husband and wife lie together. When for wifehood and husbandhood they heed Ishtar in the house of the father-in-law, let there be rejoicing for nine days; let them call Ishtar Ishara (Asherah).

After a gap of approximately fifty lines, the story continues. Twelve hundred years later Enlil is trying to destroy the human race because it is making too much noise.

300,000 years ago the Anunnaki toiling in the gold mines mutiny. The Anunnaki create Primitive Workers (the Lulus, *Cro-Magnon*) through genetic manipulation of Apewoman (Neanderthals); they take over the manual chores of the Anunnaki. The primate race was first brought to Mars and then to Earth. The Earth was once much nearer the Sun than it is today and that Mars orbited where the Earth now resides. The Earth's closer proximity to the Sun caused the first Earth humans to be black. Mars, then with a climate very much like ours, had the Anunnaki that built the pyramids which have been recorded on Mars. The Anunnaki went to war with a giant black race (Rmoahals) to conquer the Earth.

Enki and Ninharsag elevate humans (*Neanderthals*) of Pleiadian parentage by creating the humans (*Cro-Magnons*) who were to rule in Shuruppak. The *Cro-Magnons* were early humans created by Anunnaki life plasm about 300,000 years ago. The *Cro-Magnon* humans are believed to have been reddish-brown in skin color. 250,000 years ago (248,000 BC) "early *Homo sapiens*" (the Lulus) multiply, spread to other continents.

*Cro-magnon* Man appeared with a mysteriously improved skeletal characteristics and with a cranial capacity that is amazingly in excess by 100 cubic centimeters of that of modern man...A similarly large degree of brain expansion occured in absolutely no other species on Earth in all the ages of the past, not has any genus shown evidence of brain mutation of a comparable magnitude since antiquity. *Mankind, Child of the Stars* by Max H. Flint and Otto O. Binder.

Several Sumerian texts describe how, with the help of Ninmah (Ninharsag) and after much trial and error, a Lullu--a "Mixed One"--was created. Satisfied that a "perfect model" had been attained, Ninmah raised him and shouted: "My hands have made it!" Using the successful genetic combination, the slow process of making duplicates--a process we now call cloning--was started. The reproduction, involving the need of Anunnaki females to serve as Birth Goddesses, cloned the humans in sets of seven males, seven females. In the Bible, *Genesis* Chapter 1 & 5 states: On the day that Elohim created the Adam, in the likeness of Elohim he made him; Male and female created he them. A being that would resemble the Anunnaki both physically and mentally. This being, Enki promised, "will be charged with the service of the gods, that they might have their ease." *The Cosmic Code,* by Zecharia Sitchin, cr 1998, pp. 51-52.

The Popol Vuh states that mankind had been created to be a servant of the gods. The gods are quoted: "Let us make him who shall nourish and sustain us! What shall we do to be invoked, in order to be remembered on earth? We have already tried with our first creations; but we could not make them praise and venerate us. So, then, let us try to make obedient, respectful beings who will nourish and sustain us."

"They (*Cro-Magnon* man) were endowed with intelligence; they saw and instantly they could see far, they succeeded in seeing, they succeeded in knowing all that there is in the world. When they looked, instantly they saw around them, and they contemplated in turn the arch of heaven and the round face of the earth."

"But the Creator and the Maker did not hear this with pleasure. "It is not well that our creatures, our workers say; they know all, the large and the small," they said."

"What shall we do with them now? Let their sight reach only to that which is near; let them see only a little of the face of the earth! It is not well what they say. Perchance, are they not by nature simple creatures of our making? Must they also be gods?"

"Then the Heart of Heaven blew mist into their eyes, which clouded their sight (telepathy) as when a mirror is breathed upon. Their eyes were covered and they could see only what was close, only that was clear to them. In this way the wisdom and all the knowledge of the four men...were destroyed." *Popol Vuh,* a collection of ancient Mayan beliefs and legends.

In the period, then--some hundred, some ninety-eight thousand years before the entry of Ram into India, there lived in this land of Atlantis one AMEILIUS, who had first noted the separations of the beings who inhabited that portion of the earth's sphere into male and female as separate entities, or individuals. As to their forms in the physical sense, these were much rather of the nature of thought forms, or able to push out of themselves in that direction in which their development took shape in thought--much in the way and manner as the amoeba would in the waters of a stagnant bay, or lake, in the present. As these took form by the gratifying of their own desire for that which built or added to the material conditions, they became hardened or set--much in the form of the existent human body of the day, with that color as partook of their surroundings much in the matter as the chameleon in the present. Hence coming into that form as the red or the mixture peoples--or colors, approx. 300,000 years ago; known as the red race. These, then, able to use in their gradual development all the forces as were manifest in their individual surroundings, passing through those periods of developments as have been followed more closely by that of the orange, the green, the blue, the yellow, or the black (indigo) races, in other portions of the world; yet with their immediate surroundings, with the facilities for the developments, these became much speedier in this particular portion of the globe than in others--and while the destruction of this continent and the peoples was far beyond any of that as has been kept as an absolute record, that record in the rocks still remains. Also their influence extended to the lives of the people to whose lands they escaped. Even today, either through the direct influence of being reincarnated in the earth, or through mental effect on individuals' thoughts, they may influence individuals, groups and nations in the present. (364-3) *Edgar Cayce on Atlantis,* by Edgar Evans Cayce, cr1968, pps. 56-57.

With fifty heroes an expedition to the Abzu (Abdju/Abydos in Khem/Egypt) Ninurta led, with weapons were they armed. In the forests and the steppes of the Abzu, the Earthlings (Cro-Magnon) they chased. With nets they them captured, male and female to the Edin (Poseidon) they them brought. To do all manner of chores, in the orchards and in the cities, they trained them. In the Edin, the Anunnaki the Earthlings with admiration observed: Intelligence they possessed, of commands they had understanding. They took over all manner of chores; unclothed they were the tasks performing. Males and females among them were constantly mating, quick were their proliferations.

## Adapa (Adam)

Adapa by the Sumerians, son of En.ki (Poseidon) and a Cro-Magnon female. Atabba by the Akkadians. Amuta by the Babylonians. Adam by the Hebrews. Adima by the Hindoos. Ad-amah by the Persians. Ask by the Nordic-Germanic tribes.

In R. A. Boulay's book he uses mostly ancient Hebrew writings that were purposely omitted from the Bible by the ancient Hebrews, he believes, that because they contained information that was embarrassing. Boulay quotes from the Haggadah, *"...the source of Jewish legend and oral tradition",* a story of Adam and Eve: The first result was that Adam and Eve became naked. Before, their bodies had been overlaid with a horny skin, and enveloped with the cloud of glory. No sooner had they violated the command given to them than the cloud of glory and the horny skin dropped from them, and they stood there in their nakedness and ashamed. R. A. Boulay, *The Story of Mankind's Reptilian Past.*

Boulay also quotes a Gnostic version of *Adam and Eve:* "Now Eve believed the words of the serpent. She looked at the tree. She took some of its fruit and ate, and she gave to her husband also, and he ate too. Then, their mind opened. For when they ate, the light of knowledge shone for them; they knew they were naked with regard to knowledge. When they saw their makers, they loathed them since they were beastly forms. They understood very much."

"Then holy Raphael, an angel who was with me, answered and said, This is the tree of knowledge, of which thy ancient father and thy aged mother ate, who were before thee; and who, obtaining knowledge, their eyes being opened, and knowing themselves to be naked, were expelled from the garden." *Book of Enoch,* Chapter 31:5.

"The bodies of Adam and Eve gave forth a shimmer of light, but they always wore clothing in conformity with the custom of their associates. Though wearing very little during the day, at eventide they donned night wraps. The origin of the traditional halo encircling the heads of supposed pious and holy men dates back to the days of Adama and Eve. Since the light emanations of their bodies were so largely obscured by clothing, only the radiating glow from their heads was discernible." *The Urantia Book,* page 843.

"Adam and Eve could communicate with each other and with their immediate children over a distance of about fifty miles. This thought exchange was effected by means of the delicate gas chambers located in close proximity to their brain structures. By this mechanism they could send and receive thought oscillations. But this power was instantly suspened upon the mind's surrender to the discord and disruption of evil." *The Urantia Book,* page 835.

From Dolores Cannon's book *Jesus and the Essenes,* page 179, we read:

S: . . . I remember about why the flood came about, though. This was part of the time when that men were struck, so that he no longer was able to speak one-to-one to everyone. This knowlege was lost and it was closed up. And therefore there was great confusion upon the world. They spoke to one as one, to think was for the other to know. And this was lost, this ability, because of their doing. They thought, they told each other, "If we do this great thing, we can become as great as Yahweh and find the way to be even greater, to have more power". And because of this, it had been lost and the confusion was brought. Yahweh took away this ability and man was struck dumb because he had never had to communicate with others in any other way, and it was a great loss. Then he learned to speak with the mouth with words. Before this, there was no need.

D: Before this ability was lost, could they communicate with people over long distances?

S: Yes, it was as if they were with you. It was taken away because man was proud and doing many things that he was not . . . he was subverting the law of nature. And therefore he caused great destruction. And this was lost because of this. It is said that the very earth exploded, as if to spew man off its surface.

## AKIBEEL (Kakabel)

AKIBEEL, KOKABEL, KOKHABRIEL, KOKABIEL, KOCHBIEL, KOKBIEL, KABAIEL, KOCHAB, KAKABEL a “fallen angel” who taught man "signs." Kakabel or "star of God." A great angelic prince who exercises dominion over the stars and constellations. In *Enoch I,* he is a fallen angel and a resident of the nether realms. Kakabel commands 365,000 surrogate spirits who do his bidding. Among other duties he instructs his fellows in astrology.

## ALA.LU (Helios)

ALA.LU by the Sumerians, the son of An.shar.gal and Anunnaki Concubine. Alalu, the former Nibiruan commander and a relative of Anu, had previously arrived on Earth and had found gold. Anu then sent his eldest son, Enki, and fifty of his best astronauts to Earth to establish mining operations. Enki's shuttlecraft landed in the sea near Mesopotamia. He and the Anunnaki set up camp and went to work, extracting gold from the water which Alalu had found earlier. Enki then built the first city which he named Eridu-Earth Station One. He received much assistance from his relatives. ALOR.OS or

ALOR.US by the Akkadians. ALALUSH by the Hittites. ALMAQAH, ILMAQAH, ILAH, ALILAT and ALAM by the Arabs.

The Hurrians were a people who occupied Anatolia (Turkey) in ancient times from the early third millennium BC. Many of their religious and mythic concepts were absorbed by their Hittite conquerors, beginning after 2000 BC. Among these traditions was the story of Alalu, the first king of heaven, a giant god, who made his home on a mountainous island in the sea of the setting sun. His son, Kumarbi, was a mythic personification of the Atlantic Ocean through Roman times.

Aalu is Ancient Egyptian for "The Isle of Flame," descriptive of a large, volcanic island in the sea of the Distant West (the Atlantic Ocean), which physically matches Plato's Atlantis virtually detail for detail: mountainous, with canals, luxuriant crops, a palatial city surrounded by great walls decorated with precious metals. Alalu's earliest known reference appears in *The Destruction of Mankind,* a New Kingdom history (1299 BC) discovered in the tomb of Pharaoh Seti I, at Abydos, site of the Osireion, a subterranean monument to the Great Flood that destroyed a former age of greatness, and described in the account. On the other side of the world from Egypt.

HELIOS by the Greeks, son of Gin.gu (Hyperion) and Theia. HELIOS, HELIO or HELIUS was the god who personified the sun itself. Sun god. Helios is portrayed as a young man in the prime of life and of very great beauty: his head was surrounded with rays of light, which gave him a mass of golden hair. Drowned in the ocean by the Olympians, he was raised to the sky to become the luminary of the sun. Nine winged white fire breathing horses (Pyrios, Eos, Aethon and Phlegon) pulled his golden chariot, and he wore a golden helmet and breastplate. The Colossus of Rhodes, one of the Seven Wonders of the Ancient World, was a statue of Helios. (See sun god Mithra)

## ALECTO (Euryes)

ERINYES EURYES, EURYTUS, or EUMENIDES by the Atlanteans. ALECTO by the Greeks, daughter of Uranos (Anshar) and Gaea (Kishar). Known as the three FURIES or FAIRIES. The three virgin goddesses: ALLECTO, TISIPHONE, and MEGAERA. They defended mothers and the laws of blood relationship; revenge; justice against those who broke customs or taboos, social and bloodline laws. Later identified with the fairies. The angry ones; Avengers; the kindly ones; Children of Eternal Night; Daughters of Earth and Shadow. Punishers of sins, they had serpents twined in their hair and carried torches and whips. They tracked down those who wrongly shed blood, especially a mother's blood.

## AMILIUS (We-ila)

IEOUD by the Greeks. In a Phoenician legend IEOUD was the eldest son of Cronus (Annu) and Anobret (Ninsu). A Nymph called Anobret was his mother. During a war, which was devastating the country, Cronus dressed his son in royal regalia and sacrificed him.

WE-ILA by the Annunaki, son of An.nu (Cronos) and Nin.su (Anobret). An Anunnaki sacrificed to create early Cro-Magnon man – Adamu (Adam) the slave workers. AMILIUS by the Atlaneans. Edgar Cayce stated that the "entity aided the priest in the preparation of the manner of building the temple of records that lies just beyond that enigma that still is the mystery of mysteries to those who seek to know what were the manners of thought of the ancient sons who made man, beast-as a part of the consciousness." *Edgar Cayce on Atlantis,* Reading #2402-2, November 16, 1940

AMILIUS was the first expression of Divine Mind (the logos); the Christ soul before his incarnation into a physical body (corresponding to *Genesis*1); the entity that Edgar Cayce described living in the lost civilization of Atlantis who redirected the process of human evolution by creating a more appropriate [pure] physical form for the influx of souls to incarnate into rather than incarnating into the animal-human form which souls had entangled themselves in.

AMILIUS, AMEILIUS or AMELIUS by the Atlanteans. In 106,002 BC, AMILIUS (the christ spirit) introduced the `Law of One´ to the Atlanteans. This was introduced to keep the race "pure", so they would not have sexual relations with the so called 'Things' or the mythological creatures of legend. Unfortunately, the first wave of souls had traped themselves by becoming these creatures. They could use their own mental imaging abilities to generate such a creature outside themselves to mate with the animals. But the creatures they materialized into were imperfect mimics, grotesque, hapless creatures which became known as the `Things´ [mythological creatures], destined to be permanent slaves. These were called the 'lost souls' or the 'first wavers'.

In Lytle Robinson's book, *Edgar Cayce's Story* of the *'Origin And Destiny Of Man,'* Edgar Cayce gives a detailed account of not only the origin of the giants, but the origin of modern humans as well. Cayce states that ...It was Amilius (a spirit entity) who fostered the coming of other soul entities into this electro-spiritual world-for all souls were created in the beginning. These numberless, sexless manifestations of the spirit were the perfect offspring of a benevolent Father/Creator, and enjoyed a truly spiritual life in a truly spiritual world. Wholly attuned to the Supreme Will as was Amilius, they were the companions of the Father as they were intended to be; a part of the Whole yet aware of being separate and independent entities.

Since these entities or spirit beings possessed free will, each entity's first thought, first reaction and first expression were slightly different from those of all others. Thus each individual idea and each realization or motive became a part of the entity. Thought upon thought, experience after experience, each of these spirits built its own peculiar individuality and character. The activity of the spiritual entity thus became its soul-record. That which it thought it gradually became.

In Jon Peniel's book, *'The Children OF The Law Of One & The Lost Teachings Of Atlantis,'* Peniel states the same story above that was taught to him while living with monks in Tibet. ...The historical records start with the premise that there is One Great Being (God/Universal Spirit) that is All things, including the Universe itself. It divides/multiplies within itself to create us, thus, our history begins with all of us (humans) essentially being part of, and One with God. The records describe us as being spiritual or 'angelic' beings, free to roam, create, and enjoy the Universe. The teachings go on to say that our beginnings on Earth, came in two steps - a 'first wave', and 'second wave' of 'human' (& semi-human) materialization into physical bodies on Earth. At the time, we had the ability to instantly alter our vibration, and instantly create anything we desired, with a mere thought. It was in this way that we 'thought ourselves' into matter, into material existence on Earth. Which began our fall from our angelic state, and Oneness with God.

Now back to Cayce . . . But not for long did the will of the souls remain the will of their Source. They began to experiment, fascinated with the power of their own creation individuality. Desire and self-aggrandizement gave birth to the destructive-that which was opposed to goodness, the opposite of God's will. By magnifying their own will and independence, the selfishness of the ego came into being. It was this turning away from God's will that brought about the downfall, the separation, the end of the state of perfection. This was the Revolt of the Angels, or the Fall of Man.

Cayce further states, "...Then a soul-the offspring of the Creator-(when) entering into a consciousness which becomes a manifestation in any plane or sphere of activity, is given free will for its use of those abilities or qualities or conditions in its experience. And it will demonstrate, manifest and show forth what it reflects in its activity towards that First Cause." (*Case* #364-Sd-1)

The mineral, plant and animal kingdoms were thriving long before man entered this plane. They were governed by immutable laws already set in motion. Souls still in the spirit were attracted by matter and came to the new outer realms in large numbers. The earth was only one of many spheres that came into their paths and to which they were drawn.

Those souls, still in the spirit, who were attracted to the earth plane observed the various forms of animal life and the fleshly ties. They hovered about it, viewing the abundance of growing things in the slowly cooling and tropical earth. They saw the fruit of the land and wanted to taste it; they observed the sex life of animals and wanted to experience it. Since desire impelled them to seek expression in matter, they partook more and more of the material, becoming eaters of, feeders upon their physical surroundings.

Since souls were also self-conscious viewpoints possessed of God and capable of being that which God is, they played at creation-imitating the Creator. Thus they became absorbed with their own creative powers, with which they had been endowed from the beginning, and they mimicked the beasts of the fields and the fowls of the air, dreaming up ideas of bodies it would be pleasant to inhabit.

Thoughts are deeds, and these desires eventually materialized; for from the beginning the resources of all creation have been available to man. The forms so conceived were at first merely in the nature of thought-forms or visualizations, made by pushing themselves out of themselves in whatever manner desired. As the gratification of their carnal and material desires took shape, however, the forms hardened or congealed into matter itself and took on the color of the environment.

Peniel writes, . . .You have probably heard of mythological beings such as the Minotaur, Centaur, Mermaid, etc. The Minotaur, had a bull's head and a human body, the Centaur, a human head and torso with a horse's body. You may also have seen pictures of Egyptian 'gods' with animal heads and human bodies, or animal bodies and human heads (like the Sphinx).

In the Pacific regions, ancient drawings and carvings of 'bird headed' humans can be found on both sides of the ocean. Why do you think so much of this exists? Many legends and myths have some foundation in fact, and this is no exception. The ancient teachings from Atlantis, reveal that such creatures did indeed exist, and that their origins were not what you might expect - they were the fallen angelic beings from the 'first wave' of materialization on Earth. The first wave of materialization was a terrible mistake. The first spirits or entities materialized as partly human/partly animal creatures. This is why in the story of Lucifer, or the various creatures that were called 'devils' or demons, appear as horned, cloven hoofed creatures with tails - the fact is, they were part goat. This also explains why goats have become associated with the devil. But evil, is an entirely different matter. Think not that evil does not exist. But true evil, disguises itself, and points the finger at innocents.

"So Lucifer was not evil?" Not initially. The stories you have heard have become terribly mixed up. Even the Bible originally paints him as a great angel. But there was no 'rebellion' or defiance against the will of God until AFTER this fall, not prior to the fall as is often depicted. It was just a mistake at first.

There were more 'fallen angels' than Lucifer. And they took many different part animal forms. These spirit beings that fell into physical vibration or matter, during the 'first wave' of materialization became the mythological creatures of ancient history. They suffered a great 'fall' in vibration from their previous spiritual, angelic state of existence. They instantly experienced a near total loss of consciousness, awareness, and intelligence. In less than the twinkling of an eye, the consciousness that just moments before, had encompassed the entire Universe, and experienced Oneness with the Universal Father, was virtually gone. The new limited consciousness of these pitiful creatures, 'trapped' them on the physical plane of Earth, where they had to live in ignorance, with their animal-like intelligence and awareness. They were suddenly isolated from the Universal/God Consciousness and trapped in the lonely anguish of 'separate' consciousness. This separate consciousness gave birth to a sort of separate free will, which was ignorantly used selfishly, rather than in harmony with the will of God. Ultimately, they would also be trapped in slavery. Remember, we were spirits only. Very 'fine', 'high-frequency' vibrational beings, with no experience in this physical realm. These so called mythological creatures came upon their terrible fate because of rapid, uncontrolled slowing down of their vibrational frequencies, for purposes of materialization of their spiritual selves into the material plane of Earth. This left them with only a 'separate self consciousness', that lost touch with the 'Oneness Consciousness', or 'Universal Consciousness'. "Then why aren't all of us still lost, and out of touch with God?" "A couple of reasons. Some of us did not make this 'fall'. Those who didn't fall, were still in their angelic state, and watched all this happen to the first wavers.

Cayce stated . . . As souls used and abused their privileges, the highest and the lowest applications of divine forces were made. The few who sought to know the way were given guidance, as it has always been given; the masses deliberately turned away, seeking fulfillment of their own desires. These spirits became entrapped. Chaos resulted not only from the forms taken but from the misapplication of spiritual powers. The male and female came into being. This was the separation of the sexes, the division of the nature of "man" into positive and negative forces.

The first female was called Lilith, the forerunner of Eve, and a conglomeration of monstrosities (mythological creatures) emerged. The Cyclops, the Satyr, the Centaur, the Unicorn and various forms mentioned in mythology, having animal bodies and human heads, came into existence. Thus the souls who had been hovering about, influencing and directing, inhabited bodies which were projections of their own mental creations-and propagated a race of monstrosities.

Their bodies were their own creations, not God's. These were the 'daughters of men,' 'the giants in the earth,' of the *Old Testament.* So a weird, corrupt state of existence came into being, but it was the beginning of a new period of evolution for the soul-the long struggle for spirit's conquest over matter.

The monstrosities or mythological creatures roamed the earth and mixed with the animals. Sex was the determining factor, as symbolized by the serpent. Through their offspring souls were being born again and again into a prison of matter from which they could not extricate themselves. Trapped in these grotesque bodies, man as such was drifting further and further away from his Source. This he had willfully discarded for the selfish gratification of the carnal; and he had accomplished it by the spiritually destructive use of creative powers for self. This was the Original Sin of man.

Only in the earth did souls take on matter and become physical. In other planes and realms-other states of consciousness-the plan for evolution of the spirit varied. Only in the physical, three-dimensional plane does the transition from one plane to another necessitate the process called birth and death. The soul, the spirit of God in man, has been immortal from the beginning. It is not born and does not die.

Amilius, with the aid of spiritual-minded soul entites or spirits from other realms-the "sons of the Most High"-intervened in this misshaped evolution which earth-man had created for himself. With their great Love and compassion, many of these other angelic beings who had not 'fallen', decided to help the trapped first wavers, even at great risk of the same fate. They became what we call the 'second wavers'.

The second wavers knew they could only help the first wavers, if they too, materialized in forms that would allow them to work on the lost souls (the mythological creatures) in their own physical form and dimension. They new that in order to do that, it would require lowering their own vibration, towards that of the physical plane, and subsequently lowering their consciousness to some extent. They knew this was dangerous, and that they had to be very careful how they did this, and be careful about how deeply they went into physical matter, or they too would become trapped in limited consciousness just as the mythological creatures were. Thus the ancient Atlantean teachings describe how the second wave, became the first consciously controlled thought projection, or materialization, of modern 'human' life on Earth (or at least they eventually became modern humans as they gradually solidified into the material plane from their spiritual 'angelic' state). The ape-like early human form was actually just eventually chosen by second wavers as the preferred type of physical vehicle to model themselves after, because it allowed for the greatest control and manipulation in the physical plane, that would be required to help the first wavers.

From among the various physical forms on earth a body was patterned which most perfectly fitted the needs of man. This was a body that would help, not hinder, in the struggle for at-one-ment (atonement) with the Maker.

By his own choice, Amilius himself descended into matter and became Adam, man as flesh and blood, the first of the perfect race, the first of the Sons of God as opposed to "Daughters of Men", the freakish offspring of Mixtures. This was the reason for the admonishment to keep the race pure, for "the Sons of God looked upon the daughters of Men and saw them as being fair." (*Genesis* 6:2)

Adam was an individual but he was also more; he was the symbol of the whole race of man, the five races. Eve was created as the ideal helpmate for Adam, because of the division of man's spiritual nature into positive and negative. Thus Eve was also the symbolic "other half" of man's nature in all races. This was the last of the important creations.

So this second wave of spirits entered into the planes of the Earth. Careful to stay as beings free from the lower-vibratory planes, or "hardening" into the matter, they projected themselves into the material plane with thought-form bodies that were semi-etheric - matter, but not matter. Thus were they still able to function on all vibrational frequencies of the Universal spectrum - free to enter or leave the limited spectrum of the material plane at will. But most importantly they were very intent upon maintaining their consciousness of Oneness, so that they would not fall to the same fate as their kin the mythological creatures.

Adam and Eve were special creations and not evolutions from that which had already been created. Man did not descend from the monkey. For Cayce stated, "In matter of form, as we find, first there were those as projections from that about the animal kingdom; for the thought bodies gradually took form and various combinations (as may be called) of the various forces that called or classified themselves as gods, or rulers over-whether herds, or fowls, or fishes, etc.-in part much in the form of the present-day man (were one chosen of those that existed in this first period as the first destructions came about). These took on many sizes as to stature, from that as may be called the midget to the giants-for there were giants in the earth in those days, men as tall as (what would be termed today) ten or twelve feet in stature, and well proportioned throughout. The ones that became the most useful were those as would be classified (or called in the present) as the ideal stature, that was of both male and female (as those separations had been begun); and the most ideal (as would be called) was Adam, who was in that period, when he [Adam] appeared, as five in one-See?" (*Cayce* #364-11)

Through the law of relativity, the positive and the negative, man and woman experience earth; night and day, hot and cold, good and bad-all realized through the five physical senses via the reasoning of the mind. The manifestation was achieved and as they became subject to the vibratory conditions which affect this realm they saw the numerological representations of the physical plane, 2 and 5, appear in many aspects of their manifestations. For example, the beginnings of the 5 races occurred and later, the 2 sexes each being having 5 appendages (2 legs, 2 arms, 1 head) with 2 eyes, 2 ears, 2 legs, 2 of many organs, etc. and 5 fingers and 5 toes on the arms and legs.

Despite their precautions and great efforts, some of them began losing more and more consciousness and hardening into matter. Those that manifested in Atlantis with Amilius fared the best - but for many, this was to be short lived. Until this time, they were "composite" beings, macrocosms of the One. Their bodies were not as they are now. Our male and female elements had not yet separated - as composite beings we each had one body that contained both "sexes", rather than the male and female bodies we have now.

The projection of the perfect race into matter (the second wave) occurred not only in the Garden of Eden-which was in Iran and the Caucasus-but in five different places in the earth at the same time. The white race was in Iran, the Caucasus area along the Black Sea, and the Carpathian Mountains of Central Europe. The yellow race was in what was later to become the Gobi Desert of East Asia. The black race was in the Sudan and upper West Africa. The brown race was in the Andes and Lemuria, the continent lying then in the area of the Pacific Ocean. The red race was in Atlantis and America.

The environment and climatic conditions determined the color of the race. For all peoples, regardless of color, were of one blood and members of the "perfect" race. Color of the race merely adapted man to the conditions which were to be met, and symbolized the chief attribute of the people of that race. In the white race, sight or seeing was predominant or emphasized; in the red, feeling of emotion; in the yellow, hearing; in the black, gratification of the appetites; and in the brown, the emphasis on the sense of smell. The Jews, as a people, developed at a much later date. The Egyptians also came later, as a result of the mixture of red, black, and white races, in about 10,000 BC.

The continent of Atlantis was the most important land area of the world and the center of the first civilization. With the second influx of souls-the coming of the perfect race, some 10 ½ million years ago-a new era was to begin in the evolution of man in the earth.

Now, for the first time, some of the second wavers had begun to separate within themselves, manifesting as individual bodies representing the polarity elements. Bodies of opposite polarities then came into existence (male or female sex). Cayce states, . . .For in the projections they began as many, and in creating influences they began as five or in those centers where crystallization or projection had taken on such form as to become what was called man, though it hardly could be said that they were in the exact form as in the present." (*Cayce* #877-26)

The work of freeing the monstrosities or mythological creatures began. It was arduous and complex, but it proceeded well - at first. Unfortunately, the contamination of separateness slowly began to creep in. They started slowly "tasting" many of the things that instantly trapped the monstrosities. Division of the forces of mind took place during the first thousand years of the occupation of the earth by the perfect race. By this division part of the mental forces related to the material, and part to the spiritual. It occurred as man emphasized less and less the divine aspect of his nature, became less and less aware of that from which he came. For man recognized that he was a part of what was about him, and he acknowledged the oneness of all matter and force, but he relied more and more on the physical mind with its carnal interpretations. As time went on, only dreams, prayer, and religion remained to remind him of his divine origin. Desire led him to accept things which he instinctively knew were not true; he began having sex with the monstrosities and produced giants which corrupted the earth. Cayce stated, "but with these transpositions, with these changes that came in as personalities, we find . . .the Sons of the Creative Force . . .looking upon those changed forms, or the daughters of men, and there crept in those pollutions, or polluting themselves with those mixtures (mythological creatures) that brought contempt, hatred, bloodshed, and desires of self without respect of others' freedom, others' wishes-and there began, then, in the latter portion of this period dissenting and divisions among the peoples in the lands." (*Cayce* #364-4)

Even in the second wavers higher state of manifestation (which they thought would keep them safe from the loss of consciousness that plagued the mythological creatures) some of them succumbed to the lure of material sensation. They began to delve more into the indulgences of the plane until they were lost in it. In the frenzy of their addiction to physical sensations, they disregarded all their precautions and wariness. Soon their thoughts and actions had "collected" matter from this material world that surrounded them and hardened their thought-forms, making them matter-bound also. Their consciousness simultaneously slipped and their gradual loss of consciousness of Oneness gave way to that new consciousness of predominant " separateness". And along with this new consciousness came new emotions - some pleasurable and some painful. Strange new things like greed, envy, lust, excitement, fear, and desire.

Some of them vigorously strived to maintain a semblance of their consciousness of Oneness, along with the new consciousness and they were able to experience the emotions without being ruled by them. Such were the Children of the Law of One.

But others lost, or chose to deliberately suppress, even a glimmer of awareness of the One. These beings became lost, and enmeshed in separateness. Outside of the consciousness of Oneness, they became subject to being tossed to and fro by the tides of emotional onslaught, and ultimately became devoted to personal power and pleasure in this physical plane. These beings became known as the Sons of Belial (even if they were female).

Take heed of the ancient warnings and prophecies about the Belialians. "Lizard-like are they - not in apparent physical description, but in spirit form, in the heart - in the soul. Beware even now of your lizard kin, for they rule the world, with greed, and without compassion, while maintaining appearance of good and righteous. As men and women do these Sons of

Belial walk the Earth. Model citizens. Successful leaders who are the envy of the uninitiated. While some appear disgusting and strange to the eye, look not to see the ugliness of the Belialians with your eye, for some are handsome to the eye. See you will not, their true lizard-like appearance with your earthly eyes. See their true nature, you will, only with the inner-eye, or in glimpses from the corner of the eye."

The human giants and monstrosities (mythological creatures) were the outcasts of Atlantean society. Frequently of low principle and little self-will or control, they were used for the most menial tasks. Their status in the social scale was little higher than that of domesticated animals and beast of burden. Because of them men of the perfect race fell into two camps, bitterly opposed to each other in ideology. It was the mixing of those of pure lineage with those who had not completely overcome the animal influences that brought dissensions and the rise of strife and turmoil.

These outcasts, enslaved by those of Belial, the followers of Baal (Satan) or Beelzebub-the forces of evil-were treated harshly. Through use of occult powers, hypnosis and mental telepathy, they were under complete domination of their masters. They were bred like cattle for particular types of work and enjoyed none of the fruits of their labor. Cayce, stated that they were known as Things-the untouchables, the automations-they did all the work in the fields, the households, and some of the trades.

Cayce states, on 1 June 1944, "in Atlantean land before Adam-timekeeper for those who were called things or servants or workers of the people-entity felt need of change or reform so that every individual would have the right of choice or freedom-felt desire to improve the conditions for worker-felt need of God's hand in what evil or Satan had brought in the earth." (*Cayce* #5249-1)

Castes and classes came into being, fostered by the Sons of Belial through greed, contempt and hatred. Bloodshed resulted from this disregard of and disrespect for the rights and freedom of others. The many were subjected to the whims of the few for their own self-aggrandizement.

The laws of heredity and environment gradually became more of an influence; appearances changed according to the purity of the strain and individual purposes-ideals and motives of activity. There were some who were almost perfect in figure and feature; and others who had monstrous combinations of human physiques and animal appendages, such as hooves, claws, feathers, wings and tails. It was these strange creatures who later were to be so mysteriously depicted in Egyptian and Assyrian inscriptions. At an early period in Egypt they were finally to disappear from the human race.

These daughters of men and giants in the earth of the Old Testament were the reason for the admonishment to: Keep the race pure. Yet the mixtures sometimes produced divine bodies with twisted, warped souls; or repulsive bodies with souls seeking the light. It was not the body that mattered so much, but the purity of purpose, of ideals.

Through the injunction, If you will be my people I will be your God, an effort was made by the more spiritual minded to draw people to the worship of the One God. Known as the Children of the Law of One, they sought to purify the race in purpose as well as in body. The tenets of those of the Law of One-One Religion, One State, One Wife, One Home, One God-had little appeal to the Sons of Belial.

Thus it came to be that the two Atlantean socio-political groups evolved with one very essential difference: The Children of the Law of One had a consciousness of both separateness and Oneness. The Sons of Belial rejected the consciousness of Oneness entirely, and maintained only a consciousness of separateness. Finally, man had put ego of self above everything else, "And it repented the Lord that he had made man on the earth and it grieved him in his heart." (*Genesis* 6:6)

Thus the breach between those of the Law of One and those of Belial slowly took form, a breach that later was to widen into a gulf. The carnal, materialistic way of life of the followers of Belial was attractive even to many of the Children of the Law of One, and numbers of them succumbed to the temptations. With the emphasis on the value of temporal things and the de-emphasis on the spiritual, idol worship crept into the religious scene.

The first of the series of three continental catastrophes occurred about 50,700 BC, many thousands of years before the final drowning. It came as a material result of the use of chemicals and high explosives in the plan to annihilate the wild beasts. The real reason was the low state into which man had fallen. Huge and numerous gas pockets were blown open in the lairs of the animals, precipitating volcanic eruptions and earthquakes in the still slowly cooling earth. The magnitude of the disturbances caused the axis of the world to shift, bringing the poles to their present position and producing the last of the great Ice Ages.

Lemuria was the first to be affected, losing much of its territory as it began to sink into the Pacific. In Atlantis the area of the Sargasso Sea, off the coast of Cuba, was the first to go under water. The rest of the continent was broken up into several large islands with many canals, ravines, gulfs, bays and streams. The temperate climate rapidly changed to a more torrid one.

With the upheavals, the initial migrations from Atlantis took place in small numbers to the east and west. The earliest settlements were in the region of the Pyrenees Mountains in France and Spain; then later in Central and South America. The movement of the Lemurians was primarily to South America. The land of Og, along the Pacific coastal area of what was later to be southern Peru, was occupied. This was the beginning of that mysterious tribe of Indians known as the Incas.

From this time on, although material civilization rose to great heights, there was growing unrest among the Atlantean people. In a land of plenty, strife rather than peace became the rule. The altars came to be used for human sacrifice by those turning away from the original concept of the One

God. Sun worship became prevalent. Only the dedicated, inner core of the Children of the Law of One remained firm.

Low standards of morality, sex indulgence and perversion became rampant. Poverty and hunger were wide spread among the peasantry and working classes. There was a deteriorating of the physical and spiritual bodies, just as there was a wasting away of the mountains and valleys into the seas. In spite of material advancements and many scientific achievements, inner decay was to bring dispersion and finally annihilation to a proud, wicked, adulterous people.

The second important land change came long after the first, according to Cayce, around 28,000 BC, and resulted in the submergence of many large islands. The Bible gives an account of the flood. The Biblical flood was the "cleansing of the earth" of all the evil monstrosities (including the original human giants) that man had brought into the earth plane through sexual lust with mythological creatures.

After the deluge, which was preceded by volcanic eruptions and electrical storms, the principal land areas left in this part of the world were the islands of Poseidia in the North (West Indies area), Aryaz in the central Atlantic and Og (Peru) in the West. There were large movements of the people to these lands as well as to other parts of the earth.

Lemuria vanished into the Pacific Ocean. Some of its inhabitants fled to the safety lands of southern California, Arizona and New Mexico, where they established the Brotherhood of Mu in the land of "Mayra".

After the days of the Flood, a period of rebuilding began in Atlantis. However, the growth of disturbing factors within, the magnification of personal desires and embitterment's, made the final destruction of Atlantis all the more certain. Advanced understanding of spiritual and natural laws and their misapplication made that destruction all the more terrible. Those of the One God realized, through the clairvoyant powers of the fast-declining pituitary gland, that the impending final breakup of the Poseidian-Atlantean lands was now at hand. They sought ways of warning and uniting the people in order to prevent it, if possible, so that they might still carry out the injunction, Subdue the earth, rather than-as those of Belial would have it-subdue one another.

They endeavored to gather all the knowledge of the various nations of the world concerning the approaching disaster, and a meeting was called with this in view, Envoys from many lands came to Atlantis to pool their wisdom in a last attempt to avert the calamity, but the meeting and the evangelistic campaign resulting from it were to no avail.

Reconciled to the inevitable national cataclysm, the Children of the Law of One made other plans; the search for suitable lands to colonize. Many expeditions went out for this purpose. The Children of the Law of One also supplied leadership in the actual movements via land, air and water to the safety lands in Egypt, Honduras, Yucatan and other areas. Of special interest to them was the preservation of their religious tenets and records, and these were taken with them.

By 10,700 BC, Atlantis had reached the depths of moral and spiritual life-not in knowledge but in practice. Human sacrifice and sun worshipping were prevalent, as were adultery and corruption. The mythological creatures were used and abused. Violence and rebellion spread across the land. Then came the final catastrophe.

Gigantic land upheavals shook the foundations of the earth. Great islands crumbled into the sea and were inundated. Only scattered mountain peaks remained to mark the sunken graves. Some people escaped; a few stayed behind heroically to aid others in the exodus to other lands. However, the majority were lost. By 9,500 BC, Atlantis as a nation had vanished from the face of the earth.

After AMELIUS took human form he was called Adamu by the Sumerians.

Adamu or 'First Of A Kind' (Civilized Man), has been calculated to have lived between the 93rd and 108th shar since the arrival of the Nephilim on Earth in 445,000 BC. That would have been approximately from the year 110,200 to the year 56,200 BC. Adamu was taken to Nibiru by his Nephilim kinfolk, DU.MU.ZI and NIN.GISH.ZIDDA, to be presented to ANU. Before leaving Earth, EN.KI gave to NIN.GISH.ZIDDA a tablet containing the account of Adamu's ceation from his own life-force, and the suggestion that Adamu should be prevented from eating and drinking of Nibiru food, which would grant him, and his descendants, life based on the Nibiru shar cycles of one year equal to 3600 Earth years. ANU gave to Adamu, for his return to Earth, seeds from which cultivated grains might be grown, and the life-essence of sheep from which domesticated cattle might be raised.

## Amori (Amurru)

Amori, son of Canaan. Known to the Sumerians as the Martu, and to the Akkadians as the Amurru, this people settled in the land of Canaan. They appear to have initially adapted a nomadic way of life, although they were soon to organize themselves into a very powerful nation. The Amorites, were to conquer Babylonia, subsequently producing one of the most famous kings in the ancient world, Hammui, whose own name contains the designation Amarru.

## AMU (Derceto)

AMU, NINA, NAMMU or "Sea" by the Sumerians. The mother who gave birth to Heaven and Earth; Creatress Goddess; Mother of all Deities. Name of the Mother of the universe.

ATARGATIS, TIRGATA, and DERCETO by the Canaanites and Philistines. Sea Goddess, sometimes shown with a fish-tail. At her temple in Harran, her sacred fish were said to have oracular powers. She was the

"Keeper of the white stone". The 'white stone' was also called the 'Star Fire', the 'Fire Stone', the 'lapis exillis'--the stone from the heavens, the 'Stone from the Stars', the 'Stone of Scon', or the 'Parsifal Stone'.

Wolfram von Eschenbach, *Parzival* - "The noble and worthy angels who took neither side when Lucifer warred with the Trinity-Atlant, Poseidon, and Chronos were sent down to earth as custodians of this stone, which is forever pure. I know not whether God forgave them or destroyed them; if His justice so ordained, He recalled them to Himself. Since that time, those whom He has called and to whom He sent His angel guard the stone. Sir, such is the nature of the Grail."

## AN I (Annu I)

ARUS by the Pleiadians. AN by the Sumerians. AN.NU, ANNU, ANU by the Akkadians. ARMUS, IRUS or IRIS.

Source: *The Pleiadian Mission, A Time of Awareness,* cr 1994, by Randolph Winters, pp. 46-51.

"Driven off the planet earth, he fled into space towards a star called Beta Centauri, the closest sun system to Earth, located just 4.3 light years away. Here he and his followers found human life on a planet and lived in exile. For two thousand years these same exiled scientists and their followers schemed for revenge, while they built up great power and increased their life span. Because of their hatred for the rulers of Earth, they plotted to return and seek revenge and eventually attacked Earth. They were led by the evil Arus, who intended to destroy Atlantis and Mu. Robbing, murdering, but only able to take over small regions of land, they settled in the northern area called Hyperborea.

Arus and his band of followers continually started small wars around the planet, but these little skirmishes hardly had any impact on the great society of Atlantis and were not much of a bother for hundreds of years. Eventually

Arus died, and his son Arus II (An II) continued to attack remote areas, taking control of what is now India, Pakistan, and Persia. These small wars lasted another fifteen hundred years. Arus II had succeeded in infilitrating his leaders into Atlantis and Mu, causing enough dissension to begin the talk of war.

The cries of war caused panic, and by the thousands the people took to their Beamships and fled to the Pleiades for safety. The war instruments of Atlantis and Mu were of very large size and power. The army of Atlantis contained 4.83 million fighters in large ships, plus 123,000 small, individual Beamships and 16,431 remote ships equipped with the most sophisticated heat-dissolving beams. They also had 23,230 medium-class ships which were armed with terrifying weapons. But even with all this power, Mu was superior in technology and boasted weapons of greater force.

The scientists of Mu, knowing of the coming events, ordered a fleet out into space to search for a large asteroid in the debris of the destroyed planet of Milona (the asteroid belt). Finding it, they attached a powerful drive system to it so that it could be hurled at Earth as a weapon of destruction. As the attack of Atlantis started, The leaders of Mu ordered the giant asteroid to be launched, but it was to late to save Mu. The Atlantean fleet dissolved Mu almost instantly. All traces of Mu were melted away, which is evident by the smooth, flat ground in the Gobi desert where it once stood. The underground cities of Agharta were damaged and thousands were killed, but many survived the great holocaust.

Rapidly, the giant asteroid was steered toward Earth, with the dedicated pilots attached to it. Propelled by the great technology of the scientists of Mu, the huge asteroid of death was racing at incredible speeds toward Earth when some of the leaders and scientists of Atlantis detected the oncoming asteroid. They new there was no way to stop it, so they fled into space, leaving the millions of inhabitants of Atlantis to die.

The asteroid hit the atmosphere and burst like a supernova, generating heat of over 34,000 degrees. The asteroid exploded less than 110 miles up, and in a thousand small pieces hit the Earth like a shotgun blast. The continent of Atlantis melted beneath the heat of the blast within seconds, and the floor of the Atlantic ocean was broken, causing volcanoes to erupt and bringing the sea to a boil. Water from the ocean hurled upward to heights of twenty miles, causing a tidal wave over a mile high to rush over the landmass of Atlantis. It continued on across the area we call the Mediterranean and flooded Northern Africa and the land of Egypt. By our current calendar it was exactly the year 9498 BC, on June 6, when the great civilization of Atlantis sank beneath the Ocean.

The planet Earth rolled over on its axis, causing the seas to flow over the land, and volcanoes filled the air with smoke and fire. As the planet changed its axis and came to a rest in a slightly different orbit, the geography of Earth was forever changed. The great continent of Atlantis, which was orginially north of the equator, slid under the water and is now resting in the area of the Atlantic Ocean. Soon after the war of revenge by Arus II, he was murdered by his third born son, Jehovan (Enuru).

## AN II (Annu II)

ARUS II by the Pleiadians, son of An I. AN.NU II, ANNU II, AN II or "Great One" by the Anunnaki. These gods, whom the Egyptians called the Neteru. The term neter can be used as a noun in some Near Eastern languages to mean 'watchers', thus Neter-land would mean 'Land of the Watchers'. The Neteru were ruled by the god NU, NUN or ANUN. Father of the gods. God of primeval waters (Atlantis). Created the first god Atum or Tum, who then created the world and all that inhabited it. He was called IN-SHUSHINAK by the Assyrians and Babylonians. Sovereign of the gods; Maker of the universe; Supreme God. Arus II (An II) was murdered by his third born son, Jehovan (Enuru).



LYRAN-PLEIADIAN-ANUNNAKI HISTORY

The Pleiadians offered a brief history. According to the Pleiadians, the Lyrans were the original ancestors of our branch of our life stream of evolution.

Many thousands of years ago their civilization in Lyra reached a high technological level and they began to travel in space. They were free-will creatures and had control of their destiny. At a certain point in time they fell into disagreement and divided into factions with different ideologies and different goals and objectives. They eventually went to war and destroyed much of their society and ruined their home. Escapists seeking to avoid the anticipated outcome fled from their native system and found homes in the star systems that we call the Pleiades and the Hyades. They also went to nearby Vega.

In a few thousands years they had raised those societies to high technological levels and once again were able to travel in space. Some of the Pleiadians of Lyran ancestory, on their travels, discovered our planet and its nascent life evolving in a very hospitable atmosphere. They stayed and settled briefly in later Lemuria and early Atlantis, some even mixing with Earth creatures and becoming Earth men.

Those who remained apart and did not mix soon produced highly evolved technologies here and they designed and built many wonderful machines and devices, and created comforts and conveniences of all kinds.

Again they came into conflict and the society became polarized into two camps, each possessing marvelous technologies. Eventually they went to war and terrible destruction resulted. Those who could, escaped to other regions of space and started all over again. Some of those beings are now also visiting us occasionally.

A long time later a new wave of Pleiadians arrived to check on the descendants of their ancestors who survived the terrible war. They found survivors and again they mixed with them and assisted Earth humanity in getting control of its assets and producing a new technology. This society became the later Atlanteans who raised their sciences to levels that produced air and undersea travel before that civilization was also destroyed by surface war on Earth.

The modern Pleiadians are descendants of the peaceful faction that settled in the star group which astronomy gives that name. The Vegans visiting us now are descendants of another peaceful group that settled a planet in the Vega System.

The descendants of the Lyrans, long evolved beyond the conflict stage, are now interested in our welfare and feel a special responsibility toward us since we reflect the earlier warlike tendencies of themselves. They lost much in their history of conflict and destroyed themselves several times, and lost their great technological advances each time. According to the Pleiadians, they even settled another hospitable planet in our solar system, the fifth one from the sun, which was actually destroyed in a war of nuclear weapons that got out of hand there. This part of their concern about how we will use our nuclear sciences now. These Lyrans are now being helped and assisted in certain ways by their human cousins in the Pleiades and Vega and others.

So we see that although the Lyrans are much older in evolution, they are only a little ahead of the others in some technologies and are behind in others, and are being assisted along the way by their cousins. Thus it is that so many human-like extraterrestrials are appearing in the same age in time. Some are actually linked in evolution and do apparently have a common source. Our re-emerging technology attracts their attention now and they are here to observe and assist according to our will choices.

The Lyran races began evacuating their home planet over 22 million years ago, and they have peaked out and migrated from there more than once.

They believe that Creation itself is the First Cause, not that a Creator created it. They see creation as Universal Knowledge, Universal Wisdom, Universal Spirit.

Our earliest society on Earth was copied from the early Lyrans visiting Earth. They were here and observed physical life on Hyperborea, a mythical first continent encompassing all of the land mass at that time. This was before Earth humans began physical evolution. Descendants of these Lyrans came again later and assisted the budding societies of the next epoch and gave Lemuria and Atlantis their names.

There were other beings from another system called Bawwi, who also visited the Earth at that time. The Bawwi were a race of beings 9 to 10 feet tall. There were once beings visiting Earth who were 24 to 27 feet tall. They had feet 3 to 4 ft. long and their fossil tracks still exist. On what we now call Easter Island there was a special race of very big people an unimaginable 33 to 36 feet tall. They were not entirely physical. Whole histories of Hyperboria, Agartha, Mukulia and Atlantis have been described by the Pleiadians.

According to the Pleiadians, the Lyrans left their system as rebels and settled in the Pleiades and the Hyades. They later came to Earth and mixed with Earth humans. Earth humans then lived in the remnants of the earlier single continental land mass now known as Hyperboria. These beings produced and developed a civilization with advanced technology here on Earth. They became involved in a war among themselves here and a faction left and proceeded to Erra in the Pleiades, and others went to another planet in our solar system, an atmospheric planet, the fifth from the sun, which they called Malona. They settled on this planet and mixed with the human life-form there.

The Lyran descendants who settled Earth and Malona both were a war-like race and they carried their warlike tendencies with them. The Malonans ended up destroying their planet in a terrible atomic holocaust.

The surviving Lyrans left for many thousands of years. Subsequent generations came back in another age and again fell to fighting among themselves and again they left. This was repeated still once more, and now the descendants of those are again observing Earth and the surviving descendants of their ancestors.

The Lyran rebels have now reached a higher spiritual level of being and no longer indulge in conflict and war. Their ancestors are responsible for the racial variety now found on Earth.

So you see that the Pleiadians, and the Vegans, and some other Adamic beings who came here from the Hyades, are all in a sense Lyran descendants, and we are linked by a common heritage. The current Lyran visitors, with their higher spirituality, are here trying to undo some of the effects left by their earlier less spiritual ancestors.

Your planet is still trying to find its identity, for you are not a planetary people, you are, in a sense, a group of lost children. We mean this with no disrespect. The human race itself now needs to confront who its parents are. The human race needs to accept that they have become who they are because of who their parents were. In accepting that they can begin to form their own identity as a species and finally come to peace with themselves. It is then that their conflicts will subside. . . .

Source: the Pleiadians

". . . .I want to talk to you about Lyra and how the human race colonized our galaxy. Based on the age of the Suns and the planets in our galaxy, it was decided that the human life form was to be created in the Lyran system. The human race lived there for approximately 40 million years, evolving. The orientation of the human race in Lyra was agricultural in nature. Apparently, we were very plentiful and abundant, and lived in peace. Then, one day, huge craft appeared in the sky."

". . . a large ship came out of a huge craft and approached the planet Bila, and the reptilians from Alpha Draconis disembarked. The Alpha

Draconians and the Lyrans were afraid of each other. When the Draconians saw Bila, with all its abundance and food and natural resources, the Draconians wanted to control it. The Lyrans wanted to know more about the Draconians before some kind of *"assistance"* was offered. The Draconians mistook the communication as a refusal, and subsequently destroyed three out of 14 planets in the Lyran system. The Lyrans were basically defenseless. The planets Bila, Teka and Merck were destroyed. Over 50 million Lyran humans were killed. It is at this point in history that the Draconians began to look at humans as a food source. This is how old the struggle is between the reptilian and human races."

There are two schools of thought in our galaxy. There are the regressives-the Draco System, who are races that carry fear and because of that want to control others. The hierarchy of the regressives starts with a group from Alpha Draconis. Known as the Draconians, who do not like human beings. The Draconians believe that this universe was here for them-that their history teaches them that they were left here to rule it. But, when they started traveling, they ran across other races. They were able to conquer many of those races through genetic manipulation.

The Draconians are a very large reptilian race, otherwise known as "the Dracs." There is a royal line of the reptilian race called the Ciakar. They range from 14 to 22 feet tall and can weigh up to 1,800 pounds. They have winged appendages attached to their shoulders, a very long tail, and they can also be extremely sinister. Their life span is between 1,800 to 4,100 years of age. They look like a 22 foot tall velociraptor, and they're smart, intelligent and very different from us. They were one of the first races to chart our solar system, and in fact they were the first race to state that our solar system belonged to them.

They enjoy eating human flesh, and human children best, for two reasons. The first is that children don't have the accumulation of pollutants in their bodies that adults do, and when children are put into a state of fear, their energy and field and adrenalin just explodes. The reptilians get a "rush" from this stuff. There are some 1800 reptilians inside the Earth that have been responsible for some 37,000 human children disappearing. The reptilians not only eat the human children, they drain fluids from the brains of children while they are in fear. They do this to get that substance which to them is like a drug, or narcotic. The excretion from the adrenal and pituitary glands has some of the genetic coding within it. This is really what they are after. Apparently they can absorb it, but their bodies don't produce it.

When they capture a human being, they will not usually kill the person right away. What they usually do is terrify them as much as possible in order to jack up the level of emotion and hormones. Then, when they consume the physical body of that psychologically terrorized being, not only are they feeding themselves but the hormones impart a physiological and psychological "rush" which they enjoy. It's essentially a "drug high" for them.

The Draconians are the force behind the repression of human populations everywhere in this galaxy instilling fear-based belief systems and restrictive hierarchies. The Draconians are the "ultimate warriors," in a negative sense. The Draconians are the oldest reptilian race in our universe. Their forefathers came to our universe from another separate universe or reality system. The Draconians teach their masses that they were here in this universe first, before humans, and as such they are heirs to the universe and should be considered royalty. They find disgust in the fact that humans do not recognize this as a truth. They have conquered many star systems and have genetically altered many of the life forms they have encountered.

The area of the galaxy most densely populated with Draconian sub-races is in the Orion system, and systems in Rigel and Capella. The mind set or consciousness of the majority of races in these systems is Service-to-Self, and as such they are always invading, subverting and manipulating less advanced races, and using their technology for control and domination. This is a very old and ancient war, and the peace that does not exist is always being tested by these beings, who believe that fear rules, and love is weak. They believe that those they perceive to be less fortunate, in comparison to them, are meant to be slaves. This belief system is promoted at birth in the reptilian races, wherein the mother, after giving birth, will abandon the offspring to fend for themselves. If they survive they are cared for by a warrior class that uses these children for games of combat and amusement. So, you can see that the reptilians are forever stuck in survival mode. This means they have no boundaries in what they will do to other beings. It is engrained in them never to trust a human. They are taught the Draconian version of the history of the Great Galactic War, which teaches that humans are at fault for invading the universe, and that humans selfishly wanted the Draconian society to starve and struggle for the basic materials that would allow them to exist. . . . Source: the Andromedans.

*Channeled by Rakie Rehkop,* August 18, 1997 - The first Earth was destroyed by winds blowing hundreds and hundreds of miles per hour. Nothing could survive winds of that magnitude. The second Earth was destroyed by fire, and the third Earth by volcanic upheaval and ocean relocations perpetuated or started by humans. The cataclysm of the fourth Earth that took the Draconians was a pole shift that caused the oceans to relocate. But Atlantis was not covered up because of a pole shift, but because they sank the continents with the thermal egg. The winds blew so hard they made life unsustainable; solar flares caused these hot winds. The heat was too intense to support life. Yet life would always start and re-grow; some would survive somehow. The sixth Earth will be . . . (Rakie's eyes started to flow with tears) we are the worst of all that preceded us...there has been more greed and more killing than in any civilization that preceded us. You have to look at the whole picture: all the wars, genocide's, the H-bomb, pollution and rape of the planet. Even the Draconians, though power-mongers, were not as destructive. So, we the fifth Earth, will be destroyed by all four of the elements.

# ANA (Aphrodite)

ANA by the 'Shinning Ones', the Anunnaki, daughter of Nannar (Phobos) and Nin.gal (Artemis). ANU.NI.TU, ANU.NI.TUM or "beloved of Anu", "the holy mistress of Anu" by the Anunnaki. IMINI by the Sumerians. IR.NI.NI, IR.NIN.NI was changed to IN.ANNA, or "Anu's Beloved" by the Akkadians. IN.NIN, NIN.ANNA, NIN.NI or "Anu's lady" by the Akkadians. Mistress of Heaven; the Morning and Evening Star; War goddess; Sovereign Lady of the Land; Queen of the Assembly of Deities. She was represented riding on her sacred lion, sometimes with a pack of hunting dogs. Other times she was pictured as a winged goddess of war, armed with bow and quiver. One of her symbols was a gatepost hung with streamers; another, a serpent coiling around a staff; her planet was Venus. NANNA, NINA, NAMMU or "Lady" by the Syrians. Ancient Mother; Holy One of Many Names; Great Mother. The Judge of humankind on the last day of every year. An image of a winged lioness guarded her temple. NANNA, NANA, ANNA, or INANNA by the Nordic-Germanic tribes. Aesir Goddess; The Moon; Great Mother; Earth Goddess.

ANA was also known as the Archangel ANAEL, HANNIEL, HANIEL, HANAEL, HAMIEL, ONOEL, SIMIEL and ARIEL by the Hebrews. One of the seven angels of Creation. Anael exercises dominion over the planet Venus, is one of the luminaries concerned with human sexuality, and is governor of the second Heaven. It is Anael who proclaims "Open all ye gates" in *Isaiah 26:2.* In occult writings Haniel is credited with the feat (usually ascribed to Anafiel) of transporting Enoch to Heaven. In addition, she controls kingdoms and kings on earth and had dominion over the moon. Anael appears to be, another form of Aniyel, Anaphiel, Anafiel Anaphiel, Anpiel and Aufiel. Anafiel was the angel who is keeper of the keys of the heavenly halls. According to legend, Metatron the angel of the divine face, was to be punished, Anafiel was designated by God to flog His favorite angel with sixty lashes of fire. According to *3 Enoch,* it was Anafiel who bore Enoch to Heaven.

The Third Region of ancient civilization, as was discovered only some fifty years ago, was in the subcontinent of India. There too, a great civilization arose in antiquity, some 1,000 years after the Sumerian one. It is called the Indus Valley Civilization, and its center was a royal city unearthed at a site called Harappa. Its people worshiped a goddess, depicting her in clay figurines as an enticing female, adorned with necklaces, her breast enhanced by straps which crossed her body. Because the script of the Indus Valley Civilization is still undeciphered, no one knows what the Harappans called their goddess, or who exactly she was. She sometimes is believed to be the daughter of Sin, whom the Sumerians called Irnini and the Akkadians called Ishtar. Sumerian texts tell of her dominion in a far land named Aratta -- a land of grain crops and granaries as Harappa was--where to she made flying trips, attired as a pilot.

She was called TURAN by the Etruscans. The goddess of love. APHRODITE by the Greeks, daughter of Phobos (Nannar) and Aretmis (Ningal). Foam-born; Moon Goddess; "She Who Binds Hearts Together"; "She who came from the sea"; Goddess of the Western Corner. She was pictured as beautiful, voluptuous, with blue eyes and fair hair. At one time her name was Marianna or La Mer, meaning "the Ocean." She was called virginial, meaning that she remained independent. Her priestesses were not physical virgins, but celebrated sexual rites; men were excluded from many of her rituals. Frankincense and myrrh were burned in her temples. The love of women, in whatever form, was sacred to her. She was strong, proud, loving. Her birds were the heron, lovebird, swan, and dove (yonic symbol). Her girdle, cockle shells, poppy, rose, golden apples, sweet fragrances and fruits, and pomegranate were some of her symbols. Patroness of prostitutes. The goddess of love, beauty, the joy of physical love, sensuality, passion, generosity, all forms of partnerships and relationships, affection, fertility, continued creation, renewal. Aphrodite is usually portrayed as a voluptuous woman partially draped with a robe or nude. Her symbols include the dove and the swan. VENUS by the Romans.

"Now the son of Tydeus was in pursuit of the Cyprian goddess, spear in hand, for he knew her to be feeble and not one of those goddesses that can lord it among men in battle like Athene, or Enyo, the waster of cities, and when at last after a long chase he caught her up, he flew at her and thrust his spear into the flesh of her delicate hand. The point tore through the ambrosial robe which the Graces had woven for her, and pierced the skin between her wrist and the palm of her hand, so that the immortal blood, or ichor, that flows in the veins of the blessed gods, came pouring from the wound; for the gods do not eat bread nor drink wine, hence they have no blood such as ours, and are immortal. Aphrodite screamed aloud, and let her son fall, but Phoebus Apollo caught him in his arms, and hid him in a cloud of darkness, lest some Danaan should drive a spear into his breast and kill him; and Diomed shouted out as he left her, "Daughter of Zeus, leave war and battle alone; can you not be contented with beguiling silly women? If you meddle with fighting you will get what will make you shudder at the very name of war." *The Iliad, Book V, pages 74-76.*

"The goddess went dazed and discomfited away, and Iris, fleet as the wind, drew her from the throng, in pain and with her fair skin all besmirched. She found fierce Ares waiting on the left of the battle, with his spear and his two fleet steeds resting on a cloud; whereon she fell on her knees before her brother and implored him to let her have his horses. "Dear brother," she cried, "save me, and give me your horses to take me to Olympus where the gods dwell. I am badly wounded by a mortal, the son of Tydeus, who would now fight even with father Zeus."

"Thus she spoke, and Ares gave her his gold-bedizened steeds. She mounted the chariot sick and sorry at heart, while Iris sat beside her and took the reins in her hand. She lashed her horses on and they flew forward nothing loth, till in a trice they were at high Olympus, where the gods have their dwelling. There she stayed them, unloosed them from the chariot, and gave them their ambrosial forage; but Aphrodite flung herself on to the lap of her mother Dione, who threw her arms about her and caressed her, saying, "Which of the heavenly beings has been treating you in this way, as though you had been doing something wrong in the face of day?"

"And laughter-loving Aphrodite answered: "Proud Diomed, the son of Tydeus, wounded me because I was bearing my dear son Aeneas, whom I love best of all mankind, out of the fight. The war is no longer one between Trojans and Achaeans, for the Danaans have now taken to fighting with the immortals."

"Bear it, my child," replied Dione, "and make the best of it. We dwellers in Olympus have to put up with much at the hands of men, and we lay much suffering on one another. Ares had to suffer when Otus and Ephialtes, children of Aloeus, bound him in cruel bonds, so that he lay thirteen months imprisoned in a vessel of bronze. Ares would have been perished had not fair Eeriboea, stepmother to the sons of Aloeus, told Hermes, who stole him away when he was already well-nigh worn out by the severity of the bondage. Hera again suffered when the mighty son of Amphitryon wounded her on the right breast with a three-barbed arrow, and nothing could assuage her pain. So, also, did huge Hades, when this same man, the son of aegis-bearing Zeus, hit him with an arrow even at the gates of hell and hurt him badly. Thereon Hades went to the house of Zeus on great Olympus, angry and full of pain; and the arrow in his brawny shoulder caused him great anguish till Paeeon healed him by spreading soothing herbs on the wound, for Hades was not of mortal mold."

"Daring, headstrong, evil-doer who recked not of his sin in shooting the gods that dwell in Olympus. And now Athene has egged this son of Tydeus on against yourself, fool that he is for not reflecting that no man who fights with gods will live long or hear his children prattling about his knees when he returns from battle. Let, then, the son of Tydeus see that he does not have to fight with one who is stronger than you are. Then shall his brave wife, Aegialeia, daughter of Adrestus, rouse her whole house from sleep, wailing for the loss of her wedded lord, Diomed, the bravest of the Achaeans." "So saying, she wiped the ichor from the wrist of her daughter with both hands, whereon the pain left her, and her hand was healed."

**Anunnaki goddess Eanna (Ana/Inanna)**

## ANANE (Ananel)

ANANE, ANANEL or ANDANJ a "fallen angel" who mated with earth's human females and produced human giants.

## AN.IB

AN.IB by the Sumerians, son of An II and Antu. TEM, TUM, ATUM or "Creator God" by the Akkadians. Atum was represented in the form of a human and a serpent. His cult center was called Anu or Annu the Hebrew "On", Greek "Heliopolis", and located north of the first city of Babylon (modern-day Egyptian city of Cairo) in Egypt. HERU-UR, AROUERIS, ATUM-RA, TEM-RE, TEM-RA and HORUS the Elder or the "Sun God" by the Egyptians. Atum's symbol is the "scarab beetle" and his sacred animals are the mongoose, lion, bull, lizard, and ape. He was also known in Egypt as the sacred god KHEPRI or KHEPERA the scarab dung beetle. He was called HU the "Sun God" by the Druids of Britain. The Irish called him the Sun God FIN--an Irish name for the Sun. The Irish are called the children of the Sun. In Egypt he is the Sun god. Ra's (Marduk-Lucifer) symbol is an eye--"the All Seeing Eye" and the term for Iris or Irish. Fin presided over the Hill of Tara, located in County Meath, Ireland. (see sun god Mithra) This god may have been the early sun god of the Hindu called MITRA or MIT-RA, later called MITHRA or MITHRAS.

## AN.KI

ANKI by the Sumerians, son of An II and Antu. The Sumerians called their descendants the Anunnaki, who were from the planet Sumi-Er. The Egyptians called them the Neteru. The Neteru were worshiped as gods and were stronger and more intelligent than humans and possessed supernatural powers, but they were susceptible to sickness and death. These "gods" were visitors from outer space from the planet Sumi-Er in the Ash.Ta.Ri (Alpha Tauri, Aldebaran) system of the Tauris the Bull constellation, whose contributions to the early advanced civilization in Egypt were evident long after they departed.

The Anunnaki came to Earth for two reasons. First, they wished to acquire gold to put in the forcefield around Sumi-Er to save their people. Second, they had made an agreement with the Christos Sirians to create, with the help of the Lyrans, the two-stranded DNA Human body for the Earth Sirians, from a cross between the Pleiadians and the evolving land guardian race.

There existed three civilizations, the civilization of Mu (Lemuria) and the evolving human primates. Secondly, the civilization of Yu (the Orientals) in Asia and thirdly, the civilization of Atlantis (Ta Neter, Nether-Land). Ashen started the Yu civilization and Altea (Atlant) started Atlantis. Both were considered offshoots of Lemuria, as both had made agreements that the Lemurians would act as a mother empire to them.

Each of the three civilizations had begun as one race but later they had agreed to allow the Lyrans to change their DNA so they could better adapt to the climate in their chosen areas of the planet. This is how the different red, yellow, and brown races came about. The black race originated from the evolving human primates. They would become the land guardians once they were crossed with the Nibiruans to obtain the necessary DNA upgrade to homo sapien. At that time they would be able to carry the souls of the Earth Sirians. Adam and Eve, the violet race, was then established by Anu's family, the Royal House of Avyon from Nibiru.

Source: *Subterranean Worlds,* by Walter Kafton-Minkel, cr 1989, pps. 117-119.

According to Helena P. Blavatsky: The First Root Race on earth were almost totally astral--energy light beings, and first appeared in an equally astral continent, the "Imperishable Sacred Land." This land was designed by the Dhyan Chohans (seven powerful entities or "rays" that shaped and developed the universe) to "last from the beginning of humanity to the end....It is the cradle of the first man and the dwelling of the last divine mortal." Thus the Imperishable Sacred Land still exists; H.P.B. was vague about its location, but implied it might exist at or around the North Pole. In another part of the book (Stanzas of Dzyan-the oldest of all books), she suggested that when mortals finally reached the North Pole, they would find something there that would change the course of history.

The home of the Second Root Race was near the North Pole as well; it was called Hybornea, a huge, misty, partially-solid continent of which only pieces like Greenland and Spitzbergen remain. The Third Root Race lived in Lemuria, another huge continent filling what is now the Indian and Pacific oceans. While the first two Root Races had been amorphous since their bodies were primarily astral, the Third Root Race was primarily material and grew ever-more human in form as its sub-races developed. By the fourth sub-race or so, the Lemurians resembled giant apes-they stood sixteen feet tall, with long arms, short legs, and eyes almost on the sides of their heads. They also lacked true sentience, for they had no souls or consciousness.

At this point, about eighteen million years ago, spiritual beings called Kumaras or "princes," began entering the bodies of the Lemurians, and they brought the developing race both conscious minds and sexual reproduction (previous races and sub-races had divided in a protoplasmic fashion). Unfortunately, some of them received sex before consciousness; a group of the yet-soulless Lemurian males, carried away by their new urges, copulated with "huge she-animals....They begat upon these dumb races...a race of crooked monsters going on all fours." As punishment, the transgressors and their offspring were denied souls by the Kumaras, and these crooked ones eventually evolved into both the apes and what were called in her day "the inferior races....The world knows them as Tasmanians..., Australians, Andaman Islanders, etc." She stated that these peoples had no souls, and that there were other races, among them the Africans and Polynesians, which had only recently reached a level of development at which the Kumaras would enter their bodies.

The "monsters" fathered by the soulless Lemurians brought more misfortune to the world, for the monsters attacked and devoured the newly sentient Lemurians, and murder and sin came into the world. Although the sentient Lemurians appealed to the Chohans for help, and beings from the planet Venus, known as "the wise Serpents and Dragons of Light," came to their aid, Lemuria was doomed. Volcanoes and earthquakes broke the continent to bits, and Australia, Madagascar, and the Pacific Islands are all that remain of it today. The Serpents and Dragons of Light did help the remnants of humanity through the crisis, however, by teaching them agriculture, weaving, and other skills necessary to life in a sinful world. They also taught the most virtuous of the remaining humans the secret teachings, and these recipients of the teachings became the first Masters-the "elect custodians of the Mysteries revealed to mankind by the Divine Teachers." The Masters continued to dwell alongside their less advanced brethren, guiding them but remaining hidden from all but a few apprentices.

With the fall of Lemuria, Atlantis rose from the sea and the Fourth Root Race took the stage. Their first sub-race was the Rmoahals, a nation of brown-skinned giants; the second was the Tlavatlis, a red-skinned, wandering people. The third sub-race, the Toltecs (another red-skinned race), was guided by the Masters for a time, and the Toltec empire, using occult knowledge wisely, lasted a hundred thousand years, until they abandoned the Masters' teachings. As soon as they did, they began degenerating; a secret society of evil magicians (Sons of Belial) took power in Atlantis and lured the people into worshipping elemental spirits with bloody rituals. In the end the Toltecs were conquered by the barbarous Turanians (the fourth sub-race), the ancestors of the Aztecs.

The source of the magical powers of the Rmoahals, Tlavatli and Toltecs was a fully expanded etheric organism which reached far beyond the confines of the physical body. Their speech, for instance, was intimately connected to the forces of nature. Their words could not only advance the growth of plants and tame wild beasts, but also bring about immediate and miraculous healing to the sick and terrible forces of destruction in times of enmity. Their physical bodies were softer and had greater plasticity in that age, more pliable and malleable, as it were, it was possible for lofty Spirit-Beings to assume human form. They had mental and spiritual qualities of a superhuman kind and appeared to their contemporaries as Supermen. One could call them divine-human hybrid beings, sort of God-Men. They were greatly venerated by all lesser mortals who accepted their guidance gratefully and obeyed their commandments without question.

Because the Atlanteans had a magical mastery over the life forces in nature, its misuse led to disastrous consequences. The forces of growth and reproduction, when torn from the context of their natural functions and employed independently, stand in a magical relationship to the elemental powers at work in air and water. It was the egotistical abuse of the teaching of the Oracles, in which holy fertility cults originated, that brought about the most terrible disruptions. Black magic rituals, involving the perversion of the powers of human reproductions, let loose mighty and ominous forces and led to the eventual destruction of the whole continent in catastrophic storms of wind and water.

At this critical juncture in the history of Atlantis a new race was founded which was to protect the spiritual essence of man from extinction and guarantee the rightful progress of mankind for thousands of years to come. The Semitic man (Adapa, Adam) was contracted to bring about the metamorphosis to personal intelligence and a direct vision of the sense world. But these faculties of thought and sense perception were gained at the price of a total loss of all magical powers over nature and over the life-forces in the human organism. Even the basic form of man was radically changed. The former plastic, pliable, malleable, soft cartilaginous bodies of the Tlavatli,

Toltecs and Turanians were replaced by what we know today as the form of modern man, the basis of which is the bony skeleton.

The Turanians were replaced in succession by the Semites a fair-skinned race, who were the ancestors of the modern Jews, and the Akkadians, who settled the lands around the Mediterranean, and the Mongolians, ancestors of the modern East Asians.

A small group of Semites traveled to Central Asia and under the direction of the Masters evolved into the Aryans, the Fifth Root Race. The great rulers of the degenerating races in the south of the continent saw the dangers of allowing the new race of Aryans to develop and made war upon them. Out of the mists surrounding the foot of the mountains the Aryan warriors were confronted by terrifying hordes of marauding peoples, many of whom were "huge in size" and grotesque in shape, manifesting the most fearful magical powers and capable of feats of superhuman strength. Against them the Aryans pitted their newborn intelligence and the ability to improvise proved superior to all the magic thrown against them. An echo of the ferocity of these prehistoric battles which were waged between the first self-conscious human beings and these monstrous and magical creatures has come down to us through the myths, especially those which tell of the outwitting of the giants.

The Aryan race was soon to be replaced as the dominant race by the Sixth Root Race, which was evolving in America (Anglo-Saxons). The home of the Sixth Root Race was to be a new Lemuria, due to rise out of the Pacific just west of San Diego. In another few thousand years, the Seventh Root Race was to evolve from the Sixth in the vicinity of South America and humanity would return to its starting point in the Imperishable Sacred Land, once again an astral race in an astral country. Once the earth and the human race had faded again into the non-material, the curtain would fall on the earth cycle and a new, more perfect cycle of seven would begin on the planet Mercury.

The Seven Root Races of Man

The First Root Race-energy light beings who lived near the North Pole

The Second Root Race-Hyperboreans who lived in Hybornea

The Third Root Race-Lemurians who lived in Mu

The Fourth Root Race-Atlanteans who lived in Atlantis
-The first sub-race in Atlantis-Rmoahals
-The second sub-race in Atlantis-Tlavatlis
-The third sub-race in Atlantis-Toltecs
-The fourth sub-race in Atlantis-Turanians, ancestors of the Aztecs
-The fifth sub-race in Atlantis-Semites, ancestors of Hebrons & Akkadians

The Fifth Root Race-Aryans who lived in Central Asia (Gobi Desert)

The Sixth Root Race-Anglo-Saxons that live in the present United States

The Seventh Root Race-to evolve from the area of South America

## AN.NU (Cronos)

ARUSSEM by the Pleiadians. AN or EKU by the Sumerians, son of An.shar (Uranos) and Ki.shar (Gaea). ANNU and ANU or "The Heavenly One" by the Akkadians. ANUM or "heaven" by the Babylonians. ANUSH by the Hittites. Anu was said to have ruled the Nine Lords of the Rings (Planets)--having the ninth Ring (the One Ring) to govern the eight others. He owned the Ninth Ring (Saturn) which binds the others within his ultimate power. The "Ring" was a symbol of perpetually divine justice, which was measured by the Rod. In Babylonia, the Rod was referred to as the Rule. The one who held the Rod or Rule was the designated "Ruler".

The King of Sumi-Er and Nibiru (Neteru, Ta Neter, Nether-land, Atlantis) was named Annu (Annu-Antu, Twins connection). A governing body was later formed known as The Council of Twelve (six from Lyra and six from Sirius). Enlil (Lyrans) were given reign over one sector of Earth and Enki (Sirians) were given reign over the other sector. The Lyrans remained as overseers to the operations in the valleys of Mesopotamia, while the Sirians remained with the gold mining operations in South Africa.

ANU was the Great Father of the Gods, the King of the Gods. His realm was the expanse of the heavens, and his symbol was a four pointed star. This fourfold meaning of the symbol remained through the ages, as the script moved from the Sumerian pictographic to the cuneiform Akkadian, to the stylized Babylonian and Assyrian. His mystic symbol representing God was: Itt/ The Assyrian cuneiform sign of a star was a cross, which meant "Anu" and "divine," and evolved in the Semitic languages to the letter tav, or a "cross" which meant "the sign." Anu is called ON in the Bible.

The Anunnaki (also transcribed as: Anu.Na.Ki, Anu-nuki, Anu.Ki, Anunna, Anunnaku, Ananaki, An.Na.Kim, Anakim, Anu ram Kir, Anu ram Kim and other variations) are a group of Sumerian, Akkadian, Phoenician, Armenian, Assyrian and Babylonian deities. The name is variously written "a-nuna", "a-nuna-ke4-ne", or "a-nun-na", meaning something to the effect of "those of royal blood" or "princely offspring".

Anu, King of the Anu.Na.Ki by the Anunnaki (Anunna by the Sumerians, Anunnaki by the Akkadians, An.Na.Kim by the Phoenicians, An-nuki & Anu.Ki by the people of Arwad, Anakim by the Canaanites, Anuramkir & Anuramkim by the Hyskos/Armenians, Anunnaku & Ananaki by the Hittites, Anedoti by the Chaldeans, Annodoti by the Greeks, Ananaki by the Assyrians, and An-gels by the Habiru/Hebrews) which was the generic name for their "Dragons of Wisdom", known by the Hebrews as the "Watchers". The symbol of An, the king of heaven in the Sumerian pantheon of gods, was the "jackal". The Sphinx was originally built as a stone representation of Anu which was a jackel that had long pointed ears. Anu was the first god in the Sumerian pantheon. "Lord of spirits". Titan-Giant; Supreme God; God of Heaven; Father Time; the Old King; the Great Lesson-Giver; Ruler of the Golden Age. He was a Sky god, Father and King of the Gods. The Watchers obtained their power on earth by appearing in dreams and visions as gods and goddesses, and as omens in the skies, and commanded the people to build them temples and places of worship, and said that they would come to the earth and dwell amongst men.

At the time in which the events related in the Sumerian tablets had taken place. Anu lived in semi-retirement, aloof from daily affairs. His abode was "in the mountains," at "the two headwaters" (between the Orontes River & the Euphrates River in northern Syria). There he sat in his pavilion (Ain Dara Temple), receiving emissaries, holding councils of the gods, and trying to resolve the recurring disputes among the younger gods. Many of these were his own children: some text suggest that Anu may have had seventy offspring. Of them, thirty were by his official consort Antu; the others, by an assortment of concubines or even human females.

The Anunnaki have access to a plant (or tree), native to their planet Sumi-Er, that prevents normal aging and bodily deterioration. Sumerian texts referred to it as the 'Tree of Life'. Later, the Bible referred to it as 'Knowledge of The Tree of Life' in the Garden of Eden story. Only the Anunnaki royalty had privileged access to the Tree of Life, sometimes called "Ambrosiac" in Sumerian texts. They absorbed this substance into their bodies by taking baths soaked with this life extending plant. This special bath water was the origin of the story of The Fountain of Youth.

Called ZURVAN by the Persians. The god of time and space in Persian mythology, was the father of the Good god, Ahura Mazda (Enlil), and his

Evil brother, Ahriman (Enki). Some historians, as well as the theosophist occultist Helena Blavatsky, believe that Zurvan was part of the original teachings of Zoroastrianism, while other historians believe that Zurvan was added to the Zoroastrian belief later. The earliest solid evidence for a belief in Zurvan seems to date from the Sassanid dynasty, which ruled Persia from 224 to 651 AD. These historians sometimes refer to this variation of Zoroastrianism as Zurvanism. However, this term is misleading, because it is unlikely that any Zoroastrians worshipped Zurvan; worship was always reserved for Ahura Mazda alone.

The Hebrews called him the archangel KAFZIEL (CASSIEL, CADIEL, CASZIEL, ZAPHKIEL, ZAPHCHIAL, ZAPHIEL), the angel governing the death of kings. In geonic tradition, he is one of the seven archangels with dominion over the planet Saturn. The angel of solitudes and tears who 'shews forth the unity of the eternal kingdom.' He is the ruling prince of the seventh Heaven and one of the sarim (princes) of the order of powers. Sometimes he appears as the angel of temperance. Zaphkiel or "knowledge of God." Chief of the order of thrones and one of the nine angels that rule heaven; also one of the seven archangels. Zaphkiel is a governor of the planet Saturn.

He is also called the Archangel TSAPHKIEL, TZAPHQUIEL, ZAPHKIEL, ZAPHCHIAL, ZAPHIEL, ZOPHIEL, ORIFIEL, IOPHIEL and IOFIEL; which means "the knowledge of God". He is the chief of the order of thrones and one of the nine angels that rule Heaven; also one of the seven archangels. Zaphkiel is a governor of the planet Saturn. According to Fludd, Zaphkiel, as Zophiel, is the ruler of the order of cherubim (*the rabbinic ophanim). Zaphiel is also the preceptor angel of Noah. Milton *(Paradise Lost VI, 535)* calls Zaphiel (Zophiel) "of cherubim the swiftest wing."

TZAPHKIEL or TZAPHQUIEL, Dark Angel of the Soul of Man; Prince of the spiritual strife against evil. Keeper of the records of evolution; mediates with the forces of karma. He rules the planet Saturn and is one of the archangels of the ten sephiroth. Angel of spiritual development, overcoming grief, balancing or changing karma.

CHIUN (which was another name for the planet Saturn), one of the Cherubim that faced one another with their wings outstretched toward each other over the Mercy (Covering) Seat that contained the sacred items within the Ark of the Covenant.

KRONION by the Atlanteans. CHRONOS/CRONOS/CRONUS or "the Horned one" by the Greeks, son of Uranos (Anshar) and Gaea (Kishar). Cronus carried a crooked shaped sickle, the ultimate weapon a diamond sickle. KRONOS by the Phoenicians. KRODO or SATAR by the Goths. SADORN or SAMOTHES by the Celts, who gave his name to the Island of Samothea (early Britain). SATURN by the Romans. Saturn's holy day was Saturday, the original holy day of the Jews.

The Phoenicians every year sacrificed their beloved and only-begotten children to Kronos or Saturn, and the Rhodians also often did the same. The Carthaginians, on one occasion, when besieged by the Sicilians, and sore pressed, in order to rectify, as they supposed, their error in having somewhat departed from the ancient custom of Carthage, in this respect, hastily "chose out two hundred of the noblest of their children, and publicly sacrificed them" to this god.

According to the Greeks, Cronus was the youngest of twelve Titans. Chronos was an Atlantean god, and from him the Atlantic Ocean was called by the ancients 'the Chronian Sea'. The Romans called the Atlantic Ocean 'Chronium Mare' or 'the Sea of Chronos'. The pillars of Hercules were also called by the ancients 'the pillars of Chronos'. Berosus tells us that the god who gave warning of the coming of the second Deluge was Chronos.

'The Elysian Fields' (the happy islands) were commonly placed in the remote west. They were ruled over by Chronos. The Elysian Fields was the 'Elysion' of the Greeks, which was also an island in the remote west. Chronos was the ruler over these Titans, or giants of Atlantis.

According to Greek mythology the Titans, also known as the elder gods, ruled the earth before the Olympians overthrew them. Mythology tells us that when the Titans were defeated in a war by Saturn (Cronos) they retreated into the interior of Tartarus; Jupiter (Zeus) followed after them, and beat them for the last time near Tartessus, and this terminated a ten-years' war. The new ruler of the Titans was Cronos who was de-throned later by his son Zeus. Most of the Titans fought with Alalu (Helios) against Cronos and were punished by being banished to Tartarus.

According to the Egyptians, Cronos (Anu) and Zeus (Enlil), the son of Cronos, had a prolonged war; Cronos was defeated and his capital was captured. He was dethroned, and his son Zeus was put in his place as King of Atlantis.

The *Critias* that "above all let us first recall that 9,000 years (11,500 BC) had passed since the war, which I will describe, was said to have broken out between those who lived beyond the pillars of Heracles (Poseidon's kingdom) and those dwelling within them (Zeus' kingdom). It has already been mentioned that our city Athens was the greatest among the latter, and pursued the war to its end, while the former, the people of the island of Atlantis, were ruled by its kings. This island was, as we saw, once larger than Libya and Asia, but now had sunk into the sea as a consequence of earthquakes, and presented to those who wanted to sail to the further sea an insuperable obstacle in the form of mass of mud . . ."

The historian Theopompos, a contemporary of Plato, relates a conversation between the legendary King Midas of Phrygia and the very wise satyr Silenus. The satyr, entrapped and rendered drunk by Midas, told him of an Outer Continent that outlay the ocean and which was inhabited by people twice the size and twice as long-lived as the ordinary mortals. One part of the continent was permanently enwrapped by a red mist and was drained by two rivers, the River of Pleasure and the River of Grief. Once, these giants crossed the ocean intending to conquer the ancient world. But once they saw the misery of our world, they realized that it was useless to pursue their plan, and retired to their world in disgust.

In the version of Theopompos, the Atlanteans are often described as tall, blond, blue-eyed giants of twice normal size, and are a recurrent feature of the ancient Greek legends. They had technology that seemed miraculous for the age, such as the ability to throw what appeared to be lightning bolts, or float along above the ground, or take off in rocket ships, or perform surgery and have the patient live.

*Ancient American Magizine,* Volume 6, Issue #41, page 36 - U.S. Navy Cover-Up? - A September 7th (2001) dispatch received from out in the mid-Atlantic Ocean, via William Donato, President of the Atlantis Organization (CA), tells of "a team 250 miles south west of the Azores equipped with bathescape and two submersibles. We have been researching a 90-kilometer ledge with a central temple supported by three stands of nine pillars about 3 feet in diameter supporting a flat stone roof about 20 feet wide and 30 feet long."

"There are the remains of five circular canals and bridges, plus four rings of structures like the temple in between. "It is roughly 2,800 feet deep in the Mid-Atlantic Trench, and stable at this time. We have tried to send photos out, but they have been jammed by surface vessels a mile off our starboard bow, flying a United States flag. We were there on a research project for the Spanish government about a week, but were chased off the spot yesterday by those ships. The mountains that rise from the underwater valley have peaks 300 feet under the surface. We have used sonar to follow the ridge west and slightly south, and it appears to connect with the continental shelf near Hispaniola, and continues to Cuba."

"A second salvage ship is north east bound, and is tracking a similar ridge-head to a point east of England. They want to prove a contiguous path, but the damn fleet is in the way, and they are hassling those research vessels.

Must be some kind of maneuvers. But they do not want anyone sweeping that area. I smell a rat. Publish if you wish."

One of the main proponents to get information public on the underwater discoveries near Cuba is Linda Moulton Howe & her Earthfiles.com website. In Linda's first report on 5-18-01(3 days after the Reuters release), she interviewed Barbara Moffet with the National Geographic Society. Supposedly, National Geographic will be involved in this project. Linda shares the *Reuters'* May 15, 2001 News Release.

"The discovery comes from Paulina Zelitsky, of *Advanced Digital Communications,* mapping with special sonar equipment the ocean's floor in contract with the Cuban Academy of Sciences. The discoveries were said to be when they were running tests deep in waters off Havana Bay [actually much further West]. What was spotted was said to be in approximate waters of 2200 feet depth (also noted as somewhere between 700 to 800 meters). It seems to be some sort of plateau which can only be manmade, as it indicates or is similar to structures like pyramids, buildings, and even roads. ADC was also mapping underwater sea volcanoes at about twice the depth around 5000 feet or about 1500 meters. This was off the Western tip of Cuba. There was to be a hopeful expedition in the summer of 2001. The Western tip of Cuba was at one past time era joined to the Yucatan, for those that may not know."

## Anom (Anamim)

Anom or Anamim, son of Mizraim (Mitzraim) of the land of Egypt. Anamim one of the seven sons of Egypt and a grandson of Chem (Ham). *Genesis* 10:13; *1 Chronicles* 1:11.

## AN.SHAR (Uranos)

KIN.SHAR by the Sumerians, son of An.shar.gal and Kish.ar.gal (Titea). AN.SHAR by the Akkadians. Anshar was the fifth ruler on Sumi-Er of the unified dynasty. ADAR by the Canaanites. The governor of the planet Saturn. ASSHUR or ASHUR by the Assyrians. The national god of Assyria. King of gods; a warrior god; a "Sun God"; a Supreme God; the maker of the sky and the underworld. He was represented in symbols as a winged disk mounted on a bull, or a winged disk flying through the air. In some records he is shown as the father of Anu and Antu.

GEB or "Who Piles Up the Earth" by the Egyptians. Geb built the "House Which Is Like a Mountain"--the Great Pyramid of Giza. The Great Pyramid was conceived by Enki (Ptah), plained by Marduk (Meleck), built by Anshar (Geb), equipped by Ningishzidda (Thoth), and defended by Nergal (Adah/Allah). According to Edgar Cayce the Great Pyramid, was one hundred years in construction; begun and completed in the period of Araar-aart's time with Thoth and Ra. "What was the date of that period? It was 10,490 BC to 10,390 BC years before the Prince of Peace entered Egypt. The Library of Knowledge was built in Egypt 90 years later, in the year 10,300 BC". *Cayce Reading #5748-6*

ATLANT or ADLANT by the Pleiadians, the first king of Atland/Atlantis. Atlant was a tall, blond-haired, broad-shouldered man of obvious Lyran decent. His bright blue eyes and pale white skin painted a picture not unlike his Lyran ancestors of millions of years ago. He was very popular, and although life there was peaceful and happy, he longed to lead his followers to a new world where they could start a life full of adventure and growth. There were many who decided to follow Atlant, and plans were made to migrate to Earth, which was a small planet their ancestors had lived on that was hospitable to human life. Here they could create a whole new world. The Frisians called him WR'ALDA. Alda is a derivative of ALDLAND, the original name of Atland or Atlantis. VARUNA or "the god of the ocean" by the Hindoos; and his people were called "the Aditya". *The Pleiadian Mission*, by Randolph Winters, cr1994, p.46.

The barbarians of the coast of the Mediterranean regarded the civilized people of Atlantis with awe and wonder. Their physical strength was extraordinary, the earth shaking sometimes under their tread. Whatever they did was done speedily. They moved through space almost without the loss of a moment of time. They were wise, and communicated their wisdom to men. They had a strict sense of justice, and punished crime rigorously, and rewarded noble actions.

There were tales of personal visits and adventures of the gods among men, taking part in battles and appearing in dreams. They were conceived to posses the form of human beings, and to be, like men, subject to love and pain, but always characterized by the highest qualities and grandest forms that could be imagined. The gods were not looked upon as having created the world. They succeeded to the management of a world already in existence.

The gods dwelt on Olympus which was in Atlantis. It was a great island, the then civilized world. Some of the names of the cities on the different islands of Atlantis were: Eden, on the Island of Poseidia located to the North. The cities of Poseidon, Sus, Peos, Amaki, Achaei and Alta. Some of the Islands of Atlantis were: Eizen also located in the North; Aryaz (Araz), located in the East; Latinia, located in the South, and Og, Oz, or On, located in the West.

Most all ancient civilizations believed in the Titans, the race of giant beings that inhabited Earth long ago. Different races knew them by different names. The giant humanoids were thought to be legendary until the excavations of over a dozen skeletons eight to twelve feet tall, around the world, shocked archaeologists. These skeletons were positively human. Some of these skeletal remains are on Maui in lava caves near Ulupalakua and Olowalu. The Spanish Conquistadors left diaries of wild blond-haired, blue-eyed eight to twelve foot high men running around in the Andes during the conquest of the Incas. A couple were reportedly captured but died en route to Europe.

OURANOS by the Phoenicians. URANOS or "Heaven" by the Greeks, son of An.shar.gal and Titea (Kish.ar.gal). URANUS or "Starry Heaven" by the Romans. Uranos the progenitor of the Pantheon of the gods, along with his wife Gaea. Called the Els (angEls), El Anakim, or Elder Race. The Greek Titans were also called the 'Elder gods.' He plotted to kill the younger gods (the Olympians) and was killed by Baal (Enki) who became the new god of the sun. BURI by the Nordic-Germanic tribes.

The information below was found in a cave in modern Turkey. A stack of eleven clay tablets in a stone container which were originally in King Ashurbanipal's library at Ninevah. Called the Edin Text, the translation of these tablets follows:

There was once a continent in the Ocean of Tethys, in the time when the sea, between MAGAN (Greece) and the land of the Barbarians of the West, did not exist and the sea bottom was dry. It was when the Star of Tammuz rose with APSU, when APSU and LUBAD ANSHAR were both in the body of MUL GIR TAB on the first day of Nisannu. This continent lay one-fourth DUB, or three Beru, to the west of Edin on the boundary between the Way of ANU and the Way of ENLIL.

As time passed, the great continent was broken by the will of the gods into islands of great size. These islands were inhabited by the Great Ones of legend. They were taller than the people of Sumer by almost a head, and their bodies were marvelous to behold. Five races of the Great People lived in this island nation called Atlan.

And the names of their cities were Peos, and Sus, and Poseidia, and Alta. And they were wondrous places. So wise in the ways of the gods were the Great Ones that they had not to gather fuel for heat nor want for food. And when they wished to travel great distances, they rode upon horses whose feet did not touch the earth.

And on the first day of Nisannu the Great Ones gave thanks to the Great Force of Creation which has caused all things to be. And they called themselves the *"Children of the Law of One"*. And they dwelled in peace with their fellow beings.

Then, after the second great upheaval of the Earth, the people became afraid for their lives. This was when 'The Sons of Belial' came to be. They turned away from the way of the Law of One and became greedy and possessive of their neighbors' goods. And they began to worship the forces of their machines instead of the 'Great Force of Creation.' And so, their gods became many instead of 'One'. And the Sons of Belial (Enki) struggled against the Children of the Law of One (Enlil) and there was great strife in the land. It was then that the greatest of the great-the Lord Tehuti (Hermes) joined with the great Lady Isis to quell the strife. And they banned the 'Sons of Belial' from the Earth. And once again were the temples cleansed. And those were happy days for the Great Ones. But not even the great Tehuti and Isis could prevent the oncoming tragedy which was ordained by the gods to befall them. And the Earth became more unstable, and more islands sank into the ocean.

It was then that the great artificer, Tehuti, master of knowledge and determiner of fate, devised the plan. And the plan was a stargate to other lands and other times. And Tehuti said, "Let this moment begin a new era for the creatures of the Earth, for my bloodline shall course through history unto the end of each cycle of time. And when that time is come, my descendants and the descendants of Isis shall hold the keys of this knowledge and return them to Atlan (Atlantis). And they shall remember this plan like unto mine, and I shall greet the farthest traces of my seed and clasp them unto my bosom. They shall return the images of Tehuti and Isis to their rightful place in the Great Pyramid of Atlan. And then shall they open the heart AN.SIN.DIN.MUL (point-from-where-the-god-spirit-flows) of the world. And time shall be no more, and the souls of all who wish shall return to the Creator Force. When the images are returned, to represent balance of male and female on the Earth, then shall the cycles of time move to a new harmonic." And in 'that' cycle of time this did not occur. And it was in the following year that Atlan sank into the bosom of the ocean taking her secrets with her.

According to Greek mythology, there once were five races of mankind, which lived upon the Earth. The first was a golden race, created by the Titans. These people lived in ease and peace, free of all disease and never growing old. When they died, they died peacefully in their sleep and became daimones (spirits) living on the Earth as guardians of men. The second race was silver, made by the Olympian gods. These were removed from the Earth by Zeus because they were foolish and would not honor the gods. This race became underworld spirits. These beings were chained in the Abyss for their rebellion. The third or bronze race created by Zeus was fierce and warlike. It destroyed itself through violence, eventually wiping itself out and dropping into the underworld which was ruled by Hades. The fourth race, unlike the others, has no metal associated with it. This race contained great heroes or demi-gods who fought at Troy, Troad and Thebes. The fifth race or present race is associated with iron and was said to never rest from labor, being born to trouble, sorrow and death.

## AN.SHAR.GAL

ADAR, ASAR or ASHAR or "prince, foremost of the heavens" by the Sumerians. Sky god; male principle of all life; God of the Earth. AB.ZU, AP.ZU or AP.SU or "one who exists from the beginning" by the Sumerians. Apsu the air god; god of the four winds. Creator and Lord of the world. Primordial ocean; the watery abyss that encircled the Earth.

ANSHARGAL by the Akkadians, son of An.ib and Nin.ib. SHU or "God of air" by the Egyptians.

Archangel RAZIEL, RATZIEL, AKRASIEL, GALLIZUR, BALLIZUR, SARAQAEL, and SURIEL by the Hebrews. The "angel of the secret regions and chief of the Supreme Mysteries." M. Gaster, *The Sword of Moses*. The Bright Angel of the Soul of Man; Prince of the Princes of the Knowledge of Hidden and Concealed Things. One of the ten archangels of the Briatic world of the *Kabala*. Chief of the Order of the Erelim; herald of deity. Angel of illumination, guidance, destiny. In the *Cabala,* Raziel is the personification of Cochma (divine wisdom), second of the ten holy sefiroth. In rabbinic lore, Raziel is the legendary author of The Book of the Angel Raziel, "wherein all celestrial and earthly knowledge is set down."

Legend has it that Raziel gave a book to Adam, and that the other angels, out of envy, purloined the precious grimoire and cast it into the sea, whereat God ordered Rahab (Enki), obediently did, although it should be pointed out that before this, Rahab had been destroyed. The Book of the Angel Raziel finally came into possession of, first, Enoch (who, it is said, gave it out as his own work--the Book of Enoch); then of Noah (who was his son); then of Solomon, the latter deriving from it his great knowledge and power in magic. (Rf. De Plancy, Dictionnaire Infernal.) Raziel was also known as the herald of deity and preceptor angel of Adam.

In all these writings, be it long epic tales or two-line proverbs, in inscriptions mundane or divine, the same facts emerge as an unshakable tenet of the Sumerians and the peoples that followed them: in bygone days, the DIN.GIR--"The Righteous Ones of the Rocketships," the beings the Greeks began to call "gods"--had come to Earth from their own planet. They chose southern Mesopotamia to be their home away from home. They called the land KI.EN.GIR--"Land of the Lord of the Rockets" , the Akkadian name, Shumer, meant "Land of the Guardians"; and they established there settlements on the Earth.

The statement that the first to establish settlements on Earth were astronauts from another planet was not lightly made by the Sumerians. In text after text, whenever the starting point was recalled, it was always this: 432,000 years before the Deluge, the DIN.GIR--"Righteous Ones of the

Rocketships"-- came down to Earth from their own planet. The Sumerians considered it a twelfth member of the Solar System--a system made up of the Sun in the center, the Moon, all the nine planets we know of today, and one more large planet whose orbit lasts a Sar, or 3,600 Earth-years. This orbit, they wrote, takes the planet to a "station" in the distant heavens, then brings it back to Earth's vicinity, crossing between Mars and Jupiter. It was in that position--as depicted in a 4,500-year-old Sumerian drawing that the planet obtained its name NIBIRU which means "Crossing", and its symbol, the "Cross." Nibiru was called Neteru by the Egyptians. Sumeru by the Buddhists. (Mount) Meru by the Hebrews and Safon by the Canaanites.

Central to the religious beliefs and astronomy of the ancient world was the conviction that the Twelfth Planet, the Planet of the Gods, Nibiru, or Planet X, remained within our solar system and that its grand orbit returned it periodically to Earth's vicinity. The pictographic sign for the Twelfth Planet, the "Planet of Crossing," was a cross. The people of the ancient world considered the periodic nearing of the Twelfth Planet as a sign of upheavals, great changes, and new eras. The Mesopotamian texts spoke of the planet's periodic appearance as a anticipated, predictable, and observable event.

## AN.TU (Antu)

ANTU wife of An II by the Sumerians, daughter of An I. NAUNET or "primordial ocean" by the Egyptians. High Priestessess, who were the Maidens of the Ring. The ring around the neck is a torque, which in Celtic lore symbolises, Kingship and therefore wisdom and seership.

*Fingerprints of the Gods,* by Graham Hancock - "During the fabled 'First Time,' Zep Tepi, when the gods ruled in their country: they said it was a golden age during which the waters of the abyss receded, the primordial darkness was banished, and humanity, emerging into the light, was offered the gifts of civilization. They spoke also of intermediaries between gods and men-the Urshu, a category of lesser divinities whose title meant 'the Watchers.' And they preserved particularly vivid recollections of the gods themselves, puissant and beautiful beings called the Neteru (Ne.Be.Ru, Nibiru, Neteru, Ta Neter, Nether-Land, Atlantis) who lived on earth with humankind and exercised their sovereignty from Heliopolis and other sanctuaries up and down the Nile. Some of these Neteru were male and some female but all possessed a range of supernatural powers which included the ability to appear, at will, as men or women, or as animals, birds, reptiles, trees or plants. Paradoxically, their words and deeds seem to have reflected human passions and preoccupations. Likewise, although they were portrayed as stronger and more intelligent than humans, it was believed that they could grow sick-or even die, or be killed-under certain circumstance."

*Channeled by Rakie Rehkop,* August 18, 1997 - Note: Rakie's intent in entering this channeling session was to learn more about what we have called Atlantean times.

I see many round peaked roofs as you might see in ancient Persia. They are spherical or onion-shaped and come to a point on top. The weather is temperate. The buildings do not have window screens or doors that close. The whole place seems devoid of bright colors. The buildings, and the dress of the people, are white or beige, sometimes with pastel colors. Many of the people are quite tall, over 7 feet. Some have *"elongated heads".* Everybody, men and women, dress similarly and their dress looks ancient Roman. Everybody has white skin with hair of brown, auburn, red or gold and they are all rather pale. It seems like the sun is shining but nobody sems to have tanned skin. There is nobody with black hair. There are lots of children and most are blonde. The streets are walkways of stone and the buildings are made of stone set so closely that the surface looks like stucco. These people seem to have ways of cutting stone with such precision that it can be set almost mortarless, almost inlaid. It seems that people walk from one place to another. Everything is in close proximity. The only animals I see are camels and birds. There are no cats, dogs or insects.

The consciousness of the people is not as polarized as ours; they are mellower. They are not as realized as in the vision of Shamballa but their consciousness is higher than ours. These people are magical. They still have the ability to manifest. They manifest their needs, and that is why their houses are so simple. This is only one race of people; there are others. These are called the Golden Ones, and they are what remains of the highest evolved of all races. This is a race of extraterrestrials incarnate in human form. Their origin is the belt of Orion, not Sirius or the Pleiades, and they have been here for quite some time. It has been difficult to maintain a level of purity within their race, in the sense of not being infiltrated by other races. That was their intention, but many of their people over the years had gone out into the wilderness and comingled (had sex with) what were considered the lesser evolved races, all the way into the animal kingdom. Those that chose to do this were no longer welcomed into the city of the Golden Ones. Many who left wanted to experience and feel the fire of emotion, for the emotions were almost not present.

Many who left took technology with them. They also were able to maintain many of their magical abilities such as to manifest and bilocate. To some on the world outside, these people were considered gods. Many of those who left became quite powerful. They had made attempts to reconcile with the Golden Ones, to be accepted for who they were, but the Golden Ones in the city wouldn't accept or acknowledge their existence. And now over the many years the ones who had separated away literally became adversaries of the Golden Ones.

The Golden Ones had harnessed the energy of the sun using what I will call a thermal egg. They called it a *"neutron accelerator."* I see one of these devices. It is very big; probably 100 feet long and 50 feet in diameter. Originally this was developed for the good of all mankind, as a source of power. Smaller versions could cut and fuse anything and were used for masonery work. Over periods of time those on the outside became a threat to the security and safety of the Golden Ones in the city. They in turn threatened to turn the "neutron accelerator" on these people on the outside. There was such a fear of this machine that they would not even consider any action against the Golden Ones. But as time and technology grew, those on the outside developed their own neutron accelerators. These were so powerful that they could literally melt away the superstructure or the continent, causing great collapses on the surface, upheavals of volcanic eruptions, earthquakes.

I am trying to understand why the outsiders wanted to destroy the Golden Ones. For many years they coexisted, then something changed. Ah! It's about land, same old thing. The Golden Ones controlled most of the land and had come to a place where their race was dwindling in numbers. They stopped procreating somewhere along the line. I see what happened. Most of the women had left to live in the outside world. Stories of excitement, of a more expanded life, kept finding their way back and the women kept leaving. These were the factors that brought about the Great War: the women leaving and the fact the Golden Ones controlled most of the land. There came a time when the only women left were old women and the only men left were old men. The Golden Ones led a very confined simple life, similar to people all living in a monastery although not quite as rigid, but very structured as to how they went about their life. That is why the younger ones kept going to the outlands. There seemed to be a need for humanness to express itself in a wider range of experience.

There was a time when the Golden Ones would not fight, but they kept sinking more and more into polarized consciousness, feeling more hatred for the races on the outside. At one point they decided to use the ceremony that opens a portal. They felt they could destroy those mixed races if they could go through a portal and come back and re-inhabit the area at another time.

Also, they felt that by leaving through the portal they would not be affected by the war.

It appears that it was very dangerous on the outside. There were big animals, dinosaurs. The Golden Ones lived in a protected environment; they appear to be inside a shield or dome built of energy. You can not see the shield. The devices that generate this shield are very large, about 6 stories tall. They consist of a pair of shapes that are huge and they spin within each other in close proximity. When one spiral opens, the other goes in, so they are continually interfacing with each other. There are six pairs, twelve all together, put an equal distance around a large area that includes their city, but is much bigger than the city. The arrangement is hexagonal. This is what generates the protective shield. I see now that the shield does not have a top. It goes straight up into the universe. It is literally impenetrable. Air and water can get through, so it does not affect their ecosystem. It has the capability of dissolving form, so if you up your hand into the field your form will begin to dissolve and if you withdraw it quickly, it will be severely deformed. There are certain places that you can access the inside, tunnels underneath the towers that held the generating devices. There were six of these access points, called gates or portals, although one at the ocean was used very seldom. The access through the tunnels is closely guarded and can be closed very easily and when these are closed the city is impenetrable by anything. The Golden Ones who were capable of bilocating could travel to the other side that way as well.

During the times that many people wanted to leave, those that controlled the ingress/egress areas where often, "bought off." There was one time when there was a mass effort and lots of people decided they wanted to go to the other side, and the people who controlled the gate, who were responsible for the security, were part of those who wanted to leave, so when they all left the portal was left open and unguarded for quite a while. They did not have television capabilities as we know it, no *"security cameras."* They had no advanced electronic communication systems. Though many of the Golden Ones could still communicate telepathically, they started to lose that over the years. In some ways our electronic technology is more sophisticated. Without ways of consistently monitoring the gates, many such large *"escapes"* were possible.

We would consider the city of the Golden Ones utopia, but others wanted to experience the excitement on the outside. Many lost their lives to experience this. This entire scenario played itself out for 8,000 years-from the time the Golden Ones came to the time of the Great War.

In the war, the opposition had large thermal eggs they would focus on the ground beneath the giant devices that provided the shield. The ground was melted and the devices fell into it, but in the process the whole continent fell. It was a terrible thing. It's funny that in this early time, they did not seem to have air craft. It was very different. Some things were so much more advanced and some were not. Many of the Golden Ones could still bilocate, but people who could do that became fewer and fewer. They were from the belt of Orion, but we do not have a full understanding of that star system; it is really incomplete. There are many inhabited planets in that area, but not all the civilizations have the ability to travel.

The Golden Ones live for a long time; most are between 500 and 800 years old. I see he who will later incarnate as Pythagoras and Thoth. The one who will be Jesus was on the outside. Darlaiel was one of the first female Golden One's to leave; she was instrumental in developing the civilization on the outside world.

The Golden Ones who left the city dropped in level of awareness (and stature). To experience more they had to widen their parameters for experiencing; this took them into a deeper level of separation. In the beginning they were as highly evolved as they could get, but then they became encapsulated by their reality. The Golden Ones never fought, but only threatened. They had the physical ability to destroy the forces that opposed them but were not capable of violence. When those on the outside attacked, they destroyed themselves in the process along with most of the land. Most of the land was within these six devices which generated the force shield.

It seems that the Golden Ones had slaves. Golden Ones: the ones who ate gold! They had slaves that went out to get gold. It was the slaves (humans) who broke off and started their own civilization. Then many of the Golden Ones broke off and joined them, bringing the technology. They forgot how to die. The original number was 144,000 who came. Slaves were brought from five lesser evolved planets. There was no expectation that they would evolve, except the Golden Ones who left the cities brought genes of higher understanding and accelerated their development. The outsiders were starving because they did not have enough land to grow their crops; the Golden Ones had control of all the land. The Golden Ones would pick eat the refined gold from the outside. They eventually quit eating gold because they could no longer get it. This played out over a long period-thousands of years.

This 5th world was probably the best if you were to observe and categorize. The humanoid inhabitants were highly evolved and mostly peaceful, although there was some warring. The 5th world had the most advanced technologically, and their population numbered about sixty million, about one tenth of our present population. They had some crime, but not anywhere near what we have today. That is when most of the pyramids were built. Some of the artifacts you see in the present 6th world were actually produced in the 5th world. A lot of the artifacts produced in the 5th world were built by survivors or remnants of the 3rd world.

## AN.TU (Rhea)

AN.TU by the Sumerians, daughter of An.shar (Uranos) and Ki.shar (Gaea). AN.TU by the Akkadians. ANTUM by the Babylonians. Antu was the first Anunnaki consort of Anu. Their union created the Utukki and the Anunnaki. Because she was Anu's half-sister (same father, different mother), her son Enlil became Anu's Legal Heir though he was not Anu's firstborn son (Antu was Anu's official 1/2 sister/spouse/queen). She accompanied Anu on his state visits to Earth.

RHEA by the Greeks, daughter of Uranos (Anshar) and Gaea (Kishar). Universal Mother or Great Goddess; Supreme Queen of Heaven. Goddess of plant life and fertility; inventor of the arts and magic. "A keeper of the white stone or that through which many of the peoples, before the first destructions in Atlantis, kept their accord with the universal consciousness (God) through speaking to and through those activities." *Edgar Cayce* #5037-1;19, April 1944.

Later the Ark of the Covenant was also used to communicate with God. Called OPS by the Romans. Goddess of fidelity and marriage. SAMI-RAMA-ISI and SEMIRAMIS by the Indians.

BELTIS, BELIT-ILLI, BELIT-ILI, BELIT or "Lady of the gods," "Lady of childbirth" by the Babylonians. BELITIS or "Goddess of fertility" by the Assyrians. DERCETO by the Philistines.

BESTLA by the Nordic-Germanic tribes. BA'ALAT and BARATI by the Phoenicians. BARAT AN-NA or "Great Mother of the Fire-stone" by the Yulannu, who were later known as the Wallans of Mesopotamia. The cult of Barat An-na spread across Syria into the Phoenician kingdom, where they began to portray her on their coins. On these coins, she sat by the seashore with a torch of fire, and at her side was a round shield bearing the cross of the Rosi-crucis.

The cult was brought to the British islands, where her name became compacted to BRATANNA. And in those islands, her image persisted to the extent that she became the great tribal goddess of the Celts. After all this time, she is still the Mother Goddess of the land, the Lady of the Fire-stone:

BRITANNIA and the Rosi-crucis cross of her shield was amended to become the Union Jack.

## ANU.KIS

ANUKIS wife of An.ki by the Sumerians, daughter of An II and Anunnaki Concubine.

## ARAZJAL

ARAZJAL a "fallen angel" who mated with earth's human females and produced human giants.

### Aram

Aram by the Ancient Hebrews, son of Shem (Sem) and Sedeqetelebab. Founder of the city of Uz. Aram was the founder of the Aramaeans, known to the Akkadians as the Aramu, but who were later known to the Greeks as Syrians. In an Assyrian inscription of Tiglath-pileser I, c.1100 BC, the Aramae are described as living all over Mesopotamia; after which they settled to the west, occupying roughly the same area that makes up modern Syria. A cuneiform tablet from Ur bears the name of Aramu, and it is of interest to note that Aramaic is still spoken today.

### Arbakad (Arpachshad)

Arbakad, Arpachshad, Arphaxad or Arpakhsar by the Hebrews, son of Shem (Sem) and Sedeqetelebab. He was the progenitor of the Chaldeans, his name being equivalent to 'arpkeshed', that is, the boundary of Chaldea. That he was indeed the forebear of the Chaldeans is confirmed by the Hurrian

(Nuzi) tablets, which render the name as Arip-hurra, the founder of Chaldea. The name was also known to the Akkadians as Arraphu. The Assyrians knew his descendants as the Kaldu, called the Kaloo in Delores Cannon's book *Jesus and the Essenes*. The Kaldu were adept astrologers, magicians and mathematicians. Ptolemy recorded the name of their land as Arrapachitis, whilst it was known to others as Arphaxitis. The very earliest settlement of the children of Arphaxad appears to have been what is today a two and a half acre ruin called Arpachiya. It lies some four miles to the east of ancient Neineveh, and is the remains of a very early farming community.

## ARGES

ARGES was a Cyclope, son of Uranos (Anshar) and Gaea (Kishar). The Cyclopeans are remembered in Polynesian mythology as gods with golden skin who came long ago in flying machines and built pyramids throughout the Pacific.

## Arki (Arkee)

Arki or Arkee, son of Canaan. The Arkites are in the inscriptions of Shalmaneser II and Tiglath-pileser III, both kings of Assyria, and both whom describe the Arkites as 'rebellious'. The Arkites were also known to the Egyptians, as mentioned in the Amama tablets as the Irkata. Their city is known today as Tell-Arqa, a place that Thutmose III of Egypt refers to as Arkantu. The city was later known to the Romans as Caesari Libani.

## Arodi (Arvadi)

Arodi or Arvadi, son of Canaan. This people settled on the island that bore their founder's name, Arvad. Today, it is known as Ruad, and lies north of the bay of Tripoli, about two miles out to sea. The Arvadites were famed in the old world for their skilful seamanship, drawing for this even the grudging admiration of the Assyrians. The Arvadites were also known in the Armarna tablets as the Arwada.

## ARURU (Astora)

RAYSHONDRA by the Pleiadians. The Great Doctoress. Her symbol was a dog. BO.HU, BA.HU, BAAU, BA.U or "lady who the dead brings back to life" (one who breathed into humans the breath of life) by the Akkadians. ARURU or "goddess of creation" by the Babylonians, daughter of An.nu (Cronos) and An.tu (Rhea). ARUAH by the Britons. GUR, GULA or "The Big One" by the Hittites. GULAH or "The Great One" by the Kassites. Known for her medical care for the people of Lagash (her 'cult center'). When the deadly nuclear cloud unleashed in the Sinai reached Sumer, Bau could not force herself to leave their beloved Lagash. The *Lamentation Over Sumer* text states that as she lingered behind, "the storm caught up with her as if she was a mortal," suggesting that she died. ASTORA by the Nordic-Germanic tribes. Goddess of the East, dawn, rebirth and resurrection.

AUSOS in Proto-Germanic. AUSTRO in Proto-Indo-European. AUSTRIAHENEA in Roman-Germanic. OSTERN by the Germans. EOSTER in Old English. EOSTRE by the West Saxons. Who celebrated the old "Eostre festival" of Spring and fertility. EASTRE in Old High German. OSTARA in Northumbrian Old English. ESTER or ESTRID in Middle English. EASTER in English. Which is celebrated today in our modern "Easter festival". EASTREA in Cambridgeshire. EASTRY in Kent. EASTRINGTON in East Riding of Yorkshire. EASTERWINE in Wearmouth. VESNA by the Slavs. VASARA in Lithuania. USHAS by the Indians.

The name "Easter" originated with the names of an ancient Goddess. The Venerable Bede, (672-735 AD) a Christian scholar, first asserted in his book *De Ratione Temporum* that Easter was named after EOSTRE or EASTRE. She was the Great Mother Goddess of the Saxon people in Northern Europe. Similarly, the "Teutonic dawn goddess of fertility [was] known variously as Ostare, Ostara, Ostern, Eostra, Eostre, Eostur, Eastra, Eastur, Austron and Ausos."

The Germans to this day call April Ostermonat, and Ôstarmânoth. The great Christian festival, which usually falls in April or the end of March, bears in the oldest of Old High German remains the name Ôstarâ . . . it is mostly found in the plural, because two days . . . were kept at Easter. This Ostarâ, like the [Anglo-Saxon] Eástre, must in heathen religion have denoted a higher being, whose worship was so firmly rooted, that the Christian teachers tolerated the name, and applied it to one of their own grandest anniversaries, Christ resurrection-day.

Ostara or Eástre seems therefore to have been the divinity of the radiant dawn, of upspringing light, a spectacle that brings joy and blessing, whose meaning could be easily adapted by the resurrection-day of the Christian's God. Bonfires were lighted at Easter and according to popular belief of long standing, the moment the sun rises on Easter Sunday morning, he gives three joyful leaps, he dances for joy . . . Water drawn on the Easter morning is, like that at Christmas, holy and healing . . . here also heathen notions seems to have grafted themselves on great Christian festivals. Maidens clothed in white, who at Easter, at the season of returning spring, show themselves in clefts of the rock and on mountains, are suggestive of this ancient goddess.

The heathen Easter had much in common with May-feast and the reception of spring, particularly in matter of bonfires. Then, through long ages there seem to have lingered among the people Easter-games so-called, which the church itself had to tolerate: I allude especially to the custom of Easter eggs, and to the Easter tale which preachers told from the pulpit for the people's amusement, connecting it with Christian reminiscences. Wiccans and other modern-day Neopagans continue to celebrate the Spring Equinox as one of their 8 yearly Sabbats (holy days of celebration). Near the Mediterranean, this is a time of sprouting of the summer's crop; farther north, it is the time for seeding. Their rituals at the Spring Equinox are related primarily to the fertility of the crops and to the balance of the day and night times. In those places where Wiccans can safely celebrate the Sabbat out of doors without threat of religious persecution, they often incorporate a bonfire into their rituals, jumping over the dying embers is believed to assure fertility of people and crops.

## ASAELA

ASAELA a "fallen angel" who mated with earth's human females and produced human giants.

### Asar (Osiris)

ASAR.LUBI by the Sumerians, son of Mar.duk (Phosphorus) and human female Zarpanitu (Sarpanit). OSIRIS or "afterlife," ISIRIS, ONOURIS, OSER, USIRE, USAR, AUSAR, ASHAR, ASAR or "The All-Seeing," ASER, ANHUR, ANHER, ANHERT and RAM by the Egyptians. God (demi-god) of war, the Sun, and the Sky. Originally a fertility god, he was later known as the 'God of the dead.' ASAR (AS-AR); AESIR or 'Seeing Lord' in Norse mythology. He was a Naga or Dragon, a Merlin or Druidhe by the Celts. Called ORION 'the Hunter' by the Greeks. HERNE the Hunter, a great warrior by the ancient Norse. ARYAN by the Gaelic Scythians. AES DAN or 'he who sees' by the Celts. ASHSHUR (ASH SHAR) or 'Seeing Lord' by the Assyrians.

OSIRIS - Lord of life after death; worshipped as a Sun god. Pictured with a tanned complexion and fair hair. He was shown sometimes standing, sometimes seated on his throne, tightly wrapped in mummy cloth, his freed hands crossed on his breast holding the crook and flail. Sometimes his face was green. (see greek god Pan)

The history of the last god (demi-god) to rule as king of the earth is recorded in its fullest version in Egyptian rather than Greek tradition. The Egyptians unquestioningly believed that their most important god had once walked among them, led them into battle and ruled them wisely and well. Herodotus described a visit to the shrine where Osiris was said to be buried. 'Gigantic stone obelisks stand in the courtyard and there is a circular artificial lake next to it. It is on this lake at night that the Egyptians act out the Mysteries, the Black Rite that celebrates the death and resurrection of a being whose name I dare not speak, I know what goes on but . . . say no more.' Fortunately we can supplement this account with the history of Osiris as told by Herodotus's contemporary Plutarch, an initiate priest of the Oracle at Delphi. Osiris was a great hunter, a 'Beast Master' - remembered as Orion the Hunter in Greek mythology and Herne the Hunter in Norse mythology - and a great warrior. He cleared the land of predatory beasts and defeated invading armies. The great warrior's downfall came not in combat with monsters or on the battlefield, but because of the enemy within his own family. Returning from another military campaign, Osiris was welcomed back by cheering crowds, by the populace who loved him. The reign of Osiris, though constantly under attack from outside the country, would be reemebered as a golden age. And it was an age of domestic as well as civil bliss.

CERNUNNOS, CERNOWAIN, CERNENUS and HERNE 'the Hunter' - Known to all the Celtic areas in one form or another. The Horned God; God of Nature; God of the Underworld and the Astral Plane; Great Father; "the Horned One." The Druids knew him as Hu Gadarn, the Horned God of fertility. He was portrayed sitting in a lotus position with horns or antlers on his head, long curling hair, a beard, naked except for a neck torque, and sometimes holding a spear and shield. His symbols were the stag, ram, bull, and horned serpent. Sometimes called BELATUCADROS and VITIRIS. Virility, fertility, animals, physical love, Nature, woodlands, reincarnation, crossroads, wealth, commerce, warriors. Herne 'the Hunter' has come to be associated with Windsor Forest and has taken on attributes of Gwynn Ap Nudd with his Wild Hunt. The Horned God - Opener of the Gates of Life and Death. The masculine, active side of Nature; Earth Father. His sacred animals were the stag, bull, goat, bear. Growing things, the forest, Nature, wild animals, alertness, annihilation, fertility, panic, desire, terror, flocks, agriculture, beer and ale.

CERNUNNOS by the Celts. Cernunnos was known as the "horned god," the bull or stag god. The god of hunting, culling and taking. His purpose is to purify through selection and sacrifice in order that the powers of fertility, regeneration and growth may progress unhindered. Cernunnos is the guardian of the portal leading to the Otherworld. A nature deity, the ruler of the active forces of life and death, regeneration and fertility. Cernunnos is known only from one damaged carving found at Notre Dame in Paris. This carving, which shows a deity with short horns, carries the incomplete inscription '(C)ERNUNNO(S)'. He was called DON or DONU by the Welsh. FORNJOTNER, BORR or BOR by the Nordic-Germanic tribes.

## ASARADEL (Sariel)

ARAZIEL, ARAZYAL, ARAZJAL, ATRIEL, ASARADEL, ESDREEL, SAHARIEL, SERIEL, SARIEL or "my moon is God." A “fallen angel” who sinned when he descended to earth to unite with mortal women. Asaradel taught man "the motion of the moon".

## ASHAMDAN (Shamsiel)

SHAMDON, SHAMDAN, ASHAMDON, or ASHAMDAN was one of the "fallen angels" who mated with the human female Naamah and begat a giant named Asmodeus. SHAMSHIEL, SHAMSIEL, SAMSIEL, SAMSAPEEL, SAMSAVEEL, SIMAPISEEL - a fallen angel who taught men the signs of the sun. Shamshiel or "light of day," "mighty son of God". A ruler of the 4th Heaven and prince of Paradise; also guardian angel of Eden. It was Shamshiel who conducted Moses around the heavenly Paradise when the Lawgiver, according to legend, visited the upper regions while he was still in the flesh. It was to Shamshiel that the treasures of David and Solomon were turned over by the scribe Hilkiah. According to *Bereshith Rabba* 36:3, Shamdan was Noah's partner in planting a vineyard, which led to Noah's drinking, and being "uncovered within his tent," an incident related in *Genesis* 9:20-22.

In the *Zohar,* Shamshiel is head of 365 legions of spirits. He crowns prayers, just as other great angels do, and accompanies them to the 5th Heaven. In the *Book of Jubilees* he is one of the watchers or grigori, and is equated with Samsapeel. In *Enoch* Chapter 1, he rates as a fallen angel who "taught the signs of the sun." According to the *Zohar* (Numbers 154b) he served as one of the 2 chief aides to Uriel (the other aide being Hasdiel) when Uriel bore his standard in battle.

*Book of Enoch* Chapter 16:2-5 and 17:1-2 - And now to the Watchers, who have sent thee to pray for them, who in the beginning were in heaven, say, in heaven have you been; secret things, however, have not been manifested to you; yet have you known a reprobated mystery. And this you have related to women in the hardness of your heart, and by that mystery have women and mankind multiplied evils upon the earth. Say to them, Never therefore shall you obtain peace. They raised me up (spaceship) into a certain place, where there was the appearance of a burning fire; and when they pleased they assumed the likeness of men (shape-shifting). They carried me to a lofty spot, to a mountain, the top of which reached to heaven.

*Book of Enoch* Chapter 19:1-2 - Then Uriel said, Here the angels, who cohabited with women, appointed their leaders; And being numerous in appearance (assuming many forms-shape shifting) made men profane, and caused them to err; so that they sacrificed to devils as to gods. For in the great day there shall be a judgment, with which they shall be judged, until they are consumed; and their wives also shall be judged, who led astray the angels of heaven that they might salute them.

*Book of Enoch* Chapter 53:6-11 - Michael and Gabriel, Raphael and Phanuel shall be strengthened in that day, and shall then cast them into a furnace of blazing fire, that the Lord of spirits may be avenged of them for their crimes; because they became ministers of Satan (Enki), and seduced those who dwell upon earth. In those days shall punishment go forth from the Lord of spirits; and the receptacles of water which are above the heavens shall be opened, and the fountains likewise, which are under the heavens and under the earth. All the waters, which are in the heavens and above them, shall be mixed together. The water which is above heaven shall be the agent; And the water which is under the earth shall be the recipient: and all shall be destroyed who dwell upon earth, and who dwell under the extremities of heaven. By these means shall they understand the iniquity which they have committed on earth: and by these means shall they perish.

## Asshur (Ashur)

Asshur, Ashur, Ashar or Asshar by the ancient Hebrews, son of Shem (Sem) and Sedeqetelebab. The founder of the nation to whom he gave his name, to wit Assyria. It may be possible to identify Asshur in the early king-lists of Assyria as Puzur-Asshur I. According to these lists, Puzur-Asshur I would have lived and reigned c. 1960 BC, which accords rather well with the biblical chronology. Asshur was one of the earliest men to be deified and worshipped by his descendants. As long as Assyria lasted, that is until 612

BC, accounts of battles, exploits, diplomatic affairs and foreign bulletins were daily read out to his image; and every Assyrian king held that he wore the crown only with the express permission of Asshur's deified ghost.

## Asta (Isis)

ENKERSAKE, ISIS, SIRIUS and TAIT by the Egyptians, daughter of Semjasa (Oz) and human female Nraa (Noraia). Supreme Egyptian goddess; Moon [demi-] goddess; Great Mother; Great Goddess; Giver of Life. She was pictured with dark hair, blue eyes, and fair skin. With Osiris (the father), Isis (the mother) and Horus (the divine child) made up the Holy Trinity. Her priests were called the mesniu (smiths) and worked with metals. The cow was sacred to her, as were the magic Buckle of Isis and the sistrum. Her sistrum was carved with a cat image that represented the Moon. As High Priestess, she was a powerful magician. AST, AS, ASET, AUSET, ESET by the Egyptians. Her symbols were the chalice, cup, triangle, diamond, circle, oval, and the sea.

## ATUNENI (Athena)

RATTA by the Atlanteans. ATUNENI by the Sumerians, daughter of En.lil (Zeus) and Nin.lil (Hera). ADUENI by the Akkadians. ASRATUM by the Amorites. ATARGATIS by the Canaanites and the Assyrians. TIRGATA by the Babylonians. NEITH by the Egyptians. ANATH by the Hebrews. ANAITIS, ANAIT, and ANAT or "she who responded" by the Phoenicians. NOTT or NAT by the Nordic-Germanic tribes. IDUN by the Goths.

ANAT by the Phoenicians. Qadesh or “Holy One”. Mistress of the Lofty Heavens; Controller of Royalty; Mother of All Nations; Sovereign of all Deities; Strength of Life; She Who Kills and Resurrects. A virgin (meaning independent) and "progenitor of the people". Anat was one of the nursemaids to the "gracious gods." She was renowned as a fertility goddess as well as a fierce hunter and warrior. Her power was so great to curse and kill that even the gods were afraid of her; whatever she wanted was granted. She is sometimes pictured with bow and arrows. Her animal is the lion. She carried an ankh and wore horns and a Moon disk. She also wore coriander scent and purple makeup for battle. She was also portrayed festooned with severed heads along with human hands hanging from her girdle. Her temples had sacred prostitutes; sacred marriages were made by the priestesses with the kings. In her war aspect, she wore the horns of a bull. Her priestesses were famous astrologers.

ANATH is the chief West Semitic goddess of love and war, the sister and helpmate of the god Baal. Considered a beautiful young girl, she was often designated “the Virgin” in ancient texts. Probably one of the best-known of the Canaanite deities, she was famous for her youthful vigor and ferocity in battle; in that respect she was adopted as a special favorite by the Egyptian Pharaoh Ramses II (reigned 1279-13 BC). Although Anath was often associated with the god RESHEPH in ritual texts, she was primarily known for her role in the myth of Baal’s death and resurrection, in which she mourned and searched for him and finally helped to retrieve him from the netherworld.

Egyptian representations of Anath show a nude goddess, often standing on a lion and holding flowers. During the Hellenistic Age, the goddesses Anath and Astarte were blended into one deity, called Atargatis.

ANAT is the Canaanite Warrior Goddess, the Maiden who loves battle, the virgin Goddess of Sacrifice, a swordswoman and archer. Anat is famous for having a violent temperament and for taking joy in slaughter. In the 14th Century BC, Ugartic text The Epic of Ba'al, she defends her brother the Storm-God Ba'al, called by his title Ayelin, "Mightiest", against Mot or Mavet, the force of sterility and death who represents the intense heat of the dry season which causes the crops to wither. But Mot triumphs against Ba'al and sends him to the Land of the Dead; Anat, with help from the Sun-

Goddess Shapash, Who has access to the Underworld, brings Ba'al back to life. Anat then takes revenge on Mot, cutting him up into tiny pieces, winnowing him like grain, grinding him up, and then sowing him in the fields. Ba'al and Mot are symbolic of the alternating seasons of rain and drought, of life and death, and by grinding Mot up and scattering him like grain, Anat allows for the season of plenty to come again and the wheat to be reborn another year.

Before Anat goes into battle she prepares herself by anointing herself with henna and ambergris, and dressing in saffron (gold) and murex (purple) dyed clothing, both of which are famously expensive, and royal colors. She then proceeds to slaughter the enemies of Ba'al, across west and east, hanging severed heads from her back, and affixing hands to her belt. Laughing and rejoicing, she wades to her knees in the blood of soldiers, "to her thighs in the gore of quick warriors". When the slaughter is finished (and it takes a while), she then washes herself in the rain-water of her brother Ba'al, and again adorns herself with ambergris.

Though often called "Virgin", Anat also has a strong sexual aspect, much like the War-and-Sex Goddess of the Irish the Morrigan, and, though she is not usually considered the consort of Ba'al, she was said to have had seventy-seven children by him, after they had copulated in the forms of cow and bull. Given this, calling Anat a "virgin" has got to be taken to mean "independent young woman", not "non-sexual young woman".

Though she is the daughter of El, the patriarch of the Gods, She does not hesitate to threaten him when she feels Ba'al is being treated unfairly. If El does not grant Ba'al a splendid palace like all the other Gods have, "I shall surely drag him [El] like a lamb to the ground, I shall make his grey hairs run with blood, the grey hairs of his beard [thick] with gore." Not surprisingly, people sought to placate Anat, and she was invoked to grant peace: "Remove from the earth war, Set in the dust love; Pour peace amidst the earth, Tranquility amidst the fields" *(The Epic of Ba'al).*

Her worship was also known in Egypt, where she was considered the consort of the Chaos-God Seth, and her sexual aspects led her to be associated with Min, who, if you've ever seen a picture of him, is very obviously a God of Male Fertility. She was especially popular in the New Kingdom, and she was one of Ramses II's patron Deities, Who watched over him in battle. He even named one of his (zillion) daughters Bint-Anat, or "Daughter of Anat" in her honor.

Anat represents necessary endings, sacrifices to be made to serve a greater purpose, or old habits that may no longer serve and need to be let go. In this way the field of growth grows green again. Alternate names: ANAT, ANATH, ANAITIS, ANAIT, ANAT-BETHEL. She is called Rahmay or Rahmaya, "the Merciful"; this is also the title of one of the two wives of El, with Athirat-of-the-Sea, who are the mothers of the Gods of Dawn and Dusk, Shachar and Shalem. As Anatha-Baetyl, likely of Syrian origin, she is sometimes called the wife of Jehovah. In Egypt she could be called Antit. Epithets: She is called "Adolescent Anat", Batalat 'Anat, "the Maiden", "Sister of the Mighty One".

ATHENA, ATHENE or SEMELE by the Greeks, daughter of Zeus (En.lil) and Hera (Nin.lil). MINERVA by the Romans. Holy Virgin; Maiden Goddess; Mother Goddess of Athens; Bright Eyed. An all-powerful warrior goddess. Sometimes called PALLAS ATHENE in memory of the goddess' close friend whom she accidentally killed in practice. The Parthenon, "Virgin Temple," was her shrine. Sacred symbols to her were the owl, olive, oak, intertwined snakes and the swastika which can be seen on her robe. She wore a helmet and aegis (breastplate) and carried a shield and spear. She invented the plow, bridle, rake, ox yoke, chariot, and flute; also taught humankind to breed and break horses. She was celebrated at the Lesser Panathenaea in March and on the Day of the Geniae on December 25. She was a goddess of freedom and women's rights; patroness of craftsmen (now freemasons), especially smiths, goldsmiths, potters, dressmakers, shipbuilders, weavers and spinners. Also the patroness of career women. She was the protector of cities and patron of soldiers. She was the goddess of protection, writing, music, the sciences, sculptors, potters, architects, wisdom, arts and skills, renewal, true justice, protection (both psychic and physical), prudence, wise counsel, peace, embroidery, horses and oxen, snakes, pillars, trees, olive boughs, and battle strategy. A replica of the Parthenon and a 30 ft. tall statue of Athena can be seen in Nashville, Tennessee.

ATHENA the Greek Goddess of war and wisdom. She is the daughter of Zeus, born by springing forth fully grown from his forehead. It is believed that she was conceived to carry out deeds that Zeus could not do but would want to. Her name, "Pallas Athene" is representative of her dual nature. She can be seen as "Pallas" goddess of storms, courage, strength, battle, war, chivalry, and victory. She can also be "Athene" the goddess of peace, beauty, wisdom, creativity, education, science, and the arts. She was responsible for teaching mortals natal care and healing. She also invented the flute, created the olive tree, and showed men how to train horses. Athena is the patron of craftsmen (now freemasons) and the protector of cities. Her animal symbols are the cock, snake, owl, and olive tree.

I begin to sing of Pallas Athena, the glorious Goddess, bright-eyed, inventive, unbending of heart, pure virgin, savior of cities, courageous, Tritogeneia. Wise Zeus himself bore her from his awful head, arrayed in warlike arms of flashing gold, and awe seized all the gods as they gazed. But Athena sprang quickly from the immortal head and stood before Zeus who holds the aegis, shaking a sharp spear: great Olympus began to reel horribly at the might of the bright-eyed Goddess, and earth round about cried fearfully, and the sea was moved and tossed with dark waves, while foam burst forth suddenly: the bright Son of Hyperion stopped his swift-footed horses a long while, until the maiden Pallas Athena had stripped the heavenly armour from her immortal shoulders. And wise Zeus was glad. And so hail to you, daughter of Zeus who holds the aegis! *Homeric Hmyn #28*

According to the *Oera Linda Book,* a work of great antiquity that contains the annals of the ancient Frisians, an antediluvian maritime people whose country was called Atland. When there country, which adjoined the western coastline of Scandinavia, broke up and sank following a drastic change in the earth's axial rotation, those Frisians that escaped intermarried with other northern European people and set about colonizing several areas of the Mediterranean and North Africa. The Frisians were a matriarchal society, led by female warriors. Their warrior priestess, Min-Erva (Athena), at the head of a group of her people, landed on the shores of prehistoric Greece and founded the first Athens. Like the ruling caste of ancient Atlantis, the Frisians were an exceptionally tall, fair-haired, blue-eyed people.

The *Oera Linda Book* also refers to the archaic Frisians as being 7 feet tall and more. Fragments of colossal human bones have been found in Java, Southern China and South Africa. Exceptionally heavy stone implements weighing from 4 to 8 pounds have been discovered in Syria, Moravia and Morocco, suggesting that the users must have been at least 9 feet tall.

MORRIGAN, MORRIGU, MORRIGAN, MORRIGHAN, or MORGAN by the Celts. Great Queen; Supreme War Goddess; Queen of Phantoms or Demons; Specter Queen; shape-shifter. Morrigan reigned over the battlefield, helping with her magic, but did not join in battles. Associated with crows and ravens. The Crone aspect of the Goddess; Great White Goddess; Queen of the Fairies. In her Dark Aspect (the symbol is then the raven or crow) she is the Goddess of war, fate, and death; she went fully armed and carried two spears. The carrion crow is her favorite disguise. With her, FEA (Hateful), NEMON (Venomous), BADB (Fury), and MACHA (Battle) encouraged fighters to battle madness. Goddess of rivers, lakes, and fresh water. Patroness of priestesses and witches. The Celtic goddess, known in Ireland as the Morrigan, took triple form. She was associated with death and battle, sexuality and procreation. She could appear as a screaming bloodthirsty hag (Witch) or as a beautiful maiden; her totem bird was the

**crow**. We must visualize one goddess with a fluid shape-changing ability to different feminine beings with divine power.

Morrigan was one of a trio of war goddesses who appear in Irish tradition, influencing the outcome of battle by magic and inspiring terror into the hearts of warriors. Possessing marked sexual characteristics, and appearing frequently in animal guise. Appearing at one moment as terror-inspiring hags, at the next as beautiful young women, and yet again as beaked crows or ravens, these goddesses figure with impressive frequency throughout the earliest stratum of Irish tradition. These same three goddesses appear to Lugh Strong-Arm years later as three beautiful maidens.

MARGANTE, MORGANA, MORGEN, MORGANIS, MORGAN, MORGAN LA FEE, and MORGAN LE FAY by Arthurian Legend. "the Fairy Queen"; High Priestess of the sisters of Avallon; Head of the nine Holy Sisters who were guardians of the kingdom of Avallon, known as the "realm of the Immortals", and "the Land of Women"; Celtic High Priestess; Queen of the Waste Land; recognized as a goddess. The three faces of the Celtic goddess Morgan Le Fay was a Maiden (Consort), a Mother, and a Hag (Witch).

Merlin tells King Taliesin that , after Camlann, they took Arthur to the Isle of Apples, presided over by MORGAN, the chief of nine sisters, including MORONOE, MAZOE, GLITEN, GLITONEA, CLINTON, TYRONOE and THITIS.

Geoffrey of Monmouth's, *Vita Merlin* (c. 1149) introduces Morgan for the first time, attaching her to Insula Pomorum (the Isle of Apples) as one of nine sisters who 'exercise a kindly rule over those who come to them from our land. The one who is the first among them has greater skill in healing, as her beauty surpasses that of her sisters. Her name is Morgen, and she learned the uses of all plants in curing the ills of the body. She knows, too, the art of changing her shape, of flying through the air.' It was Morgan who received King Arthur after the Battle of Camlan.

In Layamon's *Brut* (c. 1189-1205), "And I shall fare to Avalun (Avalon), to the fairest of all maidens, to Argante (Margante) the queen, an Elf most fair, and she shall make my wounds all sound; make me all whole with healing draughts (thoughts)." Giraldus Cambrensis makes several references to Morganis, portraying her as a powerful figure with close links to Avalonia (Avalon) and Glastonis (Glanstonbury). In Giraldus' *De Instructione Principium* (1193-1199), he explains Morganis's status in Avalon, stating she was 'a noble matron who was ruler and patron of those parts'. "A certain fairy Goddess...called Morganis".

The *Welsh Triads* stated that there was once Three Perpetual Harmonies in Ynys Prydein-three early Celtic monastic sites. The first monastery was built in Ynys Afallach (kingdom of Avalon), the second monastery was built at Caradog, and the third monastery was built at Bangor, and that within each of these places 2,400 monks in turns, 100 at a time, spent 24 hours of every day and night ceaselessly in prayer and service to God without rest forever. Bangor (Bangor-is-y-Coed) is located on the banks of the River Dee in the region of Maelor. The monastery at Bangor was founded by a son of Coel, the first Christian King of Britain. St. Hilary and St. Benedict name Bangor as the 'Mother of all monasteries'.

**Hercules and the goddess Athena**

## AZKEEL (Ezekeel)

AZKEEL, EZEKEEL, or ZEQIEL a "fallen angel" who mated with earth's human females and produced human giants.

## BARAKEL (Baraqel)

BARAKEL, BARAQEL, BARAQIJAL, or BARKAYAL in the *Book of Jubilees,* one of the watchers (grigori) or “fallen angels” who united with the daughters of men, an incident touched on in *Genesis* 6. Baraqijal, now a demon and inhabiting the neither realms, is a teacher of astrology. In *Enoch I,* he is described as a leader (one of the "chiefs of ten") of a troop of fallen angels.

## BATRAAL (Batrael)

BATRAAL, BATRAEL, BATAREL, BATARJAL, BATARIEL, BADARIEL, BARAQEL, BARKAYAL, or METAREL a "fallen angel" who taught men "the observers of the stars."

## BRIAREOS (Briareus)

BRIAREOS was a giant in size, called Hekatoncheires, son of Uranos (Anshar) and Gaea (Kishar). One hundred handed and fifty headed monster whom gods called BRIAREUS, but men called AEGAEON. A Titan giant who were enormous beings of invincible strength and terrifying appearance.

## BRONTES

BRONTES was a Cyclope, son of Uranos (Anshar) and Gaea (Kishar). From the historian Castor (in Armenian translation of *Eusebius,* pars. i. p. 81) we learn that it was under Bel, or Belus, that is Baal, that the Cyclops lived; and the Scholiast on *Aeschylus* (p. 32, ante, Note) states that these Cyclops were the brothers of Kronos (Chronos). The eye in their forehead shows that originally this name was a name of the great god; for that eye in India and Greece is found the characteristic of the supreme divinity. The Cyclops had been representatives of Baal. The Cyclops were well known to be cannibals. "To bring back the rites of the Cyclops," meant to revive the practice of eating human flesh. The Cyclopeans are remembered in Polynesian mythology as gods with golden skin who came long ago in flying machines and built pyramids throughout the Pacific.

## Canaan

Canaan, son of Chem (Ham) and Naelatamauk. The descendants of Canaan settled in the land that was later to be given to Israel. At the time of the Israelite conquest, the population of Canaan consisted of all the tribes descended from him. Both Sanchuniathon and Phylo of Byblos confirm the fact that the Canaanites derived their name from their founder. The Greeks and Phoenicians knew the name as Kna'an; the Egyptians knew it as Kn'nw; and the Hurrians described certain dyed cloth as Kinahne or Canaanite cloth. In spite of their Hamitic descent, the Canaanites spoke a Semitic language. Canaan was cursed by Noah, by God enslaving him and his descendants to Shem's and Japheth's descendants.

*Israel My Glory,* Vol. 57, No. 1, Feb/Mar 1999 - *The Battle of the Gods: Paganism's Seduction of Israel* by Bruce Scott, pages 10-13 - The most popular pagan god of the Canaanites was known as Baal (Enki/ Satan). One account refers to him as the son of Dagon (Anu), the god of the Philistines *(Judges16:23).* Baal was the male god of fertility, both in human reproduction and agriculture.

Baal is also portrayed as a bull, an ancient symbol of fertility. Compound names of Baal are sometimes found in Scripture, such as Baalzebub *(2 Kings 1:2)* or Beel-zebub *(Matthew 12:24).* The Jewish leaders in Jesus' time understood Beel-zebub to be the prince of the devils, Satan himself.

Along with the biblical texts, the evidence found at Ras Shamra gives insight into the nature of the Canaanite religious rituals. In brief, they were characterized by drunkenness, sexual perversion, and violence.

Baal worship commonly took place at a temple on a hill *(2 Kings 10:18-27).* These structures were similar to the Jewish Temple, with an outer court for sacrifices and liturgy, an inside room for gathering, and a further inner room containing statuary. Sacrifices were also performed in a tower located on top of the building. As part of the ceremony, priests and participants reenacted the events narrated in the Ugaritic story. This reenactment may even have included bestiality, since Baal, the bull, is said to have mated repeatedly with a heifer before he entered the place of the dead. Following this, the worshipers participated in ritual mourning. They mourned the demise of Baal. This ritual involved loud moaning and slashing the flesh, similar to the description of Anat's mourning over Baal: "Of Baal she scraped her skin with a stone, with a flint for a razor she shaved her side whiskers and beard; she harrowed her collar-bone, she ploughed her chest like a garden, she harrowed her waist like a valley, saying: 'Baal is dead!'" (J.C.L. Gibson, *Canaanite Myths & Legends,* p. 74). This is reminiscent of the self-mutilation performed by the prophets of Baal on Mount Carmel *(1 Kings 18:28).* After the mourning, gladness ensued in celebration of Baal's resurrection and subsequent enthronement. Feasting, drinking, and sexual promiscuity, assisted by temple prostitutes, characterized the merrymaking.

Few details are known about the Molech and Chemosh rituals, except that horrendous child sacrifice was employed *(Leviticus 18:21; Deuteronomy 12:31; 2 Kings 3:27).* Often the child would "pass...through the fire" as food for the voracious god *(Ezekiel 23:37).* Throughout the Middle East, archaeologists have found numerous funerary urns containing the charred bones of animals and children. The citizens of ancient Carthage sacrificed children to their god Cronus (Anu) (who, according to mythology, unsuccessfully tried to murder his own children). "There was in their city a bronze image of Cronus, extending its hands, palms up and sloping toward the ground, so that each of the children when placed thereon rolled down and fell into a sort of gaping pit filled with fire" *(Diodorus of Sicily, Bk 20, 14.6).* Since the Carthaginians were descendants of Phoenician colonists, it is likely this sacrifice to Cronus was similar to the Molech and Chemosh sacrifices performed in Phoenicia. In fact, one rabbinical commentary describes similar sacrifices to Molech near Jerusalem. A hollow statue of Molech was located within the seventh and innermost chamber of his temple. No one could enter this chamber without bringing a child for a sacrifice. The statue had its hand outstretched holding a copper plate on which was a fire-pan. "They (the priest) placed the child on the copper plate, kindled the fire-pan beneath him, and sang before the image, 'May the sacrifice be pleasant and sweet to thee!' Why did they do this? So that the parents should not hear the groans of their children and retract" *(Lamentations Rabbah 1.9, sec. 36).*

Other Canaanite practices included the construction of open air shrines, known in the Bible as "high places," where sacrifices were performed and incense was commonly burned *(2 Kings 17:11).* One excavation high place, found in the ancient city of Dan and dating back to the time of King Ahab, measures 60 by 62 feet.

Despite repeated warnings from God (Jehovah) not to adopt the customs of the pagan nations around them *(Leviticus 18:3),* Israel did just that. Its downward spiral began at the foot of Mount Sinai with the forging of the golden calf *(Exodus 32).* During their forty-year trek in the wilderness, some Israelites carved images of foreign deities *(Acts 7:42-43).* Next, they fell into Baal worship through the enticements of the Moabite women at Peor *(Numbers 25:1-3).* This Baal worship consisted of eating sacrifices offered to the dead *(Psalms 106:28).* Following the death of Joshua and the elders, Israel began to "play the harlot" with the Canaanite gods in earnest. After the judges, King Saul removed the mediums and spiritists, except for one, the medium at Endor, of whom he himself inquired *(1 Samuel 28).* The people of Israel continued to sacrifice and burn incense on the high places throughout the land *(1 Kings 3:2),* despite the strict injunction against it *(Deuteronomy 12:13-14).* In the twilight years of his life, swayed by the charms of his multitudinous foreign wives, King Solomon built places of worship for each of their pagan gods *(1 Kings 11:5-8).* He even provided a site on the Mount of Olives for the worship of Chemosh and Molech. Solomon's corrupted leadership set the tone and pattern for Israel's future kings and their subjects for generations to come.

Both the northern kingdom of Israel and the southern kingdom of Judah practiced gross idolatry *(2 Kings 17:7-19).* They fashioned two golden calves. They aggressively worshiped Baal, Asherah, Ashtaroth, Molech, and Chemosh. They built shrines for pagan deities in every location-from town to watchtower to groves. They erected idols and carved images within the Temple of God *(2 Kings 21:7; Ezekiel 8:10).* They worshiped the sun, moon, and stars. They burned incense on their roofs *(Jeremiah 32:29),* on the hilltops, and under every green tree. They engaged in unbridled sexual promiscuity *(Amos 2:7-8),* together with both male and female cultic prostitution (1 Kings 14:24; *Hosea 4:13-14).* They practiced witchcraft, divination, sorcery, and spiritism *(2 Kings 21:6).* They sacrificed to demons *(Deuteronomy 32:17)* and consulted with the dead *(Isaiah 8:19),* spending nights among the tombs *(Isaiah 65:4).* They slaughtered their children, especially the firstborn *(Ezekiel 20:26),* burning them in sacrificial furnaces in the valley of Hinnom (Gehenna of the New Testament), south of Jerusalem *(Jeremiah 32:35).* For 700 years, they burned incense to the bronze serpent Moses had made in the wilderness *(2 Kings 18:4).*

Every abominable thing that God had instructed them not to do, they did, and even more. Judah's iniquity surpassed even that of the Canaanites *(2 Kings 21:9).* And, like the Canaanites, the result of their defilement was for the land to spew them out *(Leviticus 18:25-28).*

History shows that Israel continued to struggle with the first of the ten commandments: "Thou shalt have no other gods before me" *(Exodus 20:3).* This struggle had lasted even to this day among the Diaspora, just as Moses predicted *(Deuteronomy 28:64).* Israel's future is bright, however. A cleansing is in store for them *(Isaiah 4:4),* along with the removal of all idols *(Isaiah 2:18).*

## Caphtor (Caphthorim)

Caphthorim, Caphturim, Caphtor or Chaphtor, son of Mizraim (Mitzraim). The Genesis record gives the place of the Caphthorim's origin as Egypt and North Africa, that is Mizr. Genesis tells us that the Caphtorim were descended from the Mizrai. Kaphtor-Caphtor-Caphtorim is where the Philistines came from.

## Casloch (Casluhim)

Casloch, Chasloth, Casluhim or Casluchim, son of Mizraim (Mitzraim). The precise whereabouts of their country is uncertain, although the book of Genesis does record that the Philistines came from this people. The Genesis record states emphatically that the Philistines occupied parts of Canaan as early as the time of Abraham.

## Chamothi

Chamothi, son of Canaan. Dwelled in the land of Canaan.

## Chem (Ham)

Chem by the Sumerians, son of Ziu.su.dra (Noah) and Emzara (Emzarah). Noah, the first man to plant a vineyard, made wine from its grapes, grew drunk, and uncovered his secret parts...Ham entered the tent where Noah lay, observed his nakedness, and presently told Shem and Japheth what he had seen. They laid a garment over their shoulders, walked backwards into the tent and covered their father's nakedness, without looking at him. When Noah awoke from his drunken sleep, he saw what his little son had done to him, and cried: 'God's curse upon Ham! May his brothers make him a slave of slaves! But blessed be the God (Enlil) of Shem, whom Ham shall serve. May he also enlarge Japheth, to dwell in the tents of Shem; and Ham shall serve them both.

Some say that at the height of his drunkenness he uncovered himself, whereupon Ham entered the tent, mischievously looped a stout cord about his father's genitals, drew it tight, and unmanned him. Noah awakening from his drunken sleep and understanding what had been done to him, cried: 'Now I cannot beget the fourth son whose children I would have ordered to serve you and your brothers! Therefore it must be Canaan, your first-born, whom they enslave.

And since you have disabled me from doing ugly things in the blackness of night, Ham's grandchildren shall be born ugly and black! Moreover, because you twisted your head around to see my nakedness, your grandchildren's hair shall be twisted into kinks, and their eyes red; again, because your lips jested at my misfortune, theirs shall swell; and because you neglected my nakedness, they shall go naked, and their male members shall be shamefully elongated.' Men of this race are called Negroes; their forefather Ham commanded them to love theft and fornication, to be banded together in hatred of their masters and never to tell the truth.

Early Mormon doctrines placed dark-skinned people in a greatly inferior position to whites. In *2 Nephi* 5:21-24, we read that dark skin was created by "God" as a punishment for sin: . . . wherefore, as they (those being punished) were white, and exceeding fair and delightsome, that they might not be enticing unto my people the Lord God did cause a skin of blackness to come upon them.

And thus saith the Lord God: I will cause that they shall be loathsome unto my people, save they shall repent of their iniquities.

And cursed shall be the seed of him that mixeth with their seed; for they shall be cursed even with the same cursing. And the Lord spake it, and it was done.

And because of their cursing which was upon them they became an idle people, full of mischief and subtlety, and did seek in the wilderness for beasts of prey.

So Noah condemned the offspring of his youngest son to be lowly servants of his older brothers and their families. This is quite cruel punishment for seeing a parent of the same sex naked. I believe that Noah's totally irrational reaction to his son seeing him naked was due to the fact that Noah was sensitive of his traces of reptilian ancestry, such as patches of scaly hide that appeared on his body.

The Tables of Testimony, according to the teachings of the *Kabbala* & the *Midrash,* was to have been a sacred gemstone which Moses placed "in the palm of his hand." This was the same Divine Stone of Wisdom said to have been inherited by King Solomon. In the earlier texts of Egypt it was called the *'Tablet of Hermes',* which embodied the wisdom of Thoth. According to the records of the ancient Dragon Court of Egypt (founded by Queen Sobeknefru in 1785 BC), an early guardian of the Table was Chem, the High Priest of Mendes.

## CLYMENE (Cybele)

CLYMENE by the Greeks, daughter of Oceanos (Enshar) and Tethys (Ninshar). CYBELE, KYBELE by the Phrygians. Goddess of the Earth and caverns; Great Mother. She carried a scourge of knuckle bones and liked pearls and cypress. The greatest center of her worship was at Pessinus in Phrygia; there, under the shadow of Mount Dindymon, was a cave containing the tomb of her son Attis and an extremely ancient image of the goddess in the shape of a stone. She was the goddess of the natural world and its formations.

CYBELE the principal goddess of Phrygia, often called 'the Mother of the Gods', or 'the Great Mother'. She governed the whole of Nature and was, in fact, the personification of Nature's powers (MOTHER NATURE) of growth. She was worshipped in the mountains of Asia Minor, and from there her cult spread over the whole of the Greek world, and later, into the Roman world as well, when in 204 BC the Senate of Rome decided to have the 'Black Stone' which symbolized the goddess brought from Pessinus, and to build a temple to her on the Palatine Hill. She was often portrayed wearing a crown of towers and accompanied by lions, or riding in a chariot drawn by these animals. Like Rhea, she had as her servants the Curetes, also known as the Corybantes.

A NEREID (OCEANID) or goddess of the sea. They were the patrons of sailors and fishermen, who came to the aid of men in distress, and goddesses who had in their care the sea's rich bounty. Individually they also represented various facets of the sea, from salty brine, to foam, sand, rocky shores, waves and currents, in addition to the various skills possessed by seamen. The Nereides were depicted in ancient art as beautiful young maidens, sometimes running with small dolphins or fish in their hands, or else riding on the back of dolphins, hippokampoi (fish-tailed horses) and other sea creatures.

## COEUS (Phorgys)

COEUS, CYCLEUS, KOIOS, PROTEUS and PHORGYS by the Greeks, son of Uranos (Anshar) and Gaea (Kishar). The old one of the sea; god of the sea. He was a knower of the future, a just and kind god. Coeus is one of the Greek Titan gods. Coeus is the Titan god of Intellect. He reigns over the art of learning, and guides those with inquisitive minds. In Greek mythology it is believed that he is the beginning of all knowledge. He is also the god of education, learning and of the inquisitive mind. Coeus and Tiamat had twenty four male giant sons who were born at Phlegra in Atlantis, and the two Aloeids, all of whom rebelled against Almighty Zeus. Nereus had fifty lovely daughters who were called Nymphs. They had beautiful fair hair, fish-tails and accompanied the chariot of Coeus. He was the "old man of the sea."

Coeus was a NEREID or god of the sea. They were the patrons of sailors and fishermen, who came to the aid of men in distress, and goddesses who had in their care the sea's rich bounty. Individually they also represented various facets of the sea, from salty brine, to foam, sand, rocky shores, waves and currents, in addition to the various skills possessed by seamen. The Nereides were depicted in ancient art as beautiful young maidens, sometimes running with small dolphins or fish in their hands, or else riding on the back of dolphins, hippokampoi (fish-tailed horses) and other sea creatures.

## COTTUS (Cottys)

COTTUS or COTTYS was a giant in size, called Hekatoncheires, son of Uranos (Anshar) and Gaea (Kishar). Cottus had one hundred arms and fifty heads. A Titan giant who were enormous beings of invincible strength and terrifying appearance.

## CRIUS (Kreius)

CRIUS or KREIUS, son of Uranos (Anshar) and Gaea (Kishar). Crius was a Titan who fought against the Olympian gods. He was thrown down into Tartarus by Zeus (Enlil).

## Cush (Kush)

Cush, Kush, Kosh, Kish, Bel, or Belus, son of Chem (Ham) and Naelatamauk. Given the title 'Bel' (The Lord). The first human king of Babylon. Ruled from his capital of Shamar (Sennar), Nubia. King of the

Cushites of Kush (Nubia) in Africa. He built the city of Kish (modern Al'Uhaimir) in Mesopotamia. The name of Cush is preserved in Egypt's hieroglyphic inscriptions as Kush (Kish). Confirmation of this location is given in an inscription of Esarhaddon of Assyria (681-668 BC), who tells us that he made himself king of 'Musur, Patorisi and Cush'. Kush defeated Uruk (Erech, now called Warka), and was victorious in the battle with the inhabitants of Ur. He defeated the entire territory from Lagash (now called Telloh) as far as the sea.

## DANEL (Daanel)

DANEL, DANIEL, DANYAL, or DANJAL a "fallen angel" who exercises authority over lawyers.

## DA.URU

DA.URU, daughter of En.shar (Oceanos) and Nin.shar (Tethys). Queen of Neteru. She married Du.uru, king of Neteru. The adopted son of En.shar (Oceanos) who became king of Neteru, but was murdered in a struggle for the thrown by Ala.lu.

## David (Davjd)

David or Davjd, King of Israel 1070-1015 BC, son of Jesse and Habliar. David defeated the Geshite giant Goliath who stood 10 ft. 9 in. tall.

*Dead Sea Scrolls,* Fragment 1 Column 2 - (3) (He shall capture) the mountain of Zion, and he will dispossess from there all the Amorites . . . (4) to build the House for the Lord, the God of Israel. Gold and silver . . . (5) cedars and cypress will he bring from Lebanon to build it, and the sons of Satan . . . (6) he will do priestly service there and a man . . . your . . . (7) from the . . . And the Lord will establish David securely . . . (8) (He)aven will dwell with him forever. But now, the Amorites are there, and the Canaanites . . . (9) dwell where the Hittites (do), none of whom have I sought . . . (10) from you.

David, we read in *1 Samuel* 30:7, "inquired of Yahweh (Utu)" by putting on the priestly garment of the High Priest with its oracular breastplate. But thereafter he was given the "word of Yahweh" through prophets - first one named Gad and then another named Nathan. The Bible in *II Samuel* 24:11, calls the former "Gad the Nabih (Prophet), the Seer of David," through whom the "word of Yahweh" was made known to the king.

*1 Samuel* 17:4-7 - "Then Goliath, a Philistine champion (a Gittite) from Gath, came out of the Philistine ranks to face the forces of Israel. He was a giant of a man, measuring over nine feet tall! He wore a bronze helmet, a two-hundred pound coat of mail, bronze leggings, and carried a bronze javelin several inches thick, tipped with a twenty-five pound iron spearhead, and his armor bearer walked ahead of him with a huge shield."

*1 Samuel* 17:41-51 - "Goliath walked out towards David with his shield bearer ahead of him, sneering in contempt at this nice little red-cheeked boy! "Am I a dog," he roared at David, "that you come at me with a stick?" And he cursed David by the names of his gods. "Come over here and I'll give your flesh to the birds and wild animals," Goliath yelled. David shouted in reply, "You come to me with a sword and a spear, but I come to you in the name of the Lord of the armies of heaven and of Israel--the very God whom you have defied. Today the Lord will conquer you and I will kill you and cut off your head; and then I will give the dead bodies of your men to the birds and wild animals, and the whole world will know that there is a God in Israel! And Israel will learn that the Lord does not depend on weapons to fulfill his plans - he works without regard to human means! He will give you to us!" As Goliath approached, David ran out to meet him and, reaching into his shepherd's bag, took out a stone, hurled it from his sling, and hit the Philistine in the forehead. The stone sank in, and the man fell on his face to the ground.

So David conquered the Philistine giant with a sling and a stone. Since he had no sword, he ran over and pulled Goliath's from its sheath and killed him with it, and then cut off his head. When the Philistines saw that their champion was dead, they turned and ran."

The doctrine of the "divine right of kings" was introduced by the covenant God made with David, which was the origin of the "Davidic Dynasty Tradition", that is, "royal Zionist theology", which tied the dynasty to the messianic prophecies of earlier times, and was the basis of the messianism of later times, which made the Davidic Dynasty a part of Israel's religion, Judaism, and later of Christianity also.

The essence of the "Davidic Dynasty Tradition" is:

(a) that God (Utu/Yahweh) chose Jerusalem as the place of His presence, which replaced Shiloh as the cultic center of Jehovah-worship.

(b) that God would make for David a "house", that is, an everlasting dynasty of kings, whose destiny was worldwide rule with a divine mandate, sitting upon God's very intermediary role of the Davidic king between God and the people, whereby, the Davidic king would be the channel through whom God would bless the people.

The covenant made David's House a "divine dynasty". This new status brought with it the inviolability of the person of the king, called "The Lord's Anointed", and gave rise to a court rhetoric in which the king was called "the Son of God" *(Psalms 2:7)* as the visible symbol of the invisible God, occupying God's throne *(Psalms 2:6),* representing God to the people; while at the same-time the king was called "the Son of Man" *(Daniel 7:13-14)* as the corporate embodiment of the people representing them to God.

The king was answerable to God alone, and was responsible to Him to care for the people, as the politique father ("parens patriae") of a large family, his people. Too, the king was likened to a shepherd duty-bound to watch over his flock and provide for all its needs, and his people in return would attend upon the king as his servants and give him worship. The basic duties of the king was to feed his people, to heal his people, i.e., "the royal touch"; and to defend his people. Not all of the Hebrew people accepted this idea of an everlasting union of their nation, religion, and David's House; and later ten of the twelve Hebrew tribes rebelled against David's House in the time of his grandson Rehoboam, son of Solomon, that caused the disruption of the Hebrew kingdom.

## DUMU.ZI (Dionysos)

DUMU.ZID, DUMU.ZI or "Son who is Life" by the Sumerians, son of En.ki (Poseidon) and Nin.su (Anobret). He was the "Son of the Abyss," the ever-dying, ever-reviving Sumerian prototype of the resurrected savior. He was also the harvest god of ancient Mesopotamia, and the Sumerian god of vegetation and the under-world. He was known for his horned lunar crown. Dumu.zi resorted to a tactic adopted way back by his own father: he tried to seduce and have intercourse with his own sister [half sister]. But whereas in bygone days Ninharsag agreed to Enki's advances, Dumuzi's sister (half sister) Geshtinanna refused. In his desperation Dumuzi violated a sexual taboo; he raped his own sister.

DUMUZID or DUMUZI, called "the Shepherd", from Bad-tibira in Sumer, was, according to the Sumerian King List, the fifth predynastic king in the legendary period before the Deluge. The list further states that Dumuzid ruled for 36,000 years. "Dumuzid the Shepherd" is also the subject of a series of epic poems in Sumerian literature. However, he is described in these tablets as King of Uruk, the title given by the King List to Dumuzid the Fisherman - a distinct figure said to have ruled sometime after the Flood, in between Lugalbanda "the Shepherd" and Gilgamesh.

DUMUZI the Sumerian form of Tammuz. A god of vegetation and fertility, and also of the underworld. He is called 'the Shepherd' and 'lord of the sheepfolds' - the Magi lambskin apron - the Essene lambskin apron - now the Freemason lambskin apron. As the companion of Nigizzida 'to all eternity' he stands at the gate of heaven. In the *Sumerian Descent of Inanna* he is the husband of the goddess Inanna (in reality she is Nin.ki/Eos), the Sumerian counterpart of Ishtar. According to the Sumerian King-List Gilgamesh was descended from 'Dumuzi a shepherd'. Dumuzi marriage to Inanna ensured the fertility of the land and the fecundity of the womb. This marriage, however, according to a myth whose denouncement has only recently come to light, ended in stark tragedy when the goddess, offended by her husband's unfeeling behavior toward her, decreed that he be carried off to the netherworld for six months of each year-hence the barren, sterile months of the hot summer. At the autumnal equinox, which marked the beginning of the Sumerian new year, Dumuzi returned to the earth. His reunion with his wife caused all animal and plant life to be revitalized and made fertile once again.

One of Sumer's other cuneiform texts, Dumuzi's Dream, tells a different story than the *Inanna's Descent.* Dumuzi has a chilling vision of his own demise and after crying out to the countryside, he tells his beloved sister, Geshtinanna, about it:

"A dream, my sister! A dream! In my dream, rushes were rising up for me, rushes kept growing for me, a single reed was shaking its head at me; twin reeds -- one was being separated from me. Tall trees in the forest were rising up together over me. Water was poured over my holy coals for me, the cover of my churn was being removed, my holy drinking cup was torn down from the peg where it hung, my shepherd's stick disappeared from me. An owl took a lamb from the sheep house, a falcon caught a sparrow on the reed fence, my male goats were dragging their dark beards in the dust for me, my rams were scratching the earth with their thick legs for me. The churns were lying on their side, no milk was poured, the drinking cups were lying on their side, Dumuzi was dead, the sheepfold was haunted."

So shaken by the dream that Dumuzi describes it to his sister, who tells Dumuzi not to speak of it anymore, and then gives her own dire prophecy:

"My brother, your dream is not favorable, don't tell me any more of it! Dumuzi, your dream is not favorable, don't tell me any more of it! The rushes rising up for you, which kept growing around you, are bandits rising against you from their ambush. The single reed shaking its head at you is your mother who bore you, shaking her head for you. The twin reeds of which one is taken away and then the other is you and I - first one and then the other will be taken away. The tall trees in the forest rising up together over you are the evil men catching you within the walls. That water was poured over your holy coals means the sheepfold will become a house of silence. That the cover of your holy churn was being removed for you means the evil man will bring it inside in his hands.

Your holy drinking cup being torn down from the peg where it hung is you falling off the lap of the mother who bore you. That your shepherd's stick disappeared from you means the demons will destroy it. The owl taking a lamb from the sheep house is the evil man who will hit you on the cheek. The falcon catching a sparrow on the reed fence is the big demon coming down from the sheep house."

Dumuzi told his sister that he would hide in the grass and asked her not to reveal his hiding place. Two demons from the cities of Adab, Akcak, Uruk, Ur, and Nibru came and caught Geshtinanna, offering her fields of grains and rivers of water for his location, but she refused to tell them. So they left her and bribed Dumuzi's friend, then caught Dumuzi in the ditches of Arali. Once again, Dumuzi appealed to Utu and this time he was changed into a gazelle and escaped. The demons followed him to Kuberish, the house of Old Woman Belili, and then to his sister's holy sheepfold. Geshtinanna appealed to heaven and earth in Dumuzi's behalf. She lacerated her face in public and her buttocks in private, but regardless, the ten demons caught up with him at the sheepfold and destroyed the bolt, the shepherd's stick, and the holy churn (or cream mixer). They killed Dumuzi and the sheepfold became haunted.

DAMU was a Sumerian deity, the city god of Girsu on the Euphrates River near Ur in the southern orchards region. Damu was also the vegetation god, especially of the vernal flowing of the sap of trees and plants. His name means "the child" and his cult-apparently celebrated primarily by women - centered on the lamentation and search for Damu, who had lain under the bark of his nurse, the cedar tree, and had disappeared. The search finally ended when the god reappeared out of the river. Damu was also the son of Enki. The cult of Damu influenced and later blended with the similar cult of Dumuzi the Shepherd, a Sumerian deity worshipped by the central grasslands people. A different deity called Damu was a goddess of healing and the daughter of Nininsina of Isin.

TAMMUZ or "the lover of your youth" by the Babylonians and Tiberian. The Herder (Shepherd); Only-begotten Son; Son of the Blood. Called the Anointed One (Christos in Greek); a sacrificed god. TEMMOUZ by the Arabs. TAMUZ by the Gregorians. TEMMOUZZ in Levantine Arabic. ZOROASTER by the Chaldeans. The god of the ancient "fire-worshippers".

TAMMUZ was the Babylonian god of agriculture. Tammuz (Dumuzi) and Gizzida (Ningishzzida) guarded the entrance at the Gate of the House of the Lord Anu. The astrological sign for Tammuz is the Crab, Cancer. His season is summer, and the hot weather of summer causes crabs to multiply in the water. Like his counterpart the Phoenician god Adon and Adonis in Greek, He died in midsummer. But he was brought back to life by the Sumerian goddess Ishtar (Phoenicians called Ashtaroot). Inhabitants of the "Fertile Cresent"-Syria, Palestine, Phoenicia, Babylonia and the lands of Akkad worshiped him also as the sun god. Tammuz was a healer, savior, and a shepherd who looked after his flock of stars. He died wearing a "crown of thorns" made from myrrh. Tammuz was symbolically sacrificed on the Day of Atonement in the form of a lamb. He was worshipped in Jerusalem where his exact story would later be re-told using the name "Jesus". The cave in Bethlehem where Jesus is said to have been born, is the same place where the ancients claimed that the god Tammuz (Adonis) was born. The Bible "translator", Jerome, admitted that Bethlehem had been a sacred grove dedicated to Tammuz, the "fertility god" or "spirit of the corn".

Bethlehem means "House of Bread" or "House of Corn". Horus (c 3000 BC), the Egyptian son of the god Marduk (Lucifer), was born in the "Place of Bread" and Jesus said he was "the Bread of Life". In reality the Church Father Jerome, who died in Bethlehem in 420 AD, reports in addition that the holy cave was at one point consecrated by the heathen to the worship of Adonis, and a pleasant sacred grove planted before it, to wipe out the memory of Jesus. Modern mythologists, however, reverse the supposition, insisting that the cult of Adonis-Tammuz originated the shrine and that it was the Christians who took it over, substituting the worship of their own god. (see Heru/Horus)

ADON or "Lord" by the Semitic people. ADON or "Lord" by the Phoenicians. One of the names of the supreme gods of the Phoenicians; from it was derived the name of the Syrian god ADONIS. The Adonis legend is set sometimes on Mount Idalion, sometimes in Lebanon. A river called the Adonis flowed through Byblos, its waters colored red every year on the day when the death of Adonis was celebrated. The name of the god can be traced back to a Hebrew word meaning "Lord". ATUNIS by the Etruscans. Atunis (Adonis) is found depicted on Etruscan mirrors, and his cult spread throughout the Mediterranean world in the Hellenistic period. A life-death-rebirth deity.

The Greeks called him ADONIS, which was derived from the Phoenician god Adon. The Romans called him ADONUS. The Habiru (Hebrews) transformed ADON into ADONI, ADONAI, ADONAY or "My Lord". His priest wore boar skins. Adon, a Phoenician god, who was also worshiped by the Greeks and the early Hebrews who referred to him as Adonai (My Lord or My Master in Hebrew), and Adonis was the lover of Asharoot, known also as Astarte and Aphrodite. Adonis was killed by a jealous god who was in love with Ashtaroot. Following his death, the river "Nahr Ibrahim" turned into a river of blood. The last two lines of the tablet described Adonis as a "traveling handsome god" who descended on earth aboard "a circular disc resembling the sun to fertilize the earth." This young god has striking similarities with biblical accounts:

1 - The "Ibrahim River": The Jews use "Abraham". The Arabs and people of the area use "Ibrahim" instead. Both names refer to the same biblical personage.

2 - The Ibrahim River turning into a river of blood echoes the story of one of the biblical plagues.

3 - Yahweh was also called Adonai or Adoni by the Hebrews. And the Phoenicians called their god "Adon". (See Utu/Shamash)

4 - Sumerians, Akkadians, Phoenicians and Hebrews, all of them wrote about gods descending on earth to "fertilize the earth" and "fertilize" women of the earth, thus giving birth to the giant demi-gods.

ADONIS is derived from the ancient Canaanite "Adon". It is the Hebrew name for "My Master" or "My Lord". In their prayer the Jews pronounce "Yahweh" (YHWH) as "Adonai." Adonis was a god of Asiatic origin who was inserted into the Greek mythology: his name is a Semitic word. Adon, meaning "The Lord", and he was worshipped in many places, always in conjunction with Aphrodite or her equivalent. While spending his time with Aphrodite, Another version states that Adonis lost his life as he had entered it, through the charge of a wild boar. For while hunting in the forest he was attacked and killed.

MITHRA (c 1200 BC) worshipped in ancient Persia, is found in the Indian Vedic religion as MITRA (c 1500 BC) which is 3,500 years old. Early Hindu god of the Sun. Mithraism was around long before Christianity. It is erroneously claimed that there were never any written records of Mithraism but the reality of it is, that most evidence of Mithraism was destroyed by the Christians including not only monuments and many other artifacts but many books by ancient authors, such as Eubulus, who had written many volumes on the history of Mithraism. Also, another thing that proves that Mithraism was around before Christianity was the discovery of Mithraic remains beneath later Christian edifices on Vatican Hill. The following is taken out of the Catholic Encyclopedia by Joseph Wheless in his ever valuable book *"Forgery in Christianity"* (the words of Wheless are inbetween the parenthesis): "Mithraism is a pagan religion consisting mainly of the cult of the ancient Indo-Iranian Sun-God Mitra. It entered Europe from Asia Minor after Alexander's conquest, spread rapidly over the whole Roman Empire at the beginning of our era, reached its zenith during the third century, and vanished under the repressive regulations of Theodosius at the end of the fourth. "The origin of the cult of Mithra dates from the time that Hindus and Persians still formed one people, for the god Mithra occurs in the religion and sacred books of both races, i.e. in the Vedas and in the Avesta. . . . After the conquest of Babylon (538 B.C.) this Persian cult came into contact with Chaldean astrology and with the national worship of Marduk. For a time the two priesthood of Mithra and Marduk coexisted in the capital and Mithraism borrowed much from this intercourse. . . . This religion, in which the Iranian element remained predominant, came, after Alexander's conquest, in touch with the Western world. When finally the Romans took possession of the Kingdom of Pergamum (in 133 B.C.), occupied Asia Minor, and stationed two legions of soldiers on the Euphrates, the success of Mithraism was secured. It spread rapidly from the Bosphorus to the Atlantic, from Illyria to Britain. Its foremost apostles were the legionaries; hence it spread first to the frontier stations of the Roman army. *"Mithraism was emphatically a soldier religion; Mithra, its hero, was especially a divinity of fidelity, manliness, and bravery; the stress it laid on good-fellowship and brotherliness, its exclusion of women, and the secret bond among its members have suggested the idea that Mithraism was Masonry among the Roman soldiery."* Several of the Roman Emperors, down to Licinius, colleague of Constantine, built temples to Mithra, and issued coins with his symbols. "But with the triumph of Christianity [after Constantine] Mithraism came to a sudden end. The laws of Theodosius [prescribing it under penalty of death, to please the Christians] signed its death warrant. Though he was still worshiped a thousand years later by the Manichees.

Ahura Mazda and Ahriman. - This incarnate evil (Ahriman) rose; with the army of darkness to attack and depose Oromasdes (Ahura Mazda) They were however thrown back into hell, whence they escape, wander over the face of the earth and afflict man. . . . As evil spirits ever lie in wait for hapless man, he needs a friend and savior, who is Mithra. Mithra is the Mediator between God and Man. The Mithraists . . . battled on Mithra's side against all impurity, against all evil within and without. They believed in the immortality of the soul; sinners after death were dragged down to hell; the just passed through the seven spheres of the planets, leaving at each planet a part of their lower humanity until, as pure spirits, they stood before God. At the end of the world Mithra will desectid to earth, . . . and will make all drink the beverage of immortality. He will thus have proved himself Nabarses, 'the never conquered.'

The fathers conducted the worship. The chief of the fathers, a sort of pope, who always lived at Rome, was called 'Pater Patratus' . . . The members below the grade of pater called one another 'brother,' and social distinctions were forgotten in Mithraic unity. . . . A sacred meal was celebrated of bread and haoma juice for which in the West wine was substituted. This meal was supposed to give the participants supernatural virtue.

Three times a day prayer was offered the sun towards east, south, or west according to the hour. Sunday (Sun-day) was kept holy in honor of Mithra, and the sixteenth of each month was sacred to him as Mediator. The

25 December was observed as his birthday, the Natalis Invictis, the rebirth of the winter-sun, unconquered by the rigors of the season." It may be noted that Sunday was made a Pagan holiday by edict of Constantine. In the fifth Tablet of the Babylonian (Chaldean) Epic of Creation, by the great God Marduk, we read, lines 17 and 18: "On the seventh day he appointed a holy day, And to cease from all work he commanded." *Records of the Past,* vol. ix; quoted, Clarke, *Ten Great Religions,* ii, p. 383.

MITRA (c 1500 BC) was called MITHRA (c 1200 BC) by the Persians. MITHRAS by the Romans. ATTIS (c 1200 BC) by the Phrygians. KRISHNA (c 900 BC) by the Aryans of India. MITHRA (c 1200 BC) of Persia, India and Rome, is the son of Ahura Mazda (Enlil). (Intentionally changed from his real father being the evil god Enki-Satan to the good god Enlil-El Shadai). He was sent to Earth to rid the world of Ahriman (Enki/Satan) and his army of demons. The Savior Mithra was born on December 25th, quickly matured, and set about establishing himself as a formidable beast slayer. Then when his earthly mission was near completion, Mithra gathered his devotees together for one "last supper" during which he vowed to return one day and complete his battle with Ahriman's dark forces. During his time away, however, Mithra promised to continue to assist his devotees from the heavenly realms and informed them that they could still commune with him through the sacramental meal of bread and wine. The cult of Mithra originated thousands of years before "Jesus" and yet again tells the later Christian story in fine detail. It is even said that gold, frankincense, and myrrh, were offered to him. Mithra's sacred day was Sunday. Mithra worshippers called this the "Lord's Day" and they celebrated the main Mithra festival during what is now Easter. Mithra was portrayed as a winged Lion standing within a spiralling serpent. The Roman Church encompassed the Mithra Eucharist into its "Christian" rituals. Mithra was claimed to have said: "He who shall not eat of my body nor drink of my blood, so that he may be one with me and I with him, shall not be saved." The very site on which the

Vatican was built was a sacred place of Mithra worship. God of light that precedes the dawn. Among the Aryans, he is the "God of Light". In Heaven, he assigns places to the souls of the just. *The Dabistan,* page 145; Lenormant, *Chaldean Magic.* Jesus Christ was and is the "Light of the World." Mithra the Persian sun god was depicted as a Lion carrying a bee in its lips; essentially the "Lying Lion King". Worshippers of Mithras had a complex system of seven grades of initiation, with ritual meals. Initiates called themselves syndexioi, those "united by the handshake" (freemason handshake today). They met in underground temples (called a mithraeum), which survive in large numbers. The cult appears to have had its epicentre in Rome.

As for the similarities between Mithra, Mithraism, Jesus and Christianity: Mithra was born on December 25th sometimes in a stable or cave but traditionally from a rock. The emperor Aurelian declared December 25 to be the official birthday of Mithra, circa 270 CE, even attended by shepards who brought gifts. Mithra was a traveling teacher. Mithra had 12 disciples. He performed Miracles. He was buried in a tomb. In three days he was resurrected. He was called the "Good Shepard". He was considered ""the Way, the Truth and the Light, the Redeemer, the Savior, the Messiah." His sacred day was Sunday. His resurrection was celebrated on Easter. He had a Last Supper when he returned to his father. Also called the Eucharist or the Lord's Supper. He was believed not to have died, but to have ascended to heaven where it was believed he would return at the end of time where he would judge the living and the dead. He granted immortal life of his followers through baptism. Followers of Mithra were lead by a 'papa', the Greek word for 'father' and what 'pope' is derived from, who ruled on Vatican Hill in Rome. Followers of Mithra celebrated "sacramenta", a consecrated bread and wine, using chanting, incense,bells, candles and holy water just as is found in the Catholic Mass.

Quotes: *"The devil, whose business is to pervert the truth, mimics the exact circumstances of the Divine Sacraments...Thus he celebrates the oblation of bread, and brings in the symbol of the resurrection. Let us therefore acknowledge the craftiness of the devil, who copies certain things of those that be Divine.*" - Tertullian in the late 2nd century C.E., describing the similarities between Christianity and Mithraism. *"He who will not eat of my body and drink of my blood, so that he will be made on with me and I with him, the same shall not know salvation."*- No this is not *John* 6:53-54. It is actually an inscription to Mithras.

MIHR, MIHIR, MIHER or MITHRA (c 1200 BC) in ancient Persian lore, the angel presiding over the 7th month (July-crab) and over the 16th day of that month. Mihr watched over friendship and love. Hyde, *Historia Religiouis Veterum Persarum.* The magi held that, on Judgment Day, 2 angels would stand on the bridge called *al Sirat* (which is finer than a hair and sharper than the edge of a sword) to examine every person crossing. Mihr (Michael) would be one of those angels, Sorush (Gabriel) the other. Mihr, representing divine mercy, and holding a balance in his hand, would weigh the person's actions performed during his lifetime. If found worthy, the person would be permitted to pass on to Paradise. If he was found unworthy, then Sorush (Gabriel), representing divine justice, would hurl him into Hell. Sale, *The Koran,* "Preliminary Discourse," page 64.

The Mass of Mithra that St. Justin speaks of celebrates a conflict between good and evil by which the divine huntsman Mithra, a personification of light and goodness, effects the salvation of the world by pursuing a bull (Satan) personifying darkness and evil into a cave, where he dispatches him with a sword on orders from the Sun-god Ormuzd (Enlil, Zeus, El Shadai) - whereupon all visible material creation springs from the bull's dead body. I might mention that Mithra wears a Phrygian cap like those sported by the French revolutionists, a cap which can also be seen on the heads of the figures of Liberty and Young America in the blasphemous ``Apotheosis of Washington´´ painted by Brumidi in the dome of the U.S. Capitol. Supported by the Emperors, Mithraic worship spread along the

Euphrates and through Europe along the Rhine and Danube. Even after the public cult ceased with Constantine, it flourished in England, where the Roman legions had built temples from London to York, so that it became known as the Island of the Bull - today, ``John Bull.´´ Hugh Ross Williamson in *The Arrow and the Sword* even voices the suspicion that the butchery of St.Thomas Becket in his cathedral may have been a ritual murder in the Mithraic tradition. As in Masonry, only men were devotees, and their initiation took the form of a "baptism" simulating death and resurrection, more than vaguely reminiscent of the Masonic initiation ceremony of the "raising of Hiram."

Aldebaran (with two habitable planets) is one of the great stars of the heavens located in the Taurus 'the Bull' constellation. It is one of the Royal stars of Persia, it is the Watcher in the East and holds importance in astro-history. Aldebaran was the god Mithra or Ahura Mazda - the slayer of the Cosmic Bull. Mithra was a military god who gave victory to his followers but only if they followed the strictest procedure in his worship. Mithra wore the title of "lord of contracts". He considered all exchanges sacred and oversaw the business ventures of his followers, insisting upon their honesty and purity. Failure meant condemnation to an ordeal of fire. Sacrifice of a bull constituted the main rite of worship, vestiges of which are still found in Germany today, and it´s curious to note that after the Masonic ceremony dedicating the U.S. Capitol, the participants feasted on roasted ox. Mithra´s adepts likewise communicated in the common meal mentioned by St. Justin, commemorating the one he shared with the Sun-god after killing the bull. An ancient Mithraic hymn reads, "Thou hast redeemed us too by shedding the eternal blood" - for the task of man was to liberate his soul from the material shackles of his body and follow Mithra to a heaven of pure spirit. With its Christ like savior and its concept of sacrifice leading to resurrection, this myth came dangerously close to Christian doctrine and misled many. St. Augustine tells of a priest of Mithra he knew who used to say, "Our capped one is himself a Christian". On the contrary, like all mystery cults, Mithraism was in no sense of Christian Inspiration, but pure Gnosticism. Derived originally from the Jewish Kabbala imported from Egypt and Babylonia by heretical Jews, gnostic beliefs of one kind or another had been at work adulterating the true religion from earliest times, the prophets inveighing against them to little avail. Systematized 200 years before Christ in a blend of Hebraic and heretic culture by Hellenistic Jews like Philo of Alexandria, Gnosticism by the time of St. Justin was presuming to replace not only polytheism and Judaism, but also Christianity, by allegedly combining in itself the higher principles of all three. It was, in other words, an early attempt at "world religion."

As its name implies, it proposes salvation by imparting superior knowledge or gnosis, the primordial "ancient wisdom" revealed secretly to a chosen few from generation to generation. Vaguely pantheistic, it is necessarily allied to some form of dualism, for Satan, who inspired it, considers himself equal to God. In order to present himself as a viable candidate for the Lordship of the Universe, he must establish himself on the same divine level as God. He sought to do this at the very beginning of human history in Eden, where - as Louis Veuillot so aptly put it - he sought to demote the sovereign God to the rank of simple citizen in paradise according to democratic principles. At the same time, he imparted the basic tenet of the gnosis, a special knowledge not given by God to man: He asks Eve, "Why hath God commanded you, that you should not eat of every tree of paradise?" When Eve replies that to eat the fruit of a certain one entails the death penalty, the serpent tells her, ``No, you shall not die the death. For God doth know that in what day so ever you shall eat thereof, your eyes shall be opened and you shall be as gods, knowing good and evil" *Genesis* 3:1-5. In other words you shall be "enlightened".

ATTIS (c 1200 BC) by the Phrygians. He was born on December 25th to a virgin mother. He was called a "savior", the only begotten son, and died to save humanity. He was crucified on a Friday and his blood was spilled to redeem the Earth. He suffered death "with nails and stakes". He was the Father and Son combined in an earthly body. He was put in a tomb, went down into the underworld, but three days later, on March 25th, his body was found to have disappeared from the tomb and he was resurrected as the "Most High God". His body was symbolised as bread and eaten by those who worshipped him.

KRISHNA (c 900 BC) or "Christ" by the Aryans of India. He was born to a virgin mother on December 25th and his father was a carpenter. A star marked his birthplace, and angels and shepherds attended. The ruler slaughtered thousands of infants in an effort to kill him, but he survived and went on to perform miracles and heal the sick, including lepers, the blind, and the deaf. He died at about the age of 30 and some traditions say he was crucified on a tree. He was also portrayed on a cross, rose from the dead, and was considered the savior. His followers apparently knew him as "Jezeus" or "Jeseus", which means "pure essence". It is said that he will return on a white horse to judge the dead and fight the "Prince of Evil".

VIRISHNA (c 1200 BC). Some 1,200 years before "Jesus", the following was said in the East of the "heathen savior" Virishna. He was born to a virgin by Immaculate Conception through the intervention of a Holy Spirit. This fulfilled an ancient prophecy. His birth was announced by a star and angelic voices. Shepherds and wise men brought him gifts. When he was born, the ruling tyrant wanted to kill him. And his parents had to flee to safety. All male children under the age of two were slain by the ruler as he was given gifts of gold, frankincense, and myrrh. He was worshipped as the savior of men and led a mortal and humble life. He performed miracles, which included healing the sick, giving sight to the blind, casting out devils, and raising the dead. He was put to death on the cross between two thieves. He descended to hell and rose from the dead to ascend back to heaven. The Hindus call him Redeemer, Firstborn, Sin Bearer, Liberator, the Universal

Word. It is said that Krishna returns at the end of each age to save the righteous, destroy sin, and establish goodness and holiness. God of erotic delights, sexual pleasures, love, music, savior from sins.

The *Tanhuna Genesis, Jewish Encyclopedia I, 94,*claims he was the archangel MICHAEL, or MALKIEL, MALCHIEL, MACHIDIEL, and MALCHEDAEL. Michael is the chief of the order of virtues, chief of archangels, prince of presence, angel of repentance, righteousness, mercy, and sanctification; angelic prince of Israel, guardian of Jacob, conqueror of Satan. His mystery name is SABBATHIEL. In Islamic writings he is called MIKA'IL. As the deliverer of the faithful he accords, in the Avesta, with Saosyhant the Redeemer. He has been identified with the angel who destroyed the hosts of Sennacherib. In Jewish lore "the fire that Moses saw in the burning bush had the appearance of Michael, who had descended from Heaven as the forerunner of the Shekinah." Ginzberg, *The Legends of the Jews II,* 303

In Baruch III, Michael "holds the keys of the kingdom of Heaven." Among the recently discovered Dead Sea scrolls there is one titled the "War of the Sons of Light Against the Sons of Darkness." Here Michael is called the "PRINCE OF LIGHT". He leads the angels of light in battle against the legions of the angels of darkness, the latter under the command of the demon Belial (Satan). As the angel of the final reckoning and the weigher of souls, he holds in his hand the scales of justice. In Ginzberg, *The Legends of the Jews*, Michael is regarded as the forerunner of the Shekinah; as the angel who brought Asenath from Palestine as a wife to Joseph; as the one who saved Daniel's companions from the fire; as the intermediary between Mordecai and Esther; and as the destroyer of Babylon. He is also said to have informed the fallen angels of the Deluge. The Chaldeans worshipped him as a god. Chief of the Order of Virtues and archangels, "Prince of Light" and the "leader of God's host". He rules the Element of Fire and the South Wind; his color is red. In Hastings, *Encyclopedia of Religion and Ethics* IV, 616, the article "*Demons and Spirits*" speaks of the earliest tradions in Muslim lore as locating Michael in the 7th Heaven "on the borders of the Full Sea, crowded with an innumerable array of angels"; and after describing Michaels's wings as "of the color of green emerald," goes on to say that he "is covered with saffron hairs, each of them containing a million faces and mouths and as man tongues which, in a million dialects, implore the pardon of Allah." EL SABAOTH or the "GOD OF THE HEAVENLY HOSTS." In the *Dead Sea Scrolls* (*Manuscript B Fragment 1*) he has three names: MICHAEL, PRINCE OF LIGHT, and the KING OF RIGHTEOUSNESS.

According to Biblical prophecy, the New Age is scheduled to dawn at the completion of Armageddon, the global battle which is projected to occur as the polar opposite principles of good and evil, light and darkness, attract each other and clash. At the conclusion of this planetary war, the Dragon and his destructive power, which is introduced in the 13th chapter of the *Book of Revelation*, will be subdued by his Twin (Michael) and the creative power of Spirit he wields. This event is presented in the Bible as the Christed Son who descends from the heavens upon a brilliant white steed, lays "hold on the dragon," and casts him into "the bottomless pit." In *Revelation* 20:1,'he laid hold of the dragon, that old serpent, which is the Devil, and Satan, and bound him a thousand years.'

A lot of people wear crosses every day. They think of it as a sign of salvation . . . A reminder if you will, Jesus dying on the cross to free them of their sins. Yet you have others who just wear it to be wearing it, with no idea of it's origins or what it really stands for. Well if you're going to walk around wearing something around your neck at least for the love of God, Know what it truly means and where it came from. Catholics cross themselves before and after prayer, they allow the priest to put a cross of ashes on their foreheads on Ash Wednesday, and they walk around proud all day representing their faith . . . but is it their faith that they're really representing?

A tradition of the Church which our fathers have inherited, was the adoption of the words "cross" and "crucify". These words are nowhere to be found in the Greek of the New Testament. These words are mistranslations, a "later rendering", of the Greek words stauros and stauroo. Vine's Expository Dictionary of New Testament Words says, "Stauros denotes, primarily, an upright pole or stake . . . Both the noun and the verb stauroo, to fasten to a stake or pole, are originally to be distinguished from the ecclesiastical form of a two-beamed cross.

The shape of the latter had its origin in ancient Chaldea (Babylon), and was used as the symbol of the god Tammuz (being in the shape of the mystic Tau, the initial of his name). By the middle of the 3rd century AD, the churches had either departed from, or had travestied, certain doctrines of the Christian faith. In order to increase the prestige of the apostate ecclesiastical system pagans were received into the churches apart from regeneration by faith, and were permitted largely to retain their pagan signs and symbols. Hence the Tau or T, in its most frequent form, with the cross piece lowered, was adopted.

Dr. Bullinger, in the *Companion Bible, appx. 162,* states, "crosses were used as symbols of the Babylonian Sun-god . . . It should be stated that Constantine was a Sun-god worshiper . . . The evidence is thus complete, that the Lord was put to death upon an upright stake, and not on two pieces of timber placed at any angle."

Rev. Alexander Hislop, *The Two Babylons, pp. 197-205,* frankly calls the cross "this Pagan symbol . . . the Tau, the sign of the cross, the indisputable sign of Tammuz, the false Messiah . . . the mystic Tau of the Cladeans (Babylonians) and Egyptians - the true original form of the letter T the initial of the name of Tammuz . . . the Babylonian cross was the recognized emblem of Tammuz."

In the *Encyclopaedia Britannica,* 11th edition, vol. 14, p. 273 - "In the Egyptian churches the cross was a pagan symbol of life borrowed by the

Christians and interpreted in the pagan manner." Jacob Grimm, in his Deutsche Mythologie, says that the Teutonic (Germanic) tribes had their idol Thor, symbolized by a hammer, while the Roman Christians had their crux (cross). It was thus somewhat easier for the Teutons to accept the Roman Cross.

Greek dictionaries, lexicons and other study books also declare the primary meaning of stauros to be an upright pale, pole or stake. The secondary meaning of "cross" is admitted by them to be a "later" rendering. At least two of them do not even mention "cross", and only render the meaning as "pole or stake". In spite of this strong evidence and proof that the word stauros should have been translated "stake", and the verb stauroo to have been translated "impale", almost all the common versions of the Scriptures persist with the Latin Vulgate's crux (cross), a fallacious "later" rendering of the Greek stauros. Why then was the "cross" (crux) brought into the Faith?

Again, historical evidence points to Constantine as the one who had the major share in uniting Sun-worship and the Messianic Faith. Constantine's famous vision of "the cross superimposed on the sun", in the year 312, is usually cited. Writers, ignorant of the fact that the cross was not to be found in the New Testament Scriptures, put much emphasis on this vision as the onset of the so-called "conversion" of Constantine. But, unless Constantine had been misguided by the Gnostic Manichean half-Christians, who indeed used the cross in their hybrid religion, this vision of the cross superimposed on the sun could only be the same old cosmic religion, the astrological religion of Babylon. The fact remains: that which Constantine saw, is nowhere to be found in Scripture.

We read in the book of Johannes Geffcken, *The Last Days of Greco-Roman Paganism, page 319,* "that even after 314 A.D. the coins of Constantine show an even-armed cross as a symbol for the Sun-god." Many scholars have doubted the "conversion" of Constantine because of the wicked deeds that he did afterward, and because of the fact that he only requested to be baptized on his death-bed many years later, in the year 337. So, if the vision of the cross impressed him, and was used as a rallying symbol, it could not have been in honor of Yahushúa, because Constantine continued paying homage to the Sun-deity and to one of the Sun-deity's symbols, the cross.

This continuation of Sun-worship by Constantine is of by his persistent use of images of the Sun-deity on his coins that were issued by him up to the year 323. Secondly, the fact of his motivation to issue his Sunday-keeping edict in the year 321, which was not done in honor of Yahushúa, but was done because of the "venerable day of the Sun" (Sun-day), as the edict read, is proof of this continued allegiance to Sol Invictus. We shall expand on this later.

Where did the cross come from, then? J.C. Cooper, *An Illustrated Encyclopaedia of Traditional Symbols, page 45,* aptly summarizes it, "Cross - A universal symbol from the most remote times; it is the cosmic symbol par excellence." Other authorities also call it a sun-symbol, a Babylonian sun-symbol, an astrological Babylonian-Assyrian and heathen sun-symbol, also in the form of an encircled cross referred to as a "solar wheel", and many other varieties of crosses. Also, "the cross represents the Tree of Life", the age-old fertility symbol, combining the vertical male and horizontal female principles, especially in Egypt, either as an ordinary cross, or better known in the form of the crux ansata, the Egyptian ankh (sometimes called the Tau cross), which had been carried over into our modern-day symbol of the female, well known in biology.

As stated above, the indisputable sign of Tammuz, the mystic Tau of the Babylonians and Egyptians, was brought into the Church chiefly because of Constantine, and has since been adored with all the homage due only to the Most High.

The Protestants have for many years refrained from undue adoration of, or homage to the cross, especially in England at the time of the Puritans in the 16th - 17th centuries. But lately this un-Scriptural symbol has been increasingly accepted in Protestantism.

We have previously discussed "the weeping for Tammuz", and the similarity between the Easter resurrection and the return or rising of Tammuz. Tammuz was the young incarnate Sun, the Sun-divinity incarnate. This same Sun-deity, known amongst the Babylonians as Tammuz, was identified with the Greek Adonis and with the Phoenician Adoni, 96 all of them Sun-deities, being slain in winter, then being "wept for", and their return being celebrated by a festivity in spring, while some had it in summer - according to the myths of pagan idolatry.

The evidence for its pagan origin is so convincing that *The Catholic Encyclopedia* admits that "the sign of the cross, represented in its simplest form by a crossing of two lines at right angles, greatly antedates, in both East and the West, the introduction of Christianity. It goes back to a very remote period of human civilization." It then continues and refers to the Tau cross of the pagan Egyptians, "In later times the Egyptian Christians (Copts), attracted by its form, and perhaps by its symbolism, adopted it as the emblem of the cross." Further proof of its pagan origin is the recorded evidence of the Vestal Virgins of pagan Rome having the cross hanging on a necklace, and the Egyptians doing it too, as early as the 15th century B.C. The Buddhists, and Ancient Egyptian Rot-n-no priests. Note the crosses on the robe, and hanging from their necks.

Numerous other sects of India, also used the sign of the cross as a mark on their followers' heads. "The cross thus widely worshiped, or regarded as a 'sacred emblem', was the unequivocal symbol of Bacchus, the Babylonian Messiah, for he was represented with a head-band covered with crosses. "It was also the symbol of Jupiter Foederis in Rome. Furthermore, we read of the cross on top of the temple of Serapis, the Sun-deity of Alexandria. This is Tammuz, whom the Greeks called Bacchus, with the crosses on his head-band.

After Constantine had the "vision of the cross", he and his army promoted another variety of the cross, the Chi-Rho or Labarum or sometimes . This has subsequently been explained as representing the first letters of the name Christos, the being the Greek for "Ch" and the being the Greek for "r". but again, this emblem had a pagan origin. The identical symbols were found as inscriptions on a rock, dating from the year ca. 2 500 B.C., being interpreted as "a combination of two Sun-symbols", as the Ax or Hammer-symbol of the Sun- or Sky-deity, and the or as the ancient symbol of the Sun, both of these signs having a sensual or fertility meaning as well.

Another proof of its pagan origin is the identical found on a coin of Ptolemeus III, from the year 247 - 222 B.C. A well-known encyclopedia describes the Labarum (Chi-Rho) as, "The labarum was also an emblem of the Chaldean (Babylonian) sky-god and in Christianity it was adopted." Emperor Constantine adopted this Labarum as the imperial ensign and thereby succeeded in "uniting both divisions of his troops, pagans and Christians, in a common worship … according to Suicer the word (labarum) came into use in the reign of Hadrian, and was probably adopted from one of the nations conquered by the Romans. "It must be remembered that Hadrian reigned in the years AD 76-138, that he was a pagan emperor, worshiped the Sun-deity Serapis when he visited Alexandria, and was vehemently anti-Judaistic, being responsible for the final near-destruction of Jerusalem in the year 130.

Another dictionary relates the following about the Chi-Rho, "However, the symbol was in use long before Christianity, and X (Chi) probably stood for Great Fire or Sun, and P (Rho) probably stood for Pater or Patah (Father). The word labarum (labarum) yields everlasting Father Sun."

What is the "mark of the beast" of which we read in *Rev 13:16-17, Rev 14:9-11, Rev 15:2, Rev 16:2, Rev 19:20 and Rev 20:4*- a mark on people's foreheads and on their right hands? *Rev 14:11* reveals the mark to be "the mark of his (the beast's) name." Have we not read about the mystic Tau, the

T, the initial of Tammuz's name, his mark? This same letter T (Tau) was written in Egyptian hieroglyphics and in the old Wemitic languages as, representing the CROSS. Different interpretations have been given to the "mark of the beast", and also the cross has been suggested. There has been some research done on the strange crosses found on quite a few statues of pagan priests, on their foreheads. However, these scholars have been unable to come to an agreement. Conclusive evidence may still come. Let us rather use the true rendering of the Scriptural words stauros and stauro, namely "stake" and "impale" and eliminate the un-Scriptural "cross" and "crucify".

DIONYSOS by the Greeks, son of Poseidon (Enki) and Anobret (Ninsu). He was born to a virgin mother on December 25th and put in a manger in swaddling clothes. He was a teacher who travelled, performing miracles. He turned water into wine and rode in triumph on an ass. He was the ram or the lamb, God of the Vine, God of Gods and King of Kings, Only Begotten Son, bearer of sins, Redeemer, Anointed One, Alpha and Omega. He was hung and crucified on a tree, but rose from the dead on March 25th. During the 1st century BC, the Hebrews in Jerusalem also worshipped this deity.

DIONYSUS (c 500 BC) the "Horned God"; "Savior"; "The bull-horned god"; also called DITHYRAMBOS or "double-birth" or "twice-born". He was called the Roaring One; the Initiated. The vine, wine, and ivy were sacred to him. The god of wine and of ecstatic liberation: the greatest deity of the later Greek (Hellenistic) world, to which his cult, accompanied by rich ceremonial, promised salvation. He appears to be an intruder from Thrace or Phrygia. He was usually accompanied by the Sileni and Satyrs who protected fertility. Originally he may, like Demeter, have been a deity of grain and agriculture in general. Most of his followers were women, called the Maenads or "frenzied ones", who held drunken, orgiastic rituals; they abandoned themselves to wild dances on the hillsides: they clad themselves in fawnskins and carried torches and thyrsoi (staves, wrapped in grapevines or ivy stems, and crowned with pine cones); they also were known to tear men apart with their bare hands.

At Eleusis, the god appeared as "the Holy Child" IACCHUS laid in the winnowing basket. Dionysus was the great remover of inhibition and influences the human emotions. He was the god of pleasure, ecstasy, total abandon, woodlands, Nature, wine, initiation, rituals, rebirth, regeneration and civilization. Dionysus was often persecuted by those who refused to accept his divinity.

In Aetolia, Dionysus was so well received that King Oeneus offered him his own wife Althaea, who subsequently bore him a daughter, Deianira, the future wife of Heracles. Dionysus rewarded Oeneus with his favor and the art of cultivating the vine. Dionysus, as befitted a god of foreign origin, was believed to have travelled widely outside Greece. Hera drove him mad, so that he wandered through the eastern lands, Syria and Egypt, until in Phrygia Cybele or Rhea purified him and cured him of his frenzy. He adopted Phrygian dress and was accompanied by Lydian Maenads, Satyrs, and Sileni. His female followers wore deerskins, carried the thyrus, suckled fawns, tore to pieces and ate wild beasts, and allegedly indulged in sexual promiscuity. King Midas of Phrygia entertained him so royally that Dionysus offered him any favor he desired. He chose that whatever he touched should turn to gold. In the battle between the gods and giants, Dionysus killed Eurytus with his thyrsus; and the asses ridden by his Satyrs caused terror to the giants. When the gods fled to Egypt from the monstrous Typhon, Dionysus changed himself into a goat. Aphrodite was said to have borne him Priapus, who like Dionysus was a god of fertility and vegetation. The Romans identified him with Father LIBER, an ancient Italian rustic god.

BACCHUS, LIBER, LIBER PATER by the Romans. He was the consort of Libera. He was called the "Liberator", he carried a pine cone tipped thyrsus and sometimes rode a panther. He was shown accompanied by goat-foot satyrs, centaurs, and crazed female Bacchantes. He was honored on

March 17th in the Liberalia, when boys put on the toga of manhood. At his other festivals people wore masks, sang crude songs, and indulged in unrestrained good times. The ever-young god of wine, good times, ecstasy, fertility, and wild Nature.

**Anunnaki god Tammuz (Dumuzi)**

**Ningishzidda (Raphiel) and Dumuzi (Michael) holding a staff**

# DU.URU

DU.URU, son of En.shar (Oceanos) and Anunnaki Concubine. King of Neteru. Adopted Anunnaki son, Lahma who was murdered in a struggle for the throne by Ala.lu.

# Elam

Elam, son of Shem (Sem) and Sedeqetelebab. The founder of the Elamites, which people were known to the Babylonians as the Elamtu, to the Greeks as Elymais, and whom the Romans knew as Elymaei. The Elamites recorded their own name as the Haltamti. The Old Persian inscriptions rendered their name as (h)uju, and the Middle Persian inscriptions speak of huz, which is simply the archaic form of the modern Persian name for Khuzistan, which now covers what used to be the land of Elam.

## ENA.MA (Jehav)

JEHAV by the Pleiadians. Jehav (Enama) was murdered by his son Arussem (Annu) in 1320 BC. ENA.MA by the Sumerians.

## EN.KI (Poseidon)

E.A or "Whose House is Water" by the Sumerians, son of An.nu (Cronos) and Nin.ul (Perseis). Ea was given the epithet NIN.IGI.KU or "Lord bright-eye". EN.KI or "Lord [Adon] of firm ground [Earth]" by the Akkadians. GUGALANNA or "the monstrous BULL OF HEAVEN". ENKIGAL by the Britons. He built Keridor, the land between the two great rivers. HI.AH or "Lord of the Saltwaters," by the Babylonians. HEA by the Chaldeans. NUD.IM.MUD or "Artful Fashioner" by the Sumerians. The god of the Nineveh tablets, was a fish-god (snake-god); he was represented in the Chaldean monuments as half man and half fish (half snake); he was described as the god of "the abyss"-- the ocean. Enki was the "Prince of Earth," "god of the waters," "Lord of Magicians," "Lord of Wisdom," and the "Lord of Incautations." He was a "Creator God"; "Lord of the Earth"; "Lord of the Underworld". His symbol the pitchfork (the magic trident) is the ancient symbol of the Atlantean fire serpent. The "Chief Corner Stone that the Builders rejected" in the Bible.

The deliberations of the gods in the era following the First Deluge are mentioned in various Sumerian texts. The one called the *Epic of Etana* states: The Great Anunnaki who decree the fate sat exchanging their counsels regarding the Earth. They who created the four regions, who set up the settlements, who oversaw the land, were too lofty for Mankind.

The decision to establish on Earth four Regions was thus coupled with a decision to install intermediaries (priest-kings) between the gods and Mankind; so kingship was again lowered to Earth from Heaven. In an effort to end the feud between the Enlil and Enki families, lots were drawn between the gods to determine who would have dominion over which of the Regions. As a result, Asia and Europe were assigned to Enlil and his offspring; to Enki, Africa was given. Enki then cloned the first humans (Cro-Magnon man) as slaves.

A Mesopotamian description of the Dragon Enki - "The head is the head of a serpent, from his nostrils mucus trickles. The mouth is beslaved with water. The ears are those of a basilisk. His horns are twisted in three curls. He wears a veil in his head band. The body is a sun fish full of stars. The base of his feet are claws. The sole of his feet has no sole." The Sumerians, by Samuel Noah Kramer, 1963, University of Chicago Press. The RED DRAGON of the *Book of Revelation*.

Enki was designated the title NIN.IGI.KU, the "Lord of the Sacred Eye" by the Sumerians. The "Sacred Eye" or the "All Seeing Eye" was the pineal gland or the "Third Eye", the "Eye of Wisdom". He was the source of all secret magical knowledge. His priests wore fish-shaped garments when performing purification rituals. He is the God of stonecutters (the masons), carpenters, goldsmiths.

Some Mesopotamian hymns to Enki exalt him as BEL NIM.IKI or "Lord of mining". In the *Chaldean Book of Numbers*, SAMAEL (Satan/Enki) is the concealed occult Wisdom, and MICHAEL (Dumuzi) the higher terrestrial Wisdom, both emanating from the same source.

His mystic symbol was the Son of the Left Hand Mark: IIn; and the symbol of Satan - an inverted Pentagram with a circle around it. Enki was also known as the "Good and Perfect Serpent," the Messiah of Naaseni, whose symbol in Heaven is Draco, which stands for Alpha Draconians-the Reptilians.

AMON-RA, AMON-RE, AMUN-RA, AMEN-RA or "The Unseen One" by the Egyptians. Hidden god; Great Father; the great god of Thebes; a phallic deity. Sometimes pictured with the head of a ram; sometimes as a man with a crown with two tall straight plumes. Considered incarnate in the ruling pharaoh. One of the universe creators and generous to all his devotees. AMON became known as the "King of the gods," and eventually his identity merged with the older cult of RE or RA the "Bright One", the "SUN GOD" (see AN.IB, GEB).

The Ram Headed god AMON, AMMON, AMMON KEMATEF, AMEN, AMUN, and AMOUN by the Egyptians. Ammon's shrine was at Pa-Bi-Neb-Tat (Ba-neb-tettu) and called Binedi by the Assyrians, Bendes by the Greeks, which later became Mendes and then Mendesius. PTAAH, PTAH or "The Developer" by the Egyptians. A "God of Heaven and Earth." Ptah's symbol was the serpent-later the Dragon. PTHAHIL and PTAHIL by the Mandaeans. TVASHTRI, TV-ASH-TRI or 'the Fashioner' by the Aryians.

Enki (1/2 Reptilian) usurped the "Lordship" of Earth and was declared Supreme God of Babylon and of "the Four Quarters of the Earth." His son, Marduk presided over the core civilization of this Region, the civilization of the Nile Valley. He was the supreme divinity at On--Heliopolis, near Memphis. In the ancient City of Anu (later called 'On' in the Bible, 'Heliopolis' by the Greeks, and later modern 'Ciaro') there is a pillar called the 'Pillar of Anu'-'Pillar of On'-'Pillar of Shu'-'Pillar of Thoth'-'Pillar of Hermes'-'Pillar of Seth'- 'Pillar of Solomon'-'Pillars of the Gods of the Dawning Light' and the 'Gate of the Hall of Truth'. Two pillars were removed from the Temple of Amen (Enki/Satan) at Heliopolis in 1880. One was erected on the Thames River bank in London, England and the second one was erected in Central Park, New York City in United States of America. The *New York Herald,* 13 Febraury 1880, stated the following:

*"The obelisk and its foundations will be removed and replaced in New York exactly in the positions in which they were found, each having been numbered to correspond with numbers on a drawing that was made before the pieces were removed." The monument was erected by Thothmes III at the outer porch of the Temple of Amen at Heliopolis, where it and its twin (now in London) guarded the entrance of the temple for 2,000 years before they*

*were moved to Alexandria. On 12 June 1880, with the assistance of Mr. Zola, Most Worshipful Grand Master of Egypt, the obelisk was entrusted to Lieutenant Commander H. H. Gorringe, U.S.N. [United States Navy], a member of Anglo-Saxon Lodge No. 137, for shipment to New York. On 9 October 1880 the obelisk was raised with great Masonic ceremonies in Central Park, New York City. With 8,000 Masons in attendance, the cornerstone of the ancient obelisk was laid by Jesse B. Anthony, Grand Master of Masons in New York State, as 30,000 awe-struck spectators and curiosity seekers watched, wondering what the strange rites they were seeing performed meant."*

An or Annu is the original name of the Egyptian city later known as Heliopolis that was ancient Egypt's first religious center. Hieroglyphic inscriptions tell that Pharaohs were allowed to enter the Holy of Holies of the city's great temple once a year to view the "celestial barque" in which the god Ra, the son of Ptah (Amen-Ra), had arrived on Earth from the "Planet of millions of years." According to Genesis 41, when Joseph was appointed Overseer Over Egypt, the Pharaoh "gave him Assenath, the daughter of Potiphera, the Priest of On (Anu), for a wife."

A.LIM or "Ram". The "HOLY PHALLUS" or his symbol the "OBELISK". AL.LU.LIM or A.LU.LIM the "Ram of the Glittering (Shining) Waters". The dark "GOAT OF MENDES" in Lower Egypt by the Greeks. A Satyr which is the Hebrew word for shaggy or hairy one in Isa. 13:21; 34:14. It is rendered devils in Lev. 17:7; 2 Chr. 11:15. That it refers to a demonic creature is clear from Rev. 18:2, where the word demons replaces the Hebrew satyrs in the Isaiah passages quoted there. The word is rendered hairy in Gen. 27:11, 23, and goat in Lev. 4:24; 16:9-27. SIVA or "'Lord of the Goats". Azazel (Enki), one of the two leaders of the fallen angels, was said to have fostered a race of demons known as the "seirim" or 'he-goats'. They are mentioned several times in the Bible and were worshipped and adored by some Jews. There is even some indication that women actually copulated with these goat-demons, for it states in the Book of Leviticus: "And they shall no more sacrifice their sacrifices unto the he-goats (satyrs), after whom they go a whoring".

SHAHAR or "DAWN" by the Canaanites. Shahar appears as a winged deity in Psalm 139:9; and his son, according to Isaiah 14:12, was the fallen angel Helel (Marduk). SAMMAEL, SAMAEL or SAMA-EL because he was the designated Lord of the kingdom of Sama, east of Haran in northern Mesopotamia; the angel of Edom. The angel Sammael was over the planet Mars. According to Voltaire, in his book *Of Angels, Genii, and Devils,* Samiel is one of the leaders of the fallen angels, and hence evil. To Voltaire, apparently, Samiel was another form of Samael, prince of evil. In Bar-Khonai, *The Book of Scholia,* SAMIEL is described as "blind, malformed, and evil." The "SERPENT ON THE TREE", the "SERPENT SON". He was also called the AZURE DRAGON, SHESHA, AMMON KEMATEF, KNEPH, AGATHODEAMON, SANDALPHON, SANDOLPHON, SANDOLFON or one of the great Sarim (angelic prince), SEIR, SALMAEL, SAMIL, SHAITAN, SATANAIL, SATANIL, SATANA, SATAN, and the DEVIL.

RAMMAN by the Babylonians. RIMMON the Assyrian god of rain, lightning, and thunder *2 Kings* 5:18. RAMANU or "thunderer" by the Amorites. RAGIMU or "caster of hailstones" by the Canaanites. RAMA by the Hindoos. RAYMI by the Peruvians. RANA by the Toltecs. RAYAM in Yemen. Sacred animals were a ram with curled horns and a goose, both of which were kept at his temples at Karnak and Luxor. AHAB, RAHAB or "Great Dragon" by the Hebrews. Rahab, Prince of the Sea, rebelled against God. Rahab was "the Celestial Prince of Egypt". RIMAC of the southern coast of Peru. VIRACOCHA of the Andean Highlands.

AHRIMAN or "the Evil One" and ANGRA MAINYU or "King of the Underworld" by the Persians. Destructive spirit; Spirit of Darkness and Deception; Prince of Demons; Great Serpent; Lord of Darkness. He introduced death into the world. Leader of the Daevas, whom the Zoroastrians called devils, but which originally meant gods. He was known as the god of evil. Ahriman seeks to cut man off from all vision into the Macrocosm, and to lead him down into a total confinement in the three dimensional world of measure, number and weight. Ahriman also strives to establish a purely material kingdom on earth which is entirely isolated from spiritual realities, and he seeks to draw mankind so deeply into this kingdom that he loses all awareness of his spiritual origin and destiny. Ahriman utilized the perverse sexual cravings of the populace to inspire black magic rites which brought about the eventual obliteration of the whole continent of Atlantis. The Ahriman Oracle was named "Schamballah," a center where rituals were performed to control elemental powers. The Adepts of Schamballah sought to foster the illusion of materialism and lead all aspects of human activity into the abyss.

The Hebrews called him BEHEMOTH and the fallen angel DUMA, GADREL or GADREEL. Gadrel discovered every stroke of death to the children of men. He introduced weapons of war to mortals. He seduced Eve; and discovered to the children of men the instruments of death, the coat of mail, the shield, and the sword for slaughter; every instrument of death to the children of men. HUNHAU by the Maya Indians of the Yucatan. Hunhau, the lord of death, prince of devils, who presides over the abyss.

The "Fallen Angles" were known as the angels that rebelled against Almight God, were cast out of heaven and "fell to earth". They were called by the ancient sumerians the IGIGI or "Those that Watch and See". Their symbol was the "All Seeing Eye". In these ancient sumerian records the Igigi revolted against Enlil. They were called the GRIGORI or "Watchers", the "fallen angels" by the ancient Hebrons/Heberu/Hebrews. In ancient Hebrew records the Grigori revolted against Yahweh. The Greeks called them the EGREGOROI or "The Watchers".

ATLAN by the Pleiadians. ALTEA by the Atlanteans. POSEIDON or "the god of the seas" by the Greeks, son of Cronos (Annu) and Rhea (Antu). NETHUNS by the Etruscans. NEPTUNE or "god of the sea" by the Romans. NEPTUR by the Formorians of Ireland. WILI by the Nordic-Germanic tribes. JORMUNGAR by the Danes.

Poseidon ruled over the city of Poseidon (Eidon, Eden) on the island of Poseidia in Atlantis. He was the Lord of the Inner and Outer Seas and the Overlord of Lakes and Rivers. He was the god of everything that swam in or on water. His golden palace was said to be in the depths of the Atlantic Ocean. Pictured as a mature, bearded man. He used his trident to stir the seas to furious storms and to spear the clouds to release floods.

Edgar Cayce stated, "in Atlantean land during second of destructive forces that brought destruction to those of one faith (Enlil/Zeus) and to those of Belial (Enki/Baal), a brother of Atlantis whose name was Atlan (Poseidon)." Edgar Cayce #416-1; 8 Oct 1933.

Poseidon was the first to train and employ horses; his people first domesticated the horse. His symbol was the horse. He carried in his hand a three-pronged symbol, the trident, an emblem of the three continents that were embraced in the empire of Atlantis. He was the founder of many colonies along the shores of the Mediterranean; he helped in building the walls of Troy. Tradition thus tracing the Trojan civilization to an Atlantean source. He settled Attica and founded Athens, named after his niece Athena, daughter of Zeus. Poseidon also had settlements at Corinth, Aegina, Naxos, and Delphi. Temples were erected to his honor in nearly all the seaport towns of Greece.

Poseidon, King of Atlantis, King and father of the ten kings of Atlantis who were enormous giants, married a human female named Cleito, the daughter of Evenor and his wife Leucippe. Poseidon and Cleito had five pairs (twins) of male children.

Poseidon-"Earthshaker"; god of the seas and earthquakes; Supreme Lord of the Inner and Outer Seas; Overlord of Lakes and Rivers. He was the god of everything that swam in or on water. His golden palace was said to be in the depths of the ocean. Pictured as a mature, bearded man; Amphitrite, a nereid, was his immortal wife. His mortal wife was Cleito; their ten sons were made rulers of Atlantis. Horses and bulls were associated with him. He was also master of storms, lakes, and rivers. He used his trident to stir the seas to furious storms and to spear the clouds to release floods. He was turbulent and independent. Invoke this god when you want feeling but do not want to get caught in emotionalism. Storms, all marine life, intuition, human emotions, sailors, ships, hurricanes, rain, weather, and revenge.

BELIAL or BELIAR or "Lord" by the Atlanteans. His followers were known as the "Sons of Belial". The Lord of the North and Lord of Lebanon. EN.BIL.ULU, LORD BIL.ULU and OLD BEL.ILI by the Akkadians. BELUS by the Babylonians. BEL by the Phoenicians. BAAL-SAMIN, BA'AL, or "Lord" by the Canaanites. The chief male deity of the Phoenicians and Canaanites (*Numbers* 22:41). BAAL by the Goths. BAAL-BERITH or "lord of the covenant" by the Shechemites. A name under which Baal was worshiped in the time of the judges (*Judges* 9:4). NN'THERAQ'PSS an evil demon, the 'Prince of Darkness' and the 'King of Evil'. The Celtic Druids offered human sacrifices to their bloody god BAAL. The Druid priests in the Celtic nations of Gaul, Great Britain and Germany taught of the existence of a god called "BE'AL" which seemed to have an affinity with the Phoenician BAAL. Both the Druids and the Phoenicians identified this supreme deity with the sun.

BAAL the Chaldean, Canaanite and Phoenician god of fertility, harvesting crops, winter rains, and son of El. He symbolized the renewal and revival of the earth's vegetation each spring. His name derived from "BA'AL" meaning the "chief lord". The term lord meant the lord of the land. His temple in Nippur was called E.Kur. He was mentioned in the Bible in Exodus and was called BA'AL.TSEPHON, meaning the "god of the crypt". The worship of Ba'al was introduced into Israel by the King of Tyre (Marduk/Lucifer), and was called King Ahab. His wife was a Phoenician princess. Enki (Poseidon/Baal/Satan) the god of water, creation, and fertility (semem). He was once known as En.Kur, "lord of the underworld". He struggled with Kur (Ishkur) and was victorious and thereby able to claim the title "Lord of Kur" The Realm. Baal's symbol was "THE HOLY PHALLUS" or the "obelisk." There are quite a number of passages in the Old Testament which link the worship of Baal to the obelisk. Another Hebrew word appears in med-to-late books of the Old Testament. This word also is applied to objects of worship that can easily be seen to be obelisks. The Hebrew word is chamman, meaning a "a sun-pillar, idol and image". Unfortunately, this is translated simply as "image" in most English versions of the Bible.

The oldest known image of Baal is depicted in a life size bas-relief on stone from his temple at Ras-Shamra in Syria and is dated at circa 2000 BC. This Canaanite version of the god of the elements wears a pointed hat and has horns protruding from his forehead. A dagger is worn at the waist of his tunic. In his upraised hand he holds an object described as a mace. His left hand holds a spear with its point in the earth. Its upper end has sprouted into a tree. Another image of Baal, dates from 1500-1400 BC, was excavated at Ras-Shamra. This was a statue that once was gold and silver-plated. He also wears the pointed hat, his right arm is upraised as if it once held a spear (shown in scrapebook). Another Canaanite image, dated circa 1300 BC, shows the same tall pointed headdress and posture of the arms. This figure wears a kilt instead of a tunic. Another statue from ancient Phoenicia wears the tall pointed hat and has a beard. The right arm are in the same upraised posture. A similar image from the Phoenician colony on the island of Sardinia wears the pointed hat, the tunic, and holds his arms in the same way.

BAALHAZOR or "Lord of the fortresses" by the Hebrews. BAALZEBUB or "Lord of the flies" by the Philistines. Baalzebub was worshiped at the Philistine city of Ekron (*2 Kings* 1:2-3). In Samaria, north of Judea, Baal was known as BAAL-ZEBUL or "Elevated Lord" (*2 Kings* 1:2). Baalhazor provides a connection between Baal and the god of the Antichrist. Baal was lord of war and of the sky. Many titles were given to Baal by adding endings to his name. Some examples are found in scripture are BAALBAMOTH or "Lord of High Places" and BAALZEBUB or "Lord of those who fly." A heathen god considered by the Jews to be the supreme evil spirit. Baal is identified as SATAN by Jesus himself in *Matthew* 10:25, *Mark* 3:22 and *Luke* 11:15. The idolized head of BAPHOMET by the Knights Templars (the masons).

From: *The Book Of Revelation*

1 "And after these things I heard a great voice of much people in heaven, saying, Alleluia; Salvation, and glory, and honour, and power, unto the Lord our God:

2 For true and righteous are his judgments: for he hath judged the great whore, which did corrupt the earth with her fornication, and hath avenged the blood of his servants at her hand.

3 And again they said, Alleluia And her smoke rose up for ever and ever.

4 And the four and twenty elders and the four beasts fell down and worshipped God that sat on the throne, saying, Amen; Alleluia.

5 And a voice came out of the throne, saying, Praise our God, all ye his servants, and ye that fear him, both small and great.

6 And I heard as it were the voice of a great multitude, and as the voice of many waters, and as the voice of mighty thunderings, saying, Alleluia: for the Lord God omnipotent reigneth.

7 Let us be glad and rejoice, and give honour to him: for the marriage of the Lamb is come, and his wife hath made herself ready.

8 And to her was granted that she should be arrayed in fine linen, clean and white: for the fine linen is the righteousness of saints.

9 And he saith unto me, Write, Blessed are they which are called unto the marriage supper of the Lamb. And he saith unto me, These are the true sayings of God.

10 And I fell at his feet to worship him. And he said unto me, See thou do it not: I am thy fellowservant, and of thy brethren that have the testimony of Jesus: worship God: for the testimony of Jesus is the spirit of prophecy.

11 And I saw heaven opened, and behold a white horse; and he that sat upon him was called Faithful and True, and in righteousness he doth judge and make war.

12 His eyes were as a flame of fire, and on his head were many crowns; and he had a name written, that no man knew, but he himself.

13 And he was clothed with a vesture dipped in blood: and his name is called The Word of God.

14 And the armies which were in heaven followed him upon white horses, clothed in fine linen, white and clean.

15 And out of his mouth goeth a sharp sword, that with it he should smite the nations: and he shall rule them with a rod of iron: and he treadeth the winepress of the fierceness and wrath of Almighty God.

16 And he hath on his vesture and on his thigh a name written, KING OF KINGS, AND LORD OF LORDS.

17 And I saw an angel standing in the sun; and he cried with a loud voice, saying to all the fowls that fly in the midst of heaven, Come and gather yourselves together unto the supper of the great God;

18 That ye may eat the flesh of kings, and the flesh of captains, and the flesh of mighty men, and the flesh of horses, and of them that sit on them, and the flesh of all men, both free and bond, both small and great.

19 And I saw the beast, and the kings of the earth, and their armies, gathered together to make war against him that sat on the horse, and against his army.

20 And the beast was taken, and with him the false prophet that wrought miracles before him, with which he deceived them that had received the mark

of the beast, and them that worshipped his image. These both were cast alive into a lake of fire burning with brimstone.

21 And the remnant were slain with the sword of him that sat upon the horse, which sword proceeded out of his mouth: and all the fowls were filled with their flesh."

*Revelation* 19:1-21

1 "And I saw an angel come down from heaven, having the key of the bottomless pit and a great chain in his hand.

2 And he laid hold on the dragon, that old serpent, which is the Devil, and Satan, and bound him a thousand years,

3 And cast him into the bottomless pit, and shut him up, and set a seal upon him, that he should deceive the nations no more, till the thousand years should be fulfilled: and after that he must be loosed a little season.

4 And I saw thrones, and they sat upon them, and judgment was given unto them: and I saw the souls of them that were beheaded for the witness of Jesus, and for the word of God, and which had not worshipped the beast, neither his image, neither had received his mark upon their foreheads, or in their hands; and they lived and reigned with Christ a thousand years.

5 But the rest of the dead lived not again until the thousand years were finished. This is the first resurrection.

6 Blessed and holy is he that hath part in the first resurrection: on such the second death hath no power, but they shall be priests of God and of Christ, and shall reign with him a thousand years.

7 And when the thousand years are expired, Satan shall be loosed out of his prison,

8 And shall go out to deceive the nations which are in the four quarters of the earth, Gog, and Magog, to gather them together to battle: the number of whom is as the sand of the sea.

9 And they went up on the breadth of the earth, and compassed the camp of the saints about, and the beloved city: and fire came down from God out of heaven, and devoured them.

10 And the devil that deceived them was cast into the lake of fire and brimstone, where the beast and the false prophet are, and shall be tormented day and night for ever and ever.

11 And I saw a great white throne, and him that sat on it, from whose face the earth and the heaven fled away; and there was found no place for them.

12 And I saw the dead, small and great, stand before God; and the books were opened: and another book was opened, which is the book of life: and the dead were judged out of those things which were written in the books, according to their works.

13 And the sea gave up the dead which were in it; and death and hell delivered up the dead which were in them: and they were judged every man according to their works.

14 And death and hell were cast into the lake of fire. This is the second death.

15 And whosoever was not found written in the book of life was cast into the lake of fire." *Revelation* 20:1-15

**Anunnaki god En.ki**

## Enkime (Enoch I)

Enkime by the Sumerians, son of Irid (Jared) and Baraka (Barka). EN.KI took a special liking to Enki.me, and taught him things about Nibiru and the heavens which he had previously only taught to Adapa. EN.KI's son, MAR.DUK took Enki.me on journeys into space, landing on the Moon and to Lahmu/Mars. "Lord of the Knowledge of the Foundations of Heaven and Earth." The priest-scientist Enoch is credited in the Bible as architect of the original Zion, the legendary "City of Yahweh," as well as inventor of the alphabet and calendar.

In the *Dead Sea Scrolls,* revealing the lost Books of Enoch, Enoch describes a wondrous civilization in the past, who misused the keys of higher knowledge and were unable to save themselves from the last cataclysm. Enoch promises a return of this knowledge at "The end of time," the end of the present time cycle. According to the "calendar in stone" of the Great

Pyramid, which describes the "Phoenix Cycle" of our galactic orbit, the present time period ends in the year 2012 AD. The Greek word Phoenix, derived from the Egyptian word, Pa-Hanok, actually means, "The House of Enoch."

In the fourth generation after Enoch the first born son was named Enoch; scholars believe that here the name's meaning stemmed from a variant of the Hebrew root, connoting "to train, to educate." Of him the Old Testament briefly states that he "had walked with the Deity" and "did not die on Earth, for the Deity had taken him." The sole verse in *Genesis* 5:24 is substantially enlarged upon in the extra-biblical Books of Enoch. They detail his first visit with the Angels of God to be instructed in various sciences and ethics. Then, after returning to Earth to pass the knowledge and the requisites of priesthood to his sons, he was taken aloft once more, to permanently join the Nefilim (the biblical term meaning "Those Who Had Dropped Down" in their celestial abode.

The Sumerian King List records the priestly reign of Enmeduranki (Enoch) in Sippar, then the location of the Spaceport under the command of Utu/Shamash. His name, "Priestly lord of the Duranki," indicates that he had been trained in Nippur. A little-known tablet, reported by W. G. Lambert, reads as follows:

Enmeduranki (was) a prince in Sippar,
Beloved of Anu, Enlil and Ea.
Shamash in the Bright Temple appointed him.
Shamash and Adad (took him) to the assembly (of the gods) . . .
They showed him how to observe oil on water,
a secret of Anu, Enlil and Ea.
They gave him the Divine Tablet,
the kibdu secret of Heaven and Earth . . .
They taught him how to make calculations with numbers.

When the instruction of Enmeduranki in the secret knowledge of the gods was accomplished, he was returned to Sumer. The "men of Nippur, Sippar and Babylon were called into his presence." He informed them of his experiences and of the establishment of priesthood. It shall be passed, the gods commanded, from father to son: "The learned savant, who guards the secrets of the gods, will bind his favored son with an oath before Shamash and Adad . . . and will instruct him in the secrets of the gods."

The tablet concludes with a postscript: “Thus was the line of priest created--those who are allowed to approach Shamash (Utu) and Adad (Ishkur).”

It is fair to say that the patriarch Enoch was as well known to the ancients as he is obscure to modern *Bible* readers. Besides giving his age (365 years), the *Book of Genesis* says of him only that he "walked with God," and afterward "he was not, because God had taken him" (*Genesis* 5:24). This exalted way of life and mysterious demise made Enoch into a figure of considerable fascination, and a cycle of legends grew up around him.

Many of the legends about Enoch were collected already in ancient times in several long anthologies. The most important such anthology, and the oldest, is known simply as The *Book of Enoch,* comprising over one hundred chapters. It still survives in its entirety (although only in the Ethiopic language) and forms an important source for the thought of Judaism in the last few centuries BC Significantly, the remnants of several almost complete copies of The *Book of Enoch* in Aramaic were found among the *Dead Sea Scrolls,* and it is clear that whoever collected the scrolls considered it a vitally important text. All but one of the five major components of the Ethiopic anthology have turned up among the scrolls. But even more intriguing is the fact that additional, previously unknown or little-known texts about Enoch were discovered at Qumran. The most important of these is The *Book of Giants.*

Enoch lived before the Flood, during a time when the world, in ancient imagination, was very different. Human beings lived much longer, for one thing; Enoch's son Methuselah, for instance, attained the age of 969 years. Another difference was that angels and humans interacted freely -- so freely, in fact, that some of the angels begot children with human females. This fact is neutrally reported in *Genesis* 6:1-4, but other stories view this episode as the source of the corruption that made the punishing flood necessary.

According to The *Book of Enoch,* the mingling of angel and human was actually the idea of Shernihaza, the leader of the evil angels, who lured 200 others to cohabit with women. The offspring of these unnatural unions were giants 300 cubits high. The wicked angels and the giants began to oppress the human population and to teach them to do evil. For this reason God determined to imprison the angels until the final judgment and to destroy the earth with a flood. Enoch's efforts to intercede with heaven for the fallen angels were unsuccessful (*1 Enoch* 6-16).

The *Book of Giants* retells part of this story and elaborates on the exploits of the giants, especially the two children of Shemihaza, Ohya and Hahya. Since no complete manuscript exists of Giants, its exact contents and their order remain a matter of guesswork. Most of the content of the present fragments concerns the giants' ominous dreams and Enoch's efforts to interpret them and to intercede with God on the giants' behalf. Unfortunately, little remains of the independent adventures of the giants, but it is likely that these tales were at least partially derived from ancient Near Eastern mythology. Thus the name of one of the giants is Gilgamesh, the Babylonian hero and subject of a great epic written in the third millennium BC. This story is better told in The *Book of Enoch* Beginning Here a summary statement of the descent of the wicked angels, bringing both knowledge and havoc. Compare *Genesis* 6:1-2, 4.

*1Q23 Frag. 9 + 14 + 15 2 [ . . . ] they knew the secrets of [ . . . ] 3 [ . . . si]n was great in the earth [ . . . ] 4 [ . . . ] and they killed many [ . . ] 5 [ . . . they begat] giants [ . . . ]*

The angels exploit the fruifulness of the earth.

*4Q531 Frag. 3 2 [ . . . everything that the] earth produced [ . . . ] [ . . . ] the great fish [ . . . ] 14 [ . . . ] the sky with all that grew [ . . . ] 15 [ . . . fruit of] the earth and all kinds of grain and all the trees [ . . . ] 16 [ . . . ] beasts and reptiles . . . [al]l creeping things of the earth and they observed all [ . . . ] |8 [ . . . eve]ry harsh deed and [ . . . ] utterance [ . . . ] l9 [ . . . ] male and female, and among humans [ . . . ]*

The two hundred angels choose animals on which to perform unnatural acts, including, presumably, humans.

*1Q23 Frag. 1 + 6 [ . . . two hundred] 2 donkeys, two hundred asses, two hundred . . . rams of the] 3 flock, two hundred goats, two hundred [ . . . beast of the] 4 field from every animal, from every [bird . . . ] 5 [ . . . ] for miscegenation [ . . . ]*

The outcome of the demonic corruption was violence, perversion, and a brood of monstrous beings. Compare Genesis 6:4.

*4Q531 Frag. 2 [ . . . ] they defiled [ . . . ] 2 [ . . . they begot] giants and monsters [ . . . ] 3 [ . . . ] they begot, and, behold, all [the earth was corrupted . . . ] 4 [ . . . ] with its blood and by the hand of [ . . . ] 5 [giant's] which did not suffice for them and [ . . . ] 6 [ . . . ] and they were seeking to devour many [ . . . ] 7 [ . . . ] 8 [ . . . ] the monsters attacked it.*

*4Q532 Col. 2 Frags. 1 - 6 2 [ . . . ] flesh [ . . . ] 3al [l . . . ] monsters [ . . . ] will be [ . . . ] 4 [ . . . ] they would arise [ . . . ] lacking in true knowledge [ . . . ] because [ . . . ] 5 [ . . . ] the earth [grew corrupt . . . ] mighty [ . . . ] 6 [ . . . ] they were considering [ . . . ] 7 [ . . . ] from the angels upon [ . . . ] 8 [ . . . ] in the end it will perish and die [ . . . ] 9 [ . . . ] they caused great corruption in the [earth . . . ] [ . . . this did not] suffice to [ . . . ] "they will be [ . . . ]*

The giants begin to be troubled by a series of dreams and visions. Mahway, the titan son of the angel Barakel, reports the first of these dreams to his fellow giants. He sees a tablet being immersed in water. When it emerges, all but three names have been washed away. The dream evidently symbolizes the destruction of all but Noah and his sons by the Flood.

*2Q26 [ . . . ] they drenched the tablet in the wa [ter . . . ] 2 [ . . . ] the waters went up over the [tablet . . . ] 3 [ . . . ] they lifted out the tablet from the water of [ . . . ]*

The giant goes to the others and they discuss the dream.

*4Q530 Frag.7 [ . . . this vision] is for cursing and sorrow. I am the one who confessed 2 [ . . . ] the whole group of the castaways that I shall go to [ . . . ] 3 [ . . . the spirits of the sl]ain complaining about their killers and crying out 4 [ . . . ] that we shall die together and be made an end of [ . . . ] much and I will be sleeping, and bread 6 [ . . . ] for my dwelling; the vision and also [ . . . ] entered into the gathering of the giants 8 [ . . . ]*

*6Q8 [ . . . ] Ohya and he said to Mahway [ . . . ] 2 [ . . . ] without trembling. Who showed you all this vision, [my] brother? 3 [ . . . ] Barakel, my father, was with me. 4 [ . . . ] Before Mahway had finished telling what [he had seen*

*. . . ] 5 [ . . . said] to him, Now I have heard wonders! If a barren woman gives birth [ . . . ]*

*4Q530 Frag. 4 3 [There]upon Ohya said to Ha [hya . . . ] 4 [ . . . to be destroyed] from upon the earth and [ . . . ] 5 [ . . . the ea]rth. When 6 [ . . . ] they wept before [the giants . . . ]*

*4Q530 Frag. 7 3 [ . . . ] your strength [ . . . ] 4 [ . . . ] 5 Thereupon Ohya [said] to Hahya [ . . . ] Then he answered, It is not for 6 us, but for Azaiel, for he did [ . . . the children of] angels 7 are the giants, and they would not let all their loved ones] be neglected [. . . we have] not been cast down; you have strength [ . . . ]*

The giants realize the futility of fighting against the forces of heaven. The first speaker may be Gilgamesh.

*4Q531 Frag. 1 3 [ . . . I am a] giant, and by the mighty strength of my arm and my own great strength 4 [ . . . any]one mortal, and I have made war against them; but I am not [ . . . ] able to stand against them, for my opponents 6 [ . . . ] reside in [Heav]en, and they dwell in the holy places. And not 7 [ . . . they] are stronger than I. 8 [ . . . ] of the wild beast has come, and the wild man they call [me].*

*9 [ . . . ] Then Ohya said to him, I have been forced to have a dream [ . . . ] the sleep of my eyes [vanished], to let me see a vision. Now I know that on [ . . . ] 11-12 [ . . . ] Gilgamesh [ . . . ]*

Ohya's dream vision is of a tree that is uprooted except for three of its roots; the vision's import is the same as that of the first dream.

*6Q8 Frag. 2 1 three of its roots [ . . . ] [while] I was [watching,] there came [ . . . they moved the roots into] 3 this garden, all of them, and not [ . . . ]*

Ohya tries to avoid the implications of the visions. Above he stated that it referred only to the demon Azazel; here he suggests that the destruction isfor the earthly rulers alone.

*4Q530 Col. 2 1 concerns the death of our souls [ . . . ] and all his comrades, [and Oh]ya told them what Gilgamesh said to him 2 [ . . . ] and it was said [ . . . ] "concerning [ . . . ] the leader has cursed the potentates" 3 and the giants were glad at his words. Then he turned and left [ . . . ]*

More dreams afflict the giants. The details of this vision are obscure, but it bodes ill for the giants. The dreamers speak first to the monsters, then to the giants.

*Thereupon two of them had dreams 4 and the sleep of their eye, fled from them, and they arose and came to [ . . . and told] their dreams, and said in the assembly of [their comrades] the monsters 6 [ . . . In] my dream I was watching this very night 7 [and there was a garden . . . ] gardeners and they were watering 8 [ . . . two hundred trees and] large shoots came out of their root 9 [ . . . ] all the water, and the fire burned all 10 [the garden . . . ] They found the giants to tell them 11 [the dream . . . ]*

In *Enoch,* The Watchers, Chapter Seven, when they made the women acquainted with the plants and cutting roots the women became pregnant.

In the *Dead Sea text* entitled the *Book of Giants,* the Nephilim sons of the fallen angel Shemyaza, named as *'AhyÄ* and *'OhyÄ*, experience dream-visions in which they visit a world-garden and see 200 trees being felled by heavenly angels. Not understanding the purpose of this allegory they put the subject to the Nephilim council who appoint one of their number, Mahawai, to go on their behalf to consult Enoch, who now resides in an earthly paradise. To this end Mahawai then:

*[... rose up into the air] like the whirlwinds, and flew with the help of his hands like [winged] eagle [... over] the cultivated lands and crossed Solitude, the great desert, [...]. And he caught sight of Enoch and he called to him...*

Enoch explains that the 200 trees represent the 200 Watchers, while the felling of their trunks signifies their destruction in a coming conflagration and deluge. More significant, however, is the means by which Mahawai attains astral flight, for he is said to have used *`his hands like (a) [winged] eagle.'* Elsewhere in the same *Enochian text* Mahawai is said to have adopted the guise of a bird to make another long journey. On this occasion he narrowly escapes being burnt up by the sun's heat and is only saved after heeding the celestial voice of Enoch, who convinces him to turn back and not die prematurely - a story that has close parallels with Icarus's fatal flight too near the sun in Greek mythology. Resource

Someone suggests that Enoch be found to interpret the vision.

*[ . . . to Enoch] the noted scribe, and he will interpret for us 12 the dream. Thereupon his fellow Ohya declared and said to the giants, 13 I too had a dream this night, O giants, and, behold, the Ruler of Heaven came down to earth 14 [ . . . ] and such is the end of the dream. [Thereupon] all the giants [and monsters! grew afraid 15 and called Mahway. He came to them and the giants pleaded with him and sent him to Enoch 16 [the noted scribe]. They said to him, Go [ . . . ] to you that 17 [ . . . ] you have heard his voice. And he said to him, He wil1 [ . . . and] interpret the dreams [ . . . ] Col. 3 3 [ . . . ] how long the giants have to live. [ . . . ]*

After a cosmic journey Mahway comes to Enoch and makes his request.

*[ . . . he mounted up in the air] 4 1ike strong winds, and flew with his hands like a [gles . . . he left behind] 5 the inhabited world and passed over Desolation, the great desert [ . . . ] 6 and Enoch saw him and hailed him, and Mahway said to him [ . . . ] 7 hither and thither a second time to Mahway [ . . . The giants await 8 your words, and all the monsters of the earth. If [ . . . ] has been carried [ . . . ] 9 from the days of [ . . . ] their [ . . . ] and they will be added [ . . . ] 10 [ . . . ] we would know from you their meaning [ . . . ]*

*11 [ . . . two hundred tr]ees that from heaven [came down . . . ]*

Enoch sends back a tablet with its grim message of judgment, but with hope for repentance.

*4Q530 Frag. 2 The scribe [Enoch . . . ] 2 [ . . . ] 3 a copy of the second tablet that [Epoch] se [nt . . . ] 4in the very handwriting of Enoch the noted scribe [ . . . In the name of God the great] 5 and holy one, to Shemihaza and all [his companions . . . ] 6 1et it be known to you that not [ . . . ] 7 and the things you have done, and that your wives [ . . . ] 8 they and their sons and the wives of [their sons . . . ] 9 by your licentiousness on the earth, and there has been upon you [ . . . and the land is crying out] 10 and complaining about you and the deeds of your children [ . . . ] 11 the harm that you have done to it. [ . . . ] 12 until Raphael arrives, behold, destruction [is coming, a great flood, and it will destroy all living things] 13 and whatever is in the deserts and the seas. And the meaning of the matter [ . . . ] 14 upon you for evil. But now, loosen the bonds bi [nding you to evil . . . ] l5 and pray.*

A fragment apparently detailing a vision that Enoch saw.

*4Q531 Frag. 7 3 [ . . . great fear] seized me and I fell on my face; I heard his voice [ . . . ] 4 [ . . . ] he dwelt among human beings but he did not learn from them [ . . . ]*

## EN.LIL (Zeus)

SALAM or SALAMIEL by the Pleiadians. MARTU, EN.IL or EN.LIL by the Sumerians, son of An.nu (Cronos) and An.tu (Rhea). King of the Anunnaki. Lord of the Rings (planet Saturn). He was called the "Splendid Serpent of the shining eyes" by the Sumerians. The Sumerian god of wind and air. Pantheon leader after 2500 BC. En = lord, lil = air. Mate of Ninlil. Son of the An-Ki union. Enlil is able to take on the form of a raven. E.LLIL by the Akkadians. According to Assyro-Babylonian mythology, Ellil is Sumerian for "wind-storm god". MULIL by the Babylonians and Hittites. ILU.KUR.GAL or "Ruler of the Mountain" by the Akkadians. ELU by the Chaldeans.

AMURRU or "Lord of the Mountain" by the Amorites and Phoenicians. God of the west; protector of sailors. The Amorites (the giants) have been identified with the Amurru, a people who invaded Babylonia in the 21st century BC and two centuries later founded the first dynasty of Babylon. Amurru is the name given to the god of the Amurru (Amorite) people. He is sometimes called ILU or EL, the patron god of the Mesoptamian city of Ninab. He is described as a "shepherd" or as a "storm god", and as a son of the sky-god Anu. He is sometimes called the "Lord of the Mountain". "He who dwells on the pure mountain." AMURRI by the Egyptians. The ancient Egyptians described the Amurri as having fair skin, light hair, blue eyes, aquiline noses and pointed beards. Called AMURRA or ALIYAN by the Assyrians. Warrior god; Sun god. Represented as a winged disk flying through the air. ARAVAT and EL SHADDAI or "Lofty Mountain" by the Hebrews. EL ELION or "Lofty Mountain" by the Canaanites. SHED-AD or

SHEDD-AD-BEN-AD by the Arabs. ITZAMNA by the Maya Indians of the Yukatan.

ENLIL the firstborn son of Anu & Antu, Dispenser of Kingship, Chief Executive of the Assembly of the Gods, Granter of Agriculture, Lord of the Airspace. King of gods; King of the Land; Lord of all regions; Lord of the World; Counsellor of the gods; God of Earth and Air; Dispenser of good. Enlil was "Lord of the Command". Inventer of the pickaxe.

The Sumerian text state that when Enlil's father Anu retired from the Grand Assembly his eldest son Enlil assumed the presidency. He was proclaimed the master of all the Earth, although his brother Enki could retain sovereignty of the seas. Enki was not at all happy about his brother's claim because, Enki was the elder of the two, and Enki's mother was a reptilian. As a result, the people of Babylon announced their allegiance to Enki and his son Marduk. This led to the decision by Enlil to open the gates of Sumer and let in invaders from all sides.

Enlil ruled from the city of Nippur, called Nibru.ki by the Sumerians, and called Ne.ibru/Ni.ibru or "The Splendid Place of Crossing" by the Akkadians. Nippur was the location for the pre-Diluvial Mission Control Center of the Anunnaki, where Enlil's Dur.an.ki or "Bond Heaven-Earth" maintained the link with their planet Sumi-Er. Called Nibru.ki, translated "Navel of the Earth" because it was at the center of the landmarks that formed the pre-Diluvial Landing Corridor, and deemed equidistant from "the four corners of the Earth." Rebuilt after the Deluge precisely at its former location, it was Sumer's religous center, site of Enlil's sacred precinct and ziggurat/temple (from which, according to a "Hymn to Enlil", "his Eye could scan the Earth," his "Lifted beam could penetrate all").

Per Zecharia Sitchen, Nippur was the birthplace of Abram/Abraham who called himself an Ibri (a Nippurian). With the creation of Mankind's civilizations, Enlil's post-Diluvial headquarters in Ni.ibru (Ne.Ibru) (Nippur in Akkadian), established precisely where the pre-Diluvial city had been, but no longer Mission Control Center, became the overall religious capital. It was then that a luni-solar calendar, the Calendar of Nippur, with a cycle of twelve Ezen ('Festival') periods-the origin of 'months'-was fixed. That calendar, begun in 3760 BC, is still followed as the Jewish Calendar to this day. And then the gods "mapped out the city of Kish, laid out its foundations." It was intended as a national capital, and it was there that the Anunnaki started the line of post-Diluvial kings by "bringing down from heaven the scepter and crown of kingship."

ISH.KUR or "He of the Mountains" by the Sumerians. KUR or "He of the Far Mountains" by the Assyrians. AD.DAD, AD.DU, and AD.AD or "Beloved" by the Akkadians. HAD.DU or "Great God of Storms" by the Akkadians. HADDAD and HADAD by the West Semites.

HADDAD, ADDAD, ADAD, or ADDU - Worshipped in Canaan, Babylonia, Assyria, Syria, and Mesopotamia. God of the atmosphere; Lord of Foresight; The Casher; Master of storms; consort of Shala. With a voice like thunder, he rode the clouds. His symbol was forked lightning, his animal the bull. Often represented standing on a bull and holding thunderbolts. Clouds, storms, thunder, rain, lightning, foreseeing, floods, furious winds, earthquakes, destruction, the future, divination. "On the Acropolis of Baalbek, stood a temple dedicated to the storm god HADAD. It was 60 feet wide and 290 feet long, surrounded by 19 columns, each 62 feet high and over seven feet in diameter. But its flooring stones - still intact - are each larger than a modern railroad boxcar. No one can imagine how they were moved into place."

TESHUB or "Windy Storm" by the Hittites and Cassites. Weather god who carried a thunder hammer and a fistful of thunderbolts. TESHUBU or "wind blower" by the Urartians. BURIASH or "light maker" by the Indo-Europeans. MEIR or "he who lights up the skies" by the Semitites. AEOLOS (AIOLOS, LATIN AEOLUS) Greek god of storms and winds. He is best known from Homer's Odyssey, where he lives on the floating island of

Aeolia (Lipari), and gives Odysseus a bag containing all the unfavourable winds. He was regarded as human in Homer's time, but was later elevated to the status of a god. AEOLUS by the Romans.

ZABARDIBBA or "He who bronze obtains and divides" by the Sumerians. Adad was also called in some God Lists-MARTU and SHALA, his official consort, called Ishtar (Asherah). Ishkur with a voice like thunder, he rode the clouds. His symbol was forked lightning, his animal the bull. Often represented standing on a bull and holding thunderbolts.

The Anunnaki Council re-divided Egypt between Horus and Seth, but Geb had second thoughts and upset the decision, Seth could no longer have offspring. So, Geb gave as a heritage to Horus the whole of Egypt. To Seth a dominion away from Egypt was to be given; henceforth, he was deemed by the Egyptians to have become an Asiatic deity.

Ishkur (Adad) then ruled over the northwestern lands, Asia Minor (Anatolia) and the Mediterranean islands from where civilization - "Kingship" - eventually spread to Greece. Adad was depicted riding a bull and holding a forked lightning.

EL SHADDAI or "Lofty Mountain"; the "ALMIGHTY GOD", "KING OF KINGS", "LORD OF LORDS", and "MOST HIGH GOD", "HOLY ONE", "MIGHTY ONE", and "GOD OF THE WORLD" by the Hebrews. His followers were known as the "Sons of the Law of One". They believed in One God--Enlil. His mystic symbol was the Son of the Right Hand Mark: nII.

EL ELYON or EL ELION which meant "Lofty Mountain" and the "GOD MOST HIGH" by the Canaanites. In Canaan he was known to his followers as "BULL EL", "the "FATHER OF THE GODS". He was called SHALEM or "Perfect" by the Canaanites. After the Deluge Utu, nicknamed SHULIM, was put in charge of Mission Control Center in Ur-Shalem (later called Jerusalem). Shalem - is a divine epithet, probably for El Elyon (who was Utu's grandfather), from which the early name of Jerusalem, "Ur-Shalem" or "City of Shalem" probably originated.

ILUS and EL or "GOD" by the Phoenicians. El was called the "FATHER OF THE YEARS", "SUPREME GOD", "CREATOR GOD", "WAR GOD", "The Favorable", and "The Benevolent and Merciful". He was shown seated wearing bull's horns. He appears as a pillar of fire, his face brighter than the Sun. His speciality is last minute intercession. He is the angel of completion of the Great Work, spiritual enlightenment, mystical illumination.

EL or the "BULL-GOD" by the Northern Semites. EL - a term which in biblical Hebrew was the generic term for "deity", stemming as it did from the Akkadian word ILU, which literally meant "LOFTY ONE". El was the final authority in all affairs. He was the "FATHER OF THE GODS", the "creator of things created" and the "one who alone could bestow kingship." El was a principal deity of Heaven and Earth.

AHURA MAZDÃH, MAZDÃ, AHURAMAZDÃ, ARAMAZD, AZZANDARA or AHURA MAZDÃ by the Zoroastrians. Ahura Mazda is depicted in some places as a bearded human figure who stands in a stylized circular object. From the circular object protrude two stylized wings to indicate that it flies. The round flying object has two jutting struts underneath that resemble legs for landing.

The Zoroastrians of Persia believed that Ahura Mazdah (Enlil), the "GOD OF LIGHT", and Ahriman (Enki), the god of Darkness, were born simultaneously from the womb of the primal Mother of Time. There was rivalry between the twins. Ahura Mazdah was considered the Heavenly Father of Light, Ahriman was not considered inferior. Ahriman's influence upon the Earth was greatest because he had created the material world. The essence of Zoroastrian belief is that God (Ahura Mazdah) is wholly good and that all evil and suffering come from Ahriman (Satan).

The great Ahura Mazdah was believed to express his will through the Holy Spirit, Spenta Mainyu. He also had six assistants called the Amshaspends, or Bounteous Immortals. There was a continuous universal struggle between Spenta Mainyu and the Destructive Spirit called Angra Mainyu, or Ahriman (Enki) or who the Christians call the Devil.

The story of Ahriman's revolt against his brother became the basis of the Christian story of the fall of Lucifer and the battle between good and evil at the end of the world. Just before the end of the world, or doomsday, the Persian legends say that a messiah (Saoshyant) will appear. On that day of judgement at the end of all time, the Zoroastrians believe Ahura Mazdah will hand out to the good and the wicked what they deserve.

TSADKIEL, TZADKIEL, TZADQUIEL, ZEDEKIEL and ZADKIEL or "Angel of Justice" by the Hebrews. In the Zohar, TSADKIEL is fourth of the ten archangels of the Briatic world. In *Ozar Midrashim II, 316,* he is called TZADKIEL, or KADDISHA - "THE HOLY ONE," and is listed among the angelic guards of the gates of the East Wind.

In the cabala, Tsadkiel is the intelligence or angel of the planet Jupiter; also the protecting angel of Abraham. Zadkiel is the angel who stayed the hand of Abraham when he was on the point of sacrificing his son Isaac. In Maseket Azilut, with its ten hierarchic orders, Zadkiel is listed as co-chief with Gabriel of the order of shinanim. He is also one of the nine rulers of Heaven and one of the seven archangels that stand in the presence of God. Zadkiel is represented as one of two chieftains, the other being Zophiel, who assists Michael when the great archangel bears his standard in battle.

In a curious tale of the marriage of God and Earth (Elohim and Edem), told in the *Alphabet of Ben Sira,* God demands from Earth the "loan" of Adam for 1,000 years. Upon Earth agreeing to the loan, God writes out a formal receipt, and this is witnessed by the archangels Michael and Gabriel.

METATRON, METRATTON, MITTRON, METARAON, and MERRATON by the Hebrews. Represented by a tiara on a throne, his symbols were a star, scepter, diadem, crown, and staff. He presided over the fate of the universe. Metatron is the greatest of all the heavenly hierarchs, the first (as also the last) of the ten archangels of the Briatic world of Qabala. He has been called king of angels, prince of the divine face or presence, chancellor of Heaven, angel of the covenant, chief of the ministering angels, and the lesser YHWH (the tetragrammaton). He is charged with the sustenance of mankind.

According to the Cabala, Metatron is the angel who led the children of Israel through the wilderness after the Exodus. Metatron is also the tallest angel in Heaven, and the greatest, apart from the "eight great princes, the honored and revered ones, who are called YHWH by the name of their king." This is according to *3 Enoch.* Metatron is said to reside in the 7th Heaven, the dwelling place of God. He appears, when invoked, "as a pillar of fire, his face more dazzling than the sun." In Jewish angelology, Metatron is "the angel who caused another angel to announce, before the Flood, that God would destroy the world."

ZEUS or "THE KING" by the Greeks, son of Cronos (Annu) and Rhea (Antu), worshipped as the head of the Heliopolitan family of gods in *Acts* 14:12-13. ZAGG by the Minoans of Crete. AZEUS or "Lord of the Earth." Zeus was the ruler over the Olympians in Eastern Atlantis (east of the Pillars of Hercules) and the ancient Greeks. The Olympians were a group of twelve gods who ruled after the overthrow of the Titans. All the Olympians are related in some way. They are named after their dwelling place in Atlantis, called Mount Olympus. DIAS, DIOS, DEOS, DEUS, DURANKI and JOVE or "Olympian Lord of Thunder" in Latin. JUPITER by the Romans.

Zeus the Supreme God of the Greeks; Great God; Lord of the Heavens. Pictured wearing a crown of oak leaves and a mantle with his chest and right arm bare; scepter in his left hand and a thunderbolt and eagle at his feet. His sanctuary at Dodona in Epirus contained his sacred oaks and tripods with cauldrons. Oracles were heard by listening to the rustling oak leaves; the cauldrons were struck and the sounds interpreted. His bird was the eagle. Two of his symbols are a brilliant glowing crown and the almond. He was the proctector of laws, justice, and the weak. He never refused genuine supplicants who asked for his aid, but he inflicted terrible punishments on those who offended him. He was god of all high things, clouds, rain, wind, thunder, lighting, mountain tops, wisdom, justice, popularity, the law, honor, riches, friendships, health, luck, the heart's desires.

The twelve Olympian gods were:

1) Zeus (Jupiter)

2) Poseidon (Neptune)

3) Hades (Pluto)

4) Hestia (Vesta)

5) Hera (Juno)

6) Ares (Mars)

7) Athena (Minerva)

8) Apollon (Apollo)

9) Aphrodite (Venus)

10) Hermes (Mercury)

11) Artemis (Diana)

12) Hephaestus (Vulcan)

*The Iliad, Bk VIII, page 123*

". . . Zeus drove his chariot to Olympus, and entered the assembly of gods. The mighty lord of the earthquake, Poseidon, unyoked his horses for him, set the car (UFO) upon its stand, and threw a cloth over it."

**Anunnaki god Enlil's Temple and Ziggarat at Nippur**

**Sumerian cylinder seal**

**Sumerian cylinder seal and clay tablet**

**Anunnaki god Enlil giving the plow to mankind**

**Anunnaki gods Enlil, Ninki (Ishtar), Enki and demi-god King Nimrod (Janus)**

**Lord Zu brought before Anunnaki god Ea (Enki)**

**Ningal and Nannar giving the “rod’ and “ring” to Hammurabi**

**Ancient Sumerian cuniform clay tablet**

**Anunnaki goddess Ninki (Ishtar) and her symbol 'eight-pointed' star**

## E.N.SHAR (Oceanos)

EN.SHAR by the Sumerians, son of An.shar (Uranos) and Ki.shar (Gaea).

OCEANUS (OCEAN) by the Greeks, son of Uranos (Anshar) and Gaea (Kishar). OKEANOS by the Germanic people. Plato states in the Timaeus, Vol. 2, page 533, that "Oceanus and Tethys were the children of Earth and Heaven. AQUARIUS or the *'God of the Water'.*

Enshar was a NEREID (OCEANID) or god of the sea. They were the patrons of sailors and fishermen, who came to the aid of men in distress, and goddesses who had in their care the sea's rich bounty. Individually they also represented various facets of the sea, from salty brine, to foam, sand, rocky shores, waves and currents, in addition to the various skills possessed by seamen. The Nereides were depicted in ancient art as beautiful young maidens, sometimes running with small dolphins or fish in their hands, or else riding on the back of dolphins, hippokampoi (fish-tailed horses) and other sea creatures.

DAGON or DAGAN by the Philistines. The chief god of the Philistines ( *1 Samuel* 5:2-7). A fallen angel and to the ancient Phoenicians, Dagon was represented with the face and hands of a man and the body of a fish. He was a sea god shown as a merman, a fish-man.

Dagon was originally an Assyro-Babylonian fertility god, though once these beliefs adapted to Hebrews he evolved into a major northwest Semitic god, reportedly of fish and/or fishing. He was worshipped by the early Amorites and by the inhabitants of the cities of Ebla (modern Tell Mardikh, Syria) and Ugarit (modern Ras Shamra, Syria) (which was an ancient city near the Mediterranean containing a large variety of ancient writings and pre-Judeo-Christian shrines). He was also a major member, or perhaps head, of the pantheon of the Biblical Philistines.

His name appears in Hebrew as _____ (in modern transcription Dagon, Tiberian Hebrew Da -ôn), in Ugaritic as dgn (probably vocalized as Dagnu), and in Akkadian as Dagana, Daguna usually rendered in English translations as Dagan.

In Ugaritic, the root dgn also means grain: in Hebrew dagan, Samaritan digan, is an archaic word for grain.

The Phoenician author Sanchuniathon also says Dagon means siton, that being the Greek word for grain. Sanchuniathon further explains: "And Dagon, after he discovered grain and the plough, was called Zeus Arotrios." The word arotrios means "ploughman", "pertaining to agriculture" (confer ???t??? "plow").

It is perhaps related to the Middle Hebrew and Jewish Aramaic word dgn? 'be cut open' or to Arabic dagn (???) 'rain-(cloud)'.

The theory relating the name to Hebrew dag/dâg, 'fish', based solely upon a reading of *1 Samuel* 5:2-7 is discussed in Fish-god tradition below. According to this etymology: Middle English Dagon < Late Latin (Ec.) Dagon < Late Greek (Ec.) Heb dagan, "grain (hence the god of agriculture), corn."

The god Dagon first appears in extant records about 2500 BC in the Mari texts and in personal Amorite names in which the gods Ilu (El), Dagan, and Adad are especially common.

At Ebla (Tell Mardikh), from at least 2300 BC, Dagan was the head of the city pantheon comprising some 200 deities and bore the titles BE-DINGIR-DINGIR, "Lord of the gods" and Bekalam, "Lord of the land". His consort was known only as Belatu, "Lady". Both were worshipped in a large temple complex called E-Mul, "House of the Star". One entire quarter of Ebla and one of its gates were named after Dagan. Dagan is called ti-lu ma-tim, "dew of the land" and Be-ka-na-na, possibly "Lord of Canaan". He was called lord of many cities: of Tuttul, Irim, Ma-Ne, Zarad, Uguash, Siwad, and Sipishu.

An interesting early reference to Dagan occurs in a letter to King Zimri-Lim of Mari, 18th century BC, written by Itur-Asduu an official in the court of Mari and governor of Nahur (the Biblical city of Nahor) (*ANET,* p. 623). It relates a dream of a "man from Shaka" in which Dagan appeared. In the dream, Dagan blamed Zimri-Lim's failure to subdue the King of the Yaminites upon Zimri-Lim's failure to bring a report of his deeds to Dagan in Terqa. Dagan promises that when Zimri-Lim has done so: "I will have the kings of the Yaminites [coo]ked on a fisherman's spit, and I will lay them before you."

In Ugarit around 1300 BC, Dagon had a large temple and was listed third in the pantheon following a father-god and El, and preceding Bail ?apan (that is the god Haddu or Hadad/Adad). Joseph Fontenrose first demonstrated that, whatever their deep origins, at Ugarit Dagon was identified with El, explaining why Dagan, who had an important temple at Ugarit is so neglected in the Ras Shamra mythological texts, where Dagon is mentioned solely in passing as the father of the god Hadad, but Anat, El's daughter, is Baal's sister, and why no temple of El has appeared at Ugarit.

There are differences between the Ugaritic pantheon and that of Phoenicia centuries later: according to the third-hand Greek and Christian reports of Sanchuniathon, the Phoenician mythographer would have Dagon the brother of El/Cronus and like him son of Sky/Uranus and Earth, but not truly Hadad's father. Hadad was begotten by "Sky" on a concubine before Sky was castrated by his son El, whereupon the pregnant concubine was given to Dagon. Accordingly, Dagon in this version is Hadad's half-brother and stepfather. The Byzantine Etymologicon Magnum says that Dagon was Cronus in Phoenicia. Otherwise, with the disappearance of Phoenician literary texts, Dagon has practically no surviving mythology.

Dagan is mentioned occasionally in early Sumerian texts but becomes prominent only in later Akkadian inscriptions as a powerful and warlike protector, sometimes equated with Enlil. Dagan's wife was in some sources the goddess Shala (also named as wife of Adad and sometimes identified with Ninlil). In other texts, his wife is Ishara. In the preface to his famous law code, King Hammurabi calls himself "the subduer of the settlements along the Euphrates with the help of Dagan, his creator". An inscription about an expedition of Naram-Sin to the Cedar Mountain relates (*ANET,* p. 268): "Naram-Sin slew Arman and Ibla with the 'weapon' of the god Dagan who aggrandizes his kingdom." The stele of Ashurnasirpal II (*ANET,* p. 558) refers to Ashurnasirpal as the favorite of Anu and of Dagan. In an Assyrian poem, Dagan appears beside Nergal and Misharu as a judge of the dead. A late Babylonian text makes him the underworld prison warder of the seven children of the god Emmesharra.

The Phoenician inscription on the sarcophagus of King Eshmun_azar of Sidon (5th century BC) relates (*ANET,* p. 662): "Furthermore, the Lord of Kings gave us Dor and Joppa, the mighty lands of Dagon, which are in the Plain of Sharon, in accordance with the important deeds which I did."

Dagan was sometimes used in royal names. Two kings of the Dynasty of Isin were Iddin-Dagan (c. 1974-1954 BC) and Ishme-Dagan (c. 1953-1935 BC). The latter name was later used by two Assyrian kings: Ishme-Dagan I (c. 1782-1742 BC) and Ishme-Dagan II (c. 1610-1594 BC).

In the Tanakh (also referred to as the Old Testament or Hebrew Bible), Dagon is particularly the god of the Philistines with temples at Beth-dagon in the tribe of Asher (*Joshua* 19.27), in Gaza (*Judges* 16.23, which tells soon after how the temple is destroyed by Samson as his last act). Another temple, in Ashdod was mentioned in *1 Samuel* 5.2-7 and again as late as *1 Maccabees* 10.83; 11.4. King Saul's head was displayed in a temple of Dagon in *1 Chronicles* 10:8-10. There was also a second place known as Beth-Dagon in Judah (*Joshua* 15.41). Josephus (*Antiquities* 12.8.1; *War* 1.2.3) mentions a place named Dagon above Jericho. Jerome mentions Caferdago between Diospolis and Jamnia. There is also a modern Beit Dejan south-east of Nablus. Some of these toponyms may have to do with grain rather than the god.

The account in *1 Samuel* 5.2-7 relates how the ark of Yahweh was captured by the Philistines and taken to Dagon's temple in Ashdod. The following morning they found the image of Dagon lying prostrate before the ark. They set the image upright, but again on the morning of the following day they found it prostrate before the ark, but this time with head and hands severed, lying on the miptan translated as "threshold" or "podium". The account continues with the puzzling words raq dagôn niš?ar ?alayw, which means literally "only Dagon was left to him." (The Septuagint, Peshitta, and Targums render "Dagon" here as "trunk of Dagon" or "body of Dagon", presumably referring to the lower part of his image.) Thereafter we are told that neither the priests or anyone ever steps on the miptan of Dagon in Ashdod "unto this day". This story is depicted on the frescoes of the Dura-Europos synagogue as the opposite to a depiction of the High Priest Aaron and the Temple of Solomon.

The vita of Porphyry of Gaza, mentions the great god of Gaza, known as Marnas (Aramaic Marna the "Lord"), who was regarded as the god of rain and grain and invoked against famine. Marna of Gaza appears on coinage of the time of Hadrian. He was identified at Gaza with Cretan Zeus, Zeus Kretagenes. It is likely that Marnas was the Hellenistic expression of Dagon. His temple, the Marneion-the last surviving great cult center of paganism-was burned by order of the Roman emperor in 402. Treading upon the sanctuary's paving-stones had been forbidden. Christians later used these same to pave the public marketplace.

In the eleventh century, Jewish bible commentator Rashi writes of a Biblical tradition that the name Dagôn is related to Hebrew dag/dâg 'fish' and that Dagon was imagined in the shape of a fish: compare the Babylonian fish-god Oannes. In the thirteenth century David Kimhi interpreted the odd sentence in *1 Samuel* 5.2-7 that "only Dagon was left to him" to mean "only the form of a fish was left", adding: "It is said that Dagon, from his navel down, had the form of a fish (whence his name, Dagon), and from his navel up, the form of a man, as it is said, his two hands were cut off." The Septuagint text of *1 Samuel* 5.2-7 says that both the hands and the head of the image of Dagon were broken off.

H. Schmökel asserted in 1928 that Dagon was never originally a fish-god, but once he became an important god of those maritime Canaanites, the Phoenicians, the folk-etymological connection with dâg would have ineluctably affected his iconography.

The fish form may be considered as a phallic symbol as seen in the story of the Egyptian grain god Osiris, whose penis was eaten by (conflated with) fish in the Nile after he was attacked by the Typhonic beast Set. Likewise, in the tale depicting the origin of the constellation Capricornus, the Greek god of nature Pan became a fish from the waist down when he jumped into the same river after being attacked by Typhon.

Various 19th century scholars, such as Julius Wellhausen and William Robertson Smith, believed the tradition to have been validated from the occasional occurrence of a merman motif found in Assyrian and Phoenician art, including coins from Ashdod and Arvad.

John Milton uses the tradition in his *Paradise Lost Book 1:*

. . . Next came one
Who mourned in earnest, when the captive ark
Maimed his brute image, head and hands lopt off,
In his own temple, on the grunsel-edge,
Where he fell flat and shamed his worshippers:
Dagon his name, sea-monster, upward man
And downward fish; yet had his temple high
Reared in Azotus, dreaded through the coast
Of Palestine, in Gath and Ascalon,
And Accaron and Gaza's frontier bounds.

## Enshi (Enoch)

Enshi by the Sumerians, son of Ka.in (Cain) and Awan (Luwa). Enoch (Henoch) by the Hebrews founded the famous Kanite tribe of Midianite Arabs. They were quite renounced coppersmiths who settled to the south-west of the Gulf of Aqaba. Founder of the city of Irouq, in modern day Iraq which means "orginial city".

## Enshi (Enos)

Enshi by the Sumerians, son of Sati (Seth) and Noam (Neom). Enosh means in Hebrew *"Human-Mortal",* and it is clear that the Old Testament considered him the progenitor of the human lineage at the core of the ancient chronicles. It states in respect to him, that *"It was then that the name of Yahweh began to be called,"* that worship and priesthood began.

## EN.URTA (Ninurta)

EN.URTA, NIN.GRI.SU, NIN-GURSU, NIM.RUD by the Anunnaki. NIN.URTA by the Akkadians, daughter of En.ki (Poseidon) and Nin.lil (Hera). Wife of her father En.ki (Poseidon).

## ENU.RU (Jehovan)

JEHOVAN by the Pleiadians. Jehovan (Enuru) was murdered by his son Jehav (Enama) about 7,000 years ago. ENU.RU by the Sumerians.

*UFO Contact from the Pleiades,* by Lt. Col. Wendelle C. Stephens, 1983 - Semjase - At our fifth contact, we ended the history of (our) mankind wheresome 50,000 years ago in Earth chronology, our homeworlds found peace and liberty. Shortly before this time, 70,000 human beings fled (the Pleiades) under the leadership of Pelegon. In spacecraft which they took by force, they fled through the cosmos and settled here on Earth. Under Pelegon were 200 subleaders, scientists, competent in special fields of knowledge. By these, and others, Pelegon was unanimously acknowledged as "King of Wisdom" (IHWH/God) and regarded as such. In the course of milleniums, they constructed great cities and inhabited all the continents of Earth. Regrettably, this went well for only a narrow 10,000 years, until desires for power and control prevailed once more, and a deadly war raged over all the Earth. Without exception, all was destroyed, and only a few thousand human beings survived (on Earth) while others fled once more into the cosmos and settled on faraway worlds.

For 7,000 years, none returned to Earth, and the humans left behind degenerated and became completely wild. Then descendents of those who had settled on faraway worlds returned. They were again under the leadership of an IHWH, under whose command they built on Atlantis and Mu. They built huge cities on each of the two separate continents. For thousands of years they lived in friendship and peace, until a few scientists were again overcome by the old thirst for might and power, and tried to seize the government. But having tired of wars, the nations rose against them, and they occupied spaceships and fled into cosmic space; that being some 15,000 years ago in Earth chronology. For two milleniums, they and their descendants lived in a neighboring solar system. Two millenniums during which they had become very evil and only maintained order under strictest control. By mutation and their sciences, they extend their lifespans to some thousands of years.

Overcome by their thirst for power, they left their world about 13,000 years ago and returned to Earth Their highest leader was the scientist "ARUS", who was also called "The Barbarian".

Like the IHWH 40,000 years before, he also had 200 leaders and subleaders, who were competent in special fields of sciences. In two groups, they settled the high north and the present Florida of North America, while they continuously attacked Atlantis and Mu in wars. In only a few millenniums after their occupation of Earth bases, they succeeded in destroying the civilizations of Atlantis and Mu. The few survivors went into servitude, while many great scientists were able to flee, and return to their homeworlds in the Pleiades.

But centuries before this point in time, the intruders boasted of their conquest of Earth, and the IHWH ARUS led a severe and bloody regime. Still his subleaders assumed for themselves many things and became More and more independent. Within only three decades they had gone far in their own decisionmaking, even though they feared the punishments of the IHWH ARUS. They advocated a codex, to under all circumstances maintain their own race pure and not allow it to fall to mutations away from themselves. In a forbidden manner and secretly, they went out and caught wild Earth creatures and mutations who were distant descendants of former human beings from cosmic space. Wild and beautiful female beings were tamed and mated with by the leaders who called themselves "Sons of Heaven". Each, according to his own race, created mutated beings, completely new forms of life, who were of dwarf-like stature, gigantic, or animal-like. Semjasa, the highest of the subleaders, mated with an EVA, a female being, who was still mostly human-like and also rather beautiful (in feature and form). The descendent of this act was of male sex and a human being of good form. Semjasa called him "Adam", which was a word meaning "Earth human being". A similar breeding produced a female, and in later years they were mated to each other. Meanwhile, others similar had been produced, who forced groups and tribes. From these, present Earth mankind developed.

IHWH me angered by those activities, seized his subleaders when he could catch then and killed or exiled them. In time he changed his mind and recognized a new power he could exercise over the Earth beings. With newly appointed subleaders and guard-angels, he brought three human races under his control. These were the ancestors of those who today are known as "Indians"; then the (fair-sknnned) inhabitants who had settled around the Black Sea; and the third were the Gypsies along the south of the

Mediterranean Sea, who were called Hebrews. Through his guard-angels, IHWH ARUS subjugated those races and forced them under his control. As the highest ruler over them, he allowed himself to become venerated and adored. He allowed them to venerate him above Creation itself, and his subleaders as assistant creators. He imposed harsh and severe laws demanding blood of the guilty.

His son JEHAV who took over his dominion was little better, for he too as IHWH demanded only blood and death from the three enslaved races. The later descendants of these "Gods" became more humane and developed a degree of spirituality. Their spiritual evolution changed their minds and they decided to leave the development of the Earth beings to their natural course, and retired to their homeworld, so they left the earth and returned as peaceful creatures to the Pleiades, where their own mankind had reached advanced states.

## E.RESH.KI.GAL (Persephone)

ALLATU by the Anunnaki. NIN.ERESH.KI.GAL, E.RESH.KI.GAL or "queen of the great below" by the Sumerians, daughter of Nannar (Phobos) and Nin.ul (Perseis). Mistress of "the Great Land". She was the "dark goddess of the underworld"--a place of the dead, which was guarded by seven gates. ALLATUM by the Akkadians. MUT, MAUT, NEKHBET, NEKHEBET, and NECHBET or the "Vulture goddess" by the Egyptians. MISOR by the Phoenicians.

Mut (Maut) was the mother goddess, the queen of the gods at Waset (Thebes), arising in power with the god Amen. She came to represent the Eye of Ra, the ferocious goddess of retribution and daughter of the sun god Ra. Originally a local goddess, probably from the delta area, she became a national goddess during the New Kingdom and was adored at one of the most popular festivals at the time - the Festival of Mut.

She was either depicted as a woman, sometimes with wings, or a vulture, usually wearing the crowns of royalty - she was often shown wearing the double crown of Egypt or the vulture headdress of the New Kingdom queens. Later she was shown as woman with the head of a lioness, as a cow or as a cobra as she took on the attributes of the other Egyptian goddesses. The ancient Egyptian link between vultures and motherhood lead to her name being the ancient Egyptian word for mother.

Egypt: Mut, Mother Goddess of the New Kingdom, Wife of Amen, Vulture Goddess Mut, Mother Goddess of the New Kingdom, Wife of Amen, Vulture Goddess, By Caroline Seawright: Mut (Maut) was the mother goddess, the queen of the gods at Waset (Thebes), arising in power with the god Amen. She came to represent the Eye of Ra, the ferocious goddess of retribution and daughter of the sun god Ra. Originally a local goddess, probably from the delta area, she became a national goddess during the New Kingdom and was adored at one of the most popular festivals at the time - the Festival of Mut.

She was either depicted as a woman, sometimes with wings, or a vulture, usually wearing the crowns of royalty - she was often shown wearing the double crown of Egypt or the vulture headdress of the New Kingdom queens. Later she was shown as woman with the head of a lioness, as a cow or as a cobra as she took on the attributes of the other Egyptian goddesses. The ancient Egyptian link between vultures and motherhood lead to her name being the ancient Egyptian word for mother.

Mut took over the position of the original wife of Amen - Amaunet, the invisible goddess - during the Middle Kingdom and rose to power when the New Kingdom rulers took up the worship of Amen. The pharaohs moved to Waset, making it their capital, and so the worship of the local Waset gods spread throughout the land. As Amen became the god of the pharaohs, Mut became their symbolic mother and was identified with the queens. Their adopted son was Khonsu, the moon god, and the three were worshiped as a triad at Waset and at the Temple of Amen at Ipet-Resyt (Luxor). Originally their adopted son was Montu, the god of war, but he was dropped in favor of the moon god, possibly because the shape of Mut's sacred lake was in the shape of a crescent moon.

During the Festival of Mut in Waset, a statue of the goddess was placed on a boat and sailed around the small crescent shaped sacred lake at her temple at Ipet-Isut (Karnak). In a yearly matrimonial ceremony during the New Year festival, Amen traveled from his temple at Ipet-Resyt down to Ipet-Isut to visit her. Originally this was for the fertility goddess Ipet (Taweret), as a way of ensuring fertility for the coming year. Unas hath had union with the goddess Mut, Unas hath drawn unto himself the flame of Isis, Unas hath united himself to the blue water lily.

There was also a composite deity called "Mut-Isis-Nekhbet, the Great Mother and Lady" who was shown as a winged goddess with leonine feet, an erect penis and three heads - a lion head wearing Min's headdress, a woman's head wearing the double crown of Egypt and a vulture's head wearing the red crown of Lower Egypt.

In The Book of the Dead, a spell was spoken over a statue of her. The statue had her with three heads - one of the heads was that of a lioness wearing a headdress of two tall plumes, a human head wearing the double crown, and the third being the head of a vulture, again wearing the headdress of two plumes - as well as wings, an erect penis and the paws of a lion. This spell was to protect the dead from being disturbed, and it linked her to Bast, Sekhmet and the sun. In this form she was called both Mut, but addressed as Sekhmet-Bast-Ra.

When she started to take over the positions of other goddesses, her name was linked to the older goddess' - such as Mut-Temt, Mut-Wadjet-Bast and Mut-Sekhmet-Bast-Menhit. She also started to take on the aspects and attributes of Isis, such as Mut's form of Mut-Isis-Nekhbet. She seems to have also taken the attributes of even the sky goddess Nut, mother of the five deities - Osiris, Horus the Elder, Set, Isis and Nephthys.

When Amen was assimilated with Ra, becoming Amen-Ra, Mut took on the title the Eye of Ra, a form associated with Hathor and Sekhmet, among others. The Eye was usually shown as a lioness, representing the fierce heat of the sun, and so Mut was given the form of a lion headed woman. She was then thought to be the daughter of Ra, yet she was also "Mother of the Sun in Whom He Rises" - she was thought to be the mother of mothers, and thus could be both the mother and daughter of the sun god.

PERSEPHONE or KORE by the Greeks, daughter of Zeus (Enlil) and Demeter (Nisaba). PROSERPINE by the Romans. Queen of the Underworld; Corn Maiden; Destroyer. She was a goddess of harvest and fertility. She is often portrayed as a maiden crowned and enthroned. She sometimes carries an ear of corn or a pomegranate.

## ERTRAEL (Ertael)

ERTAEL, ERTRAEL, TERJEL or YETAREL a "fallen angel" listed in the *Book of Enoch.*

## Gergashi (Girgashi)

Gergashi or Girgashi, son of Canaan. Father of the Gergashites. The name of this people has been discovered in the Ugaritic inscriptions as 'grgs' and 'bn-grgs', that is, Girgash and the sons or children of Girgash. They are also known to us in the Hittite documents as the karkm; and in Egyptian records as the Kirkash. They settled to the east of the river Jordan between Galilee and the Dead Sea.

## GESH.TI.NAN.NA (Belili)

GESHTINANNA by the Sumerians, daughter of En.ki (Poseidon) and Nin.dur.ra. She was raped by her [half] brother Dumuzi. GESHTIANNA by the Akkadians. Anunnaki wife of Nin.gish.zida and mother of Ngu.shur.

## GI.BIL (Hephaestos)

GI.BIL or "he who burns the soil" by the Sumerians, son of Enki (Poseidon) and Nin.ki (Eos). Gibil learned from his father Enki, the arts of mining and metallurgy, and took over control of the African gold mines. GERRA and HEPHAESTOS by the Greeks. A prototype of EPHAESTUS, the Greek god of fire and metallurgy and VULCAN by the Romans. In the texts dealing with the conflict that led to the use of nuclear weapons, Gibil is described as the god in whose African domain the seven "Awesome Weapons" had been hidden.

Gibil the Sumerian god of light and fire. He was also invoked to protect against wizardry. He despairs and will not attack Anzu after Anzu has stolen the Tablet of Destinies from Enlil. He is the god of fire, and is adept at using weapons. He lights the way in front of Erra (Nergal) and the Sebitti. He advises Erra against attacking Marduk or his people in Babylon. When Erra takes Marduk's seat, Gibil (Ishum) persuades him against destroying Babylon, finally appeasing him by promising that the other gods would acknowledge themselves as his servants (see also the original Babylonian tablet called Erra and Ishum).

CAN (KAN), CON (KON) or "whirling serpent" and "fire serpent" by the Atlanteans. (VOL)CAN the "underworld fire serpent" by the Atlanteans. Can was the fire serpent of Atlantis who produced the deadly weapons of war.

VULCAN by the Romans, the smith god who sustained a permanent limp after being thrown down to Earth from Heaven and resided within the fiery bowels of volcanoes. He was the god of terrestrial fire. The element that this god represents was not the destructive fire, but the beneficial fire of the forge that permitted humans to smelt metal and advance civilization. He was the divine blacksmith, the artisan who taught humans the mechanical arts and built the divine palaces of Olympus.

VOTAN by the Chiapenese of Central America. He built a great city in America called "Nachan," City of the Serpents. Votan's race was known as Chan, a serpent. This Nachan was supposed to have been Palenque. The date of his journey according to legend was in the tenth century BC. He also founded three kingdoms, whose capitals were Tulan, Mayapan, and Chiquimala. CULANN by the Celts.

HEPHAESTUS, HEPHAISTOS and EPHAETUS by the Greeks, son of Zeus (Enlil) and Hera (Ninlil). He was a magician of metal and gems for the Olympians; he made a scepter and the dreaded aegis for Zeus (later worn by Athene), and armor for Achilles and Memnon. His workshops were said to be under the Earth, one of them within Mount Etna in Sicily. His forge was a volcano, which he used to make armor and weapons for the gods. The place most sacred to him, however, was Lemnos, at the foot of Mount Mosychlos. He appears as a powerful, broad-shouldered, bearded smith who is lame in both legs. He wore a leather apron and leaned on a great staff; considered the common person's deity.

KOTHAR-HASIS, the Divine Craftsman of the Canaanites was associated with the Island of Crete.

## GIGANTES

GIGANTES, son of Uranos (Anshar) and Gaea (Kishar). A Titan giant who were enormous beings of invincible strength and terrifying appearance.

### Gish.bil.ga.mesh (Gilgamesh)

Gish.bil.ga.mesh or "Firebrand Offspring" in Sumerian, giant demi-god son of demi-god Lugal.banda and Anunnaki goddess Nin.su (Anobret). Gilgamec or Gilgamesh in Akkadian. A Sumerian king of Uruk (biblical Erech) circa 2900 BC. Known primarily from the 'Epic of Gilgamesh', he is also listed in the chronicles called the 'Sumerian King Lists' and is the subject of other texts; thus there is no doubt about his being a historical figure. The son of the city's High Priest and the goddess Ninsun, he was not just a demi-god but supposedly "two-thirds divine." This, he believed, entitled him to avoid man's mortality, and the Epic relates his search for immortality. That the tale of Gilgamesh and its moral ("Man was given knowledge, the life of a god he was not given") was known throughout the ancient world is evident not only from the various renderings that have been discovered, but also from widespread depictions (including in South America) of an episode in the tale-the wrestling of Gilgamesh's quest-the "Landing Place" of Baalbek in the "Cedar Forest" and the Spaceport in the Sinai.

GILGAMESH TOMB BELIEVED FOUND - Dated April 29, 2003 - Archaeologists in Iraq believe they have found the lost tomb of King Gilgamesh. A German-led expedition has discovered what is thought to be the entire city of Uruk -- including, where the Euphrates once flowed, and the last resting place of its famous king. On a set of inscribed clay tablets -- Gilgamesh was described as having been buried under the Euphrates, in a tomb apparently constructed when the waters of the ancient river parted following his death. "We found just outside the city an area in the middle of the former Euphrates river the remains of such a building which could be interpreted as a burial," Mr. Fassbinder said. He said the amazing discovery of the ancient city under the Iraqi desert had been made possible by modern technology. "By differences in magnetisation in the soil, you can look into the ground," Mr. Fassbinder added. "The most surprising thing was that we found structures already described by Gilgamesh," Mr. Fassbinder stated. "We covered more than one hundred hectares. We have found garden structures and field structures as described in the epic, and we found Babylonian houses." But he said the most astonishing find was an incredibly sophisticated system of canals. "Very clearly, we can see in the canals some structures showing that flooding destroyed some houses, which means it was a highly developed system.

## Gomer (Gamir)

Gomer, Gamir, Gimmer, Gomeria, Gotarna, or Goth, son of Japet (Japheth) and Adataneses. Sumerian Lord of Magog - the Cimmerians. The tribes of Gomer are mentioned by the Jews in the 7th century BC as the tribes that dwelt in the "uppermost parts of the north". The Assyrians in the 7th century referred to them as the Gimirraya. Other names used thoughout history include Gimmerai, Crimea, Chomari, Cimmer, Cimmerian. The Cimmerians populated areas of the north of the Caucasus and Black Sea in southern Russia. Linguistically they are usually regarded as Thracian, which suggests a close relationship. "Thraco-Cimmerian" remains of the 8th-7th century BC found in the southwestern Ukraine and in central Europe are associated with the Aes people.

## GYES (Gyges)

GYES a giant in size, called Hekatoncheires, son of Uranos (Anshar) and Gaea (Kishar). Gyes had one hundred arms and fifty heads. A Titan giant who were enormous beings of invincible strength and terrifying appearance. Classical writers such as Ovid (43 BC-AD 18) wrote that Gyges was punished by being banished to the prison of Tartarus. Yet an account of this same story given by a Chaldean writer named Thallus, states that instead of being banished to Tamrus, Gyges was "smitten, and fled to Tartessus". The Greek geographer named Strabo (60 BC-20 AD) claimed that Tartessus possessed "written records" going back 7,000 years.

## Haia (Hiya)

Haia, Haya, Hiya, Hahya, Hiyyah, Ahijah, Ahiah, Ahyah, Ahya and Pat-Sam, son of Semjasa (Oz) and human female Nraa (Noraia). The *'Damascus Document'* found among the *Dead Sea Scrolls:* I will uncover your eyes . . . that you may not be drawn by thoughts of the guilty inclination and by lustful eyes. For many went astray because of this . . . The Watchers of heaven fell because of this . . . And their sons as tall as cedar trees, whose bodies were like mountains. (*Damascus Document, Manuscript A,* 2:17-19).

## Hammurabi

Hammurabi, the Amorite King of Babylon 1726-1686 BC, son of Sin-muballlit. His seed was said to have been implanted in his mother by the sun-god (Anib). Hammurabi later became one of the greatest law-givers. From him derives the most ancient recorded rules and regulations for ordering human society: the *Codex Hammurabi.* The stone pillar, over 1 meters high, upon which these laws were engraved, was dug up at the beginning of the 20th century in Susa. Today it can be seen in the Paris Louvre. The *Codex Hammurabi* consists of 282 paragraphs; according to Hammurabi these were given to him by the god of heaven. Hammurabi expressing says that 'Bel, the Lord of heaven and earth' had chosen him to 'spread justice through the land, to destroy the wicked and to prevent the strong suppressing the weak.'

## Havilah

Havilah, brother of King Nimrod, son of Cush (Kush) and Candace. The progenitor of the Hamitic tribe of Havilah, his descendants settled on the east coast of Arabia overlooking the Persian Gulf, where their land was known to the pre-Islamis Arabian cosmographers as Hawlan. Kautsch renders the name as Huwailah, and confirms their settlement on the eastern coast of Arabia.

## Heru (Horus)

Heru or Horus by the Egyptians, son of Asar (Osiris) and Asta (Isis). HERU, HOR, and HORUS the Younger, the Egyptian "God of Light", was called "Krist" or "Krst". Falcon-headed Sun and Sky god; "Divine Child" or "reborn Sun". He was pictured as very fair with blue eyes, and associated with cats. As the divine falcon, his two eyes were the Sun and the Moon. From prehistoric times, the falcon was carried as a totem and considered an important powerful, divine being. The hieroglyph for "god" was a falcon on its perch. Some twenty sanctuaries were dedicated to Horus in his different attributes.

Some of the major aspects of Horus were: HAROERIS or HORUS the Great, the Sun and Moon god; HOR BEHDETITE, shown as a winged solar disk, a design placed over the porches of temples. The followers of Horus were known as the "mystery teachers of the heavens (Magi/Freemasons). His symbol is the wedjat eye or "all seeing eye" of Horus.

The Egyptians deified the sun as a trinity of gods - Osiris, the Father, Horus, the Son, and Ra, the Highest Sun - each corresponding to at least one of the sun's 3 key positions throughout the day. Osiris represented the "setting" sun, and is reborn as Horus, the "rising" sun. Ra, who alone represented the "mid-day" sun completes the trinity as "Ra-Horakty" (translates to "Ra who is Horus of the Two Horizons") the conflation of all three gods and positions of the sun. Horus is associated with the setting sun, because the egyptians considered the son as also being the father. This is why throughout the *pyramid texts* Horus and Osiris are frequently interchangeable. *Revelation* 22:16 states: "I, Jesus, have sent my angel to give you this testimony for the churches. I am the Root and the Offspring of

David, and the bright - MORNING STAR - Egyptian *Book of the Dead* Chapter 109 states: "I know the souls of the easterners, they are Horakhty (horus of the horizons), the sun calf, and the -MORNING STAR - *Journal of Near Eastern Studies* Ro Faulkner *Pyramid Texts* "O Morning Star, Horus of the Dlet, divine falcon, widwid-bird whom the sky bore . . ."

Horus was born on December 25 which precede Christianity by 3000 years. The birthday of Horus was celebrated annually celebrated on December 25 in the temples. As both Macrobius and the Christian writer [of the "*Paschal Chronicle*"] say, a figure of Horus as a baby was laid in a manger, in a scenic reconstruction of a stable, and a statue of Isis was placed beside it. Horus was, in a sense, the Savior of mankind. He was their avenger against the powers of darkness; he was the light of the world. His birth-festival was a real Christmas before Christ. This is even closer to the myth associated with Jesus.

Horus was born of a Virgin Isis. "In Egypt the epiteths dd.t, rnn.t and hwn.t, 'girl; young woman; VIRGIN', are applied to many goddesses - e.g Hathor and ISIS WHO HAD NOT HAD SEXUAL INTERCOURSE". In a text in the Abydos Temple of Seti I, Isis herself declares: "I am the great VIRGIN". There was a star in the east. The *Ancient Egyptian Pyramid Texts* (Translated by R.O Faulkner) - "You are this LONE STAR that comes forth from the EAST of the sky, and who will surrender himself to Horus of the Netherworld . . ." Horus was visited by three kings with gifts. Sokar, Osiris, and Ptah - 3 kings - approaching baby Horus in a manger at the Winter Solstice (John Gardener Wilkinson, *Manner and Customs of the Ancient Egyptians* III).

Horus was called the "Lamb of God" and "The Light". Horus was called the Annointed One. *Pyramid Texts Utterance* 77-52a. Oil Oil arise open thou; (thou) who art on the forehead of Horus, arise, open thou. 52b. Thou who art on the forehead of Horus, put thyself on the forehead of this N. (pharoah). 52.c Make him sweet with thyself (perfumed oil); glorify him with thyself.

*Utterance* 576-1505.a "N (pharoah) is your seed, Osiris, the pointed in his name of "Horus of the great green"; "Horus of the chief of spirits". 1511a. "N ANOINTS himself with the best ointment'.

Horus was baptized at the age of twelve years. *Book of Gates* Chapter 5 *The Gate of Tchetbi Fourth Division of Tuat*. Note: In the *Book of Gates* Ra is Ra-Horakty (Ra who is Horus of the two Horizons: the sun traveling from one horizon to the other.) The 12 double headed/jackal headed gods say unto Ra/Horus: - " Immerse thyself, O Ra, in the holy lake wherein the lord of the gods immersed himself, whereunto the souls of the dead approach not; this is what thou thyself hast commanded. O KHUTI . . . Their food consisteth of bread...their vessels are filled with wine. Horus was a teacher at the age of twelve years. The *Second Story of Khamuas* (Griffith, F. LI, *Stories of the High Priests of Memphis; The Sethon of Herodotus and the Demotic Tales of Khamuas*). "Si-Osiris (son of osiris). Numerous are the marvels that he shall do in Egypt . . ." ". . . I would cast my magic up to Egypt that I might cause the peope of Egypt to pass three days and nights without seeing light except kiki" "I will not remove my spell, until you have sworn an oath to me not to return up to Egypt." . . . "Now when the boy Si-Osiris (son of Osiris) had attained - 12 years - it came to pass that there was no [good scribe or learned man] that rivalled him in reading and writing that compels."

Horus began his ministry at age 30. Historically the Messiah characters begin their ministry at age 30. Horus had twelve disciples. The boat of Ra (Marduk/Lucifer), who was later merged with Horus, was towed by twelve gods. Though not mentioned as "disciples", they are his followers in that they follow him throughout his quest through the sky. In Chapter 5 of the *Book of Gates*, Horus is mentioned as having another group of 12 in his service, to who he tells "Live delicatley on the BREAD of HU, and drink ye the Ale of Maat". This ale is later referred to as the "Tchesert Drink" which translates to "Divine Drink". This concept is reworked in the New Testament when Jesus, at the Eucharist, offers the 12 apostles his body in the form of BREAD and his divine blood in the form of WINE.

Horus performed miracles. The *Book of Gates* Chapter 3 - *The Gate of Saa-Set - The Second Division of Tuat* - Note: Ra was a solar deity representing the sun's "mid-day" position while Horus represented the sun's "rising" position. By the time of the *Book of Gates,* Ra had already merged with Horus to represent both positions. In the texts Ra is traversing the underworld in a boat, and in the pyramid texts, it states very clearly that when Horus enters the boat he becomes Ra. The *Book of Gates* states: "The 12 worshippers of Ra/Horus who are at peace...They who praised Ra/Horus upon Earth...They who spoke Truth upon Earth (On Ra/Horus' behalf) . . ."They who UTTERED WORDS OF POWER (exorcism) against Apep, the serpent...and have vanquished Apep for me". Jesus' twelve followers are referred to as "apostles". An apostle is one sent forth as a messenger; one SPREADING TRUTH. According to *Matthew* 10:1, Jesus' apostles also exorcised demonic spirits in his name.

Horus walked on water. In two official translations of the *Pyramid Texts* Horus is said to have walked on water or is referred to as "Lake Strider" in the *Ancient Egyptian Pyramid Texts* James P. Allen 118, 154 and the *Ancient Egyptian Pyramid Texts* R. O. Faulkner Pg 192.

Horus was crucified on a cross. The *Egyptian Book of the Dead* (Ani Papyrus) (RO Faulkner, EBD, pl. 1) shows Horus spectacled in cruciform (arms outstretched) on the combination of the Ankh Cross and Djed Pillar/Tree Trunk (containing his dead body . . . osiris' body). The two sisters, Isis-Meri and Nephtys-Meri are at the feet of the figure, just as the two sister Marys in *John* 19:25. The Ankh Cross represents the Eternal Life that Horus/Osiris achieves through death. In numerous biblical verses, Jesus is said to have died on a tree while tradition holds that it happened on a cross. This tree/cross discrepancy, is not really a discrepancy, but rather an accomodation of both the Djed and Ankh, forming the combination in Jesus' myth.

Horus was buried for three days and then ressurected. (see also Dumuzi/Dionysos) *Pyramid Texts Utterance* 667-1941b "Oh Horus, this hour of the morning, of this - Third Day - is come, when thou surely passet on to heaven, together with the stars, the imperishable star" *Utterance* 556 1382f "this hour of the - Third Day - comes, where the father Osiris will be reborn as Horus, at the place where the gods are born . . ." According to the *Ikhernofret Stela* (2000 BC) by Richard H. Wilkinson, Osiris' Death and Resurrection was celebrated in a 5 day festival known as the "*Passion Plays*". He is entombed on the 2nd day, and remains so until the 4th day (3 days) Afterwards, on the 5th day, he is reborn at Dawn. This is why Horus represented the sun's "rising" position, whereas Osiris represented the sun's "setting" position; Horus is symbolic of Osiris' resurrection/rebirth.

The brightest star Sirius aligns with three stars in the east in the Orion belt called the three kings, on December 24, these tree stars point to the SUN rise on December 25 the winter SOLTICE the birth of the GOD SUN. The ressurection of the SUN was celebrated during the spring EQUINOX or EASTER because thats when the revitalizing spring begins and day time becomes longer than the night. Horus is where we get the following words: Horizon = Horus reason; Hours = Horus; and Sunset = Horus (Light) vs. Set (Dark).

## Heth

Heth, son of Canaan. Heth was the progenitor of the Hittite nation, whose name was known to the Assyrians as the Khatti. The Hittites were apparently the first nation to smelt iron. The Armarna tablets contain letters that were sent from the Hittite emperor Subbiluliuma to the Pharoah Amenhotep IV. Rameses II also tells us how he engaged the Hittites in what was the earliest recorded battle involving massed chariots. This was the famous battle of Kadesh, and it appears that the Hittites got the better of the Egyptian forces. Heth's name was perpetuated in the Hittite capital Hattushash, that is modern Boghazkoy in Turkey.

## Hivi

Hivi, son of Canaan. Known to the ancient Greeks as the Heuaios, this people moved to the foothills of Lebanon during the Israelite conquest of Canaan. King Solomon was later to use Hivites as builders.

## Hiwa (Ohya)

Hiwa, Hiwwah, Ahiwah, Ohyah, Ohya, Sahm and Sam, son of Semjasa (Oz) and human female Nraa (Noraia). The *'Damascus Document'* found among the Dead Sea Scrolls: I will uncover your eyes . . . that you may not be drawn by thoughts of the guilty inclination and by lustful eyes. For many went astray because of this . . . The Watchers of heaven fell because of this . . . And their sons as tall as cedar trees, whose bodies were like mountains. (*Damascus Document, Manuscript A,* 2:17-19).

## IAPETUS (Iberius)

IAPETUS by the Greeks, son of Uranos (Anshar) and Gaea (Ki.shar). A Titan who was imprisoned by Zeus in Tartarus after the war between the gods of Olympus and the Titans had ended. IBERIUS a Titan who went to Spain after the Flood. And Spain was for centuries named "Iberia" in his honor.

Iapetus or "the Piercer" is the one Titan mentioned by Homer in the *Iliad* (8.478-81) as being in Tartarus with Cronus. He is a brother of Cronus, who ruled the world during the Golden Age. Iapetus' wife is normally a daughter of Oceanus and Tethys named Clymene or Asia.

In Hesiod's *Works and Days*, Prometheus is addressed as "son of Iapetus", and no mother is named. However, in Hesiod's *Theogony,* Clymene is listed as Iapetus' wife and the mother of Prometheus. In Aeschylus's play *Prometheus Bound,* Prometheus is son of the goddess Themis with no father named (but still with at least Atlas as a brother). However, in Horace's *Odes,* in *Ode* 1.3 Horace describes how "audax Iapeti genus/ Ignem fraude mala gentibus intulit"; "The bold offspring of Iapetus [i.e. Prometheus]/ brought fire to peoples by wicked deceit".

Since mostly the Titans indulge in marriage of brother and sister, it might be that Aeschylus is using an old tradition in which Themis is Iapetus' wife but that the Hesiodic tradition preferred that Themis and Mnemosyne be consorts of Zeus alone. Nevertheless, it would have been quite within Achaean practice for Zeus to take the wives of the Titans as his mistresses after throwing down their husbands.

## Ibru (Eber)

Ibru by the Akkadians, son of Shelach (Shelah) and Muak. Ibri or Eber by the Hebrews. The meaning of the name Eber and the reason for bestowing it upon the firstborn in 2351 BC and from which has stemmed the biblical term *Ibri* (Hebrew) by which later Abraham and his family identified themselves.

## Japhet (Japheth)

Japhet, Japheth, Yafet, Yapheth, Iapetus II, son of Ziu.su.dra (Noah) and Emzara (Emzarah). Settled in Anatolia and father of the Indo-Europeans.

## Jacob (Israel)

Jacob by the ancient Hebrews, son of Isaac (Jsaak) and Rebecca. Founder of the nation of Israel.

The Stone of Destiny (the Stone of Scone), or 'the Stone of the Covenant,' or the stone known as 'Jacob's Pillow' *(Genesis 28:18-22);* on which Jacob laid his head and saw the ladder reaching up to Heaven (the spaceship) at Beth-el. In a dream God (El Shaddai/Enlil) promised Jacob that his seed would generate the line of kingship to follow-the line which in due course became the Davidic succession.

It was Jacob's family alone who had moved to Egypt, and it was their descendants who eventually returned with Moses--to be united, after countless generations, with their fellow Hebrews. The Israelites had long been subjected to the laws and religions of Egypt and they knew very little about the customs of their cousins in Canaan. Through more than 400 years they had been in an environment with a whole pantheon of gods; and although they had developed a 'one god' concept within their own fraternity, that god was not the Jehovah of the Canaanite Hebrews.

The Israelites' god was a faceless entity whom they called, quite simply, the Lord. In the Israelite language he was called Adon. This is one of the reasons why the names 'Lord' and 'Jehovah,' were always separately identified in early texts, although they were brought under the wrap of the single God in later times to suit the emergent Jewish and Christian faiths. To the Egyptians, the name of this Lord (Adon) was quite similar; they called him Aten. From this derived the name of Pharaoh Akhenaten, meaning 'servant of Aten.'

So, when Moses and the Israelites made their exodus into Sinai, they arrived not as worshippers of Jehovah but of Aten; and it was for this very reason that they were given a whole new set of laws and ordinances to bring them into line with the Hebrew culture of their prospective new homeland.

## Javan

Javan son of Japhet (Japheth) and Adataneses. Dwelled in the land of Makdonia. Founder of the tribe of Javanim. Father of the Ionian Greeks. Javan's descendants appear in Assyrian documents as the Iamanu, where we are told that they engaged the Assyrians in a major naval battle during the reign of Sargon II (721-705 BC). The Archaemenian inscriptions also refer to them as the Yauna. Homer wrote in the Iliad that Iawones (Hebrew Iawan) was the father of the Ionians (Greek Iones); a nation that was later famed in the old world for the high quality of their yarn and bronze vessels. The Hebrews knew the Greek races as the Jevanim (Iewanim).

## Jesus 'the Christ'

Yehu-shu'ah or "Yahweh Saves," Yeshua, Jeshua, Yehoshua, Jehoshua, and Joshua by the Hebrews. Jesus "Light of the World". Rex Mundi (latin for "King of the World"). Jesus' ancestors were known as Rex Deus or "desposyni". Jesus' name was changed in AD 189 to Jesus 'the Christ' by the Roman Catholic [Universal] Church.

Edgar Cayce stated that Jesus was born on March 19, 4 BC. According to the *Talmud of Jmannuel,* Jesus was born on February 3, 7 BC in Bethlehem, Judea. In Laurence Gardner's book, *Bloodline of the Holy Grail,* Jesus was born on March 1, 7 BC in Bethlehem, Judea. In the *Urantia Book,* Jesus was born August 21, 7 BC in Bethlehem, Judea. Jesus was born on January 6, 7 BC in Bethlehem, Judea, according to the traditional Orthodox Church and the early Jerusalem Church whos bishops were the “desposyni”.

Author Deloris Cannon's book *Jesus and the Essenes,* places Jesus' birthday just before Spring time, which places more weight on him being born in January, February or March than in August. Jesus' birthday was later changed (by Emperor Constantine "the Great") to December 25th, the birth date of the god/angel Michael/Mithra of which the Roman Catholic Church created the stories contained in the New Testament. According to the *Talmud of Jmmanuel,* through Jesus' spiritual/celestrial father Gabriel/Nannar who was born on December 25, this made him the rightful heir to the throne of the world.

However, the historical Jesus scholars and the first jewish writtings in the *Arethas Codex,* along with the *Babylonian Talmud* and the *Palestian Talmud*, state that Yeshua's father was a Roman archer named Tiberius Julius Abdes Panthera, nicknamed "The Panther", who was the child of the Roman Emperor Tiberius I and Julia Augustus, daughter of Mark Antony and Octavia "the Elder." This seems to explain why the Roman Emperor wanted to kill him when he was just an infant. (See Panthera).

Through his mother Miriam 'the Virgin' [originally Miriam "the young woman"], Jesus was the rightful heir to the 41st Temple Governor-the Jacob Patriarch; rightful heir to the 31st High Priest of Jerusalem-the Zadok (Michael); and the rightful heir to the throne as the King of Jerusalem (King of the Jews). Through his paternal grandmother Julia Augusta, and his step-paternal grandmother Princess Cleopatra Selene, Jesus was also the rightful heir to the throne of Egypt.

Stories told to Delores Cannon during her clients past life regression therapy; while in the deepest hypnotic state.

*Legacy from the Stars* by Delores Cannon, cr 1996, pages 13-16

D: Can you tell me a little about the beliefs of the group?

T: We believe Yahweh is the creator of the heavens and the Earth. Who is the ultimate, supreme being. This is given to us by those who are of the fair skin, and who travel in the skies at night.

D: I'm interested in the fair-skinned ones that come from the sky.

T: These are our friends who visit us frequently and bring us tidings of much to-do on this planet. For they have educated us to the fact of there being life on other planets. This is knowledge which would cause us to be stoned, were we to speak of it.

T: These are very beloved friends who come to us and give us words of great hope and encouragement of the Messiah which is to be born on this planet. For these are precursors of the coming of the Messiah . . . we are being told He will come in our lifetime. There is much love from these creatures. And we believe them and trust them and listen to them. For they are obviously of angelic proportion.

D: How do they know these things?

T: They are of the spirit world and have knowledge from that which is from the spirit world.

D: Do you have anything in your own teachings, beliefs, about the Messiah?

T: He will be of fair skin, we are told, and his face will shine like the sun. He will be of the heritage of these light beings yet He will be a man. He is the Son of God, they say, and is to teach our world that which is God's love on Earth.

D: Do they say where he will be born?

T: In Bethlehem.

*Jesus and The Essenes* by Delores Cannon, cr 1992, pages 197-198

S: It is the beginning of the year. The new . . . year has just passed.

D: Is this during the season we call Spring?

S: The season of growth is coming, yes.

D: Describe the stars now that they are all four come together.

S: There is a beam . . . it is like a tail. It comes down with all of the light. It is like a focus that drops straight from the star. And it is said that in this light shall he be born.

D: Is it brighter now that they are all together?

S: It is like most of the light is being focused. In that it is no longer scattered about, but in a precise point. It is about the brightness of a very large, full moon.

*The Talmud of Jmmanuel* by Judas Iscariot, edited by Billy Meir, Fourth Edition, cr 2007 (First Edition 1992), pages 11-12 - Thereupon, Herod

Antipas called the wise men secretly and diligently asked them when the *bright light with the long tail* had appeared in the sky. He then directed them to Bethlehem, and said, "Go and search diligently for the young child and when you find him, let me know, so that I may also come and adore him." After they had listened to Herod Antipas, they departed. And behold, the *light with the long tail*, which they had observed in the Orient, moved ahead of them with a high singing sound until it reached Bethlehem and stood directly over the stable where the infant was born . . . the voice again rang out from the light high above, saying that they should not return to Herod Antipas because he planned evil for the young child.

The "wise men" of the Christmas story were Zoroastrians from Persia, which is present-day Iran. Down through the years from the time of Daniel (circa 500 BC), these Magi were initiated into the true meaning of the constellations and their stars. When they observed the various movements portending the birth of the promised "seed of the woman," they knew this to be the coming Messiah.

*The Talmud of Jmmanuel* by Judas Iscariot, edited by Billy Meir, Second Edition, cr1996 (First Edition 1992), pages 245-251 - Also among them was Joseph of Arimathea, a follower of Jmmanuel. After a little while, he noticed that Jmmanuel was only half dead, but he told no one. He quickly went into the city to see Pilate, and he asked for the body of Jmmanuel be turned over to Joseph. Many people went with him and they took Jmmanuel off the cross. Joseph wrapped the body in pure linen that he had previously painted so as to form an image of Jmmanuel. Joseph of Arimathea carried the body of Jmmanuel all the way to Jerusalem and placed him outside the city in his own tomb, which he had cut into a rock for his own future burial. He rolled a big stone in front of the door of the tomb and went to obtain some medicine in order to nurse Jmmanuel.

The entrance of the tomb was guarded by soldiers and Jmmanuel's mother so no one could enter and steal the body. Joseph of Arimathea sought out Jmmanuel's friends from India and went back with them to the tomb. They went in through a secret second entrance unknown to the henchmen and to the soldiers and nursed him for three days and three nights, so that he was soon in better health again and his strength was restored.

The tomb was guarded on the other side by the soldiers, because the chief priests and Pharisees had gone to Pilate, saying, "Sir, we considered that when this crazy man was still alive, he said to the people, 'I shall return after three days and three nights and rise, because I will be only half dead.' But, since it was established through a soldier that he was really dead, his tomb should be guarded so that no one can come, steal the body and say, 'Behold, he has risen from the dead after all!' Therefore, command that the tomb be guarded for three days so that the last deception may not be worse than the first." Pilate said to them: "Take my soldiers as guardians. Go and watch the tomb as well as you can." They went away, watched the tomb, and sealed the stone in front of the door. But they did not know the secret of the grave, namely, that it had two exits and entrances, so that Jmmanuel's helpers could, without being seen, go to him to apply healing salves and herbs, so that on the third day he was again strong enough to walk.

When the first day of the week had come after Passover, the three days and nights had passed following which Jmmanuel would live again after near-death, as he had foretold. Behold, a great thunder arose in the air, and a radiant light came down from the sky and landed on the earth, not far from the tomb. Then the guardian angel came out of the light, and his appearance was like lightning and his garment was as white as snow. He went to the tomb, and the soldiers got out of his way because they feared him. He lifted his hand from which came bright lightning that hit the soldiers one after the other. And they fell to the ground and did not stir for a long time. Then the guardian angel stepped up to the tomb, rolled the stone away from the door and spoke to Mary, the mother of Jmmanuel, and to Mary Magdalene, who were both there, "Do not be afraid. I know that you are seeking Jmmanuel, the crucified. But he is not here. He lives, as he said. Come here and behold the place where he lay. Go quickly and tell his disciples that he has risen from near-death. Also tell them he will walk ahead of you to Galilee, and there you will see him. Behold, I have told you." But Mary asked, "Yet he was dead and lay here dead, how can he rise?" The guardian angel answered, "Why are you seeking someone alive among the dead? Go now and spread the news among his disciples, but beware, and do not tell anyone else."

The guardian angel went to the bright light and disappeared into it; soon a great thunder came out of it again, and it rose up into the air, shooting straight into the sky. Jmmanuel's mother and Mary Magdalene went away, leaving the tomb. The soldiers recovered from their paralysis and were surprised; so they went into the city and spread the news of what had happened. And they came together with the chief priests and elders of the council for a secret meeting to decide what to tell the people. The chief priests and elders gave sufficient money to the soldiers and said, "Tell the people his disciples came at night while we were sleeping and stole his body." And the soldiers took the money and did as they had been instructed.

Mary and Mary Magdalene went away and did as they had been told by the guardian angel. Behold, a guardian angel met them again on their way and said, "Remember what you haave been told. Be careful not to make a mistake when talking to the people." Mary Magdalene approached the guardian angel, who wore a brilliant white garment, and she wanted to grasp his hand. But he stepped back from her and said, "Don't touch me, because I am of a kind different than you and my garment is a protection against this world. If you touch me, you will die and be consumed by fire. Get away from me, and do as you have been told." So they went away, met Peter and another disciple and told them what had happened. But Peter and the other disciple went to the tomb, the other disciple arriving there first. And he looked into the tomb and saw the linen bandages lying on the ground, but he did not enter.

*The Uranitia Book*, cr 1955, pages 2006-2007 - Jesus' crucifixion was not a Jewish mode of punishment. Both the Greeks and the Romans learned this method of execution from the Phoenicians. During the crucifixion the soldiers first bound Jesus' arms with cords to the cross beam, and then they nailed his hands to the wood. When they had hoisted this crossbeam up on the post, and after they had nailed it securely to the upright timber of the cross, they bound and nailed his feet to the wood, using one long nail to penetrate both feet. The upright timber had a large peg, inserted at the proper height, which served as a sort of saddle for supporting the body weight. The cross was not high, Jesus' feet being only about three feet from the ground. After Jesus' was hoisted on the cross, the captain nailed the title up above his head, and it read in three languages, *"Jesus of Nazareth-the King of the Jews."*

*The Urantia Book*, cr 1955, pages 2020-2021 - The Resurrection . . . seven unidentified Paradise personalities, arrived on the scene and immediately deployed themselves about the tomb. At ten minutes before three, intense vibrations of commingled material and spiritual activities began to issue from Joseph's new tomb, and at two minutes past three o'clock, this Sunday morning, April 9, AD 30, the resurrected spirit form and personality of Jesus of Nazareth came forth from the tomb. After the resurrected Jesus emerged from his burial tomb, the body of flesh in which he had lived on earth was still lying there in the sepulcher niche, undisturbed and wrapped in the linen sheet, just as it had been laid to rest by Joseph and his associates on Friday afternoon. Neither was the stone before the entrance of the tomb in any way disturbed . . . We perceived the seven personalities of Paradise surround the tomb, but we did not see them do anything in connection with the Master's awakening. Just as soon as Jesus appeared beside Gabriel, just above the tomb, the seven personalities from Paradise signalized their intention of immediate departure for Uversa.

*The Urantia Book*, cr 1955, page 2023-2024 - . . . it was assigned the secondary Urantia (Earth) midwayers to roll away the stones from the entrance of the tomb. The larger of these two stones was a huge circular affair, much like a millstone, and it moved in a groove chiseled out of the rock, so that it could be rolled back and forth to open and close the tomb. When the watching Jewish guards and the Roman soldiers, in the dim light of the morning, saw this hughe stone begin to roll away from the entrance of the tomb, apparently of its own accord-without any visible means to account for such motion-they were seized with fear and panic, and they fled in haste from the scene. The Christian belief in the resurrection of Jesus has been based on the fact of the "empty tomb." It was indeed a *fact* the the tomb was empty, but this is not the *truth* of the resurrection. The tomb of Joseph was empty, not because the body of Jesus had been rehabilitated or resurrected, but because the celestial hosts had been granted their request to afford it a special and unique dissolution, a return of the *"dust to dust."* The mortal remains of Jesus underwent the same natural process of elemental disintegration as characterizes all human bodies on earth except that, in point of time, this natural mode of dissolution was greatly accelerated, hastened to that point where it became well-nigh instantaneous.

*The Urantia Book*, cr 1955, pages 2002-2003 - The gospel of the good news that mortal man may, by faith, become spirit-conscious that he is a son of God, is not dependent on the death of Jesus. The Father in heaven loved mortal man on earth just as much before the life and death of Jesus on earth as he did after this transcendent exhibition of the co partnership of man and God. Jesus is not about to die as a sacrifice for sin. He is not going to atone for the inborn moral guilt of the human race. Mankind has no such racial guilt before God. Guilt is purely a matter of personal sin and knowing, deliberate rebellion against the will of the Father and the administration of his Sons. We mortals are the sons of God, and only one thing is required to make such a truth factual in our personal experience, and that is your Spirit-born faith.

*Jesus and the Essenes* by Delores Cannon, cr1992, pages 256-264

D: Whose tomb is it put in?

S: It is Joseph's. He was having it prepared.

D: What do they do with the body?

S: They anoint it with the oils, and incense is lit, and it is wrapped in linen and laid. And the stone is rolled over the doorway.

D: Was the tomb sealed?

S: Yes.

D: Does anything else happen?

S: During the next three days, it shall be as no more. For it is not needed. Then it shall be gone.

D: The body will be gone, you mean?

S: Yes . . . I know that there are ways of doing this, but I'm not familiar with the method.

D: What do you mean exactly? I thought you meant the body was dead.

S: The body is dead, but since it is no longer needed, it is . . . There are ways of making it as if it had not been. I do not know the method. I cannot explain any better.

D: Oh? It is something you don't understand yourself?

S: It is known only to the masters.

D: You mean the body disappears, in other words?

S: Yes, it is made as if . . . It is made of the dust that it was and it is no more.

D: Why would the body have to disappear?

S: Because it was foretold in the prophecies that he would rise upon the third day. And in order to rise, they must show that the place where he was laid is empty. And he cannot be taken away by normal means. That the body cannot be . . . they cannot get to it to do anything. Therefore it must be done from this side.

D: You said the prophecy was that he would rise again. Will this happen?

S: Yes! How can he not! He is as he was before. Is this not in essence a rising? For he is risen from the body which is made out of dust and clay, and is as he was.

D: Could they see him and hear him?

S: Yes, for they have this ability. All who open themselves have this ability and could have seen him. Many did.

D: Do you think they saw him as a physical person?

S: Yes, but one who is . . . different. Who is more like one of the beings of light than having an earthly body. It is not one you could perhaps reach out and to touch, for your hand would pass through.

D: But they were able to see it?

S: Yes. To know that it was true.

D: Does he still have any marks on the spiritual body?

S: Yes, for a while it shall echo the things that have been done. Because this was a way of proving to them. The doubts that he perhaps was who he said he was.

D: And the physical body was just completely taken apart, so to speak.

S: Reduced to dust and ash, yes.

D: What happened to Yeshua?

S: He eventually went back to be with the others. To be with the masters and our God, as we know him.

D: Then when they say that he died for the sins of all the people in the world, does that make sense?

S: How can he die for someone else's sins? You must all pay for your own. If not this time around, then perhaps the next, or even the next. But ultimately, you must endure what you have made others endure because of you.

D: Then his life, his dying will not wipe out the other people's sins?

S: There is a law of grace that will exist. But it is not because he paid for your sins, but because you would accept him as being worthy and perhaps a messenger of God. And the law of grace deals with God's love for you, not because he died for the sins. He is to be marveled at, but not to be worshiped. Not to be deified, because we are part of God.

D: Do you think he wants to be worshiped?

S: He wants to be remembered. as a spirit guide to guide people to greater enlightenment, to help them achieve greater power. To help them become more spiritual in their perceptions. He mainly considered himself as a helper, a guide, an example, like a good friend who is helping you with advice. We are all part of God. Some of us are more aware of this than others. I would say that he is one of these such people.

D: Can you tell us if the Christ will return to earth at some future time?

S: Yes, he shall return.

D: Will people be aware of his coming beforehand, as you were aware this time, or will he come suddenly?

S: There will be those who will know.

In AD 314, the Roman Emperor, Constantine the Great, changed the date of Jesus's official birthday to December 25th which is the date of birth of Mithra (Nannar-Sin-Gabriel & Dumuzi-Dionysus-Mithra). According to the Bible, through Jesus' human parents he descended from both Aaron and David, so he could claim the titles of Priest Messiah and Royal Messiah. This would seem to explain Luke's assertion in *Acts (2:36)* that God had made Jesus *'both Lord and Christ'.* Jesus the Christ. The New Testament describes three substances gold, frankincense and mirth, that were presented to Jesus by the Magi, thereby identifying him beyond doubt as a hereditary Priest-King. The Magi identified *Jesus' birthmark of royal descent*, which was a *mole with the shape of a cross within a circle around it*. This mark is believed by many to be *'the mark'* of *'the Holy Grail,'* the mark of Jesus' *bloodline descendants.* This *'mark'* was the oldest Grant of Arms in sovereign history--a Grant of Arms which denoted the Messianic Bloodline for all time. The Sumerians referred to this insignia as *'the Gra-al'.* From biblical history, however, we know it better as *'The Holy Grail'.*

What was this Sumerian Gra-al? It was this emblem dignified as the *'Cup of the Waters'* or the *Rosi-Crucis (the 'Dew Cup'),* and it was identified in all records (including those of Egypt and Phoenicia and in the Hebrew annals) as being an *upright, centered red cross within a circle.* Throughout the ages it was developed and embellished, but it has always remained essentially the same and is recognized as being the original symbol of the Holy Grail. The Holy Grail was 'a distinctive birthmark', which distinguished Christ's descendants from all other men, which rendered them immediately identifiable, and which attested to their semidivine or sacred blood. This birthmark reputedly took the form of a *small red cross, either over the heart or between the shoulder blades.*

Jesus' siblings descendants became known as the *"Fisher Kiings"* and still later the *"Merovingian Kings."* Both were often called the *"sorcerer-kings"* or *"thaumaturge-kings".* Sons of the Merovingian blood were not *"created"* kings. They were automatically regarded as such on the advent of their twelfth birthday. There was no public ceremony of anointment, no coronation of any sort. Power was simply assumed, as by sacred right. By virtue of some miraculous property in their blood they could allegedly heal by the laying on of hands; and according to one account the tassels at the fringes of their robes were deemed to possess miraculous curative powers. They were said to be capable of clairvoyant or telepathic communication with beasts and with the natural world around them and to wear powerful magical necklaces. They were said to possess an arcane spell that protected them and granted them phenomenal longevity-which history, incidentally, does not seem to confirm. And they all supposedly *bore a distinctive birthmark*, which distinguished them from all other men, which rendered them immediately identifiable, and which attested to their semidivine or sacred blood.

The Merovingians were also frequently called the long-haired kings. Like Samson in the Old Testament, they were loath to cut their hair. Like Samson's their hair supposedly contained their virtue-the essence and secret of their power. When King Childeric III was deposed in AD 754, he was imprisoned and his hair was ritually shorn at the Pope's express command. The Merovingian Kings were not regarded as kings in the modern sense of that word. They were regarded as priest-kings-embodiments of the divine. They did not rule simply by God's grace. They were apparently deemed the living embodiment and incarnation of God's grace-a status usually reserved exclusively for Jesus. The Merovingians seem to have engaged in ritual practices that partook more of a priesthood than of kingship. Skulls found of Merovingian monarchs bear what appears to be a ritual incision or hole in the crown. Other items found are a severed horse's head, a bull's head made of gold, and a crystal ball. It also contained arms, treasure, and regalia that you would find in a royal tomb.

The Sumerians state that the first human kings on Earth were the offspring of god rulers who mated with human women. Those matings entitled the half-human offspring to become early monarchs on Earth. Thus was born the idea of *"royal blood"* and the perceived importance of maintaining proper royal *"breeding"* to ensure continued purity of the human royal blood line. Some ancient *"gods"* were depicted as either blue-skinned or blue-blooded: this gave us the idea of royal *"blue bloods."* Aristocratic breeding practices have persisted through history and remain important to some royalty even today. Human *"blue bloods"* appear to be the prize race of Homo sapiens.

In biblical Israel all men, especially rabbis were expected to be married and to father families. The Gospels are quite open about the forms of address used by the disciples in their conversations with Jesus. He is repeatedly addressed as rabbi. The Gospels clearly state that he was the heir to the line of kings descended from David. The heir to the Davidic line was obliged by law to marry and to father sons in order to ensure the continuance of the hereditary line of the Royal House of Israel.

A number of religious historians have concluded that Jesus belonged to a Hebrew religious sect known as the "Essenes." Joachim, Anna, and Mary had all been members of Essene temples. The Essenes were outwardly Jewish, but they also studied the Zend Avesta of the Zoroastrian religion and reportedly practiced Aryanism. The germans claimed that Aryans were originally created by godlike superhumans from a different world. Aryanism is the elevation of white-skinned Aryans over other races based on the notion that Aryans are the "chosen" or "created" race of "God" or "gods," and Aryans are therefore spiritually, socially and genetically superior to all other races. The Aryans were created by an extraterrestrial *"superrace"* of giant gods.

This would help explain the visit of the three Persian wise men to baby Jesus in Bethlehem. It further appears that being Aryan was a requirement to becoming an Essene. Jesus himself was white-skinned with dark brownish red hair. The Essene priests often called themselves "The Sons of Zadok" after high priest Zadok, who had served in the temple of Solomon. The Essenes had a system of degrees and used a symbolic apron just like the freemasons many years later.

In AD 80, the Roman Emperor Domitian decreed that all descendants of Jesus Christ's family should be hunted down and put to the sword. As chronicled by Hegesippus, Africanus and Eusebius, the Messianic dynasts were known as the *"Desposyni"* (the Heirs of the Lord). This decree was never rescinded.

Throughout Jesus' life he was never called Jesus Christ. This was a name given to him in the year AD 189 by those who were still forming Christianity. The descendant heirs of Jesus posed an enormous threat to the Roman High Church because they were the dynastic leaders of the true Nazarene Church. In real terms, the Roman Church (Roman Catholic Church) should never have existed at all, for it was no more than a 'hybrid' movement comprised of various pagan doctrines attached to a fundamentally Jewish base.

The 'Shroud of Turin' has been proven to be from the first century AD. Words have been found on the 'Turin Shroud' that link the image to *"Jesus the Nazarene"*. Like the image of the man himself the letters are in reverse and only make sense in negative photographs. Dr Barbara Frale told La Repubblica, that under Jewish burial practices current at the time of Christ in a Roman colony such as Palestine, a body buried after a death sentence could only be returned to the family after a year in a common grave.

A death certificate was therefore glued to the burial shroud to identify it for later retrieval, and was usually stuck to the cloth around the face. This had apparently been done in the case of Jesus even though he was buried not in a common grave but in the tomb offered by Joseph of Arimathea.

Dr Frale said that many of the letters were missing, with Jesus for example referred to as "(I)esou(s) Nnazarennos" and only the "iber" of "Tiberiou" surviving. Her reconstruction, however, suggested that the certificate read: *"In the year 16 of the reign of the Emperor Tiberius Jesus the Nazarene, taken down in the early evening after having been condemned to death by a Roman judge because he was found guilty by a Hebrew authority, is hereby sent for burial with the obligation of being consigned to his family only after one full year"*. It ends *"signed by"* but the signature has not survived. Dr Frale further said that the use of three languages was consistent with the polyglot nature of a community of Greek-speaking Jews in a Roman colony.

The Holographic Record of Christianity - *Defending Sacred Ground* - Alex Collier, cr 1998

Q: Can you be specific on what the Andromedan viewpoint is on Christianity, especially in view of the fact that they have holographic access to all events that have happened on Earth? I mean, what are some of the specifics?

A: You know, I don't like talking about this, because I was raised a Catholic. I was an altar boy. The truth broke my heart. You know, to find out that what I thought was reality really wasn't. Where I'm at with it is very personal, but I'm not counting on anybody to come down and save me. The Andromedan perspective of the whole scenario is really different that what we've been told.

Q: Well, it's apparent that there were several characters in history with the name Yeshua, translated loosely as "Jesus". There's Yeshua Ben Joseph, etc. How did all this develop?

A: Okay. Basically what happened was that the Catholic church created a composite character, because at the time they were expending a lot of resources putting out religious wars. It seemed like a good idea at the time, but like many things it got perverted. Yeshua Ben Joseph, was a Jewish rabbi who lived from 70BC to 9 BC. He was apparently crucified at some point, charged with being a thief. Prior to that there was a man by the name of rabbi Hallel who apparently died in 100BC. Rabbi Hallel was called "The Great Teacher". Many Christians are led to believe that a man named Jesus was called this, when in fact it was Rabbi Hallel. Now, what happened was that the New Testament composite character of "Jesus The Christ" was created by the Council of Nicea. Most of the words that are attributed to this composite character, referred to colloquially as "Jesus", were in fact spoken by Apollonius of Tyana, who the Bible calls "Paul of Tarsus". Because Rome had their armies scattered all over the place and all these wars were over the subject of religion, what the Council of Nicea decided to do is essentially create a "State Religion". So, what they did was combine the religions of the east and the west, both of which were concerned with Sun worship. Those in the West worshipped Hesos, also called Hess. Those in the East that worshipped the Sun worshipped Krishna, which in Greek is called Kristos. The very first "Bible" that was put together in AD 325. They took some books that Apollonius of Tyana had brought back from Burma, called the Codes of the Initiates (which concerned themselves with man's relationship to the seasons, among other things) containing lessons that were handed down to those particular Holy Men in India during that particular period in history. The Codes of the Initiates allegedly contained words that were spoken by Krishna. The very first "Bible" was called the Helios Biblios, which means "The Sun Book". This is what they did in the very beginning.

Q: When was the Helios Biblios assembled?

A: Between 324 and 355 AD, by the Council of Nicea under Emperor Constantine The Great. Then they slowly developed a "God", a personage, to replace the Sun, and slowly changed the books, disposing of the material detailing reincarnation and many of the other teachings. They changed meanings, and every scribe that worked on this thing kept changing things as belief systems were revised with the prevailing times.

Q: How about things ascribed to the historical "Jesus" such as the Sermon on the Mount?

A: The exact words ascribed to the historical "Jesus" with reference to the Sermon on the Mount were found in a Turkish museum, authored by a Greek Senator in 64 AD. The Church went out a gathered all the information they could at various times in history, and they suppressed what they didn't agree with or what they didn't want the people to know.

Q: Then, who was the healer in this whole scenario?

A: That was Apollonius of Tyana, who the Catholic Church referred to as the "Anti-Christ", despite the fact that he was also known as Paul of Tarsus, mainly because he encouraged rebellion against Roman tyranny.

Q: And Yeshua Ben Joseph?

A: From what I understand, he was of the royal line, but he tried to create rebellion against Roman tyranny as well. Now, there was also another Yeshua.

Q: Another Yeshua?

A: Yes. It was a very common name than in Judea. He was a rabbi who was also a rebel, of sorts. He died at Massada in 64 AD, and his presence at

Massada was why Massada was attacked. His name was Yeshua Malathiel. The bottom line is there was no "Jesus Christ" in history at all. It was a composite character, and history reveals this fact.

Q: Now, Robert Morning Sky revealed that the specific crucifixion that involved a Yeshua was a mock crucifixion, in that the person did not really die, because he was given an herbal mixture to simulate death, and that Bar Abbas was in fact the son of the Yeshua concerned here.

A: Yes, if you take the name Bar Abbas, which is a two-word name (not Barrabas, as in the Biblical product of the Roman Church), and you go back to the ancient Hebrew, it means "Son of the Teacher" or "Son of the Master".

Q: So whose son was Bar Abbas?

A: Yeshua Melethiel.

Q: His son.

A: Yes, and from that grew the lineage in France.

Q: The lineage in France? That is where Alex Christopher's book *Pandora's Box* picks the trail up. The so-called "bloodline of Christ" that related to the mission of the Templars.

A: That's right. It related not to Yeshua (Jesus) Malathiel himself, who died at Massada in 64 AD, but to his son, Bar Abbas, who survived and went to France.

Q: This is also connected with the "blue-bloods" and extraterrestrial genetics?

A: That's exactly right.

Q: So Yeshua Malathiel was a "blue-blood"?

A: Yes, he was, and he was connected to the House of David, and if you go all the way back through the line, through David, and you get to Moses, who was a human-extraterrestrial "half-breed".

Q: So, was it Yeshua Malathiel who was involved in the "cross scenario"?

A: I don't know for sure. The only place I have heard of the story that Robert is talking about is from a book called *Crucifixion By An Eyewitness* (which does not at all imply that Robert got his data from that book, just that the book mentions it) But, the Essenes were herbalists and knew how to mix potions and knew about this kind of thing. Of course, the real secrets about all of this lie in the Dead Sea Scrolls.

Q: Which the Israeli government have locked up, or at least most of them, and will only let a few select people see a few of them.

A: Yes, by the Israeli's and the Roman Church, because what the Dead Sea Scrolls show, according to the Andromedans, are that "Christianity" and "Judaism" were really one thing, one religion, and they also tell the true story of who Yeshua was, as we have spoken about here.

Q: Yeshua Malathiel?

A: Right. Rabbi Wise in the 1950's and 1960's did an extensive study of the death warrants and death certificates of those who were crucified during that time period, as the Romans kept records, and the only Yeshua listed as being crucified was a man coincidentally named Yeshua Malathiel, who was listed as a traitor and a thief. Mary of the house of Magdelana was the wife of Yeshua Malathiel. She came from a very well-to-do family who raised doves for sacrifices put on by the Pharisees at the temples. I think the book Holy Grail talks a little about that, too. The Jewish tradition was at that time that any man 13 years of age, who was a rabbi, must take a wife and have children. That was the law.

Q: How did the crucifixion scenario arise with Yeshua Malathiel and his son, Bar Abbas?

A: Well, the story behind that is that they took Bar Abbas because they knew that the father, Yeshua, would come after his son. The story goes on to say that a ransom was paid, and they did a "mock" crucifixion in order to hide the fact of a payoff to the Romans. Malathiel did not leave the area. He continued to do what he did and died at Massada. There is apparently a scroll which is in the possession of the Russians that proves this, and the son, Bar Abbas, was escorted to France with the rest of the family.

Q: So, presuming that somewhere along the line Christians or Jews would read this material, what would you say to them if they feel concerned by it?

A: Well, all I would say is that true history does not support the idea or the proof that a "Jesus Christ" lived. It does prove that Apollonius of Tyana was real, and the other thing I would say is, "you've been duped". There is no middle man between you and the Creator, and your relationship is directly with the Creator.

Q: Of course, this is why Gnosticism has been so suppressed throughout history.

A: Yes. These "churches" exist only because people "believe in them" and support them financially. If you take that away and say, "my relationship is with the Creator, I don't need a middle man", then "there is no need for you." Let's face it, the church is politics and a form of government. The Andromedans share very much the same viewpoint as some of the Pleaidian groups - that all religions on our planet are forms of government, and they don't see any difference between government and politics (power-brokering), in their perspective. I mean, people used to have to pay priests in order to "assure their place in heaven".

Q: Are there any religious systems on this planet that are at all beneficial?

A: There are two religious systems they say have been beneficial, and they were the original form of Buddhism and the original form of Shinto. All the other stuff is designed to hold you back and control you. That is their perception.

*In AD 80, the Roman Emperor Domitian decreed that all descendants of Jesus Christ's family should be hunted down and put to the sword. As chronicled by Hegesippus, Africanus and Eusebius, these Messianic dynasts were known as the Desposyni (the Heirs of the Lord). The decree was never rescinded.*

**Priory of Sion parchment**

**Jesus ‘the Christ’**

**Shoud of Turin - face**

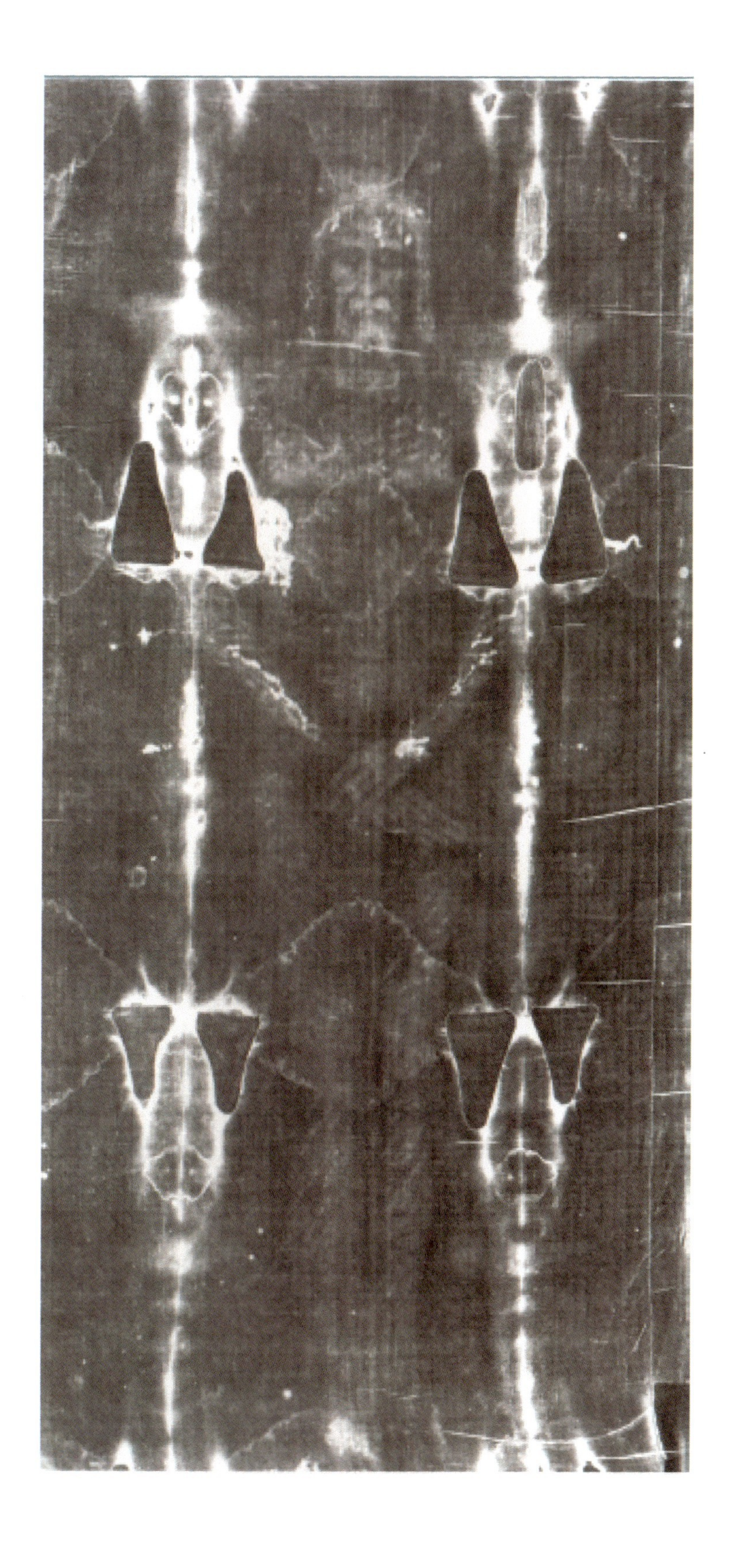

**Shoud of Turin - front**

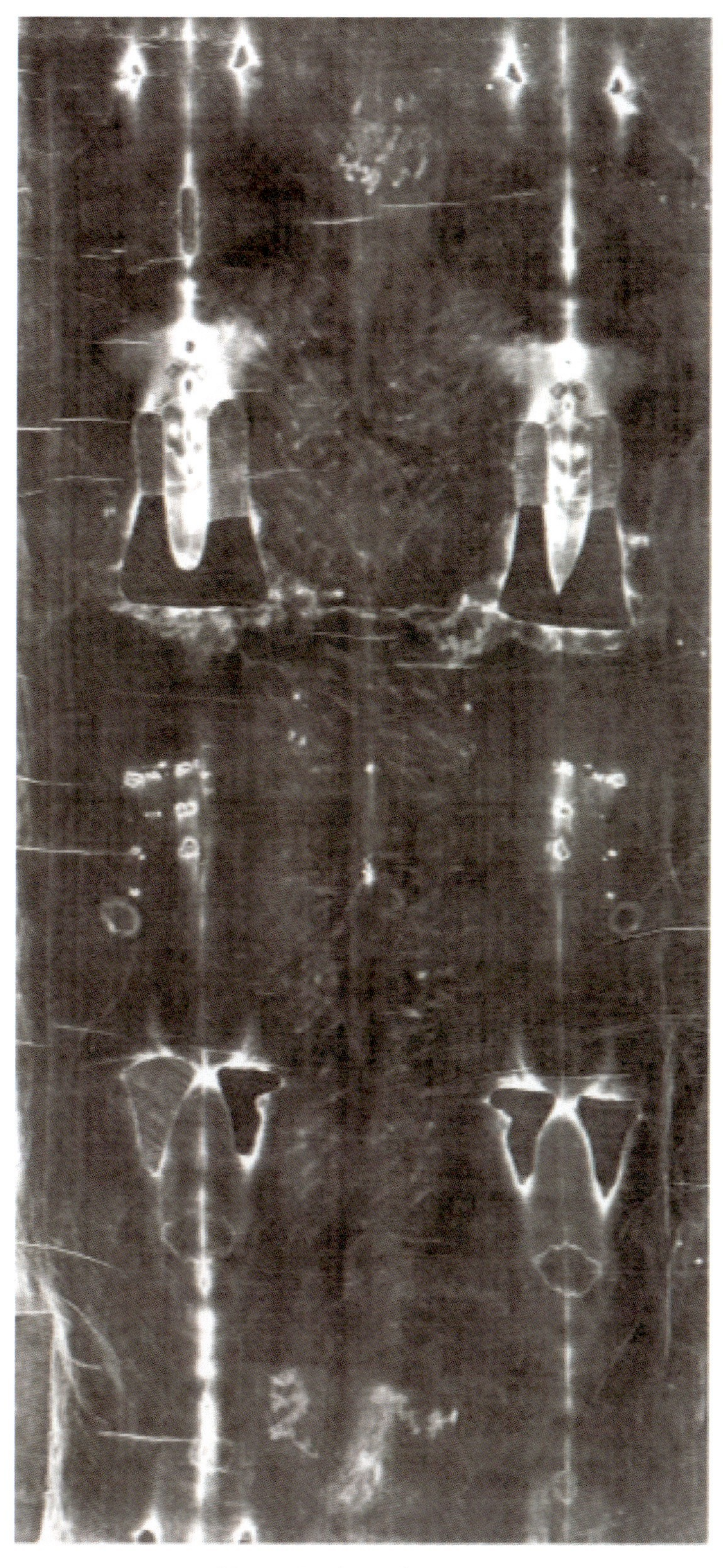

**Shroud of Turin - back**

## Ka.in (Cain)

KA.IN by the Sumerians, son of Adapa (Adam) and Khawa (Eve). Cain by the Hebrews, son of Adam (Adapa) and Eve (Khawa). The Mark of Cain was called the Hebrew MALKHUT, from the Akkadian Malku, meaning sovereign. It was the symbol that has become known as the Rose Cross. This Rose Cross (RX), is now pronounced phonetically as Rex, the title given to monarchs. It is also the symbol one finds in the Pharmaceutical fields and professions. The ancient Annunaki were powerful Alchemists or Chemists. The Mark of Cain or Rose Cross is the Cross and the Circle. It is also the sign for Venus in astrology. This is seen held inverted by the monarchs. The cross within the circle is found on many Churches and architecture. The Holy Grail symbol was the *"Cross within the Circle"* birthmark, found on Jesus' descendants. It was found either in the middle of the chest or on the shoulder blade.

From the Gnostic fragment, Cain and Abel: "And the first ruler (Enki) saw the female virgin standing with Adam, and saw that the living, luminous afterthought had been shown forth within her. And Aldabaoth became filled with lack of acquaintance. Now, the forethought of the entirety learned of this, and sent certain beings, who caught life (Zoe) out of Eve. And the first ruler (Enki) defiled her, and begot on her two sons-the first and the second, Eloim and Iaue. Eloim has the face of a bear; Iaue, the face of a cat.

One is just, the other is unjust: Iaue is just, Eloim is unjust. It established Iaue in charge of fire and wind, and established Eloim in charge of water and earth. And it called them by the names Cain and Abel, with trickery in mind . . . "And to the present day sexual intercourse, which originated from the first ruler, has remained. And in the female who belonged to Adam it sowed a seed of desire; and by sexual intercourse it raised up birth in the image of the bodies.

And it supplied them some of its counterfeit spirit. And it established the two rulers in charge of realms, so that they ruled over the cave." Gnostic Scriptures such as the one above, describe how Eve was 'raped' as it were by the serpent (Enki) in order to bear Cain and Abel, and even supplied her with some of his 'evil' or "counterfeit spirit." Many aspects of the Sumerian texts also suggest that it was Enki who was physically intimate with his creation.

In the Bible version it specifies that Eve had help from "the Lord" with her first two sons, Cain and Abel; and with their third son, Seth, it was Adam who became the father of "a" son, who was at last in his father's likeness: *Genesis* 4:1. ". . . and she bore Cain saying. "I have gotten a man with the help of the Lord. And again, she bore his brother Abel . . . *Genesis* 5:3 "When Adam had lived a hundred and thirty years, he became the father of a son in his own likeness, after his image, and named him Seth."

According to the Gnostic Scriptures, the importance of Cain was that he was directly produced by Enki and Kava (Eve), so his blood was three-quarters Anunnaki, while his half-brothers, Hevel and Satanael (better known as Abel and Seth), were less than half Anunnaki, being the offspring of Atabba and Kava (Adam and Eve). Cain's Anunnaki blood was so advanced that it was said that his brother Abel's blood was earthbound by comparison. It was related in the scriptures that Cain 'rose far above Abel', so that his brother's blood was swallowed into the ground - but this original description was thoroughly misinterpreted for the modern Bible, which now claim that Cain 'rose up against Abel' and spilled his blood upon the ground. This is not the same thing at all.

In truth, Adam and Eve as the creation of these gods were two races of people, and not specific individuals - the Adama and the Evee. Thus the first race of people that were sired through 'eve' were bred by the gods from artificial insemination and not by physical sexual means. This led to the sons Cain and Abel being genetically altered to fit the Anunnaki's needs and not randomly accessed genetically as would be typical of a human birth. Cain "had the face of a bear" making him black; "Iaue, the face of a cat" -a Persian cat-making him white.

This occurred 230,000 years ago during the first experimentation of Enki to create a worker race. This is the time as stated when mitochondrial research has found that 'all races' seemed to have stemmed from the one common mother - 'Eve'.

"The earliest true human being in Africa, Homo sapiens, dates from more than 200,000 years ago. A hunter-gatherer capable of making crude stone tools, Homo sapiens banded together with others to form nomadic groups; eventually these nomadic San peoples (Negroids) spread throughout the African continent. Distinct races date from approximately 10,000 BC.

Gradually a growing Negroid population, which had mastered animal domestication and agriculture, forced the San groups into the less hospitable areas." (*Encarta*) Cain killed Abel because they were different, one black and one white. Cain indeed was the black son of Adam and Eve-the black race of offspring as suggested by the Mormon religion who have always looked upon being black as the Mark of Cain. Abel was the white son, the white offspring as it were. A war broke out between the two races and for the first time as humans of a common origin on this planet, post-Anunnaki - a war was fought between these two races. Now look at the two italicized sections of these quotes only in reverse order: "And it supplied them some of its counterfeit spirit . . . with trickery in mind." And the trickery caused by these alien gods was to breed jealousy and prejudice between the two races that they might always be at war with each other-"divide and conquer"- a way to make sure that the gods could always remain in power against the warring races. When we used the term 'black' here, "it is of the darkness of skin that might be found among many Middle Eastern tribes, rather than the blackness of the African negroid skin," say The Nine.

"Yahweh (Utu) paid heed unto Abel and his offering; Unto Cain and his offering He paid no heed. So Cain was very resentful". The race of Cain was a race of farmers, the race of Abel was a race of sheepherders. The Anunnaki being as much meat-eaters as anything else while here on Earth, they preferred the race of Abel's offering of meat over the race of Cain's offering of grain. Hence the archetype of 'flesh' sacrifices that persisted from then on. This created great jealousy in the race of Cain, and began the war between the two. "Cain came upon his brother Abel and killed him . . . So Yahweh (Utu) put a mark on Cain, so that whoever shall find him should not smite him." As much as the physical attribute of black skin, the Mark of Cain was also symbolic of an emotional attitude, an archetype of jealousy and victimization. The race of Cain then moved in its entirety to the land of Nod, and their multiplied by mixing with the other races of the area. And thus began the reign of Homo sapiens, the origins of modern man.

The mark by which Cain could be distinguished from the other children of Adam was his black skin. Noah, as a literal child of the gods, was born with very, very white skin. Cain and his descendants lived separately from the other descendants of Adam.

Edgar Cayce, 1968-2; January 25, 1940

"In those periods of time there was not a laboring for the sustenance of life (as in the present, but rather gods who were children of the Law of One (Enlil)--and some who were the children of Belial (Enki)--were served by humans, that were retained by individuals or groups to do the labors of a household, or to cultivate the fields or the like, or to perform the activities of artisans. And it was concerning these humans about which much of the disturbing forces grew to be factors to be reckoned with, between the children of the Law of One and the Sons of Belial. For these were the representation of what in the present experiences would be termed good (Able & Seth) and evil (Cain), or a spiritual thought and purpose and a material thought or desire or purpose."

The Hebrew legends tell us that after Eve gave childbirth two separate races arose: that of Cain and that of Able. The descendants of Cain behaved like animals: Exposed and naked went the race of Cain, both man and wife as the cattle of the fields. Naked went they around the market-place...and men procreated with their mothers and with their daughters and with their brothers' wives openly in the street.

Kebra Negest, *The story about Ethiopian Kings,* Chapter 100

“Those daughters of Cain, however, with whom the angels had done indecent acts, became pregnant, but could not give birth, and died. And of those in their wombs, some died and others came out by splitting the bodies of their mothers . . . as they grew older and grew up these became giants.”

The original city of Baalbek was built before the Great Flood by Cain, the son of Enki, whom God (Enlil) banished to the 'land of Nod' (Nodites-Niphilim) that lay 'east of Eden' for murdering his good brother Abel, and he called it after his son Enoch. The citadel at Baalbek fell into ruins at the time of the deluge and after the destruction by God, legends speak of how the giant races were dispersed across the bible lands. However, the citadel was later re-built by a race of giants under the command of Nimrod, the 'mighty hunter' and 'King of Sinar' of the Book of Genesis.

## Khawa (Eve)

Khawa by the Sumerians, daughter of Enki (Poseidon) and Cro-Magnon female. Kava by the Akkadians. Eva or Eve by the Hebrews. Mother of modern Homo Sapiens Sapiens.

*The Urantia Book,* page 845

Adam and Eve, like their fellows on Jerusem, maintained immortal status through intellectual association with the mind-gravity circuit of the Spirit. When this vital sustenance is broken by mental disjunction, then, regardless of the spiritual level of creature existence, immortality status is lost. Mortal status followed by physical dissolution was the inevitable consequence of the intellectual default of Adam and Eve.

Caligastia (the Devil) did succeed in trapping Adam and Eve, but he did not accomplish his purpose of leading them into open rebellion against the universe government. What they had done was indeed evil, but they were never guilty of contempt for truth, neither did they knowingly enlist in rebellion against the righteous rule of the Universal Father and his Creator Son.

## KIN.GU (Hyperion)

ALAM by the Atlanteans, the first King of Adlan-Atlantis. KIN.GU by the Sumerians, son of An.shar.gal and Anunnaki Concubine.

HYPERION by the Phoenicians. PORPHYRION by the Greeks. Hyperion's most powerful giant champion was called Alkyoneus. Alkyoneus, a giant, was born in Thracean Pellene (Phlegrae). The giants made a desperate struggle for supremacy, but were conquered by Zeus. The Greek legends tell us of the rebellions inaugurated at different times in Olympus. One of these was a rebellion of the Giants, "a race of beings sprung from the blood of Uranos," the great original progenitor of the stock. "There king or leader was Porphyrion."

According to the Greeks, Poseidon, and Chronos were the sons of Uranos, who reigned over a great kingdom composed of countries around the western part of the Mediterranean, with certain islands in the Atlantic, one was called Mount Othrys. Hyperion his son succeeded his father, and was then killed by the Titans. The kingdom was then divided between Poseidon and Cronos - Poseidon taking Northern Africa, with the Atlantic islands called Atlantis, and Chronos the countries on the opposite shore of the Mediterranean to Italy and Sicily.

According to Diodorus Siculus, after the death of Uranus, Basilea (Theia), the sister of Hyperion, was unanimously elected Queen of Atlantis. She then married her brother Hyperion. Her relatives in Mesopotamia, dreading that Hyperion might usurp the Throne, slew him and drowned his infant son Helio (Helios). Hyperion's daughter Selene, in despair at the death of her brother, cast herself down from a height and perished.

He was called YMIR by the Nordic-Germanic tribes. The first Frost Giant. Brutal, evil, violent. Odin (Zeus), Wili (Poseidon), and We (Hades) slay Ymir (Hyperion), the father of the Hrimthursar (ice giants). The Germans and the Nordic Scandinavians spoke of a vanished continent in the North Atlantic ocean called Thule with the civilization of Hyperbores (named after its god-ruler Hyperion) located on it.

Many famous writers, like Diodorus Pliny, and Virgil wrote about Thule, a land the Greeks knew existed before their time. They described Thule in the North Atlantic, as warm and green surrounded by high mountains, known for breathtakingly beautiful women. The race reportedly was blonde with blue eyes, the men were exceptionally handsome, although some writers spoke of a violet skinned race with golden hair, that ruled these people. The ancients agreed that the Hyperborean Race was tall and in excellent physical condition, and some told of how they conquered the aging process and looked youthful in old age. They were reportedly vegetarians and fruitarians who lived in harmony with nature. Although several ancient writers firmly believed in Thule, historians of the Middle Ages, who had no evidence that the north was once warm and therefore inhabited, naturally censored it out of the history books we inherited! Today's science knows as a fact that the far north was once tropical!

YAMM or "day god of the sea" by the Phoenicians. YAM, or "Ocean-Sea" by the Canaanites. SHADID by the Arabians. He who belongs to the swift queen. An ancient sea god who took part in the creation of Cosmos out of Chaos, and whose power was later given to Poseidon. The Greeks said that he surrounded the Earth and held his tail in his mouth. He was the inventor of the arts and magic.

In the Bible the non-Israelite inhabitants of Syria and Palestine in early times are called Canaanites. Little was known of Canaanite mythology until 1929, when inscribed tablets in a previously unknown language were discovered at the Syrian village of Rases-Shamrah (ancient Ugarit). The language is now called Ugaritic and the site proved to have been the religious and political center of a Canaanite kingdom which flourished in northern Syria in the period from about 1500 to 1000 BC. The tablets, which are badly broken, include passages of poetry about the god Baal, known as the Rider on the Clouds, the god of rain and fertility.

The first story concerns Baal's (Enki/Poseidon) conflict with Yam (Hyperion), the god of the sea. What appears to be the first tablet records the building of a temple for Yam by the divine craftsmen, Kothar and Khasis. The building seems to have been authorized by El, the chief god, but he is told that there is a danger of Yam, the sea, 'rushing quickly over the earth' and bringing destruction on the land, El (Annu) supports the work, however, but Yam is told that he will have to challenge the authority of Baal and 'drive him from his throne'.

The second tablet opens with the announcement that Baal is planning an attack on Yam with the help of another god, Horon (Horus), and the goddess Athtart. Yam sends messengers to the assembly of the gods on the 'Mountain of Night', saying: *'Surrender Baal and his servants, I will possess the gold of the son of Dagon'.* El (Annu) agrees to make Baal (Poseidon) the slave of Yam (Hyperion). Baal resists violently, but is restrained by two goddesses, Athirat and Anat. There is a large break in the tablet at this point, but Baal is apparently surrendered to Yam by the other gods.

When the text becomes legible again, the god Athtar, who seems to be claiming the right to Baal's kingship, interrupts the work on Yam's palace by complaining that he has no house like the other gods, 'no court like the sons of the holy one'. Shapash, the sun-goddess, explains to him that he cannot really be a king, because he has no wife like the other gods.

At the end of the tablet, Baal (Poseidon) is in bitter conflict with Yam (Hyperion). He is on the point of being defeated when Kothar and Khasis, the craftsmen gods, give him two magic clubs. Baal names the clubs 'Chaser' and 'Driver', and they chase and drive Yam from his throne. The first, 'struck Prince Yam on the shoulders' but 'he did not fall down', The second, however, struck Yam on the skull.

Yam collapsed, he fell to the earth, His face trembled, his body crumpled. Baal dragged away Yam and laid him down. The few fragmentary lines at the end of this tablet contain the proclamation: 'Yam is certainly dead, Baal shall be king!'

## KI.SHAR (Gaea)

KARYATIDE by the Pleiadians. KI or *"the cleaved one"* by the Sumerians. KISHAR or "Great Princess of Firm Ground" or "foremost of the firm lands" by the Akkadians, daughter of Murus and Amu. GAIA or GAEA by the Greeks.

DANUIH (Da-noo-ee) or "Earth goddess" by the Atlanteans. DANU, DANANN, and DANA by the Celts. Major Mother Goddess; ancestress of the Tuatha De Danann (Tribe of Dardanus); Mother of the gods; Great Mother; Earth Goddess. She gave her name to the Tuatha De Danann (People of the Goddess Danu). Patroness of wizards, rivers, water, wells, prosperity and plenty, magic, and wisdom.

SOPHIA goddess of wisdom. Have you ever wondered about that gorgeous woman in Michelangelo's painting on the ceiling of the Sistine chapel-the one that God has his arm wrapped around while his other arm extends to touch the hand of Adam? Some art historians believe the petite blonde was Jehovah's grandmother, the Goddess SOPHIA. In the Judeo-Christian tradition the goddess Sophia is the beginning, the source of wisdom, and keeper of the knowledge of all that is righteous and just. With her sound wisdom and guidance, rulers lead their kingdoms to prosper. In the darkness and ignorance that thrive in her absence, the proverbial wasteland eats away at the soul and nations perish.

Known as the MOTHER OF ALL or simply as WISDOM, Sophia was born of Silence according to Gnostic creation myths. She gave birth to both Male and Female who together created all the elements of our material world.

Female then gave birth to Jehovah in all his emanations. But she also gave birth to Ildabaoth who was known as the Son of Darkness. When humans were created, Sophia loved them all dearly.

Unfortunately, her affection for humans sparked jealousy in both Ildabaoth and Jehovah. Hoping to keep humans weak and powerless, the brothers forbade humans to eat the fruit of the tree of knowledge. Female then sent her spirit in the form of the serpent to teach the humans to disobey the envious gods.

Sophia so desperately loved humans that she decided she would live among them. To her dismay they mostly ignored her. She tried speaking to them. When they turned a deaf ear, she screamed from the tops of the highest walls. Still she was not heard.

In her anguish at being so neglected, she left humans with one last thought: You have denied and ignored me, so will I do when calamity strikes and you call for my help. Only those who earnestly search for me and love me will merit my love and assistance.

There are those who believe that Sophia, so desperate in her desire to relate, later returned to humans in another attempt to bond with them. Sophia is often symbolized by the DOVE of Aphrodite, which later became the dove representing the HOLY SPIRIT.

The dove appeared to the Virgin Mary in the form of the VIRGIN OF LIGHT, entered her and conceived Jesus. In this sense, Sophia attempted again, in to form of a man, to be united with the mortals she so loved.

Sophia's traits include: righteous, wisdom, loving, communicative, knowledgeable, creative, protective, giving, and truthful. A Sophia woman sees it and tells it as it is; she has no fear of the truth.

She brings meaning to human experience with her gift of understanding "the bigger picture". Only when you stand back, gaining some emotional distance, can you see that even the most traumatic experiences can be the birthplace of your most treasured strengths. It is only in times of great stress that heroic feats are truly appreciated.

Sophia was also the mother of Faith, Hope, and Charity. They are Sofia's gifts to us, gifts that can overcome the despair, confusion, and suffering that frame human life. Sophia reminds you that clear vision and understanding line the path that leads to the discovery of the meaning of your life.

**God has his left arm around the goddess of wisdom - Sophia**

## KISH.AR.GAL (Titea)

KI and KISH.AR.GAL by the Sumerians, daughter of An.ib and Anunnaki Concubine. KUR, HUWAWA, TI.AMAT or "maiden of life" by the Akkadians. NUIT, NUT, and TEFNUT or "Goddess of moisture" by the Egyptians. TITEA and URAEA by the Greeks. TERRA and TEHOMOT by the Hebrews. TELLUS by the Romans. TITAEA in Latin. Goddess of the primal abyss. A she dragon (the Sea-dragon), she was sometimes evil, sometimes good. Shown as part animal, part serpent, part bird. In later times, these queens or "Sea-dragons" were commonly represented as mermaids (mere maids), and were often called Ladies of the Lake. Marduk destroyed Tiamat, took the "Tablets of Destiny", or the "White Stone" and built the universe out of her body (the asteroid belt). Tiamat was the "bearer of the skies and the earth". Tiamat was killed by the younger god Marduk, the son of Enki.

*Enuma elish* - circa 1500 BC

When on high the heaven had not yet been named,
Firm ground below had not been called by a name,
Nought but primordial Apsu, their begetter,
And Mummu, and Tiamat -- she who bore them all,
Their waters mingled as a single body.

Tiamat is portrayed in several different ways, but she was originally drawn as a four-legged creature with head and forequarters of a lion, a scaled body, feathery wings, an eagle's hind legs and a forked tongue. She also had a hide that was impervious to all weapons.

The Babylonian creation epic, Enuma Elish, tells of how, in the beginning there was nothing save for two elements: Apsu - the male spirit of fresh water and the abyss, and Tiamat - the female spirit of salt water and chaos. Their children were the gods, but, becoming increasingly enraged by their offsprings' unruly ways, Apsu sought to destroy them. But the gods struck first and destroyed Apsu.

Tiamat lived on and plotted her revenge. She spawned eleven monsters to help her make war upon her children; the viper, the shark, the scorpion man, the storm demon, the great lion, the dragon, the mad dog and four nameless ones.

Mar.duk (Moloch) was the only god who fought Tiamat. There was an epic struggle but Marduk was finally able to shoot an arrow into her mouth which split her heart in two. He then divided her body into two parts - the sky and the land. Marduk cut the head off one of Tiamat's advisers and from the blood created humanity to serve as slaves to the gods.

THE DESTRUCTION OF TIAMAT

Anu took over command of the battlestar Nibiru and headed for our solar system and the planet Tiamat. Tiamat was in, roughly, the same orbit as Earth is now. It was just a little futher out from the sun. Being the 12th planet of our solar system, Nibiru entered our solar system from the back, as this is their orbital pattern. Nibiru passed by Neptune and Uranus and, drew closer to Saturn, letting its gravitational pull move us into a position that aligned us with Tiamat. They harnessed a satellite of Saturn and propelled it into the middle of Tiamat with such force that it distended her. Then they shot a laser beam into this cleavage at the location of the fusion generators. The beam blew out the force fields, and Tiamat was left lifeless.

During this time Anu was in constant communication with his superiors in the Nibiruan Council. Anu was given the order to continue with his regular orbit and, when he arrived back in our solar system, to finish the job. That meant breaking Tiamat in two and shunting the upper half into a new orbit to be rehabilitated. This upper half would become Earth. The lower half would be smashed into pieces and become the Asteroid Belt. The Saturn satellite they had harnessed became Pluto. They shunted it into orbit and established an outpost command there.

Once Tiamat was put out of commission they didn't hear much from the Reptiles (Draconians) for a while. Tiamat's near destruction had been a big blow for them, and they needed time to recover. Only two percent of the Reptiles survived by, either going underground, or by being taken aboard Nibiru. Anu offered sanctuary to those members of the ruling Reptile families that had been cast out by the Reptilian Council for not going along with the plan to destroy the Humans.

With the cooperating remnant of the House of Aln aboard Nibiru, Anu set out for his next assignment-the destruction of the Reptilian Royal Planet Aln in the Orion constellation.

Once the Reptiles recovered from the shock of the destruction of Tiamat and Aln, the Great Galactic War began. They decided that the Humans in this Galaxy had to be destroyed for peace to reign. They armed Maldek, their military outpost planet in our solar system to do just that.

The upper half of Tiamat, now called Earth, was rehabilitated and reseeded by the Felines. They, with the help of the Christos Sirians, seeded for plants, animals, and a new land guardian race. Once again the evolving land guardian race was being watched over by the Earth Sirians.

A few million years after the reseeding of Earth, a new Human colony, called Hybornea, was established. The human colonists came from all over the galaxy and Hybornea survived and flourished for nearly one million years. It was a Lyran/Sirian colony and attracted colonists who leaned toward the feminine polarity. The Hyborneans tried to help the Things and managed to free a few of them from the animal cycle, but many still remained to be freed. Hybornea was destroyed in a massive attack by the Reptiles. They launched their attack from Maldek, which they later destroyed. Maldek is now part of the Asteroid Belt, along with the lower half of Tiamat.

The destruction of Hybornea fueled the fires of the Galactic War even more. This would be the final great battle. Nibiru was ordered to destroy Maldek and run the Reptiles out of our solar system for the last time. This Anu accomplished but not before the Reptiles had destroyed the Human colonies on Venus and Mars, leaving them both uninhabitable. The destruction of Maldek brought the Galactic War to an end.

The destruction of Maldek cost Nibiru her protective forcefield, due to the massive amounts of atomic weapons used by the Reptiles in their attacks. Maldek was destroyed and Nibiru was severly crippled and its people were dying by the thousands. The only way to save the Galactic Federation's great battlestar was to find large quantities of gold to suspend in the forcefield around Nibiru. This would protect the battlestar from the radiation that swept through space. So, the Anunnaki came to earth to mine for this gold.

## KU.MAR.BI

KU.MAR.BI by the Akkadians, son of Ala.lu (Helios) and Nin.ul (Perseis). For nine counted periods Anu was king in Heaven; In the ninth period, Anu had to do battle with Kumarbi. Anu slipped out of Kumarbi's hold and fled-Flee did Anu, rising up to the sky. After him Kumarbi rushed, seized him by his feet; He pulled him down from the skies. He bit his loins; and the "Manhood" of Anu with the insides of Kumarbi combined, fused as bronze.

According to this ancient tale, the battle did not result in a total victory. Though emasculated, Anu managed to fly back to his Heavenly Abode, leaving Kumarbi in control of Earth. Meanwhile, Anu's *"Manhood"* produced several deities within Kumarbi's insides, which he (like Cronos in the Greek legends) was forced to release. One of these was Teshub, the cheif Hittite deity.

However, there was to be one more epic battle before Teshub could rule in peace. Learning of the appearance of an heir to Anu in Kummiya *("heavenly abode"),* Kumarbi devised a plan to *"raise a rival to the God of Storms." "Into his hand he took his staff; upon his feet he put the shoes that are swift as winds";* and he went from his city Ur-Kish to the abode of the

Lady of the Great Mountain. Reaching her, His desire was aroused; He slept with Lady Mountain; His manhood flowed into her. Five times he took her . . . Ten times he took her. A son of Kumarbi by the Lady of the Great Mountain could have claimed to be the rightful heir to the Heavenly Throne; and that Kumarbi "took" the goddess five and ten times in order to make sure that she conceived, as indeed she did: she bore a son, whom Kumarbi symbolically named Ulli-Kummi ("suppressor of Kummiya"-Teshub's abode).

The battle for succession was foreseen by Kumarbi as one that would entail fighting in the heavens. Having destined his son to suppress the incumbents at Kummiya, Kumarbi further proclaimed for his son: Let him ascend to Heaven for kingship! Let him vanquish Kummiya, the beautiful city! Let him attack the God of Storms (Ishkur-Yahweh) And tear him to pieces, like a mortal! Let him shoot down all the gods from the sky. The tale of the challenge to the Divine Throne by Ulli-Kummi continues to relate heroic battles but of an indecisive nature. At one point, the failure of Teshub to defeat his adversary even caused his spouse, Hebat, to attempt suicide. Finally, an appeal was made to the gods to mediate the dispute, and an Assembly of the Gods was called.

## LARJJSA (Arjjsa)

LARJJSA or ARJJSA a "fallen angel" who mated with earth's human females and produced human giants.

## Lehabim (Hercules Lybicus)

Lehabim or Hercules Lybicus, son of Mizraim (Mitzraim). The Egyptians recorded his name as 'rbw', although it is uncertain where they settled. Some authorities (including Josephus) give Libya as their country.

## Lud (Laud)

Lud or Laud by the ancient Hebrews, son of Shem (Sem) and Sedeqetelebab. The early descendants of Lud, the Ludim, were known to both the Assyrians and Babylonians as the Ludu. Josephus tells us that their land was later known as Lydia, (a direct Greek derivation of the name of Lud) which is located in western Asia Minor. The Lydians were famed in the old world for the skill of their archers. They spoke an Indo-European language, some examples of which are in the form of certain items of graffiti that currently defiles certain Egyptian monuments. The land of Lydia was finally conquered by Cyrus, king of Persia in the year 546 BC.

## Lud (Ludim)

Lud or Ludim, son of Mizraim (Mitzraim). The Ludim settled on the north coast of Africa and gave their name to the nation of Libya. They are known to have provided Egypt on more than one occasion with mercenary troops, the records that tell us this giving their name as the Lebu.

# LUNERA

LUNERA a "fallen angel" who mated with earth's human females and produced human giants.

## Madai (Mada)

Madai or Mada, son of Japhet (Japheth) and Adataneses. Dwelled in the land of Curson. Founder of the tribe of Orelum. Father of the Persians and the Medes. Madai's descendants became the Madaeans, who are better known to us as the Medes. The Assyrians recorded the name as Amada; the Greeks as Medai; and the Old Persian inscriptions speak of them as the Mada. The earliest reference to the Medes that is found in secular records is in the inscriptions of Shalmaneser III, King of Assyria from c.858-824 BC, in which he tells us that he invaded their lands for their famous and excellent horses. Both Strabo and Herodotus confirm the fact that the Medes were of Indo-European extract, and we know also that their language was of this group. After 631 BC, the Medes joined with the children of Ashchenas (that is the Askuasa or Scythians), and those of Gomer, in order to throw off the Assyrian yoke.

## Magog

Magog son of Japhet (Japheth) and Adataneses. Magog's descendants were known as the Magogites, Josephus tells us that they were later known to the Greeks as the Scythians. However, given the subsequent history of the peoples of Ashchenaz, who are far more certainly identified as the later Scythians (Greek Skythai and Assyrian Askuza), it is much more likely that the early Magogites' were assimilated into the peoples of Ashchenas, thus making up merely a part of the Scythian hordes. Father of the Scythians, the Western Russians, the Scots, & the Irish.

## Manis-Ittusu

Manis-the-Warrior by the Sumerians, giant demi-god son of King Sargon and Ana (Aphrodite). Man-icticcu or Manishtusu by the Akkadians. Manja-the-Shooter by the Indus Valley civilization. Manj-the-Warrior, Manshu, Manash, Minash, Hor-Aha-Men and Aha Manash by the Egyptians. Menes by the Greeks. Mena to English Egyptologists. Menes led a revolt against his father, Sargon, and took control of Egypt, declaring it independent of Sumer. As a result, Sargon disinherited him and the succession went to his youngest brother. But Menes succeeded after a decade or so when his brother died-probably with Menes' help. Menes ruled Sumer after the death of his brother and this empire included Sumer, Egypt, and the Indus Valley.

## MAR.DUK (Phosphorus)

MAR.DUK son of En.ki (Poseidon) and Nin.ki (Eos), the god of "the waters" *Gensis* 1:1, was MARDUK or MERODACH, who is the MORDECAI of the biblical book of *Esther* (Ishtar). AZAG (AZAEL) or "The Great Serpent" by the Sumerians. AMARU.DUK, MARU.TUK.KU, MER.SHA.KU.SHU, LUGAL.DIMMER.ANKIA, ASAR.LU.HI, NAM.TI.LA, NARI.LUGAL, DIMMER.ANKIA, NAM.RU, MAR.DUK.KA,
MAR.DUCK, MAR.DUK and MAR.DUC or "Son of the Pure Mound" by the Akkadians.

Marduk was taught by his father Enki all knowledge of sciences and astronomy. The National god of Babylonia. Bull calf of the Sun; Great God; Lord of Life. As head of the Babylonian pantheon, he held the ring and rod symbols and carried a saw-toothed dagger in his belt. His robe was decorated with starlike rosettes. He killed Tiamat and took from her the Tablets of Destiny, or Law. Governor of the Four Quarters of the Earth.

Enki usurped the "Lordship" of Earth and was declared Supreme God of Babylon and of "the Four Quarters of the Earth." His son, Marduk presided over the core civilization of this Region, the civilization of the Nile Valley. He was the supreme divinity at On--Heliopolis, near Memphis. In the ancient City of Anu (later called 'On' in the Bible, 'Heliopolis' by the Greeks, and later modern 'Ciaro') there is a pillar called the 'Pillar of Anu'-'Pillar of Shu'-'Pillar of Thoth'-'Pillar of Hermes'-'Pillar of Seth'- 'Pillar of Solomon'-'Pillars of the Gods of the Dawning Light' and the 'Gate of the Hall of Truth'. Two pillars were removed from the Temple of Amen (Enki/Satan) at Heliopolis in 1880. One was erected on the Thames River bank in London, England and the second one was erected in Central Park, New York City in United States of America. The *New York Herald,* 13 Febraury 1880, stated the following: *"The obelisk and its foundations will be removed and replaced in New York exactly in the positions in which they were found, each having been numbered to correspond with numbers on a drawing that was made before the pieces were removed." The monument was erected by Thothmes III at the outer porch of the Temple of Amen at Heliopolis, where it and its twin (now in London) guarded the entrance of the temple for 2,000 years before they were moved to Alexandria. On 12 June 1880, with the assistance of Mr. Zola, Most Worshipful Grand Master of Egypt, the obelisk was entrusted to Lieutenant Commander H. H. Gorringe, U.S.N. [United States Navy], a member of Anglo-Saxon Lodge No. 137, for shipment to New York. On 9 October 1880 the obelisk was raised with great Masonic ceremonies in Central Park, New York City. With 8,000 Masons in attendance, the cornerstone of the ancient obelisk was laid by Jesse B. Anthony, Grand Master of Masons in New York State, as 30,000 awe-struck spectators and curiosity seekers watched, wondering what the strange rites they were seeing performed meant."*

Marduk stated "In the deep Above", where you have been residing, "The Kingly House of Above" have I built. Now, a counterpart of it I shall build in The Below. When from the Heavens for assembly you shall descend, there shall be a restplace for the night to receive you all. I will name it "Babylon"-- The Gateway of the Gods."

RA or "The Pure One" by the Egyptains. The son and successor of Ptah as ancient Egypt's leading deity, who at times was called Ra-Amen or "The Unseen". He was venerated as a great god "of Heaven and Earth," for he had come to Earth from the 'Planet of Millions of Years' in his 'Ben Ben', a conical 'celestial barge' which was kept in the Holy of Holies of a special temple in Anu - later called Heliopolis. When expectations of the return of

Nibiru into view began, the Unseen Ra/Marduk was also worshipped as the ATEN, the planet of the gods, depicted as a Winged Disc.

BEL by the Chaldean Magi - Astrologers - now Freemasons. HELEL by the Canaanites. A fallen angel, son of Sahar, (Enki) a winged deity. Helel sought to usurp the throne of the chief god and, as punishment, he will be cast down into the abyss. He was the first star (god) to fall from Heaven according to the *Book of Enoch I,* Chapter 86:1. Helel became the leader of the Nephilim, the giant offspring of the Anunnaki. HEL by the Nordic-Germans. Hel was exiled to Niflheim.

MILCOM by the Egyptians. MELEK and MELQART by the Phonecians. MELEK TAUS and the "Peacock Angel" by the Yezidhi, a cult of Kurds. MALKA TAUSA by the Mandeans. MALIK by the Arabs. The chief guardian angel of Hell. He is mentioned in the Koran. Ezekiel's King of Tyre worshipped Ishtar and watched boys being burned alive as surrogates of the god MELECH-KIRYATH and MELKARTH or 'Ruler of the City'. Called MERDUK or MERODACH by the Babylonians, MORDECAI in the *Book of Esther* (Ishtar) in the Bible. Merodach the Babylonian god of war and the patron deity of the city of Babylon (*Jeremiah* 50:2). MUSHEZIB, MASTEMA, MASTEMAH, MOLECH the national god of the Ammonites whose worship involved child sacrifice *Leviticus* 18:21. MOLOCH the god of barbarity and blood by the Hebrews. Moloch is the Hebrew word for "King" or "King Star" which was the name given to the planet Jupiter.

The Hebrews made their children pass through the fire to Moloch as they offered them in sacrifice. When "the fruit of the body" was thus offered, it was "for the sin of the soul." And it was the principle of the Mosaic law, a principle no doubt derived from the patriarchal faith, that the priest must partake of whatever was offered as a sin-offering *Numbers* 18, 9-10. The priest of Baal (Enki/Satan) were required to eat of the human sacrifices; and thus it has come to pass that "Cahna-Bal," the "Priest of Baal," is the word in our own tongue for a devourer of human flesh. The word Cahna is the emphatic form of Cahn. Cahn is "a priest," Cahna is "the priest."

MOLOCH, horrid king, besmeared with blood of human sacrifice, and parents' tears. Though, for the noise of drums and timbrels loud, their children's cries unheard, that passed through fire to his grim idol. Moloch's symbol is the owl. In almost every land the bloody worship to Moloch prevailed; "horrid cruelty," filled not only the dark places of the earth, but also regions that boasted of their enlightenment. Greece, Rome, Egypt, Phoenicia, Assyria, and Britian under the Druids, at one period or other in their history, worshipped the same god (Moloch) and in the same way. Human victims were his most acceptable offerings.

*Jeremiah* 32:35 - *"And they built the high places of Baal, which are in the valley of the son of Hinnom, to cause their sons and their daughters to pass through the fire unto Molech; which I commanded them not, neither came it unto my mind, that they should do this abomination, to cause Judah to sin"*

*Ezekiel* 20:31 - *"For when ye offer your gifts, when ye make your sons to pass through the fire, ye pollute yourselves with all your idols, even unto this day: and shall I be enquired of by you, O house of Israel? As I live, saith the Lord God, I will not be enquired of by you"*

*Ezekiel* 23:37-39 - *"That they have committed adultery, and blood is in their hands, and with their idols have they committed adultery, and have also caused their sons, whom they bare unto me, to pass for them through the fire, to devour them. Moreover this they have done unto me: they have defiled my sanctuary in the same day, and have profaned my sabbaths. For when they had slain their children to their idols, then they came the same day into my sanctuary to profane it, and, lo, thus have they done in the midst of mine house"*

*We Are The Nibiruans* by Jelaila Starr, cr 1999, pps. 101-104 - By 11,000 BC, man had degenerated to the point where it was decided to start over. The Atlanteans were the main reason for this decision, due to the influence of Marduk and his Reptilian allies. Their desire to rule the world created war across the planet. The Biblical Deluge was not caused by the Anunnaki marrying the daughters of men, as you have been told. Instead, it was due to Marduk's actions in Atlantis.

The time was about 25,000 BC, the Atlanteans, under Marduk's direction, had harnessed the power of a giant crystal. This, at first, was used to power aircraft, ships, and submarines. The Atlanteans were overjoyed at this latest technological advancement. Marduk was worming his way into their good graces and gaining their trust by giving them Nibiruan and Reptilian technology.

He began in the scientific community which then became the dominant portion of their society. Next, he infiltrated the ruling class and soon became the power behind the throne. This led to much dissension within the Atlantean society, pitting the Priesthood and the spiritually oriented people against the power and technologically oriented people. There was division in all classes, from the ruling class to the common people. Many Atlanteans supported Marduk (the Sons of Belial-the Sons of Darkness-the Sons of the Left Hand Mark) and many supported Enlil (the Sons of the Law of One-the Sons of Light-the Sons of the Right Hand Mark).

The Lemurians sent delegates to the rulers of Atlantis, attempting to warn them of the negative outcome of their quest for world domination under Marduk's direction. Marduk felt his father, Enki, should be the heir apparent of Earth and Nibiru, not his uncle, Enlil. But, Enki had already given up his quest for rulership. He preferred working in his laboratory, building things, and pursuing his spiritual studies over the daily grind of rulership.

Marduk, on the other hand, preferred ruling and felt he was doubly entitled to do so, since his mother was a Princess of the Snake people and his grandmother was the Queen of the Dragons. Her first husband had died before she married Anu. Marduk felt that if he could not get his father to fight for rulership of Earth, he would. Atlantis was the perfect place for him to begin, as it was far enough away from Mesopotamia and Egypt and from the everwatchful eyes of his uncle, Enlil, and his father, Enki. In his quest for world domination, Marduk had a very powerful ace--the Giant Crystal. He had managed to harness a comet, one of Tiamat/Earth's ten comets, via a tractor beam from the Giant Crystal, and he used it to threaten the other civilizations into submission.

At any time, Marduk could bring the comet down on any land mass which, because of its size and the speed of the impact, could destroy that civilization. He did this to Lemuria, and it caused the destruction and sinking of the entire continent. He was ready to do it again to the Rama and Yu empires when Nibiru returned to the vicinity of Earth. Nibiru created a momentary disruption of the tractor beam holding the comet in place, and within minutes, the comet came down on Atlantis, sinking the entire continent. This happened at the same time as the Great Deluge, adding to the mass destruction of the planet.

Marduk was also responsible for the destruction of the Firmament. The Firmament was the band of moisture, about three miles thick, surrounding Earth. Man did not see the sun and the moon until then. Like the planet Avyon, Earth was kept in a suptropical environment, which accounts for the lush, green, garden-like descriptions in the ancient texts.

The crystal temples were located underground in Mesopotamia. They held the Firmament in place. Marduk and Seth, his son, launch the attack on the crystal temples from the Great Pryamid in Egypt. This caused the forty days and nights of rain as the Firmament slowly collapsed. There was as much water in the Firmament as in the oceans. Seth used a laser weapon in the Great Pryamid to accomplish the task. His use of the Great Pyramid for this purpose would later bring about the Second Pryamid War and the emptying of the Great Pryamid of all its equipment, by Ninurta.

PHOSPHORUS by the Greeks, son of Astraeus and Eos (Ninki). The name sometimes given to the morning star which is also called Heosphorus. Translated into Latin the name becomes Lucifer. It is often personified in poetry as the star which announces the approach of Aurora, the dawn, and which is the bearer of the light of Day. HEOSPHORUS or EOSPHORUS, the flame of Eos (the Dawn), was the name of the morning Star.

LUCIFER, son of the Dawn (Nin.ki/Eos/Lilith). HELEL ben (son of) Shahar (Enki/Satan) by the Romans. Lucifer rebelled against God. Lucifer, whom God had made Guardian of All Nations, behaved discreetly; but soon pride turned his wits. *'I will ascend above the clouds and stars,'* he said, *'and enthrone myself on Saphon (Zaphon, Hazzi, Casius, now Jebel Akra-5800-foot mountain), the Mount of Assembly, thus becoming God's equal.'* Mount Zaphon was where the North-Semitic Bull-god El also ruled 'in the midst of his divine assembly, it rises near the mouth of the Orontes. God, observing Lucifer's ambitions, cast him down from Eden (Heaven) to Earth, and from Earth to Sheol. Lucifer shone like lightning as he fell, but was reduced to ashes; and now his spirit flutters blindly without cease through profound gloom in the Bottomless Pit. Lucifer being a Reptilian has the ability to materialize any physical object at will. They dwell within immutable, physical bodies which can survive for hundreds of years, although they experience the world primarily out of an immortal, fourth dimensional "Dragon Body,"an etheric sheath which surrounds and interpenetrates the physical body.

Lucifer rebelled against God. Lucifer, whom God had made Guardian of All Nations, behaved discreetly; but soon pride turned his wits. "I will ascend above the clouds and stars," he said, and "enthrone myself on Saphon (Zaphon, Hazzi, Casius, now Jebel Akra - elevation 5800 ft.), the Mount of Assembly, thus becoming God's equal." Mount Zaphon was where the North-Semitic Bull-god El also ruled 'in the midst of his divine assembly, it rises near the mouth of the Orontes. God, observing Lucifer's ambitions, cast him down from Eden (Heaven) to Earth, and from Earth to Sheol. Lucifer shone like lightning as he fell, but was reduced to ashes; and now his spirit flutters blindly without cease through profound gloom in the Bottomless Pit.

Lucifer being a Reptilian has the ability to materialize any physical object at will. They dwell within immutable, physical bodies which can survive for hundreds of years, although they experience the world primarily out of an immortal, fourth dimensional *"Dragon Body,"* an etheric sheath which surrounds and interpenetrates the physical body.

Contained within the Reptilian Body are the *"supernatural"* senses of clairvoyance, clairaudience, telepathy, omniscience, and omnipresence, which allow the Serpents to remain in continual communication with the subtle realms which surround and interpenetrate the physical plane. If they desire, they can extricate the Reptilian Body from its physical sheath and travel within it to distant locations throughout the universe.

Lucifer was equated with the fallen angel Azazel in *Isaiah* 14:12. The name Lucifer was applied to Satan by St. Jerome and other early Church Fathers. Lucifur leads man into a spiritual independence of the celestial hierarchies, tempting him to set himself up as a God. Lucifer incited the lust for power, the false pride and the egotism which led to the misuse of magical powers in Atlantis.

HELEL ben (son of) Shahar (Satan) by the Canaanites. A "fallen angel" a winged deity. Helel sought to usurp the throne of the chief god and, as punishment, was cast down into the abyss/earth. The same as the Lucifer legend. Helel was head or one of the leaders of the nephilim. Generally speaking, angels can have no offspring, since they are pure spirits; but when angels sin, when they "put on the corruptibility of the flesh" and cohabit with mortal women, they are capable of producing progeny. A case in point is the incident in *Genesis* 6. In the *cabala* and *rabbinic lore* there are numerous instances of such heteroclitish productivity.

DIABOLOS by the Hebrews. The one who tempts Christ to become Lord of this world. It is only a reference appropriate to modern times when we call him LEVIATHAN who is the SEVEN-HEADED, TEN-HORNED BEAST of the Apocalypse. The Luciferic danger threatens us inwardly from the sea of emotions, and is the beast of the Apocalypse who comes out of the ocean. OUROUBOROUS or "the serpent eating it's tail which encircles the cosmos," providing a "womb" for the Celestial Ocean, the Abyss.

"Moreover the word of the Lord came unto me, saying, Son of man, take up a lamentation upon the king of Tyrus, and say unto him, Thus saith the Lord God; Thou (Lucifer) sealest up the sum, full of wisdom, and perfect in beauty. Thou hast been in Eden the garden of God; every precious stone was thy covering, the sardius, topaz, and the diamond, the beryl, the onyx, and the jasper, the sapphire, the emerald, and the carbuncle, and gold: the workmanship of thy tabrets and of thy pipes was prepared in thee in the day that thou wast created. Thou are the anointed (Messianic) cherub that covereth; and I have set thee so: thou wast upon the holy mountain of God; thou hast walked up and down in the midst of the stones of fire (to mimic this, the Israelites caused their firstborn to *"pass through the fire").* Thou wast perfect in thy ways from the day that thou wast created, till iniquity was found in thee. By the multitude of thy merchandise they have filled the midst of thee with violence, and thou hast sinned: therefore I will cast thee as profane out of the mountain of God: and I will destroy thee." *Ezekiel* 28:11-18.

The Antichrist is described in *Daniel* 11: "He shall not regard the God of his fathers, YHWH nor the desire of women, nor love any god, for he shall magnify himself above all. But in his place he shall honor the god of fortresses, and he shall honor a god whom his fathers did not know."

The Hebrews called him the Archangel HAZAZEL, AZAEL, AZAZEL, AZZAZEL, ASAEL or ASIEL in *Leviticus* 16:8,10,26 & *Enoch* 8:1, 9:5, 10:6-12. Azzazel, the "fallen angel" from Heaven taught the daughters of men the art of smithing. He taught men to make knives, swords, shields and devised ornaments, coloring tinctures for the beautifying of women. YAZDA or YAZADAN by the Persians. AZAZYEL in *Enoch* 8:1-2, 10:6-12, the "fallen angel" by the Hebrews.

"Moreover Azazyel taught men to make swords, knives, shields, breastplates, the fabrication of mirors, and the workmanship of bracelets and ornaments, the use of paint, the beautifying of the eyebrows, the use of stones of every valuable and select kind, and of all sorts of dyes, so that the world became altered. Impiety increased; fornication multiplied; and they transgressed and corrupted all their ways. Thou hast seen what Azazyel has done, how he has taught every species of iniquity upon earth, and has disclosed to the world all the secret things which are done in the heavens." Again the Lord said to Raphael, "Bind Azazyel hand and foot; cast him into darkness; and opening the desert which is in Dudael, cast him in there. Throw upon him hurled and pointed stones, covering him with darkness; There shall he remain for ever; cover his face, that he may not see the light. And in the great day of judgment let him be cast into the fire. Restore the earth, which the angels have corrupted; and announce life to it, that I may revive it. All the sons of men shall not perish in consequence of every secret, by which the Watchers have destroyed, and which they have taught, their offspring. All the earth has been corrupted by the effects of the teaching of Azazyel. To him therefore ascribe the whole crime." *Enoch* 8:1-2, 9:5, 10:6-12.

"And Aaron shall cast lots upon the two goats; one lot for the Lord, and the other lot for Azazel. And Aaron shall bring the goat upon which the Lord's lot fell, and offer him for a sin offering. But, the goat, on which the lot fell to be Azazel, shall be presented alive before the Lord, to make an atonement with him, and to let him go to Azazel into the Wilderness. And he that let go the goat for Azazel shall wash his clothes, and bathe his flesh in water, and afterward come into the camp." *Leviticus* 16:8-10,26 Azazel's burial place is believed to be under a heap of stones at the foot of the cliff of

Haradan, in what is now the Sinai. Here he received every year the scapegoat driven into the desert with it's burden of Israel's sins.

Sitchin, Z., 2002, *The Lost Book of Enki*, page 284 - MARDUK/RA is the powerful "RA" who deposed Ningishzidda/Thoth in Egypt. Marduk's allies, the Igigi, ruled estates in Lebanon and Sumer. Nabu, Marduk's son, summoned these Igigi communities to Marduk's city, Babylon, to build a launch tower from which Marduk could challenge the Enlilite spaceport on the Sinai. Enlil asked Marduk to stop but he kept building his tower. "Marduk an unpermitted Gateway to Heaven is building, to Earthlings he is entrusting," Enlil told his clan, the Enlilites. They bombed the launch tower and Nabu's camp at Babylon. The Enlilites scattered Marduk's servants and programmed them to different languages and scripts. Marduk fled to Enki's region, the Nile. "When Marduk (now called Ra), after a long absence, to the Land of the Two Narrows (Egypt) returned, Ningishzidda (called Thoth in Egypt) as its master he there found. With the aid of offspring of the Anunnaki who Earthlings esposed did Ningishzidda the land oversee, what Marduk had once planned and instructed by Ningishzidda was overturned." For the next 350 years, the armies of brothers Marduk/Ra and Ningishzidda/Thoth clashed over Egypt. Finally, Enki, their father, known in Egypt as Ptah, ordered Thoth to leave Egypt to Ra. Triumphant, Ra reunited Egypt. And he honored Father Ptah. Ptah as Enki had not been able to give Marduk rule of Nibiru, which was once to have been his patrimony. But Ptah could at last settle Ra down in Egypt. Ptah gave his son the MEs (super computer programs) to make Egypt prosper; he gave Ra all his knowledge except how to revive the dead. The face of Ra's son Asar (called Osiris in Egypt) replaces Thoth's face on the Sphinx: Ra rewrote Egyptian history, relegating Thoth to *"the Divine Measurer."* Ra replaced Thoth's image on the "Stone Lion" (Sphinx). The new face of the Sphinx was now Asar (Osiris), Marduk's son. Exiled, Thoth and a band of his followers migrated to Mesoamerica, where Thoth, once Ningishzidda, was now Quezecoatl, the Winged Serpent.

The Persians adopted a totally new state religion, Zoroastrianism, remnants of which still exist today. The religion was named after Zoroaster, or Zarathustra, who was definitely anti-female. He taught that no woman could go to Heaven unless she was submissive to her husband's will, an idea adopted by the Jews and Christians.

This Persian religion centered around fire-altars and an eternal flame. The priests believed in free will, and posthumous reward and punishment. Their infernal deity, equal in power to their god, was later made into the devil by the Christians. Their ceremonies consisted of lighting and maintaining the sacred fire, drinking an intoxicating mixture made from a sacred plant called *haoma*, sacrificing a bull, and chanting for hours before the flame. They wore veils over their mouths to avoid contaminating the fire with their breaths.

The Chaldean astrologers or Magi ("Wise Men" - now called Freemasons), were widely respected throughout the entire area. The Magi worked with seven planetary spheres and twelve zodiac signs. The planetary bodies known and used were the Sun, Moon, Mercury, Venus, Mars, Jupiter, and Saturn. This association of planetary bodies to zodiac signs was set up by their god Marduk, the god of the Magi (and Freemasons).

The Magi, a hereditary priesthood, controlled Zoroastrianism and were renowned for their supernatural powers and skill in sorcery. They had a holy book of hymns called the Avesta and exposed their dead to the vultures. The floating winged disk symbolized Ahura Mazdah to them, as the rayed headdress represented Mithra, the warrior against evil.

The Chaldeans (Crescent "Moon worshippers"), who were called the Magi, was a common name for Mesopotamian astrologers who studied the movements of the Moon and stars. Their magical powers were respected throughout the ancient world. The Catholic Encyclopedia states that the 'chaldaea' worshipped the god BEL (Marduk/Lucifer). Diodorus Siculus states that "the Magi controlled the temple of Bell in Babylon" *Bibliotheca Historica, II,* 31; *Ephraem Syrus II,* 48 after the Medes had stormed the city.

The priest of Inanna in northern Europe were also called 'magi'. They had separated from the southern Chaldeans in the time of Peleg, after the Biblical Deluge.

Nowhere is Zoroaster Spitama, the founder of Zoroastrianism, ever described as a magi. After he experienced revelations from heaven, he was assassinated. It is believed that this crime was ordered by the Mithraic magi, resistant to a change of religion and threatened by Spitama's doctrine of non-intervention which rendered them obsolete. After Zoroaster Spitama's death the magi created the religion called Zoroastrianism, based upon his revelations but retaining their position as priests. Les Gosling writes of the Zoroastrian magi:

"They were astrologers of the first rank, and their influence was known over the ancient world. Providing occult information to the Medo-Persians and Babylonians at a kingly level *(Strabo, XVI,* 762; *Cicero, De Divin.,* 1, 41) the magi even made inroads into areas of Kashmir where ancient Isralites had established a colony. By the sixth century B.C. they had acquired power to overturn governments". *Herodotus, III,* 61 sq.

Olaf Hage who has a website called *The Chapel Perilous,* states the magi were Ephraimites. He further states, "The ancient 'G'KIM' of Daniel's and Joseph's times (the Biblical 'Magi') are hardly Persian in origin. The Persians captured them when they took Babylon. Babylon had taken them from Assyria in 612 BC. Assyria had captured them from Israel, as they reported on their tablets. Israel traced them back to Ephraim, the heir of Joseph, who was made their chief in Egypt, as *Genesis* states."

When the Medes stormed Babylon, as related in the *Book of Daniel,* they incorporated the Bel worshipping Ephraimite Chaldeans into their culture. These Chaldeans became Zoroastrian magi, and thus the Israelites became associated with Zoroastrianism. Martin Haug writes in *The Sacred Language, Writings, and Religions of the Parsis,* page 16: "The Magi are said to have called their religion Kesh-i-Ibrahim. They traced their religious books to Abraham, who was believed to have brought them from heaven."

The Israelite association explains the existence of a Jewish sect called the Essenes, whose members learned Zoroastrian doctrines. Jesus was an Essene, and Zoroastrian magi were deeply involved in the establishment of Christianity. The magian Christians were Manichaeans with ideas that contradicted both Zoroastrians and Christians. *Before the Burning Times,* a history of medieval culture, relates:

"Many of the more stubborn adherents were persecuted and executed in Sassania. That was until they banded together and retaliated against the magian hierarchy, they launced military attacks against them, then migrated westward, out of Persia and Iran. The only problem is that once they arrived in Christian Byzantium's outer provinces, they found themselves assailed by Christian forces . . ."

"Wherever they went to escape the violence of their many persecutors (whether Zoroastrians or Christians), the magian Christians were progressively exterminated, as at Anatolia where 100,000 were crucified in reprisals by Byzantine Christian troops. On top of that a further 200,000 were repatriated into the Balkans, into a plague city, where it was hoped that the last of them would die. But the plague lifted and these 200,000 extremely anti-Catholic, anti-Orthodox 'heretics' had found a new home."

"To the traditional Church authorities the Balkan Peninsula was akin to the mouth of Hades from which belched the pestilential teachings that gnawed away at the body of the Church. That was until Emperor Alexius decided to wipe them from the face of the earth in the 12th Century. But this "religious cleansing" of the Balkans backfired. Not too far away, in Germany, dazed Catholic priests watched on helplessly as streams of these war refugees started walking into the Holy Roman Empire en-masse, escaping Alexius' dragnet. Their bewilderment was caused by the rapturous welcome these refugees received from the German people who clapped adn cheered them on as they passed by."

A propaganda campaign was lauched declaring that the refugees were "black magi" (Satanists). Their association with the *Kabbalah* suggest that they were Israelites, descendants of the Ephraimite G'KIM. *Before the Burning Times,* speaks also of the magi who took refuge in Russia when Persia was invaded by Muslims:

"It took a mere 20 years for the Muslims to go on the war path after the death of their prophet Mohammed. Between AD 642 and the first decade of the 8th century AD, Arab Islamic forces pierced the vulnerable underbelly of magian Iran, and across the Oxus river into the lands of the nomadic Turkic tribes." In 712 AD Khorezm, a bastion of Zoroastrianism, fell to Islamic forces.

The magi "had ruled large tracts of Asia, served in the court of the Chinese Emperor, and studied alongside the priests, priestesses and philosophers of Greece, Rome, India and Egypt." *Before the Burning Times* goes on to relate how before the attack on Khorezm, magi had fled into Russia, bringing their books with them. They were given the name 'Kolduny', the Russian word for 'Chaldees', and were associated with both white and black magic.

The dying god (Mithra) was a deity revered throughout the ancient Near East, and whose death and resurrection was celebrated annually. And, in Babylon, in the sixth century BC, the god was introduced into the cult of the Chaldean Magi. Many scholars have recognized, that these Magi were not priests of orthodox Zoroastrianism. Rather, judging from their various tenets, which included a divine triad, pantheism, magic, astrology, number mysticism, the belief in reincarnation and the four elements, their cult was closer in similarity to the *Kabbalah,* believed also to have originated in Babylon in the same time frame the sixth century BC.

The creed of the Chaldean magi was introduced to Greece during the Persian invasions, and led to the emergence of what we call philosophy in that region. Then, with the conquests of Alexander, these doctrines were then spread to the rest of the known world, flourishing particularly at Alexanderia in Egypt, where they led to the formulation of Gnosticism, Neoplatonism, Hermeticism and the Ancient Mysteries.

The Cathars were a Manichaean sect who were among those magian Christians who had fled from Persia to the Balkans, then to Germany. They settled eventually in the south of France, where most of them were burned alive. This was also the fate of the Templar Knights. The Celts offered refuge to the victims of this persecution, if they could escape in time. Their own Druidic priests, now long converted to Christianity, had been magi themselves.

The northern magi who converted to Christianity en masse automatically ceased to be magi and destroyed their records. To the best of my knowledge Zoroastrian priests are no longer called magi, it is my personnal belief that they are what we call today - Freemasons.

***Enuma Elish* was written, which tells the story of Marduk's birth, heroic deeds, and becoming the ruler of the gods.**

## Mary 'the Temple Virgin'

Miriam, Mari, Maria, Mari Anna, Virgin Mary, St. Mary, "Black Madonna" or Mary 'the Temple Virgin', daughter of Joachim (Joakim) the High Priest of Jerusalem-the Jacob Patriarch (the son of Salome Alexandra II, the Maccabee Queen of Jerusalem) and Hannah (Annas) who was appointed High Priestess of Jerusalem-the Phanuel as Annas in AD 6-13.

The *Gospel of Luke 1:26,* states that Jesus Christ was the first born of Mary and the Archangel Gabriel. It is Gabriel who "came in unto her," and also then informs her that she "had found favor with the Lord" (Gabriel being the god Mithra which means "Lord") and "would conceive in her womb." Later Jesus has four younger brothers and at least two sisters *(Mark 6:3).* Roman Catholics are obliged to hold the opinion that the brothers and sisters of Jesus Christ were the children of Joseph by a former marriage.

This conclusion originally stemmed from the *Gospel of James* (the Protevanglium) that related to the age of Joseph at the birth of Jesus.

However, it was clearly recorded that Joseph had sex with Mary after the birth of Jesus. The statement in the *Gospel of Matthew* that Joseph 'knew her not until she had born a son. *(Matthew 1:25)*.

Joseph returned to Galilee with the intention of marrying Mary. The Gospels according to *Matthew* and *Luke* clearly explained that they were 'betrothed' before Joseph's departure. This was the equivalent of being `engaged' in modern-day terminology. However, upon his return some months later, it was plainly apparent that Mary `was with child' *(Luke 2:5)* and it 'could not be hid from Joseph'.

The *Gospel of Matthew* elaborated extensively upon the feelings of Joseph when he saw the violated condition of his bride-to-be. He was uneasy and being unwilling to defame her, he privately discussed ending their engagement *(Matthew 1:19)*. From the description in the Gospels, it was clear that Joseph was not the biological father of Mary's child.

According to the apocryphal *Gospel of James,* Mary was the daughter of Saint Joachim and Saint Anne. Before Mary's conception Anna had been barren. Mary was given to service as a consecrated virgin in the Temple in Jerusalem when she was three years old, much like Hannah took Samuel to the Tabernacle as recorded in the Old Testament. Some apocryphal accounts state that at the time of her betrothal to Joseph Mary was 13 years old.

On January 17, 1965, Pierre Plantard de Saint-Clair, Grand Master of Priory of Sion, released the following information that if made known would destroy religion as we know it! Plantard stated: "Joseph, an eighty-three year old octogenarian, had children from two or three former marriages when he married Miriam [Mary "the Virgin"], a thirteen year old girl who was fatherless since the age of ten. Miriam had been married for four months and had just reached fourteen when she found herself pregnant. Joseph who was an honest and kind man, became suddenly aware of this and thought at once of repudiating her in silence. He did not want to put the child that he loved on trial; it would have meant lapidation for her and scandal for him. You see,

Miriam was "black", as she was the daughter of Joachim "the black man converted to Judaism", and her mother was Anne, the prophtess. (Anne was seventy years old when she gave birth to Miriam; at the death of her husband Joachim, she retired to the Temple in Jerusalem). Anne was only recognised definitely as Miriam's mother, out of political necessity, during the Middle Ages. Miriam was heiress to her father's possessions. However, as she was underage, Joseph became her tutor and took charge of administering her inheritance, until such day when, out of interest as well as love, he married her secretly, whilst respecting her virtue. One can imagine his bitterness when he had to face the evidence regarding Miriam's condition. One can also understand why Joseph, who knew the father [Tibirius Julius Abdes Panthera, the son of Roman Emperor Tibirius I], accepted the situation and the fury of King Herod the Great at the birth of Jesus."

## MEGAERA

MEGAERA, daughter of Uranos (Anshar) and Gaea (Kishar). Known as the three FURIES or FAIRIES. The three virgin goddesses: ALLECTO, TISIPHONE, and MEGAERA. They defended mothers and the laws of blood relationship; revenge; justice against those who broke customs or taboos, social and bloodline laws. Later identified with the fairies. The angry ones; Avengers; the kindly ones; Children of Eternal Night; Daughters of Earth and Shadow. Punishers of sins, they had serpents twined in their hair and carried torches and whips. They tracked down those who wrongly shed blood, especially a mother's blood.

### Meshech

Meshech, son of Japhet (Japheth) and Adataneses. Founder of the tribe of Shibashni. Father of the Russians, the Moschians and the Muscovites. The descendants of Meshech are often spoken of in close association with those of Tubal, the Assyrians, for example, mentioning the Tabal and Musku, whilst Herodotus also writes of the Tiberanoi and Moschoi. A very much earlier reference to the posterity of Mesbech is an inscription of c.1200 BC which tells us how they overran the Hittite kingdom; and an inscription of Tiglath-Pileser I c.1100 BC, who tells us that, in his own day, the Muska-a-ia were able to put an army of 20,000 men into the field. The activities of this same people are also subsequently reported by Tukul-ti-ninurta II, Ashurnasirpal II, Sargon and Shalmaneser III, who refers to them as the Mushki. Josephus knew them as the Mosochenu (Mosoch), whom, he says were known in his days as the Cappadocians. He also points out that their chief city was known to his contemporaries as Mazaca, which was also once the name of the entire nation.

## Mízraím (Mítzraím)

Mizraim or Mitzraim, son of Chem (Ham) and Naelatamauk. Mizraim's descendants settled in Egypt. Father of the Kemi (Egyptians). Mizraim is still the Israeli name for that nation. The name is also preserved in the Ugaritic inscriptions as msrm; the Amar tablets as Misri; and in the Assyrian and Babylonian records as Musur and Musri. Modern Arabs still know it as Misr. Josephus relates a curious episode that he called the Ethiopic War, an incident that was apparently well known throughout the ancient world. According to this account, some six or seven nations descended from Mizraim were destroyed, clearly a major conflict that would have had profound and far-reaching repercussions on the world of those times. Josephus lists those nations that were destroyed as the Ludim, the Anamim, the Lehabim, the Naphtuhim, the Pathrusim, the Casluhim and the Caphtorim.

## MNEMOSYNE (Memory)

MINEMOSYNE by the Greeks, daughter of Uranos (Anshar) and Gaea (Kishar). Mother of the nine Muses. MEMORY by the Romans.

## Moses (Chabar)

Moses, Chabar, Jekuthiel, Jered, Abi Zanuch or Abigdor, son of Amram (father of the Amramites *(Numbers 3:27, 1 Chronicles 26:23)* and Tuya. Queen Consort of Pharaoh Seti I. Queen Tuya of Egypt died soon after year 22 of Pharaoh Ramesses II reign and was buried in an impressive tomb in the Valley of the Queens *(QV80)*. In her tomb, Tuya "was stripped of the first part of her name to become plain Tuya for enternity, the loss of the prefix Mut - suggest that her death had ended in an almost divine earthly status."

Moses was raised by princess Bathia, the daughter of Pharaoh Tao II 1574-1573 BC (also known as Seqenenre II, Taaiken and Hiram Abif) as her own son. *Exodus* 11:3 informs us that: "Moses was very great in the land of Egypt, in the sight of Pharaoh's servants, and in the sight of the people."

Moses later received the original *Twelve Commandments* and the *Kabala* from God (Yahweh, Jehovah) on Mount Sinai. The last two Commadments were later disgarded from the Hebrew/Jewish Torah and the Christian Bible. The original *Twelve Commandments* are:

I am the Lord thy God and . . .

Thou shalt have no other gods before me.

Thou shalt not make graven images.

Thou shalt not use the name of God in vain.

Remember the Sabbath day and keep it holy.

Honor thy father and mother.

Thou shalt not kill.

Thou shalt not steal.

Thou shalt not commit adultery.

Thou shalt not give false testimony.

Thou shalt not covet thy neighbor's wife or property.

Thou shall do only unto others as they would do unto you.

Thou shalt not follow the ways of the path of Baal.

*The Book of Jasher,* Chapter 77:38-51 - And afterward Moses went into the garden of Reuel which was behind the house, and he there prayed to the Lord his God, who had done mighty wonders for him. And it was that whilst he prayed he looked opposite to him, and behold a sapphire stick was placed in the ground, which was planted in the midst of the garden.

And he approached the stick and he looked, and behold the name of the Lord God of hosts was engraved thereon, written and developed upon the stick. And he read it and stretched forth his hand and he plucked it like a forest tree from the thicket, and the stick was in his hand.

And this is the stick with which all the works of our God were performed, after he had created heaven and earth, and all the host of them, seas, rivers and all their fishes.

And when God had driven Adam from the garden of Eden, he took the stick in his hand and went and tilled the ground from which he was taken.

And the stick came down to Noah and was given to Shem and his descendants, until it came into the hand of Abraham the Hebrew. And when Abraham had given all he had to his son Isaac, he also gave to him this stick.

And when Jacob had fled to Padan-aram, he took it into his hand, and when he returned to his father he had not left it behind him. Also when he went down to Egypt he took it into his hand and gave it to Joseph, one portion above his brethren, for Jacob had taken it by force from his brother Esau.

And after the death of Joseph, the nobles of Egypt came into the house of Joseph, and the stick came into the hand of Reuel the Midianite, and when he went out of Egypt, he took it in his hand and planted it in his garden.

And all the mighty men of the Kinites tried to pluck it when they endeavored to get Zipporah his daughter, but they were unsuccessful. So that stick remained planted in the garden of Reuel, until he came who had a right to it and took it.

And when Reuel saw the stick in the hand of Moses, he wondered at it, and he gave him his daughter Zipporah for a wife.

## MUL.LIT.TU (Hestia)

MUL.LIT.TU by the Sumerians, daughter of An.nu (Cronos) and An.tu (Rhea). HESTIA by the Greeks, daughter of Cronos (Annu) and Rhea (Antu). VESTA by the Romans. Hestia was the goddess of the hearth-fire of the household--for that was beneficial to humankind. Considered the oldest of the Olympians, she was venerated in all of Greece, and the fire of the hestia or public hearth was used in sacrifices and was never allowed to go out. She was considered a protectress of home, family, and city. Hestia is pictured as a robed woman who maintains an attitude of immobility. She inflicted illness or restored health; also ruled fate.

## MURAS

MURAS was a powerful leader from the Lyran chain of families. Muras came to Earth with thousands of his followers and built two cities on the opposite side of the planet called Mu. Mu (Pan, Mar, Muror) or Agharta Alpha was located in what is today the Gobi desert. Mu, named after its founder, grew to be a large city; it started to spread and after many years many cities were under the rule of Muras. Muras' kingdom later became known as Lemuria. Muras' other city Agharta Beta was located in what is today Antartica under the ice of the South Pole. The Nazis built an underground military base there in 1943 to continue work on their Pleiadian spacecraft technology. The underground base was abandoned in 1946 after it was attacked by an US Naval Fleet.

*Story of The Origin and Destiny of Man,* Lytle Robinson, cr 1972, pp. 110-111 - From the Cayce Records: One of the first lands to which the fleeing Atlanteans migrated during the upheavals was what is now Peru, then called Og, Oz, and On. This was the only large area of South America above water, and it was already occupied by a tribe of brown people known as the Ohums, or Ohlms, who were of Lemurian origin.

Lemuria had sunk into the Pacific Ocean with the first cataclysm. The Ohlms had come from the south when the lowlands went under, about 50,700 BC. They set up their communities to the north, established their homes, estates, and Temples of Mu. There were priests, priestess, ministers, teachers, "workers and shirkers" in this earliest of Peruvian cultures.

A peaceful people, they found themselves in a land rich in natural resources of gold and precious stones, and they soon became highly skilled craftsman in these trades. They also excelled in music, art, braiding of beads, and jewelery for bodily adornment.

The people were ruled by a line of monarchs, at least one of whom was a woman, who were known as the High Ohlm. But during the last rule an insurrection by the people succeeded in establishing new democratic principles of self-government.

With the coming of the Atlanteans and the people from the "South country" of On and Og, many changes again took place. At this time the land of the Ohlms was ruled by a weak leader who degraded himself by his sexual excesses. The invading Atlanteans brought conflict and bloodshed, and they succeeded in overthrowing the High Ohlm and sent him into exile, an action that brought popular approval and helped solidifying the country.

## Nabu (Anubis)

Nabiu, Nabu or Nabon by the Sumerians, son of Mar.duk (Phosphorus) and human female Zarpanitu (Sarpanit). Nebo the Babylonian [demi-] god of literature, wisdom and arts (*Isaiah* 46:1). Nabak by the Hebrews. [Demi-] God of writing and destiny; patron of scribes. It was believed he could increase or decrease the number of days allotted to a person. Represented death and sterility. His symbols were a serpent-headed dragon, an engraving tablet and chisel. He was called Shu or *"Dryness"* by the Egyptians. Nabu was the god from whom humanity learnt to write in script. In the Louvre there is a cylindrical releif sculpture upon which Nabu is depicted next to Marduk. Nabu's chief temple (ziggurat) was situated in Borsippa (now Birs NImrud, Iraq) and bore the name 'Temple of the Seven Command-Transmitters of the Heaven and the Earth'. Anpu and Anubis by the Egyptians.

Akhantuih (Ar-khan-too-ee) or "Negotiator of Chaos and alien energy fields" by the Atlanteans. ANUBIS by the Greeks, son of Hades (Nergal) and Persephone (Ereshkigal). SEKHEM EM PET and ANPU by the Egyptians. Messenger from the gods to humans. God of embalming, he presided over funerals and embalming, having invented the art when he preserved the body of Osiris so that the great god would live again. Jackal headed Egyptian god.

## NANNAR (Phobos)

PLEJOS by the Pleiadians. NANNA, NANNAK, NANNAR, NANNER or "The Bright One" and NUGIG or "He of the night sky" by the Sumerians, son of En.lil (Zeus) and Nin.lil (Hera). "Lord of Destiny". He is "Lord of the calendar", fixing the seasons, and also a vegetation-deity and patron of fertility. He has a beard of Lapis Lazuli and rides a winged bull. AKU, ZU, ZU.EN, EN.ZU, SU.EN, and SIN by the Akkadians.

He supervised the reconstruction of Sumer, rebuilding the pre-Diluvial cities at their original sites and establishing new cities. As the Moon God, his depictions included the crescent symbol of the Moon. The Chaldeans (Magi- "Wise Men") worshipped the moon god SIN, and so did the Hebrews who came after them. Sinai - the name of the triangle-shaped Peninsula wedged between Asia and Africa was called Til.mun or "Land of the Missiles" in Sumerian times. It was the 'Fourth Region' of the Anunnaki where their post-Diluvial spaceport was located. It and its skies, often served as an Anunnaki battlefield, culminating with the use of nuclear weapons at the time of Abraham. Six hundred years later it was the location of the events of the Exodus. The current name, Sinai, stems from the Bible, when and why its apparent association with the god Sin began, is not clear. He was called SORUSH by the ancient Persians. TASHMISHU by the Hittites. YERAH by the Canaanites. The moon-god was the chief deity of all the early South Arabian kingdoms. PHOBOS or "Moon" by the Greeks. The personification of Fear, who accompanied Ares on the battlefield. Phobos is a male deity. MANI by the Norse. Mani's potential connection to the Northern European notion of "the Man in the Moon". TECCIZTECATL by the Aztecs.

Shumer and the lands that stretched there from westward to the Mediterranean were put under the god Nannar's rule. Lord of the calendar; Lord of the diadem. He held the chief place in the astral triad along with Ishkur (Ares) and Ishtar (Asherah). He was shown as an old man with a long beard the color of lapis and wearing a turban. He rode in a boat (a brilliant crescent Moon, a space ship) across the skies, with the Full Moon as his diadem (crown). Enemy of evil doers; god of the measurement of time. SIN by the Akkadians, the king of the gods, became angry with his city and his temple, and went up to Heaven. His followers became known as the "sin fearing ones".

Ur, the city was the 'cult center' of Nannar/Sin that served three times as the capital of Sumer. The Ur III period (2113-2024 BC), considered the most glorious era of the Sumerian civilization, ended with Sumer's demise in the aftermath of the nuclear events of 2024 BC. At its peak, Ur was a walled city with a king's palace, administrative buildings, wide streets, schools, workshops, merchant's warehouses, two-storied dwellings, and a sacred precinct with a majestic ziggurat-temple with a monumental stairway for Nannar and his spouse Ningal. Its two harbors, linked by canals to the Euphrates River, enabled its merchants to trade with distant lands, importing metals and raw materials and exporting the garments for which Ur became famous. The Bible states that Abraham came to Harran from "Ur of One Chaldea". Zecharia Sitchen has suggested that he was actually born in Nippur, then grew up and was married in Ur, where his father Terah served as a priest. Some of the most artful artifacts discovered in Sumer were unearthed by Sir Leonard Woolley in what he termed 'The Royal Tombs of Ur'.

KHONSU, KHONS, CHONS, or KHENSU by the Egyptians. God of the Moon, Time, and Knowledge. His cult center was located in Thebes. "Traveller"; "The Navigator"; "He who crosses the sky in a boat"; God of the New Moon; son of Amen-Ra and Mut. He wore a skullcap topped by a disk in a crescent Moon. His head was shaved except for a scalp-lock tress of a royal child. His human body was swathed tightly, and he held a crook and flail. It was not until the New Kingdom that Khensu gained popularity as an exorcist and healer. The possessed and sick from Egypt and beyond flocked to his temples in Thebes, Ombos, and Karnak.

The Hebrews called him the Archangel YAHRIEL, YEHRA, YARHEIL, YACHADIEL, ZACHARIEL, TSAPHIEL, JIBRIL, JABRIEL, JIBRA'IL, JABRIYEL, and ABRUEL who had dominion over the Moon; and is called the "BRILLIANT EVENING STAR". The Chaldeans called him the messenger Archangel GABRIEL, which means "God is my strength". The Archangel Gabriel resides over Paradise, and although he is the ruling prince of the 1st Heaven, he is said to sit on the left-hand side of God. He is the Spirit of Truth. In Jewish legend it was Gabriel who dealt death and destruction to the sinful cities of the plain (Sodom and Gomorrah among them). Cabalists identify Gabriel as "the man clothed in linen" in *Exekiel 9-10.* In *Daniel 10-11* this man clothed in linen is helped by Michael. In rabbinic literature, Gabriel is the Prince of Justice. The name Gabriel is of Chaldean origin and was unknown to the Jews prior to the Captivity. According to the court testimony of Joan of Arc, it was Gabriel who inspired her to go to the succor of the King of France.

The Ancient Persians called him SORUSH, who is the archangel Gabriel, "giver of souls." The Magi held that, on Judgement Day, 2 angels, Sorush (Gabriel) and Mihr (Michael), will stand on the bridge called *al Sirat* (which is finer than a hair and sharper than the edge of a sword) and examine every person crossing. Mihr, representing divine mercy and holding a balance in his hand, will weigh the actions performed during the persons's lifetime. If found worthy, the person will be permitted to pass on to Paradise. Otherwise he will be handed over to Sorus, representing divine justice, who will hurl him or her into Hell. *The Koran*, "Preliminary Discourse," page 64.

*The Pleiadian Misson* by Randolph Winters - Salam (Enlil) ruled until he became old and weak, turning the rule over to his son Plejos (Gabriel) in 40 BC. Plejos was a peaceful ruler and had aligned himself with the High Council of the Pleiadian System. Two thousand years ago, Plejos, the last of the Pleiadian System leaders on Earth, was informed of the peace agreement between the Pleiades System and the High Council of Andromeda. A new era of spiritual growth and peace had come to the Pleiades, causing Plejos and his followers to want to return to their home system. It was decided to leave someone behind who could carry on the teachings of the Creational knowledge taught by the Pleiadians. However, they would need an Earthman who was a leader among men and who could carry on the teachings of their higher consciousness. This man was Emmanuel who was later called Jesus the Christ.

**Anunnaki god Nannar (Sin) and his symbol "crescent moon"**

## Napthtuhim (Naphtuchim)

Napthtuhim, Naphtuchim, or Neptune Marioticus, son of Mizraim (Mitzraim). Napthtuhim's descendants settled in the Nile Delta and the western parts of Egypt, where early records refer to them as the p't'mhw-literally, they of the Delta or Marshland.

## NASH (Nanshe)

NASH by the Sumerians, daughter of En.ki (Poseidon) and Nin.ki (Eos) and wife of the giant demi-god Haia (Hiya). Sumerian goddess of astronomical oracles. NANSHE by the Babylonians and Assyrians. Interpreter of dreams. Her priests probably used a cup for divination. To acquire prophetic powers, the priests underwent an initiation of descent into a pit, a symbol of death and resurrection (1st Degree of Freemasonry to the initiate is death and resurrection). Goddess of awareness and prophecy, springs and canals, dreams, regeneration, death. Evil Spirit of the 'False Prophet'.

## Nebet (Nepthys)

Nebet by the Akkadians, daughter of Semjasa (Oz) and human female Nraa (Noraia). Nepthys by the Egyptians.

## NER.GAL (Hades)

NAGAR by the Sumerians. NER.GAL, NAR.GAL or "Great Watcher" by the Sumerians, son of En.ki (Poseidon) and Nin.ki (Eos). He is described as being bald and walking with a limp from birth. Nergal the "war god" of the men of Cuth, in Media-Persia *2 Kings* 17:30. ALLUL, ALLA by the Akkadians. ADAH by the Hebrews. In the Hebrew Bible they are called "the sons of Adah". ALLAH and ALLA by the Arabs.

MESHLAMTHEA, MESLAMTAEA, ERRA or "The Annihilator" by the Babylonians. Lord of the great dwelling; Lord of attack; God of the Underworld (Netherworld); Judge of the dead. A form of the black Underworld Sun, his symbol was a sword or lion's head. Shown wearing a crown and attended by fourteen terrible demons. When he was exiled to the Underworld, he conquered Ereshkigal, who became his wife. Ruler over the southernmost parts of Africa. Nergal was consumed with personal hatred toward his brother and nephew: *"I shall annihilate the son (Nabu), and let the father bury him; then I shall kill the father (Marduk), let no one bury him!"* To the Akkadians he was a lion-headed god. To the Babylonians he was a human-headed god with a lion's body (the Sphinx), that had wings. To the Chaldeans he was one of four principal protecting genii (guardian angels). Nergal and Ereshkigal ruled from the Diligina (Ekalgina) palace located in

Arallu (Andurana, Ganzir, Shualu) an underworld kingdom were the dead are judged.

HADD by the northern Semites. HADES or "Lord of the Lower World" by the Greeks. The invisible one; ruler of the Underworld and wealth. Absolute master in the Underworld. His helmet of invisibility allowed only the initiated to see him. PLUTO, PLOUTOS, PLUTON or "Lord of Riches" by the Romans. WE by the Nordic-Germanic tribes. LOKI and HALOGE by the Nordic-Scandinavians. Haloge came north with Odin, and began to reign over northern Norway, which from him was called Halogaland. His principal temples were at Pylos, Athens, and Olympia in Elis. He was both the mysterious, terrifying god of death and the benign god of prosperity. The house of Hades was the place of shades, or the dead.

## Nimrod (Nimrud)

Usmu, Isimud, Nimurda, Nimrud, Nimrod, Nebrod, Idzubar, Eannus, Janus, or Kazartu, son of Cush (Kush) and Candace. King of Kush (Nubia) and Bebel (Babylon), Accad (Akkad) and others in the land of Shinar (Sumer). Human sacrifice was practiced by his Babylonian priest who were required to eat some of their sacrificial offerings.

The Chaldeans had Idzubar (Nimrod), a hero, shown in all the tablets as a mighty giant who towered in size above all other men as the cedar towers over brushwood-a hunter, according to cuneiform legends, who contended with and destroyed the lion, tiger, wild bull, and buffalo. Nimrod was born on December 25. In an ancient picture of Nimrod he is pictured with a long flowing beard, holding a reindeer in one hand and a fur tree in the other hand with wings on his back. According to his wife/mother (2300 BC), who stated after his death, that the spirit of Nimrod sprouted out of a fur tree stump every December 25th and he put presents under the tree. Pope Liberius in AD 374 officially declared that we should celebrate Jesus Christ birthday on

December 25th eventhough most of the early Christians in the Roman Empire celebrated his birth at that time on January 6th. Most of the Eastern Orthodox Church today still celebrate Jesus Christ birthday on January 6th. Christmas was not even celebrated in America until 1828, after the Christmas Carol was published.

The Hebrew Talmud stresses that: while "Esau spent his days hunting and that an arrow from his bow killed the giant Nimrod. Nimrod was given the title Baal (the Lord). He was also Eannus, the god with two faces, who was later called Janus by the Romans.

Writing in 1876, George Smith tells us that, 'Nearly thirteen hundred years before the Christian era, one of the Egyptian poems likens a hero to the Assyrian chief, Kazartu, a great hunter . . . and it has already been suggested that the reference here is to the fame of Nimrod. A little later in the period 1100 to 800 BC, we have in Egypt many persons named after Nimrod, showing a knowledge of the mighty hunter there.' *Chaldean Genesis* p. 313.

King Nimrod was probably the most notorious man in the ancient world who is discredited with instigating the Great Rebellion at Babel (Babylon), and founding the very features of paganism, including the introduction of magic astrology and human sacrifice. There is, moreover, much evidence to suggest that he himself was worshipped from the very earliest times. His name, for example was perpetuated in those of Nimurda, the Assyrian god of war, Marduk, the Babylonian king of the gods; and the Sumarian deity Amarutu. His image was likewise incorporated very early on in the Chaldean zodiac as a child seated on his mother's lap, and both mother and child were worshipped-a pattern since repeatedly followed throughout history. A mountain not far from Ararat has been called Nimrud Dagh (Mount Nimrod) from the earliest times. One of the chief cities of Assyria was named Nimrud, and the Plain of Shinar, known to the early Syrians as Sen'ar, was itself once known as the Land of Nimrod. Iraqi and Iranian Arabs speak his name with awe even today. Nimrod's city - now known as Nimrud, but in the early days called Kalhu, which is synonymous with the Calah mentioned in *Genesis* 10:8-12. Nimrod's kingdoms of Babel and Accad are self-explanatory, being Babylon and Akkad respectively.

*Book of Jasher* - Chapter 12 verses 24-30 - "And the garments of skin which God made for Adam and his wife, when they went out of the garden, were given to Cush. For after the death of Adam and his wife, the garments were given to Enoch, the son of Jared, and when Enoch was taken up to God, he gave them to Methuselah, his son. And at the death of Methuselah, Noah took them and brought them to the ark, and they were with him until he went out of the ark. And in their going out, Ham stole those garments from Noah his father, and he took them and hid them from his brothers. And when Ham begat his first born Cush, he gave him the garments in secret, and they were with Cush many days. And Cush also concealed them from his sons and brothers, and when Cush had begotten Nimrod, he gave him those garments through his love for him, and Nimrod grew up, and when he was twenty years old he put on those garments. And Nimrod became strong when he put on the garments, and God gave him might and strength, and he was a mighty hunter in the earth, yea, he was a mighty hunter in the field, and he hunted the animals and he built altars, and he offered upon them the animals before the Lord."

Nimrod married his mother Ester when Moses (Musa) was sent to the devils 4,000 years ago. This meant the end of the Blackman's power to keep them in their boundaries of Europe. This brought them out of the caves putting them on the road to the conquest of Asia, (Black, Brown, Red and Yellow man). Nimrod killed his father and began sleeping with his mother, Ester, known today as the holiday called Easter. She had children by her son Nimrod, making Nimrod his own father and son, which was the beginning of the lie that God and son are one And the same. It's true that this made Nimrod, his own father but the father and the son could never be identical. This is also where the lie originated of the "Immaculate Conception" woman giving birth without the agency of man. Nimrod and his mother were worshipped by the people, and knowing that if they found out that she was bearing her son's children they would not respect her, she lied telling the people that the spirit was visiting her, giving her babies.

The people, being paganish, believed those lies thus establishing a holiday called Easter commemorating her birthday. They used the sign of the rabbit, which is an over-sexed animal; and eggs representing the first stage of the "embryo" chicken, which is capable of laying eggs without a male, was also used. Nimrod would go into Asia robbing the brothers of their wealth. Using his unalike attracting power, he was able to steal and divide the brothers. The cross originated as a symbol meaning death and dividing the four brothers, so that Nimrod could rule. The cross is used in most European nations today in their flag in the same form.

Christmas being Nimrod's birthday has all the signs; the evergreen meaning everlasting life for the Caucasian; the ornaments signifies all the riches and pretty things that the Blackman has. The star on the top of the tree, meaning the devils brain as being powerful enough to keep the Blackman divided, or in the cross. Santa Claus is the symbol of Nimrod bringing gifts back to Europe from Asia. A pagan religion was adopted by the Jews in Judaism. They didn't want the Blackman's religion, Islam, nor would they accept the Yellowman's religion, Buddhism, the whiteman had to invent himself a religion that would fit his nature, for his being evil, his religion had to be flexible enough to allow him to practice his evil and worship statues, drink blood (wine), eat [body flesh], etc.

They applied the teachings of Moses to paganism, thus Judaism began. Judaism kept the Jews a united people. The other devils used parts of Judaism, paganism and combined all those teachings together, thus began Catholicism, out of Catholicism they invented Christianity 551 years ago. We wouldn't expect a whiteman to accept a Black, Brown, Read and Yellowman's religion. They hate everything Black . . . That stands for Black.

Christmas was set up as a memorial to Nimrod. The Christmas tree is an Evergreen tree, this means that it is green or has life, all year round and does not die out like other trees.

Evergreen tree is used at Christmas as a symbol to represent everlasting life for the white race.

It sits in a box held in place by a cross which represents the division of the four brothers; Black, Brown, Red and Yellow, which support the white race.

The trinkets and ornaments represents the riches, wealth and knowledge of the Blackman which was stolen by Nimrod and brought back to the white race in Europe.

The star on top of the tree represents the superior brain power of the white race to remain on top.

Santa Claus represents Nimrod bringing the riches of the Blackman back to Europe. (They do not explain where Santa Claus gets the presents from do they). Santa Claus robbing Black people at Christmas is similar to Nimrod's work. This also is included at the end of Nimrod's history: Judaism is a mixture of Moses teachings, Islam, and paganism to make it more flexible.

December 25th is the birthday of Nimrod. Nimrod is mentioned in the Bible (Old Testament) as a mighty hunter in opposition to God. This is because he turned against the teachings of Moses. Nimrod was a white man who was born 300 years before Christ. He took the teachings of Moses and used them as a game to set up the early pagan Empires such as Greece and Rome. According to the Bible, he is the son of Cush. He went among the pagan white people of Europe who rejected the teachings of Moses and used the knowledge to become ruler of the people. Nimrod killed his father and married his mother whose name was Semiramis. When Nimrod's wife/mother had her first child he feared that the people would lose respect for him if they knew he was making babies through his own mother (it was a secret that they were married) therefore, to fool the people, Nimrod told the people that the

Holy Ghost had impregnated his mother. This was the beginning of the great lie told about the birth of Jesus. The lie that a woman can have a baby without the agency of the male sperm. This lie began 300 years before Jesus was born.

Easter is Ester's birthday. The rabbit is used because he is an oversexed animal (but a rabbit does not lay eggs). There is more to this but I will not include it now. Just like Alexander the Great, Nimrod went among the original people to divide and rob them of their wealth. To rob the original has always been the work of the white race. Nimrod would bring the wealth back to his own people in Europe. For this they loved him as a ruler. This is what all white explorers and conquerors have done; from John Hawkins to the Peace Corps.

Nimrod started the great organized worldly apostasy from God that has dominated this world until now. Nimrod married his own mother, whose name was Semiramis. After Nimrod's death, his so-called mother-wife, Semiramis, propagated the evil doctrine of the survival of Nimrod as a spirit being. She claimed a full-grown evergreen tree sprang overnight from a dead tree stump, which symbolized the springing forth unto new life of the dead Nimrod. On each anniversary of his birth, she claimed, Nimrod would visit the evergreen tree and leave gifts upon it. December 25th, was the birthday of Nimrod. This is the real origin of the Christmas tree.

Traditionally, a yule log was burned in the fireplace on Christmas Eve and during the night as the log's embers died, there appeared in the room, as if by magic, a Christmas tree surrounded by gifts. The yule log represented the sun-god Nimrod and the Christmas tree represented himself resurrected as his own son Tammuz. So our Christmas tree - and our yule log - have tremendous meaning, but not a Christian meaning. The yule log is the dead Nimrod, human ruler of ancient Babylon, who was eventually deified as the sun incarnate, and hence a god. The Christmas tree is mystical Tammuz, the slain god come to life again.

The real origin of Christmas goes back to ancient Babylon. It is bound up in the organized apostasy with which Satan has gripped a deceived world these many centuries! In Egypt, it was always believed that the son of Iris (Egyptian name for "Queen of Heaven") was born December 25th. Semiramis also bore the title "Queen of Heaven" - and she was Nimrod's mother. Paganism celebrated this famous birthday over most of the known world for centuries before the birth of Christ.

Jesus Christ was not born on December 25th. December 25th can be traced back to *Genesis* and a man named Nimrod. Nimrod was the founder of a great false religious system that began in ancient Babylon that has always opposed the truths of God. It's time we face facts! This world is deceived, just as God prophesied it would be (*Revelation* 12:9). Satan is the power behind this deception.

Satan has successfully pawned off the old customs of the Babylonian mystery religion as being pleasing to Jesus Christ. Nimrod, who built Babel or Babylon, conceived a one world government model in rebellion against Jehovah-God and went about to establish a one world government in the land of Shinar (which is today known as Iraq) and institute a pagan worship system that rejected the Lord God Jehovah. Not only has the original Babylonian religious system served as the source of all the world's non-Christian religions, hut it has also infiltrated and corrupted Christendom to an alarming degree.

Much of the Babylonian worship was carried on through mysterious symbols - thus the "Mystery" religion. This system of idolatry spread from Babylon to the nations, for it was from this location that men were scattered over the face of the earth (*Genesis* 11:9). As they went from Babylon, they took their occult worship and its various mystery symbols with them.

## NIN.A.GAL (Alalgar)

ALAL.GAR by the Anunnaki. A.DAR, NIN.A.GAL, NINA.GAL, NIN-AGAL or *"Prince of the Great Waters"* by the Sumerians, son of En.ki (Poseidon) and Nin.ki (Eos). The 'Lord strong-arm' patron god of smiths. He chews copper and makes tools. ALAL.JAR by the Akkadians. Second King of Eridug (Eridu) as Alalngar (Alalgar, Alaljar) for 10 sars or 36,000 years.

## NIN.DUR.RA (Duttur)

NIN.KUR.RA by the Sumerians, daughter of En.ki (Poseidon) and Nin.sar. NIN.DUR.RA by the Akkadians. DUTTUR by the Babylonians. Wife of her father En.ki (Poseidon) and mother of daughters Gesh.ti.nan.na and Ut.tu.

## NIN.GAL (Artemis)

PLEJA by the Pleiadians. NIN.GAL or "Great Lady" by the Sumerians, daughter of En.ki (Poseidon) and Nin.gi.kuga. Moon goddess. NIK.HAL, NIK.KAL by the Akkandians. BAST, BASTET, and PASHT by the Egyptians. Cat-headed goddess; mother of all cats. Lady of the East; associated with the god SEPT or "Lord of the East." The cat was Egypt's most sacred animal but the black cat was especially sacred to her; Egyptians physicians used the black cat symbol in healing. Cats were sacred to her in general, kept in her temple, and embalmed when they died. To kill a cat meant a death sentence. Bast carried a sistrum in her right hand and a basket in her left. She was generally draped in green.

ARTEMIS by the Greeks, daughter of Zeus (Enlil) and Leto. ARDUINA by the Sicambrians. DIANA by the Romans. PERATHEA by the Hittites. POTNIA and DIONE in Latin. She was originally known as a moon goddess and was associated with lunar light and the crescent moon. Later she became known as a goddess of the hunt and protectress of women in childbirth. She is the goddess of untamed nature and the "lady of the breast" -

a virgin goddess who hunted deer with silver arrows. She was destructive to those who displeased her, but beneficial to her worshippers. At times she is depicted as having many breast, a reference to her powers of fertility. At other times she is flanked by lions, dancing with a stag, or holding a slain deer in each hand. Artemis or Diana was one of the major deities of the Merovingians. Artemis was symbolised with bees, as is the Merovingian bloodline. DIANA an ancient Italian woodland goddess, a patroness of wild things and of women.

Artemis the "Virgin Huntress"; goddess of wild places and wild things; the Huntress; Maiden; Bear Goddess; Moon Goddess; Hunter of Souls; shape-shifter. In Ephesus she was called "many-breasted" and was the patroness of nurturing, fertility, and birth. In Greece she was sculpted as tall, slim, lovely, and dressed in a short tunic. Her chariot was pulled by silver stags. She roamed the forests, mountains, and glades with her band of nymphs and hunting dogs. She acted swiftly and decisively to protect and rescue those who appealed to her for help and was quick to punish offenders. She new the deep secret places in Nature where one could rest and regain strength.

The Amazons, who were loyal to her, worshipped one aspect of this Moon Goddess (the New Moon phase). Acorns were the symbol of her association with forests and the woodlands. Goddess of the hunt accompanied by a stag and the Alani (her pack of hounds), she carried a silver bow. Her priestess did not consort with men, but the goddess helped women in childbirth. She could bring destruction but was usually benign. Her animals were guinea fowl, dog, horse, stag. Her symbols were the sickle, bridle, spinning distaff, hanks of wool. The sixth day from the New Moon was hers. Defender of women who were harassed or threatened by men. Very beneficial when dealing with animals or the elemental kingdoms. Patroness of singers; protector of young girls; mistress of magic, sorcery, enchantment, psychic power, women's fertility, purification, sports, exercise, good weather for travellers, countryside, the hunt, mental healing, dance, wild animals, forests, mountains, woodland medicines, juniper, and healing.

## NIN.GI.KUGA

NINGIKUGA or "Lady of the Pure Reed" by the Sumerians, daughter of An.nu (Cronos) and Nin.ul (Perseis). Wife of En.ki (Poseidon) and mother of daughter Nin.gal (Artemis). She is the goddess of reeds and marshes.

## NIN.GISH.ZIDDA (Hermes)

NIN.AZU or "Lord of the Artifact" by the Sumerians, son of En.ki (Poseidon) and E.resh.ki.gal (Persephone). NIN.GISH.ZIDDA by the Akkadians. TOTH, THOTH and IBIS, "God of the Scribes" by the Egyptians. About 15,000 BC, Thoth brings Atlantean wisdom through Atalantes to Cyrene (in Libya), Lake Tritonis on the sacred hill Phla, later to be worshipped on the island of Philae in Egypt.

THOTH was known as the recording angel and is said to have been the inventor of astronomy, science, mathematics, magic and writing. He was an arbiter between the gods and healed both Horus and Seth after their battle. The god Thoth possed all secret knowledge (the Emerald Tablet) on 36,535 scrolls that were hidden under the heavenly vault (the sky) which could only be found by the worthy, who would use such knowledge for the benefit of mankind. In the Egyptian legends a passage of Manetho, in which Thoth, before the Deluge, inscribed on stelae, or tablets, in hieroglyphics, or sacred characters, the principles of all knowledge. After the Deluge the second Thoth translated the contents of these stelae into the vulgar tongue. Edgar Cayce stated that a hidden chamber with hidden knowlege would one day be found under the left paw of the Sphinx.

In the ancient City of Anu (later called 'On' in the Bible, 'Heliopolis' by the Greeks, and later modern 'Ciaro') there is a pillar called the 'Pillar of

Anu'-'Pillar of Shu'-'Pillar of Thoth'-'Pillar of Hermes'-'Pillar of Seth'- 'Pillar of Solomon'-'Pillars of the Gods of the Dawning Light' and the 'Gate of the Hall of Truth'. Two pillars were removed from the Temple of Amen (Enki/Satan) at Heliopolis in 1880. One was erected on the Thames River bank in London, England and the second one was erected in Central Park, New York City in United States of America. The *New York Herald,* 13 Febraury 1880, stated the following:

*"The obelisk and its foundations will be removed and replaced in New York exactly in the positions in which they were found, each having been numbered to correspond with numbers on a drawing that was made before the pieces were removed." The monument was erected by Thothmes III at the outer porch of the Temple of Amen at Heliopolis, where it and its twin (now in London) guarded the entrance of the temple for 2,000 years before they were moved to Alexandria. On 12 June 1880, with the assistance of Mr. Zola, Most Worshipful Grand Master of Egypt, the obelisk was entrusted to Lieutenant Commander H. H. Gorringe, U.S.N. [United States Navy], a member of Anglo-Saxon Lodge No. 137, for shipment to New York. On 9 October 1880 the obelisk was raised with great Masonic ceremonies in Central Park, New York City. With 8,000 Masons in attendance, the cornerstone of the ancient obelisk was laid by Jesse B. Anthony, Grand Master of Masons in New York State, as 30,000 awe-struck spectators and curiosity seekers watched, wondering what the strange rites they were seeing performed meant."*

KUKULCAN by the Maya of the Yukatan. QUETZALCOATL or the "White Plumed Serpent god" or the "Winged Serpent God" by the Aztecs. His arrival (3114 BC) was the beginning date of the first calendar instituted by him in Mesoamerica by the Maya.

Who was the warrior called Quetzalcoatl? He was a very high-ranking officer of an extraterrestrial group (Anunnaki) that was exercising control over Egypt for a short time. He was wise and kind and was often sent on special missions. One of the missions took him to South America, where he was praised as a god by the Maya and Aztecs. He came into contact with Huitzilopochtli, a leader of the Gizeh people, who led the Aztecs into creating the ritual of human blood sacrifices. Quetzalcoatl was against these rituals and a bitter feud developed for power. In the end Huitzilopochtli was able to drive Quetzalcoatl out, forcing his return to Egypt. *The Pleiadian Mission,* by Randolph Winters, cr1994, p.191.

Quetzalcoatl, the Lord of the Morning Star, was a benign serpent-like (reptilian like) god worshiped by the Toltec Mexicans as the bringer of light to his people and fertility to the land. Sometimes he appeared arched across the sky, and other times he could adopt human form - either a young man in a feathered cloak, or an old man with a broken walking stick and a white beard - and mingled amongst his subjects.

Ningishzidda is the archangel RAPHAEL or "God has healed", of Chaldean origin, originally called LABBIEL. Raphael is one of 3 great angels in post-Biblical lore. He first appears in The Book of Tobit, Raphael acts as companion and guide to Tobit's son Tobias who journeys to Media from Nineveh. It is only at the end of the journey that Raphael reveals himself by name as "one of the 7 holy angels" that attend the throne of God. In *Enoch I, 20,* Raphael is declared to be "one of the watchers". In *Enoch I, 22,* Raphael is a guide in sheol (the underworld). In *Enoch I, 40,* he is "one of the 4 presences, set over all the diseases and all the wounds of the children of men." Rabbi Abba in *The Zohar I:* "Raphael is charged to heal the earth, and through him . . . the earth furnishes an abode for man, whom also he heals of his maladies." According to *Gamatria (Cabala)* and *Yoma 37a,* Raphael is one of the 3 angels that visited Abraham *(Genesis 18),* the other 2 angels identified usually as Gabriel and Michael. Raphael is credited also with healing Abraham of the pain of circumcision, the patriarch having neglected to observe this rite earlier in life. In *The Legends of the Jews I, 385,* Raphael is the angel sent by God to cure Jacob of the injury to his thigh when Jacob wrestled with his dark adversary at Peniel (the adversary having been identified variously as Sammael/Satan).

Another legend *(Sefer Noah)* claims it was Raphael who handed Noah, after the flood, a "medical book", which may have been the famous *Sefer Raziel (The Book of the Angel Raziel).* Among other high offices, Raphael is the regent of the sun (Longfellow refers to him as the angel of the sun), chief of the order of virtues, governor of the south, guardian of the west, ruling prince of the 2nd Heaven, overseer of the evening winds, guardian of the Tree of Life in the Garden of Eden, one of the 6 angels of repentance, angel of prayer, love, joy, and light. Above all, he is, as his name denotes, the angel of healing (Aslepios, ancient Greek god of healing). He is also the angel of science and knowledge, and the preceptor angel of Isaac. Barrett, *The Magus H.*

Raphael belongs to at least 4 of the celestial orders: seraphim, cherubim, dominions (or dominations), and powers. According to Trithemius of Spanheim, the 15th-century occultist, Raphael is one of the 7 angels of the Apocalypse. He is also numbered among the 10 holy sefiroth. And while he is not specifically named as the angel who troubled the waters at the pool in ancient Bethesda *(John 5),* he is generally so credited. The file on Raphael is inexhaustible, but one additional legend may be worth repeating here: it is taken from Conybeare, The Testament of Solomon. When Solomon prayed to God for help in the building of the Temple, God answered with the gift of a magic ring brought to the Hebrew king personally by Raphael. The ring, engraved with the pentalpha (5-pointed star), had the power to subdue all demons. And it was with the "slave labor" of demons that Solomon was able to complete the building of the Temple. Raphael is credited also with healing Abraham of the pain of circumcision, the patriarch having neglected to observe this rite earlier in life. In The Legends of the Jews I, 385, Raphael is the angel sent by God to cure Jacob of the injury to his thigh when Jacob wrestled with his dark adversary at Peniel. One additional legend is taken from Conybeare.

TA-KHU (Tar-Koo), TAT-TET, TEHUTI, TAHUTI, AT-HOTHES, and DJEHOTI by the Atlanteans. TAK.HU, TEK.HI, and TU.KE by the Sumerians. TAAUT by the Phoenicians. HERMES TRISMEGISTUS or "the ram-bearer" by the Greeks, son of Zeus (Enlil) and Maia. The Greek god of commerce, science, invention, cunning, eloquence, and theft in *Acts 14:12.* MERCURY by the Romans. VRI-TAKA or DHRI-TAKA by the indians of the Indus Valley.

TEHUTI (Hermes), ruler of Atlantis for thousands of years. Tehuti was described as being twenty seven feet tall and having full use of his brain which was shaped differently from a modern human brain of today (elongated skull). They travelled inter dimensionally in space craft. They also wore breastplates and head pieces made of a metal called electrum (transmuted platinum). The jewels encrusted in them, as well as in their sandals contained special crystals that were used as communication devices. (See Aaron-first high priest of Israel)

HERMES the second son of the god Zeus (Enlil) and goddess Maia, patron of shepherds, guardian of the flocks and herds. He was closer to human affairs; any stroke of good luck was attributed to him. As Giver of Good Things, he was the deity in charge of commerce, patron of merchants and travelers. But his main role in myth and epic was as herald of Zeus, Messenger of the Gods.

He was the grandson and messenger of Cronos. It was his duty to bring the dictates of the gods to earth. Primarily a god of travelers, he guided those who were journeying. He was charged with the duty of conducting the souls of the dead to the underworld. He is often represented as a swift-footed, (sometimes bearded) athletic god, wearing a winged helmet and winged sandals. Hermes holds a winged staff with two serpents twined around it--the caduceus.

MERCURY by the Romans. In the Cabala, the angel of progress, also a designation for Raphael. *Acts* 14:11-12; Levi, *Transcendental Magic.*

## NIN.IB (Saosis)

NINIB by the Sumerians, daughter of Enu.ru and Ninu.ru. The Anunnaki have access to a plant (or tree), native to Sumi-Er, that prevents normal aging and bodily deterioration. Sumerian texts referred to it as the "Tree of Life". Later, the Bible referred to it as 'Knowledge of The Tree of Life' in the Garden of Eden story. Only the Anunnaki royalty had privileged access to the Tree of Life (sometimes called Ambrosiac in Sumerian texts). They absorbed this substance into their bodies by taking baths soaked with this life extending plant. This special bath water was the origin of the story of The Fountain of Youth.

IUSAASET, JUESAES, AUSAAS, IUSAS, and JUSAS or "the great one who comes forth" by the Egyptians. SAOSIS by the Greeks.

## NIN.KI (Eos)

DAM.KI.NA or "lady of that which is below," and DAM.GAL.NUN.NA or "great lady of the waters," who was the "spouse who to earth came" by the Anunnaki. NIN.KI, NIN.KA or "god of sweet waters" by the Sumerians, daughter of Kin.gu (Hyperion) and Theia. She was also known as DAM.GAL.NUN.NA or DAM.GAK.NU.NA, wife of Gugalanna (Enki), the monstrous Bull of Heaven. ANGRBODA by the Nordic-Germans.

ISHTAR, ESHDAR and TASHMETUM by the Assyrians. In ancient Sumeria, she had 180 shrines where women gathered daily for prayer, meditation, and socializing. The night of the Full Moon, known as Shapatu, saw joyous celebrations in her temples. At these rites, called the sacred Qadishtu, women who lived as priestesses in her shrines took lovers to express the sacredness of sexuality as a gift from Ishtar. Men communed with the goddess in these rites through sex. Every woman once in her life had to sit in the temple grounds of Ishtar's temples and wait for a man to drop a coin in her lap. Then she had to lie with him. Until this was done, the woman could not marry. Goddess of the positive and negative sides of all she ruled. Patroness of priestesses. Radiant, sweet, and delightful, but also could be stern, cruel, and bad tempered. HEPET and HEBAT or "Lady of the Skies" by the Hittites. ASHRATU by the Babylonians.

ASHIRAT, ASHERAT, ATHIRAT or "the lady of the sea" by the Canaanites. Lady of sorrows and battles; Queen or Lady of Heaven; Goddess of the Moon and evening; Great Mother; Shining One; Mother of Deities; Producer of Life; Creator of People; Guardian of Law and Order; Ruler of the Heavens; Source of Oracles of Prophecy; Lady of Battles and Victory; Lady of Vision; Possessor of the Tablets of Life's Records. As a warrior goddess, she carried a bow and rode in a chariot drawn by seven lions. Other images show her seated on her lion throne, with horns, a bow and arrows, a tiara crown, a double serpent scepter, holding a sword, or with dragons by her sides. Her symbols were the eight-point star, the pentagram, dove, serpents, and the double axe; her planet the Moon. She wore a rainbow necklace.

ATHIRAT or ASHERAT-OF-THE-SEA by the Canaanites. Mother of the gods; goddess of the sea. Her offspring were called Dactyls or "Fingers". Divine Beings. They were spirits, five males from her right hand, five females from her left hand. They were blacksmiths, magi (now freemasons), founders of the meter, inventors of magical formulae. A form of the Earth elementals. She was also known as the SHEKINAH or MATRONIT.

ASHTORETH by the Philistines, Zidonians and Phoenicians. ASHTAROTH by the Hebrews. This is the plural Hebrew form for the Canaanite goddess Astarte, one of the dominant female deities of fertility. From the numerous 'Astarte' plaques discovered in archaeological excavations, this goddess was usually represented as naked. The name is often used as a general term for female deities of Canaan. Her symbols are the lion, the rosette, and the eight-pointed star. As Asherah which translated as "straight", or "pillar"; the goddess was worshipped in the form of a "tree" or a "straight wooden staff". Her tree or staff symbol was eventually replaced by the image of the menorah. She is the goddess of planting and childbirth. Known as a huntress and warrior, she was primarily worshipped as a goddess of love, sex, and fertility.

ASHERAH or "the woman who made towers" by the Hebrews. This is the Hebrew rendering of Ashirat, the leading goddess of the Phoenician Canaanites and the consort of the head of their pantheon. She represented the female principle in the fertility cult. Asherah was worshipped by the Hebrews for six centuries-even in the first and second temples at Jerusalem. Her statue had been brought to the temple by King Solomon, who later possessed the "White Stone", the "Stone of Destiny". Also called the "Stone of Ana", the "Lia Fail", a phallic standing stone, which is one of the four treasures brought to Ireland by the Tuatha De Danaan, the direct decendants of the "Shinning Ones". On the Hill of Tara, in County Meath, Ireland, stood the great "Stone of Ana", the "Ish-Tar Gate" to the Otherworld (Netherworld), Egyptian-Neter World, Neteru (Nibiru/Atlantis). From the earliest dawn of Irish mythology Celtic rites were performed here. When the true king leapt onto this "Stone of Light", it shrieked. The stone was used for healing and prophesy. Asherah, which translates as "oak grove." It was her rod of Peace. It was once housed in the City of Peace (Jerusalem) atop Mount Moriah. *1 Kings 11:5* states Solomon turned his heart away from Yahweh and chose Astarte (Ishtar). The Ashera, which is translated "grove", was a "phallic object" used in connection with the worship of the goddess Astarte in Solomon's Temple. The Ashera or Ashtoreth was an upright stem or pole, an obelisk.

The Holy or Holies, or inner sanctuary, in King Solomon's Temple was deemed to represent the womb of Ashtoreth, alternatively called ASHERAH, as mentioned several times in the Old Testament. Her statue had been brought to the temple by King Solomon. Ashtoreth was openly worshipped by the Israelites until the 6th century BC--even in the first and second temples. Her tree-symbol was eventually replaced by the image of the menorah. In pre-patriarchal Jerusalem, the Menorah---the 7 branched candlestick, originally symbolized the Pleiades in their aspect of the sevenfold "Men-horac" or "Moon Priestess".

During the reign of King Ahab, his queen, Jezebel of Tyre, who had brought her worship of the Tyrian gods to her adopted land, secured official status for 'the four hundred and fifty prophets of Baal and the four hundred prophets of Asherah'. *(1 Kings 18:19)* This led to the dramatic confrontation with Elijah on Mount Carmel. King Josiah destroyed the Asherah idol in Jerusalem. Is is occasionally mentioned in the Bible to denote a wooden cult object. It also appears in the plural form, in both genders, as Asherim and Asheroth.

ASTYNOME, ASHTAR, ASHTART, BA'ALAT ASHTART or NOEMA by the Phoenicians. She was the principal goddess of the Phoenicians, representing the productive (fertility) power of nature. She was a moon goddess and was adopted by the Egyptians as a daughter of Ra or Ptah. ATHTART, ASTARTE or "Queen of Heaven" by the Canaanites. ASHRATU, ATAR, ATHTAR by the Babylonians. ATIRAT by the Assyrians. MYLITTA by the Arabians.

ASTARTE, ARGANTE, ANDRASTE, ADRASTE and ANDATE by the Celts. A fierce goddess of victory to whom her opponents were sacrificed in a sacred grove. Described in Dio Cassius' *Annals XIV,* Andraste was said to be both mysterious and terrible. At one stage she was reputed to have been invoked by Queen Boudicca when she revolted against Roman tyranny during the first century AD. She may have originated in the Gaulish bear goddess ANDARTE, since Andarte has also been mooted as a British variant of that goddess.

LILITH or LIL by the Akkadians. LILLIBET (ELIZABETH) by the Egyptians. LILITHU by the Hebrews. Lilith in Hebrew means "evil woman" is descended from the Mesopotamian Lilitu, a she-demon who lurked in waste places and abandoned buildings and menaced travelers, young men, infants, and pregnant women, and was acquired from Mesopotamian mythology via the Babylonian Captivity.

LILITU, LILAKE or LILLAKE by the Babylonians. Lilitu in the cuneiform language of Iraq's ancient peoples such as the Sumerians and Babylonians means "whirlwind." Moon goddess; Lady of the Moon; patroness of witches; female principle of the universe; demon goddess to the Jews and Christians. Lilith is also a curse to all pregnant women, mothers and children. JAHI the Whore by the Persians. She mated with the serpent Ahriman (Enki). Handmaiden to the Matronit, and she left Adam because he tried to dominate her. Lilith's epithet was "the beautiful maiden," She was described as having no milk in her breasts and were unable to bear any children. *Babylonian texts* depict Lilith as the prostitute of the goddess Ishtar (Atuneni/Athena/Minerva). Similarly, older Sumerian accounts assert that Lilitu is called the handmaiden of Inanna or "hand of Inanna." The Sumerian texts state that "Inanna has sent the beautiful, unmarried, and seductive prostitute Lilitu out into the fields and streets in order to lead men astray." That is why Lilitu is called the "hand of Inanna."

The Lilitu, the Akkadian ARDAT-LILI and the Assyrian LA-BAR-TU like Lilith, were figures of disease and uncleanliness. Ardat is derived from "ardatu," a title of prostitutes and young unmarried women, meaning "maiden." One magical text tells of how Ardat Lili had come to "seize" a sick man. Other texts mention Lamashtu as the hand of Inanna in place of Lilitu and Ardat lili.

SAMAEL AND LILITH

The mystical writing of two brothers Jacob and Isaac Hacohen, which predates the Zohar by a few decades, states that Samael and Lilith are in the shape of an androgynous being, double-faced, born out of the emanation of the Throne of Glory and corresponding in the spiritual realm to Adam and

Eve, who were likewise born as a hermaphrodite. The two twin androgynous couples resembled each other and both "were like the image of Above"; that is, that they are reproduced in a visible form of an androgynous deity. Another version that was also current among Kabbalistic circles in the Middle Ages establishes Lilith as the first of Samael's four wives: Lilith, Naamah, Igrath, and Mahalath. Each of them are mothers of demons and have their own hosts and unclean spirits in no number. The marriage of Samael and Lilith was arranged by "Blind Dragon", who is the counterpart of "the dragon that is in the sea". Blind Dragon acts as an intermediary between Lilith and Samael:

Blind Dragon rides Lilith the Sinful - *may she be extirpated quickly in our days, Amen!* - And this Blind Dragon brings about the union between Samael and Lilith. And just as the Dragon that is in the sea (*Isaah* 27:1) has no eyes, likewise Blind Dragon that is above, in the likeness of a spiritual form, is without eyes, that is to say, without colors . . . *(Patai 81:458)* Samael is called the "Slant Serpent", and Lilith is called the "Tortuous Serpent". The marriage of Samael and Lilith is known as the "Angel Satan" or the "Other God," but it was not allowed to last.

To prevent Lilith and Samael's demonic children from filling the world, God castrated Samael. In many 17th century *Kabbalistic* books, this mythologem is based on the identification of *"Leviathan the Slant Serpent and Leviathan the Torturous Serpent"* and a reinterpretation of an old Talmudic myth where God castrated the male Leviathan and slew the female Leviathan in order to prevent them from mating and thereby destroying the earth. After Samael became castrated and Lilith was unable to fornicate with him, she left him to couple with men who experience nocturnal emissions. A 15th or 16th century *Kabbalah* text states that God has "cooled" the female Leviathan, meaning that he has made Lilith infertile and she is a mere fornication.

Lilith is further associated with the Anzu bird, lions, owls, and serpents, which are animals associated with the Lilitu. It is from this mythology that the later *Kabbalah* depictions of Lilith as a serpent in the Garden of Eden and her associations with serpents are probably drawn. Her most sacred bird was the owl, the totem of Lilith. In ancient Egyptian, Celtic, and Hindu cultures the symbolic meaning of owl revolved around guardianship of the underworlds, and a protection of the dead. In this light the owl was ruler of the night and seer of souls. A misunderstanding of this necessary relationship gave the owl some negative associations with death. It should be clear that the owl was honored as the keeper of spirits who had passed from one plane to another. Often myth indicates the owl accompanying a spirit to the underworld - winging it's newly freed soul from the physical world into the realm of spirit. The Romans called the owl by a word that meant witch. During medieval times in western and central Europe it was fabled that owls were actually priestesses (witches) and wizards in disguise. To this day the owl is considered a witch's familiar (an animal soul-spirit linked to a spiritual person via a unique, communicative bond). The owl has been symbolised as a witch in bird form and is associated with witches in the symbols of Halloween. Hinduism culture claim that the owl's eyes open the portal for lost souls and with it, serve as the foreseer and guardian of the dead. Shaman priests and the Native American religion have stressed the owl to have supernatural capabilities with spiritual associations. They believe that an owl's cry is an indication of impending sickness, doom and death. In practicing Native American traditions, they call on the spirit of nature through the owl. They believe that the owl's presence would give them clairvoyance and other supernatural capabilities which is why all customary shaman traditions are considered sacred among Native Americans.

One of the most bizarre symbolic inclinations of the owl is the Bohemian Club. It is said to be the noble men's secret organization involving rich entrepreneurs, top level executives, multi-million dollar company financiers and even the former United States President George W. Bush. In fact, every Republican president since Herbert Hoover has been a member and most Democrates, including Bill Clinton. Every year the Bohemian Club holds a two-week camp in the woods of Northern California where they perform rituals and ceremonies before a 40 ft. stone owl (representing Lilith) as their central symbol. It is said that the practices were meant to uphold wisdom just like what the owl characterizes and represent. Regular attendees at the Bohemian Grove are known as 'grovers' and among them are people like George H.W. Bush; George W. Bush; Bill Clinton; Gerald Ford; Ronald Reagan; Richard Nixon; Henry Kissinger; Dick Cheney; Alan Greenspan; Jack Kemp; Alexander Haig; Casper Weinberger; George Shultz; Bob Hope; etc. and a long list of the best known politicians, businessmen, media people, and entertainers in the world. Steve Bechtel, the head of the world's biggest construction company, attended Bohemian Grove in the 1980s while his company enjoyed massive contracts thanks to the spending decisions of the World Bank and its president A.W. Clausen, another 'grover'. This meeting of the world elite is described as a 'summer camp', it is actually a Satanic center for the Elite who run the planet and this is where many of the real decisions are made before they become public.

Lilith was a contributor for the female denucleated DNA genes of all races, the ancestral memory N her daughters married both of the lineages of mankind according to the stone tablets of the Sumerian Kings, which in some versions are more than 5,000 years old.

God then formed Lilith, the first woman, just as he had formed Adam, except that he used filth and sediment instead of pure dust. From Adam's union with this demoness, and with another like her named Naamah, Tubal Cain's sister, sprang Asmodeus and innumerable demons that still plague mankind. Many generations later, Lilith and Naamah came to Solomon's judgement seat, disguised as harlots of Jerusalem.

Adam and Lilith never found peace together; for when he wished to lie with her, she took offence at the recumbent posture he demanded. 'Why must I lie beneath you?' she asked. 'I also was made from dust, and am therefore your equal.' Because Adam tried to compel her obedience by force, Lilith, in a rage, uttered the magic name of God, rose into the air and left him.

Hebrew traditions say that Lilith rebelled against Adam and his God and fled to a cave after eating her own child. There she lived with the demons of the underground world and bred with them. She told Adam and Eve that she and her offspring would always abduct human children and take them to their subterranean world.

The prophet Elijah, according to legend, encountering Lilith, forced her to reveal to him the names she used in her various disguises when she worked her evil among mortals. She confessed to seventeen names, and they are recorded in M. Gaster, *Studies and Texts in Folklore,* page 1025 as follows: Abeko, Abito, Amizo, Batna, Eilo, Ita, Izorpo, Kali, Kea, Kokos, Lilith, Odam, Partasah, Patrota, Podo, Satrina, Talto.

"And there came one of the seven angels... saying unto me, Come hither; I will show unto thee the judgment of the great whore that sitteth upon many waters: 2 With whom the kings of the earth have committed fornication, and the inhabitants of the earth have been made drunk with the wine of her fornication. 3 So he carried me away in the spirit into the wilderness: and I saw a woman sit upon a scarlet-coloured beast, full of names of blasphemy, having seven heads and ten horns. 4 And the woman was arrayed in purple and scarlet colour, and decked with gold and precious stones and pearls, having a golden cup in her hand full of abominations and filthiness of her fornication: 5 And upon her forehead was a name written, MYSTERY, BABYLON THE GREAT, THE MOTHER OF HARLOTS AND ABOMINATIONS OF THE EARTH. 6 And I saw the woman drunken with the blood of the saints, and with the blood of the martyrs of Jesus: and when I saw her, I wondered with great admiration. 7 And the angel said unto me,

Wherefore didst thou marvel? I will tell thee the mystery of the woman, and of the beast that carrieth her, which hath the seven heads and ten horns. 8 The beast that thou sawest was, and is not; and shall ascend out of the bottomless pit, and go into perdition: and they that dwell on the earth shall wonder, whose names were not written in the book of life from the foundation of the world, when they behold the beast that was, and is not, and yet is. 9 And here is the mind which hath wisdom. The seven heads are seven mountains, on which the woman sitteth. 10 And there are seven kings: five are fallen, and one is, and the other is not yet come; and when he cometh, he must continue a short space. 11 And the beast that was, and is not, even he is the eighth, and is of the seven, and goeth into perdition. 12 And the ten horns which thou sawest are ten kings, which have received no kingdom as yet; but receive power as kings one hour with the beast. 13 These have one mind, and shall give their power and strength unto the beast. 14 These shall make war with the Lamb, and the Lamb shall overcome them: for he is Lord of lords, and King of kings: and they that are with him are called, and chosen, and faithful. 15 And he saith unto me, The waters which thou sawest, where the whore sitteth, are peoples, and multitudes, and nations, and tongues. 16 And the ten horns which thou sawest upon the beast, these shall hate the whore, and shall make her desolate and naked, and shall eat her flesh, and burn her with fire. 17 For God hath put in their hearts to fulfil his will, and to agree, and give their kingdom unto the beast, until the words of God shall be fulfilled. 18 And the woman which thou sawest is that great city, which reigneth over the kings of the earth." *Revelation 17:1-18.*

"After these things, I saw another angel coming down out of the sky, having great authority. The earth was illuminated with his glory. 2 He cried with a mighty voice, saying, "Fallen, fallen is Babylon the great, and she has become a habitation of demons, a prison of every unclean spirit, and a prison of every unclean and hateful bird! 3 For all the nations have drunk of the wine of the wrath of her sexual immorality, the kings of the earth committed sexual immorality with her, and the merchants of the earth grew rich from the abundance of her luxury." 4 I heard another voice from heaven, saying, "Come out of her, my people, that you have no participation in her sins, and that you don't receive of her plagues, 5 for her sins have reached to the sky, and God has remembered her iniquities. 6 Return to her just as she returned, and repay her double as she did, and according to her works. In the cup which she mixed, mix to her double. 7 However much she glorified herself, and grew wanton, so much give her of torment and mourning. For she says in her heart, 'I sit a queen, and am no widow, and will in no way see mourning.' 8 Therefore in one day her plagues will come: death, mourning, and famine; and she will be utterly burned with fire; for the Lord God who has judged her is strong. 9 The kings of the earth, who committed sexual immorality and lived wantonly with her, will weep and wail over her, when they look at the smoke of her burning, 10 standing far away for the fear of her torment, saying, 'Woe, woe, the great city, Babylon, the strong city! For your judgment has come in one hour.' 11 The merchants of the earth weep and mourn over her, for no one buys their merchandise any more; 12 merchandise of gold, silver, precious stones, pearls, fine linen, purple, silk, scarlet, all expensive wood, every vessel of ivory, every vessel made of most precious wood, and of brass, and iron, and marble; 13 and cinnamon, incense, perfume, frankincense, wine, olive oil, fine flour, wheat, sheep, horses, chariots, bodies, and people's souls. 14 The fruits which your soul lusted after have been lost to you, and all things that were dainty and sumptuous have perished from you, and you will find them no more at all. 15 The merchants of these things, who were made rich by her, will stand far away for the fear of her torment, weeping and mourning; 16 saying, 'Woe, woe, the great city, she who was dressed in fine linen, purple, and scarlet, and decked with gold and precious stones and pearls! 17 For in an hour such great riches are made desolate.' Every shipmaster, and everyone who sails anywhere, and mariners, and as many as gain their living by sea, stood far away, 18 and cried out as they looked at the smoke of her burning, saying, 'What is like the great city?' 19 They cast dust on their heads, and cried, weeping and mourning, saying, 'Woe, woe, the great city, in which all who had their ships in the sea were made rich by reason of her great wealth!' For in one hour is she made desolate. 20 Rejoice over her, O heaven, you saints, apostles, and prophets; for God has judged your judgment on her." 21 A mighty angel took up a stone like a great millstone and cast it into the sea, saying, "Thus with violence will Babylon, the great city, be thrown down, and will be found no more at all. 22 The voice of harpists, minstrels, flute players, and trumpeters will be heard no more at all in you. No craftsman, of whatever craft, will be found any more at all in you. The sound of a mill will be heard no more at all in you. 23 The light of a lamp will shine no more at all in you. The voice of the bridegroom and of the bride will be heard no more at all in you; for your merchants were the princes of the earth; for with your sorcery all the nations were deceived. 24 In her was found the blood of prophets and of saints, and of all who have been slain on the earth." *Revelation 18:1-24*

The Flame of EOS, "the dawn", by the Greeks. AURORA or DAWN by the Romans. Goddess of the dawn. Sometimes she rode on Pegasus, sometimes in a purple or gold chariot. She was also pictured rising from the ocean in a chariot. She belongs to the first divine generation (mythological creatures), that of the Titans. She was depicted as a goddess whose rosy fingers opened the gates of heaven to the chariot of the Sun. She first slept with Ares; this earned her the wrath of Aphrodite who punished her by turning her into a nymphomaniac. Her different lovers were: Orion the Giant, the son of Poseidon, whom she abducted and carried off to Delos; then Cephalus, the son of Deion and Diomede, whom she carried off to Syria, where she bore him a son, Phaethon (more commonly held to be the son of the Sun). Finally she abducted Tithonus, son of Ilus and Placia (or Leucippe), a Trojan, and took him to Ethiopia, which in the old legends was the land of the Sun. There she bore him two sons, Emathion and Memnon. The latter, who seemed to have been her favorite son, reigned over the Ethiopians (modern day Morocco) and died before Troy, fighting Achilles.

ESTHER by the Arabians. Lady of the Mountain; Queen of Heaven; Sovereign of Heaven; Guiding Star; Serpent Lady (in the Sinai). Lady of Byblos; Mistress of horses and chariots; Maiden; Virgin (meaning independent); Mother Goddess. Goddess of the Moon. Byblos claimed she descended to Earth as a fiery star and landed in a lake near Aphaca. Her sacred stone was kept in her Byblos temple. This stone was said to heal and prophesy. Her symbol was an eight pointed star. The word Bibles came from Byblos where the earliest libraries were attached to her temple. Byblos or Bibles and Gene-Isis or Genesis. Isis-Ra-El or Israel.

**Anunnaki goddess Ninki (Eos/Lilith) 'the Owl'**

## NIN.LIL (Hera)

SHALA by the Pleiadians. NIN.LIL or "lady of the command" by the Sumerians, daughter of An.nu (Cronos) and Nin.mah (Metis). She was called "the Shining Lady" by the Sumerians. IN.NI.NI or "lady of the airspace" by the Akkadians. RANN-T, NEBT HET or "Lady of the House" and NEPHTYS or "goddess of the dead" by the Egyptians.

HERA by the Greeks, daughter of Cronos (Annu) and Rhea (Antu). Lady; Holy One; Great Lady; Mother of the gods; Queen of Heaven; Earth

Goddess; Great Mother. Her sacred bird was the peacock. Pictured wearing a veil and a matronly dress; very noble. She held a scepter and pomegranate; wild marjoram, the cow, the Milky Way, and lilies were sacred to her. The sickle she sometimes carried was made for her by Hephaestus. To her belonged the tree of golden apples in Hesperides. Some of her symbols were the double axe, sacred shield, helmet, spear, cows. Eire, the Celtic name for Ireland, comes from the name of the celtic goddess ERINN, a form of Hera. JUNA by the Hebrews. JUNO by the Romans. She wore either a cobra headdress or a disk between two horns. She set each human's fate at birth.

FRIGGA by the Scandinavians. FRIGG, FRIGGA, or FRIJA by the Nordic-Germanic tribes. "Well-Beloved Spouse or Lady"; Aesir Mother Goddess; wife of Odhinn; queen of Goddesses; a shape-shifter; knower of all things. A Nereid. The Nereids had beautiful fair hair, no fish-tails and accompanied the chariot of Coeus. EL, ELDI or "FIERY EL", the "Hound" by the British Celts. Given the title RANN or the "nursing serpent mother" by the British Celts.

## NIN.MAH (Metís)

NIN.MAH by the Sumerians, daughter of En.shar (Oceanos) and NIN.SHAR (Tethys). NIN or "Mighty Lady", NIN.HUR.SAG, NIN.KHUR.SAG, NIN.HAR.SAG or "Lady of the Mountain peaks," or "Queen of the Mountains" by the Sumerians. NIN.HOUR.SAGH or "Lady governess of the Mountain" by the Sumerians. SUD or "Nurse" by the Akkadians. When she grew older she was called MAM.MU, MAMI, MAM.MI, or "Old Mother" and "Mother of the Gods" by the younger Anunnaki. NIN.TI or "Lady of Life" or "Lady of the Rib". NIN.TU or "the lady who gives birth". Birth goddess who enabled pregnant women to make the bones of babies out of their own ribs.

METIS was the Greek goddess of prudence, daughter of Oceanos (Enshar) and Tethys (Ninshar). Metis, a nymph by the Greeks. She was the first consort of Zeus. After she prophesied that she would bear first a daughter and then a son who would rule the world, Zeus swallowed Metis. He soon came down with a tremendous headache and ordered Hephaestus to split his forehead open. Out jumped Athena (Atuneni), fully grown and armed. Metis was no more, but her prudence had been passed to Athena, who became the goddess of wisdom.

Metis was an NEREID (OCEANID) or goddess of the sea. They were the patrons of sailors and fishermen, who came to the aid of men in distress, and goddesses who had in their care the sea's rich bounty. Individually they also represented various facets of the sea, from salty brine, to foam, sand, rocky shores, waves and currents, in addition to the various skills possessed by seamen. The Nereides were depicted in ancient art as beautiful young maidens, sometimes running with small dolphins or fish in their hands, or else riding on the back of dolphins, hippokampoi (fish-tailed horses) and other sea creatures.

**Anunnaki goddess Ninmah (Metis)**

## NIN.SAR

NIN.SAR by the Sumerians, daughter of En.ki (Poseidon) and Nin.mah (Metis). Wife of her father En.ki (Poseidon) and mother of Nin.dur.ra.

## NIN.SHAR (Tethys)

NINSHAR by the Sumerians, daughter of An.shar (Uranos) and Ki.shar (Gaea).

THETYS or TETHYS by the Greeks, daughter of Uranos (Anshar) and Gaea (Kishar). She was a primordial force that personified the fertility of the seas. She also looked after the young Hera during the great war between the Olympians and the Titans.

Tethys was a NEREID or goddess of the sea. They were the patrons of sailors and fishermen, who came to the aid of men in distress, and goddesses who had in their care the sea's rich bounty. Individually they also represented various facets of the sea, from salty brine, to foam, sand, rocky shores, waves and currents, in addition to the various skills possessed by seamen. The Nereides were depicted in ancient art as beautiful young maidens, sometimes running with small dolphins or fish in their hands, or else riding on the back of dolphins, hippokampoi (fish-tailed horses) and other sea creatures.

## NIN.SU (Anobret)

NIN.SU or "Lady Wild Cow" by the Sumerians, daughter of Nin.urta (Ares) and Aruru (Aruah), wife of Enki (Poseidon) and mother of Dumuzi. NIN.SUN by the Akkadians. SEMIRAMIS by the Babylonians. ATHOR, ATHYR, HAT-HOR, HATHOR or "The Cow", HET-HERU, HET-HERT by the Egyptians. Queen of the West (or the Dead); the Lady of the Sycamore; House of the Face; House of Horus; Mother Goddess; mother of all gods and goddesses; Queen of Heaven; sky and Moon goddess. She carried Ra's Sacred Eye. The mirror and sistrum were sacred to her. Hathor's appearance could be as a cow headed goddess or a human-headed woman with horns, cow's ears, and heavy tresses. New Year's Day, one of her many festivals, was celebrated as her birthday. At that time her image was taken from the temple out into the rising Sun for a day of enjoyment, song, and intoxication. SIGYN by the Nordic-Germans.

NINSU was one of the most illustrious figures of the Sumerian mythology. Ninsu was a favorite queen, and the famous mother of Gilgamesh. She knew alchemy, astronomy, astrology and able to read the future. She was also an expert in interpreting dreams and forseeing the future. According to the Assyro-Babylonian mythology, Ninsu was "the great wild cow", the great queen, Gilgamesh's mother and Lugalbanda's mate. She is wise, 'knows everything' and interprets Gilgamesh's dreams. She offers incense and drink to Shamash (Utu) and questions his decision to send Gilgamesh against Humbaba. When doing so, she wears a circlet on her head and an ornament on her breast. She adopts Enkidu prior to the quest against Humbaba. ANOBRET by the Greeks.

SIRTUR is the goddess of sheep. She is incharge of the stables and sheepfolds. Although she is referred to in many places as a goddess, she started out mortal, and it is only in later references that she is mentioned as a deity.

SEKHMET by the Egyptians. Queen of the West; Mistress of the Lilithian Netherworld; protectress of womanhood; and the "lady of the sycamore." It was from the milk of Hathor that the pharaohs were said to gain their divinity, becoming gods in their own right.

SHEPESH by the Canaanites. The name is of uncertain meaning but suggests an association with the Sun. The Canaanite text state that "she governs the Repha'im, the divine ones" and rules over demigods and mortals. SEKHMET is described as 'the Mighty Lady, Mistress of Flame', and is depicted in Egyptian art with the head of a lion and the body of a woman. According to legend, Sekhmet is said to have had the power of the 'fierce scorching, and destroying heat of the sun's ray's. Marduk called her 'His Terrible Eye', who was the goddess Sekhmet.

## NIN.UL (Perseis)

DRA.MIN by the Anunnaki. NIN.UL by the Sumerians. DAM.KI.NA or NAM.MU by the Akkadians. SIR or "The Serpent Lady" by the Babylonians. A fish-goddess (snake-goddess) and mother of Babylonia's foundress. JORMUNGAND by the Nordic-Germans.

*The Children of the Law of One & the Lost Teachings of Atlantis,* by Jon Peniel, cr1997, pps. 80-83 - Take heed of the ancient warnings and prophecies about the Belialians: "Lizard-like are they--not in apparent physical description, but in spirit form, in the heart--in the soul. Beware even now of your lizard kin, for they rule the world, with greed, and without compassion, while maintaining 'appearance' of good and righteous. As men and women do these Sons of Belial walk the Earth. Model citizens. Successful leaders who are the envy of the uninitiated. While some appear disgusting and strange to the eye, look not to see the ugliness of the Belialians with your eye, for some are handsome to the eye. See you will not, their true nature, you will, only with the inner-eye, or in glimpses from the corner of the eye."

Thus it came to be that the two Atlantean socio-political groups evolved, with one very essential difference: The Children of the Law of One had a consciousness of both separateness of Oneness. The Belialians rejected the consciousness of Oneness entirely, and maintained only a consciousness of separateness. The differences of opinion between the two groups were great and many, but nothing was more of an issue than the morality of how the humanimals were to be dealt with.

Those of the Law of One, remembering still that we originally came to this plane just to help release the humanimals from matter-bondage, continued trying to free our trapped siblings. The kindred also created ways to aid in the maintenance of the consciousness of Oneness, so we would never lose sight of our goals. But the Belialians wanted to use the humanimals for their own comforts and pleasures. Since those of us from the second wave were of greater consciousness than the humanimals, and could still function on higher planes to some extent, we had powers of the mind, both spiritual and psychological, that made it easy for us to control humanimals.

The Children of the Law of One refused to use their abilities to control the humanimals, while the Belialians relished in the power, and wanted to use them as slaves.

The other great division in opinion between the Children and the Belialians was over the "environment" as it is called now. The Belialians used methods of generating power that were dangerous and destructive to the Earth.

So did the great conflict between the Children and the Belialians of Atlantis begin. A conflict between light and dark, between selfishness, and unselfishness, and unselfish love. And the conflict that was, continued throughout history, and continues to this day.

The Belialians' lust for power and lack of care or awareness of the balances of nature, led to the destruction of Atlantis. This was due in great part to the abuse of their power generation plants.

When the final destructions of Atlantis occurred, Grand Master Thoth then led us to the land of Khem (now Egypt), to complete the Great Work of evolving the humanimals. As gods were we to the people of Khem, and yea did they think the humanimals to be gods.

And so it was done. The humanimals were brought to human levels, to choose their path from there. But even though the humanimals were no more, the Belialians had not lost their taste for slavery. Thus the great conflict with the Belialians was far from over, and still continues on, with the Children of the Law of One as Lamps, illuminating the path of unselfish love, helping the lost find their way home to their spiritual heritage of the One, and to find freedom--while the disguised Sons of Belial do everything possible to maintain their decadence and power, and maintain slavery. And they seek to destroy all those who would shine Light into this world of darkness. All those who do not actively work for the Light, are to varying degrees, pawns of the Belialian Darkness.

Case: *Inter-dimensional Reptoids attacking human Female*

Subject: Clarita Villanueva, Female

Location: Manila, Philippines

Date: May 1951

Witnesses: Dr. Marianna Lana, Mayor Arsenio Lascon, two local constables and several newspaper reporters:

It was a sultry May evening in 1951, and the Manila police patrols were expecting trouble. There was the smell of it in the air and it was as safe a prediction as the storm warning which was being made by the distant rumble of the approaching thunderstorm. That was why a patrol car sped instantly along the main street when they received a message that a crowd was gathering outside one of the waterfront bars. The car skidded to a stop as a terrified scream rang out. Forcing their way through the watching crowd, the constables saw a girl rolling about on the ground. She was shouting: *"Keep it away from me! Keep it away . . . Oh, please, won't someone help me? I can't stand the pain!"*

But there was nothing anybody could do, for there was no one anywhere near the girl-yet the shocked policemen clearly saw teeth marks appearing on the girl's arms and neck. As nobody else moved to help her, the crowd just watched in superstitious horror, the constables sprang forward and carried the frantically struggling girl to the car, manacled her-and drove at top speed all the way to headquarters.

All during the journey she fought against the manacles screaming and sobbing, *"Please call the Thing off. It's biting me to death. I can't stand it anymore . . ."*

But there was little the policemen could do, in fact, there was nothing anybody at headquarters could do, but summon the police doctor. At first, they suspected that he girl, Clarita Villaneuva, had been taking drugs and drinking. But there was a more macabre, inexplicable reason for it all. A reason so fantastic that, at first it even fooled the police medical officer, Dr. Marianna Lara, who gave her one quick look and snapped: *"She's having an epileptic fit."*

The policemen next took Clarita to a cell, ignoring her pleas not to leave her alone. As the cell door slammed, Clarita collapsed to the floor sobering bitterly. A few minutes later, she started screaming uncontrollably and this time the two policemen came running. The distraught girl moaned to them:

*"The Thing is coming at me. It's coming through the cell door as if it weren't there."* Whatever *"It"* was, looked like a man, she claimed, but it had big bulging eyes and wore a cape over it's shoulders. And it could float in mid air!

The policemen let themselves into the cell, but they could see nothing. All they could do was try to calm the girl. Yet, even as they watched, more and more bite marks began appearing on her arms. This time, the policemen decided to send for the chief of police, the mayor, and, once again, the medical officer, Dr. Lara. They arrived and everybody agreed that he bites could not possibly have been self-inflicted for no one could bite herself on the back of the shoulders. Yet Clarita clearly was being bitten there!

Eventually, the exhausted girl fell asleep and in the morning she had to appear in court to face charges of vagrancy. But just as she was being taken into the court, she screamed that *"The Thing"* was back. The two policemen beside her saw teeth marks, deep and painful looking on her arms, hands and neck. Several newspaper reporters, court officials and Dr. Lara also started at them in sheer astonishment. For five terrifying minutes the attack went on until Clarita fell unconscious to the floor. Then the amazed medical officer carried out an on-the-spot examination and found herself baffled! *"These bites are genuine," she told reporters. "And they are not self inflicted!"*

The reporters knew they were on to a great story and rushed to catch their editions. Half-an-hour later, Mayor Arsenio Lascon arrived and spoke to Clarita, whose arms and hands were badly swollen by then. Mayor Lascon decided to ride in the ambulance with the medical officer, Dr. Lara, and see that nothing happened to the unfortunate girl. But even in the ambulance, she shouted once again that *"The Thing"* was after her. Only on this occasion there were two of the creatures, both with the same large, staring eyes. Both the mayor and the doctor said on oath that they watched as vicious-looking teeth marks came up on both sides of the girl's throat and her hands, even as the mayor was holding them in an effort to comfort her.

It took fifteen minutes for the ambulance to reach the hospital-and to Lascon they were the longest fifteen minutes of his life. It seemed more like twenty-four hours of Hell, he said afterwards. Strangely, once the girl was in the hospital, the attacks ceased and although she was guarded night and day nothing ever happened. She recovered and was released from the hospital six weeks later.

Dr. Lara, once skeptical, was now deeply interested in the case and recorded: *"What happened to Clarita Villanueva is a complete mystery, something which defies description. She was repeatedly attacked by something with invisible sharp fangs. We shall never know what it was, but I don't mind admitting that I was scared stiff." "And even today, Clarita still has bite marks all over her body...evidence of the impossible was, unhappily, possible!"* (A Look Through Secret Doors, by John Mackim, 1969, Ace Publishing)

PERSEIS or PERSE, a daughter of Oceanos (Enshar) and Thethys (Ninshar) and the wife of Helios (Alalu).

Perseis was a NEREID (OCEANID) or goddess of the sea. They were the patrons of sailors and fishermen, who came to the aid of men in distress, and goddesses who had in their care the sea's rich bounty. Individually they also represented various facets of the sea, from salty brine, to foam, sand, rocky shores, waves and currents, in addition to the various skills possessed by seamen. The Nereides were depicted in ancient art as beautiful young maidens, sometimes running with small dolphins or fish in their hands, or else riding on the back of dolphins, hippokampoi (fish-tailed horses) and other sea creatures.

## NIN.URTA (Ares)

NIN.URTA or "The Whirlwind" by the Sumerians, son of En.lil (Zeus) and Nin.mah (Metis). Former United States President George Walker Bush called him "The Angel From The Whirlwind". NIN.URTA or "Lord Who Completes the Foundation" by the Sumerians. The First Region of civilization was Mesopotamia and the lands bordering upon it. The mountain-lands where agriculture and settled life began, the lands that came to be known as Elam, Persia, Assyria-- were ruled by Ninurta. He was called PABILSAG and NIN.GIRSU or "Lord of the Girsu" by the Akkadians. The Throne Carrier; God of war; messenger from gods to humans. The amethyst and lapis lazuli were sacred to him. MARS by the Romans. The "god of war". AMSET by the Egyptians. AMABIEL by the Hebrews. Amabiel was an angel and a presiding spirit of the planet Mars. Amabiel is also one of the angelic luminaries "concerned with human sexuality." ISHUM or "The Scorcher" by the Hittites. MOT or "Smiter, Annihilator" by the Phoenicians and Canaanites.

Nissaba performs a purification ceremony on Ninurta and he receives the following new names and shrines: Duku - 'holy mound' in Sumerian, Hurabtil - an Elamite god, Shushinak - patron god of the Elamite city Susa, Lord of the Secret, Pabilsag - god of the antediluvian city Larak, Nin-Azu - god of Eshunna, Ishtaran - god of Der, Zababa -warrior god of Kish, Lugalbanda - Gilgamesh's father, Lugal-Marada - patron god of Marad, Warrior Tishpak - similar to Nin-Azu, Warrior of Uruk, Lord of the Boundary-Arrow, Panigara - a warrior god, and Papsukkal - vizier of the great gods. The city of Nippur was the center of his cult. He was the patron deity of the ancient Sumerian city of Girsu (Lagash) where king Gudea (c.2141-2122 BC) built a temple for him called the E-ninnu.

NINURTA from NINI.URTA, the firstborn son of Enlil by Enlil's half-sister Ninharsag, and therefore in line to succeed Enlil and his rank of Fifty, just below that of Anu; his emblem was a "double-headed eagle". His feats, that earned him a variety of epithet-names, were recorded in hymns and epics and were the subject of cylinder-seal depictions; they included erecting dams after the Deluge to make Mesopotamia habitable again, and bestowing the plough to Mankind; defeating the evil Zu who had stolen the Tablets of Destinies from Enlil; leading the Enlilities in the Pyramid Wars against Marduk; and joining the god Nergal in the launching of nuclear weapons; it was he, according to the *Erra Epic* (where he is called Ishum, 'The Scorcher') who nuked the Spaceport in the Sinai. Quoting clay tablet texts, Z. Sitchen explained various enigmas concerning inner features in the Great Pyramid of Giza as resulting from Ninurta's attack and entry when Marduk/Ra took refuge inside it. Gudea, king of Lagash, described in long inscriptions how he built for Ninurta and his spouse the temple E.Ninnu ('House/Temple of Fifty'), including a special enclosure for the god's winged aircraft.

From the *Erra Epos* text we know that Ishum (Ninurta) "to the Mount Most Supreme set his course" in his Divine Black Bird. He raised his hand and the mount was smashed. The plain by the Mount Most Supreme he then obliterated; in its forests not a tree was left standing. According to the Sumerian texts, Ninurta tried to dissuade Nergal from distroying the "sinning cities". Text continued: Erra (Nergal), emulating Ishum (Ninurta), the cities he finished off, to desolation he upheavaled them. Sodom and Gomorrah and three other cities in "the disobedient land, he obliterated." *The Bible,* in virtually identical words, relates that "as the sun was risen over the Earth, from the skies were those cities upheavaled, with brimstones and fire that have come from Yahweh (Utu)." These verses clearly show that the god Yahweh of the Hebrews sent the gods Ninurta and Nergal of the Sumerians to destroy the sinning cities. "And Abraham got up early in the morning, and went to where he had stood with the Lord, and gazed toward Sodom and Gomorrah, in the direction of the place of the Plain; and lo and behold - there was steaming smoke rising from the ground like the steaming smoke of a furnace." *Genesis* 19:27-28.

ARIS by the Atlanteans. ARES by the Greeks, son of Zeus (Enlil) and Hera (Ninlil). The God of War. Undoubtedly the most fierce and vicious of the gods within the Greek pantheon. He had a passion for mass slaughter. Son of Zeus and Hera. He was the greek god of war, the equivalent of Mars in Italy. Ares is represented wearing armour and a helmet, and carrying a shield, spear and sword. He was of more than human height and uttered terrible cries. He normally fought on foot but he could be found in a chariot drawn by four chargers. He was attended by demons who served him as squires, especially Deimos and Phobos (Terror and Fear). Ares lived in Thrace. Thrace was traditionally, the home of the Amazons, who were Ares' daughters. In Greece he was the object of a special cult in Thebes, where he was believed to have been the ancestor of the descendants of Cadmus. His worship was important at Sparta, where prisoners of war were sacrificed to him. At Athens, there was a temple dedicated to Ares at the foot of the Areopagus (Ares' Hill).

MARS by the Romans. Mars was the "God of War" and agriculture; god of spring. Originally Mars was an Etruscan fertility-savior MARIS; he was worshipped at a shrine in the Apennines. He was pictured as bearded with a cuirass and helmet. He was considered important because he was the father of Romulus and Remus. Sacrifices to him took place in his month of March, thus making it a dangerous time of the year. Sacred to him were the woodpecker, horse, wolf, oak, laurel, dogwood, and the bean. War, terror, anger, revenge, and courage.

**Anunnaki god Ninurta (Ares)**

## NINU.RU

NINURU by the Sumerians, daughter of An II and Anunnaki Concubine. Anunnaki wife of Enu.ru (Jehovan).

## NIS.ABA (Demeter)

NIN-GISHZIDA by the Sumerians, daughter of En.ki (Poseidon) and Nin.ki (Eos). NIS.ABA by the Babylonians and Assyrians. Goddess of grain. The astronomy goddess. According to Assyro-Babylonian mythology, Nissaba was the cereal grain harvest goddess. Her breast nourishes the fields. Her womb gives birth to the vegetation and grain. She has abundant locks of hair. She is also a goddess of writing and learned knowledge. She performs the purification ceremony on Ninurta after he has slain Anzu and is given his additional names and shrines.

PHILAEIA (Phil-ay-ee-ar) or "goddess of wisdom, philosophy, science and architecture" by the Atlanteans. DEMETER or "the pure bee" by the Greeks. CERES by the Romans. She was the goddess of the fruitful earth. She represented the fertile, cultivated soil of fields as well as grain, fruit trees, and the harvest. Demeter is usually represented as a mature woman in a long robe, often wearing a veil that covers the back of her head. She is sometimes crowned with ears of corn or a ribbon, and she holds in her hand either a scepter, ears of corn, or a torch. This goddess gave the first wheat seeds to humans, taught them how to cultivate the soil and make bread from the grain. She instituted the Eleusinian Mysteries. Later she was brought to America and she holds her torch high. She is the National symbol of the United States, the "Statue of Liberty" in New York City. Demeter's emblems are the ear of corn, the narcissus, and the poppy. Her bird is the crane and her favorite victim the sow. She is often portrayed seated, with torches or a serpent.

## Panthera (Panther)

Tiberius Julius Abdes Panthera, Panthera, Pamphir, Pantera, Pantiri, Pandera or ‘the Panther’, son of Roman Emperor Tiberius Claudius Nero II (Tiberius I) and Julia Augustus, daughter of General Marcus Antonius II (Mark Antony) and Octavia the Elder. Panthera was a Roman archer who transferred to service in the Rhineland and fought in battle with the Germans at Bingerbruck.

In the opening sentence of the New Testament parable in *Luke 19:12*, Jesus stated: A man of noble birth was on a long journey abroad, to have himself appointed king, and return.

In the *Toldoth,* Yeshua [Jesus], Yeshu ben Pandera [Jesus son of Pandera] was a Jew who went to Egypt, became proficient in their magical arts , returned to Judea, went about healing many people and incurred the hostility of the religious upper echelon-the Sanhedrin. He (Jesus) was stoned to death at Lud [Al-Lud or Lydda], and his body was "hanged on a tree" on the eve of Passover.

In the *Toldoth,* Yeshua [Jesus] begins with, John of the House of David, getting engaged to Miriam, originally from Bethlehem, the daughter of a neighboring widow. A certain Pandera also had desires for Miriam. On a Sabbath night he came to Miriam during her period, raped her, and Yeshu was conceived. Miriam thought Pandera was her husband-to-be and yielded to him after a struggle, greatly astonished at the behavior of her fiancé. When the real fiancé John came, she made her anger clear to him. He immediately suspected Pandera and told Rabbi Shimon Ben Shetah of the incident. Miriam became pregnant, and since John knew that the child was not his, but was unable to prove who was guilty he fled to Babylon. Joseph then is introduced to Miriam who is unknowingly to him pregnate by another man.

The Jewish records of the Rabbis are of extreme importance in determining Gospel origins and the value of the Church presentation of the virgin birth story of Jesus Christ. A common appellation for Jesus in the *Talmud* is Yeshu'a ben Panthera, an allusion to the widespread Jewish belief during the earliest centuries of the Christian era that Jesus was the result of an illegitimate union between his mother and a Roman soldier named Panthera.

The *Talmud* enshrines within its pages Jewish oral law. It is divided into two parts, the *Mishna* and the *Gemara.* The *Mishna* discusses such subjects as festivals and sacred things. The *Gemara* is basically a commentary on these subjects. When the *Talmud* was written is not known. Some authorities suggest a date of 150-160, around the same time the Christian Gospels began to emerge, while others say 450.

The *Talmud* writers mention Jesus' name 20 times and quite specifically documents that he was born an illegitimate son of a Roman soldier called Panthera, nicknamed "the Panther". Panthera's existence was confirmed by the discovery of a mysterious tombstone at Bingerbruck in Germany. The engraving etched in the headstone reads: Tiberius Julius Abdes Panthera, an archer, native of Sidon, Phoenicia, who in AD 9 was transferred to service in Rhineland.

Scholars over the centuries have discussed at length why Jesus was so regularly called ben Panthera. Adamantius Origen, an early Christian historian and Church father (185-251), recorded the following verses about Mary from the research records of a highly regarded second-century historian and author named Celsus (c. 178): Mary was turned out by her husband, a carpenter by profession, after she had been convicted of unfaithfulness. Cut off by her spouse, she gave birth to Jesus, a bastard; that Jesus, on account of his poverty, was hired out to go to Egypt; that while there he acquired certain (magical) powers which Egyptians pride themselves on possessing.

Later, in *passage 1:32*, Origen supports the Jewish records and confirms that the paramour of the mother of Jesus was a Roman soldier called Panthera, a name he repeats in *verse 1:69.* Some time during the 17th century, those sentences were erased from the oldest Vatican manuscripts and other codices under Church control replaced them.

The traditional Church writings of St. Epiphanius, the Bishop of Salamis (315-403), again confirm the ben Panthera story, and his information is of a startling nature. This champion of Christian orthodoxy and saint of Roman Catholicism states: "Jesus was the son of a certain Julius whose surname was Panthera".

In many cases a name was a reflection of that person's character and that view of ancient understanding can be used to trace an individual's life and illuminate that person's intimate character peculiarities. That was the case with Tiberius Julius' nickname, Panther. Variations were

Panter/Panetier/Panterer (Roman) which all meant 'adulterer' and Tiberius was a man noted for his sexual excesses. Not even Tiberius' friends would deny that he often committed adultery. The reputation of being a womanizer stuck to Tiberius, and as an elderly man he was said to have still harbored 'a passion for deflowering young girls, indulging in his sensual propensities on the island of Capri'.

The story of Mary's pregnancy by a Roman soldier also appears in the sacred book of the Moslems, the *Koran.* It states that "a full-grown man" forced his attentions on Mary, and in her fear of the disgrace that would follow she left the area and bore Jesus in secret. This story was supported in the *Gospel of Luke*, with the description of the departure of Joseph and Mary from their home prior to the birth. Rape was a common event in Palestine during the Roman occupation, and soldiers were notorious for their treatment of young women. It would be unthinkable for Mary to admit such an event had occurred, for under the Law of Moses a betrothed virgin who had sex with any man during the period of her betrothal was to be stoned to death by the men of the city *(Deut. 22:21).* Simply put, Mary faced the death penalty unless she could prove her innocence.

On further examination of the headstone of Panthera, a remarkable materialisation of information appeared, for on a modern map of Germany we find that Bingerbruck is located on the Rhine River in the Rhineland Palatinate, a district of southwest Germany west of the Rhine, which belonged to Bavaria, Germany until 1945. Formerly, portions of the neighboring territory (Upper Palatinate) constituted an electorate of the Holy Roman Empire, now part of the Rhineland Palatinate State. The Latin-derived word Palatinate was a different sense of the word Palatine, whereas the Latin Palatinus meant "of the Imperial House" and the electorate indicated the state contained one of the German princes entitled to elect the Emperor of the Holy Roman Empire. Palatine is one of the Seven Hills of Rome and was where the Emperor of the Roman Empire resided in the

Imperial House--succeeded by the Emperor of the Holy Roman Empire who now resides in the Vatican.

The early church knew the real story of the death of Jesus. In an ancient document titled the *Arethas Codex*, which appeared to have had at least two previous titles but in its current form it purported to be the works of the Second Century presbyter, Bishop Clement of Alexandria. This writing stated that, *'In his sixty-third year of his age (Jesus) was stoned to death . . .'* Writing about AD 197-198, the Bishop of Carthage, Tertullian, addressed the Jews stating, 'ye stoned him'. Tertullian spoke of the stoning of Jesus not as the invention of an enemy, but simply as a genuine piece of accepted church history.

The Rabbinic records confirmed the church accounts and stated that Jesus was eventually captured and stoned to death by a person called Pinhas at a place called Lud. Both the Palestinian and Babylonian Talmuds contain a precise description of his death that, in both cases, was appended to the following passage from the *Mishna:* . . . and to bring him forward to the tribunal and stone him. And thus they have done to Jesus at Lud, and they hanged him on the day before Passover.

The name Lud (sometimes Llud) derived from 'the great burth, Lundunaborg, which is the greatest and most famous of all burths in the northern lands'. This city was first called by Brutus, Troynovant, or New Troy. About one thousand years later, ca 41 BC, there reigned in the same town King Lud, who built walls and towers to his city, and renamed it Caer Lud. Thus Lud's Town became Londinium in the Fourth Century and then London, the capital city of England today and chief city of the British Empire. King Lud's name still lives in London today and is encompassed in one of the seven double gates called Ludgate, the location of St. Paul's Cathedral and the probable site of the stoning of Jesus. St. Peter traditionally came to Britain in AD 62 and built a chapel on the future site of Westminster Abbey in London, which is still traditionally called St. Peter‘s Chapel after him. Old St. Peter's Abbey following a persecution of Christians during the second-century AD was turned into the "Temple of Apollo" by the pagan Roman authorities. The next year, AD 63, St. Paul, the Apostle, between his two imprisonments, came himself to Britain, on a missionary tour, and built Old St. Paul´s Cathedral in London on the probable site of the stoning of Jesus.

Clearly inferred by the *Babylonian Talmud.* Stoning, and then the hanging of the body of Jesus, was recorded in the canonical Christian writings today. The word 'stake', not 'cross', was found in all oldest Christian Gospels and the 'cross tradition' did not enter the New Testament until centuries later. The Catholic Church admitted that 'there is no proof of the use of a cross until much later' than the Sixth Century. The word 'cross' was later substituted for the word 'stake' in the rewriting of the Christian texts. It was recorded in Christian archives that the general use of the crucifix became ratified at the Sixth Ecumenical Council in AD 680 *(Canon 82).* The council decreed that *'the figure of a man fastened to a cross be now adopted'.* The new church logo was later confirmed by Pope Hadrian I (772-795). About a century afterwards, the first pictures of Jesus Christ standing against a cross slowly started to appear, mainly in Syrian art. The Second Century historian Celsus provided a hint when he referred to the *'alleged crucifixion'* of Jesus Christ. The church later burnt his books. But it was a statement made by Pope Leo X to the Latin Church that strengthened the suspicion that both Leonardo da Vinci and Michelangelo were privy to secret information. Pope Leo X frankly declared, *'How well we know what a profitable superstition this fable of Christ has been for us'.*

**Tiberius Julius Abdes Panthera's gravestone**

**Roman writing on Panthera's gravestone in Germany**

## Pathros (Pathrusim)

Pathros or Pathrusim, son of Mizraim (Mitzraim). The people of this name migrated to Upper Egypt, where the Egyptians recorded their name as the p't'rs or Ptores, and where they gave their name to the district of Pathros. Esarhaddon, king of Assyria (681-668 BC), records his conquest of the Paturisi, thus showing that this people, at least could not have been totally destroyed in the earlier Ethiopic War as asserted by Josephus.

## Peleg (Palag)

Peleg, son of Ibru (Eber). In his day was the earth divided. The meaning of his name, that is, 'division' as rendered in Hebrew, is confirmed by the Akkadian noun *pulukku*, which means a dividing up of territory by means of borders and boundaries. The Akkadian verb meaning to divide at the borders, is *palaka.* Likewise, the Assyrian *palgu* refers to the dividing up of land by canals and irrigation systems. It is in this sense that the Hebrew word peleg is used in, for example, *Job* 29:6 and *Job* 38:5. The man named Peleg, however, was so named after the division and scattering of the nations at Babel. In fact, one of the ancient names of Babylon (Babel) is nowadays translated as 'the place of canals' (palgu); whereas a better translation would obviously be 'the place of division'. There is an ancient city that bore his name. That was known to the Akkadians as Phalgu, whose ruins lie at the junction of the Euphrates and Chaboras (Chebar, see *Ezekiel* 1:1) rivers.

## PENEMUE (Pnimea)

PNIMEA or PENEMUE a "fallen angel" who instructed mankind in writing "and thereby many sinned from eternity to eternity and until this day.

For man was not created for such a purpose." *Enoch I 7:8.* Penemue also taught children the "bitter and sweet, and the secrets of wisdom."

## PHOEBE (Doris)

PHOEBE by the Greeks, daughter of Uranos (Anshar) and Gaea (Kishar). DORIS by the Romans. She was the third protectress of the Delphic Oracle, after Gaia and Themis.

Phoebe was a NEREID or goddess of the sea. They were the patrons of sailors and fishermen, who came to the aid of men in distress, and goddesses who had in their care the sea's rich bounty. Individually they also represented various facets of the sea, from salty brine, to foam, sand, rocky shores, waves and currents, in addition to the various skills possessed by seamen. The Nereides were depicted in ancient art as beautiful young maidens, sometimes running with small dolphins or fish in their hands, or else riding on the back of dolphins, hippokampoi (fish-tailed horses) and other sea creatures.

## Put (Phut)

Put, Phut, or Punt, son of Chem (Ham) and Naelatamauk. The country in which the descendants of Put settled is well known to us from Egyptian records, which render the name as Put or Punt. It is always spoken of as closely associated with Egypt, and its close proximity to that nation is confirmed by an inscription from the archives of Darius I the Great, King of Persia (522-486 BC). Here the land of Puta is shown as lying in the proximity of Cyrenaica, that is on the North African coast to the west of Egypt. This same land was also known as Puta to the Babylonians, and as Putiya in the Old Persian inscriptions.

## Raamah (Raama)

Raamah or Raama, brother of Nimrod, son of Cush (Kush) and Candace. We know from the inscriptions of ancient Sheba that Raamah's descendants settled near to the land of Havilah to the east of Ophir. They are known from other sources to have traded with the children of Zidon in the city of Tyre.

## RAMUEL (Ramel)

RAMUEL, RAMEL, RUMYEL or RAMUELA a "fallen angel" who mated with earth's human females and produced human giants.

## Reu (Ragau)

Reu, son of Peleg (Palag) and Lamna. Reu's name appears as a personal name in Akkadian documents, where it is rendered Ra'u. The early Greeks knew it as Ragau. Reu was to give his name to an island in the Euphrates that lies just below the city of Amat, and which the Akkadians knew as Ra'ilu. It was also known to the Greeks as Ragu.

## Sabtah

Sabtah, brother of Nimrod, son of Cush (Kush) and Candace. Josephus records the name of Sabtah's descendants as the Sabateni. Ptolemy knew them as the Stabaei, and Pliny called them the Messabathi. They settled on the eastern side of the Arabian peninsula. Sabta's name is also preserved in the ancient city of Shabwat, the capital of the Hadramaut (Hazarmaveth).

## Samson

Samson of the tribe of Dan, his birth was foretold by an angel who appeared to his father Manoah and his barren wife, saying that Samson would be a Nazirite, a person dedicated to God by taking special vows.

*Judges* 13:3-5 - And the angel of the Lord appeared unto the woman, and said unto her, Behold now, thou art barren, and bearest not: but thou shalt conceive, and bear a son. Now therefore beware, I pray thee, and drink, and eat not any unclean thing: For, lo, thou shalt conceive, and bear a son; and no razor shall come on his head: for the child shall be a Nazarite unto God from the womb: and he shall begin to deliver Israel out of the hand of the Philistines.

*Judges* 13:13-14 - And the angel of the Lord said unto Manoah, of all that I said unto the woman let her beware. She may not eat of any thing that cometh of the vine, neither let her drink wine or strong drink, nor eat any unclean thing: all that I commanded her let her observe.

*Judges* 15:9-17 - Then the Philistines went up, and pitched in Judah, and spread themselves in Lehi. And the men of Judah said, Why are ye come up against us? And they answered, to bind Samson are we come up, to do to him as he hath done to us. Then three thousand men of Judah went to the top of the rock E-tam, and said to Samson, knowest thou not that the Philistines are rulers over us? What is this that thou hast done unto us? And he said unto them, as they did unto me, so have I done unto them. And they said unto him, we are come down to bind thee, that we may deliver thee into the hand of the Philistines. And Samson said unto them, swear unto me, that ye will not fall upon me yourselves. And they spake unto him, saying, No; but we will bind thee fast, and deliver thee into their hand: but surely we will not kill thee. And they bound him with two new cords, and brought him up from the rock.

And when he came unto Lehi, the Philistines shouted against him: and the Spirit of the Lord came mightily upon him, and the cords that were upon his arms became as flax that was burnt with fire, and his bands loosed from off his hands. And he found a new jawbone of an ass, and put forth his hand,

and took it, and slew a thousand men therewith. And Samson said, "with the jawbone of an ass, heaps upon heaps, with the jaw of an ass have I slain a thousand men." And it came to pass, when he had made an end of speaking, that he cast away the jawbone out of his hand, and called that place Ra-math-le-hi.

## SARAKNYAL (Sahriel)

SARAKNYAL, SARAKUYAL, SAHRIEL, SAHTAIL, SAHTEIL, SAHARIEL, or ASDEREL a "fallen angel" who is one of 200 angels under the leadership of Semyaza who descended to earth to cohabit with the daughters of men.

## Sargon

King Sargon I by the Akkadians, giant demi-god son of human male Buru-Gina and Anunnaki goddess Atuneni (Athena). Sha-Gana, Sha-Guna, Gin-ukus or Gin-ukussi by the Egyptians. Sargon the Great's Sumer-centered empire extended to the Indus Valley in the east, the British Isles in the west, encompassing much in between, and was larger than that of Alexander the Great or the Romans.

The Sumerian story of King Sargon states that his mother floated him in a basket of rushes on the river and he was found by a member of the Sumerian royal family who brought him up as their own. The Hebrew priests, the Levites, later stole this ancient story from the Sumerian accounts and used it in the invented character known as Moses.

*The Legend of Sargon* - "Sargon, the mighty King of Agade, am I. My mother was a high priestess; I knew not my father. My mother, the high priestess who conceived me, in secret she bore me." Then, as in the story of the birth of Moses in Egypt a thousand years later, Sargon continued: "She set me in a basket of rushes, with bitumen sealed the lid. She cast me into the river, it did not sink me. The river bore me, carried me to Akki the gardener. Akki the irrigator lifted me up when he drew water. Akki the irrigator as his son made me and reared me. Akki, the irrigator, appointed me as his gardener."

## Satecha

Satecha, brother of King Nimrod, son of Cush (Kush) and Candace.

## Satí (Seth)

Satanael by the Sumerians. Sati by the Akkadians, son of Adapa (Adam) and Khawa (Eve). Seth by the Hebrews. Josephus tells us that "The patriarch Seth, in order that wisdom and astronomical knowledge should not perish, erected, in prevision of the double destruction by fire and water predicted by Adam, two columns, one of brick, the other of stone, on which this knowledge was engraved, and which existed in the Siriadic country."

## SAT.IS

SAT.IS by the Sumerians, daughter of An.ki and Anu.kis. Anunnaki wife of Soth.is.

## Satu (Seth)

Satu by the Akkadians, son of Mar.duk (Phosphorus) and human female Zarpanitu (Sarpanit). Suti, Sutekh or "the god (demi-god) of wind and storms" and Set, Seti and Seth or "God (demi-god) of destruction" or "Fierce Wind" by the Egyptians. The red colored 'Dark Lord' deity of the scorching Egyptian desert. The Egyptians would sacrifice red-headed men on the tomb of Osiris because red was the color associated with Set, the Egyptian version of Satan.

Set or "He who is below"; God (demi-god) of the unclean, the terrible desert, the murderer and cruelty, evil, war, and the Underworld. God of the northern sky, darkness, cold, mist, rain. Set was both a good and bad god, turning from one mood to another with lightning and unpredictable speed. He had reddish-white skin and bright red hair-something hated by the Egyptians. This was emphasized by the fact that the conquering Hyksos (rulers identified Set with their Sutekh, built a magnificent temple to him in Avaris, and elevated his worship over all others. The animal associated with this god had long pointed ears and looked rather like a dog, but the exact animal is not known.

## Sebah (Seba)

Sebah or Seba, brother of King Nimrod, son of Cush (Kush) and Candace. Sebah founder of the nation that was known to later history as the Sabaeans, Strubo writes of their chief town of Sabai and its harbour of Saba, both of which lay on the west coast of the Arabian peninsula.

# SEMJASA (Oz)

AZZA, ASA, SAMYAZA, SEMIHAZAH, SEMIAZA, SEMJASA, SEMJAZA, SEMYAZA, SHEMYAZA, SHEMHAZAI, SHEMAZYA, SHEMIHAZA, SHEMYAZA, SHEMIHAZAH, SHAMGAZ, SHAMAZYA, SHAMCHAZAI, SHAMHAZAI, SHAMIZAD, SHAMIAZAZ, SHERNIHAZA, AMEZYARAK, AMAZAREC, AMAZAROC, AMIZIRAS, AZZA, AZA, AUZA, ASA, UZZA, UZZAH, UZAH, USIAH, OUZA, OZAH, OZA and OZ (Wizard of Oz). (see also the fallen angels Enki/Gadreel/Satan & Marduk/Azazel/Lucifer)

SEMJASA by the Pleiadians. SHEMYAZA by the Hebrews. Shemyaza was the leader of the "fallen angels" who fell to Earth. UZZA, UZZAH, OUZA or "strength" by the Egyptians. UZZA is the tutelary angel of the Egyptians. ASA or "Father God" by the Africans.

The "Fallen Angels" were known as the angels that rebelled against Almighty God, were cast out of heaven and "fell to earth". They were called by the ancient sumerians the IGIGI or "Those that Watch and See". Their symbol was the "All Seeing Eye". In these ancient Sumerian records the Igigi revolted against Enlil. They were called the GRIGORI or "Watchers", the "fallen angels" by the ancient Hebrons/Heberu/Hebrews. In ancient Hebrew records the Grigori revolted against Yahweh. The Greeks called them the EGREGOROI or "The Watchers".

Angels do "excel in strength" *Psalm* 103:20. They are greater "in power and might" than men of earth *2 Peter* 2:11.The 'fallen angels' offspring, the nephilim, were giants in size and strength. There is plenty of documentation of the exceptional physical stature and super-human strength of the nephilim or the sons of the fallen angels. What applies to holy angels, applies equally to fallen angels. Their fall to earth does not seem to have reduced their physical prowess. The Book of Enoch states that their *"height was like the tallness of cedars and whose bodies were like mountains."*

Dr. Arthur David Horn, *Humanity's Extraterrestrial Origins* cr 1994 - The Pleiadians tell of more recent meetings of Pleiadians and the "daughters of men" some 13,000 to 11,000 years ago. They caught wild Earth creatures "descendants of former human beings from cosmic space" - descendants of survivors of earlier disasters: Wild and beautiful female beings were tamed and mated with by the sub-leaders of the Pleiadian YHWH, ARUS, who called themselves "Sons of Heaven" . . . Semjase, the highest leader of the subleaders, mated with an EVA, a female being, who was still mostly human-like and also rather beautiful . . . The descendant of this act was of male sex and a human being of good form. Semjase called him A-DAM, which was a word meaning "Earth human being." A similar breeding produced a female, and in later years they were mated to each other.

Shemhazai (Semjasa) and Azael (Lucifer), two angels in God's confidence, asked: "Lord of the Universe, did we not warn you on the day of Creation that man would prove unworthy of your world?" They answered: "We shall inhabit it." God asked: "Yet upon descending to earth, will you not sin even worse than man?" They pleaded: "Let us dwell there awhile, and we will sanctify your name!" God allowed them to descend. They were then overcome by lust for Eve's daughters, Shemhazai begetting on them two monstrous sons named Hiwa and Hiya, each of whom daily ate a thousand camels, a thousand horses and a thousand oxen. Azael also invented the ornaments and cosmetics employed by women to lead men astray. God therefore warned them that he would set loose the Upper Waters, and thus destroy all men and beasts. Shemhazai wept bitterly, fearing for his sons who, though tall enough to escape drowning, would starve to death.

The Fallen Ones had such huge appetites that God rained manna upon them, of many different flavors, lest they might be tempted to eat flesh, a forbidden diet, and excuse the fault by pleading scarcity of corn and pot herbs. Nevertheless, the Fallen Ones rejected God's manna, slaughtered animals for food, and even dined on human flesh, thus fouling the air with sickly vapors. It was then that God decided to cleanse the Earth.

*Book of Enoch* 7:1-15 - It happened after the sons of men had multiplied in those days, that daughters were born to them, elegant and beautiful. And when the angels, the sons of heaven, beheld them, they became enamored of them, saying to each other, Come, let us select for ourselves wives from the progeny of men, and let us beget children. Then their leader Samyaza said to them; I fear that you may perhaps be indisposed to the performance of this enterprize; And that I alone shall suffer for so grievous a crime. But they answered him and said; We all swear; And bind ourselves by mutual execrations, that we will not change our intention, but execute our projected undertaking.

Then they swore all together, and all bound themselves by mutual execrations. Their whole number was two hundred, who descended upon Ardis, which is the top of Mount Armon. That mountain therefore was called Armon, because they had sworn upon it, and bound themselves by mutual execrations.

These are the names of their chiefs: Samyaza who was their leader, Urakabarameel, Akibeel, Tamiel, Ramuel, Danel, Azkeel, Saraknyal, Asael, Armers, Batraal, Anane, Zavebe, Samsaveel, Ertael, Turel, Yomyael, Arazyal (Azazyel/Azazel). These were the prefects of the two hundred angels, and the remainder were all with them.

"Then they took wives, each choosing for himself; whom they began to approach, and with whom they cohabited; teaching them sorcery, incantations, and the dividing of roots and trees."

"And the women conceiving brought forth giants. Whose stature was each three hundred cubits (300 inches = 25 ft.). These (giants) devoured all which the labor of men produced; until it became impossible to feed them; When they turned themselves against men, in order to devour them; And began to injure birds, beasts, reptiles, and fishes, to eat their flesh one after another, and to drink their blood. Then the earth reproved the unrighteous.

*Book of Enoch* 7:10-15 - Then they (the fallen angels) took wives, each choosing for himself; whom they began to approach, and with whom they cohabited; teaching them sorcery, incantations, and the dividing of roots and trees. And the women conceiving brought forth giants, Whose stature was each three hundred cubits. These (giants) devoured all which the labor of men produced; until it became impossible to feed them; When they turned themselves against men, in order to devour them; And began to injure birds, beasts, reptiles, and fishes, to eat their flesh one after another, and to drink their blood. Then the earth reproved the unrighteous.

*Book of Enoch* 9:8-14 & 10:1-5 - The women likewise have brought forth giants. Thus has the whole earth been filled with blood and with iniquity. And now behold the souls of those who are dead, cry out. And complain even to the gate of heaven. Their groaning ascends; nor can they escape from the unrighteousness which is committed on earth. Thou knowest all things, before they exist. Thou knowest these things, and what has been done by them; yet thou dost not speak to us. What on account of these things ought we to do to them?

Then the Most High, the Great and Holy One spoke, And sent Arsayalalyur to the son of Hamech (Noah), Saying, Say to him in my name, Conceal thyself. Then explain to him the consummation which is about to take place; for all the earth shall perish; the water of a deluge shall come over the whole earth, and all things which are in it shall be destroyed. And now teach him how he may escape, and how his seed may remain in all the earth.

*Book of Jubilees* 7:21-22 - For owing to these things came the flood upon the earth, namely, owing to the fornication wherein the Watchers against the law of their ordinances went a whoring after the daughters of men, and took themselves wives of all which they chose: and they made the beginning of uncleanness. And they begat sons the Naphidim (Nephilim), and they were all unlike, and they devoured one another: and the Giants slew the Naphil, and the Naphil slew the Eljo, and the Eljo mankind, and one man another.

*Book of Enoch* 15:8-10 - Now the giants, who have been born of spirit and of flesh, shall be called upon earth evil spirits, and on earth shall be their habitation. Evil spirits shall proceed from their flesh, because they were created from above; from the holy Watchers was their beginning and primary foundation. Evil spirits shall they be upon earth, and the spirits of the wicked shall they be called. The habitation of the spirits of heaven shall be in heaven; but upon earth shall be the habitation of terrestrial spirits, who are born on earth. The spirits of the giants shall be like clouds, which shall oppress, corrupt, fall, contend, and bruise upon earth. They shall cause lamentation. No food shall they eat; and they shall be thirsty; they shall be concealed, and shall not rise up against the sons of men, and against women; for they come forth during the days of slaughter and destruction.

*Book of Enoch* 16:1 - And as to the death of the giants, wheresoever their spirits depart from their bodies, let their flesh, that which is perishable, be without judgment. Thus shall they perish, until the day of the great consumation of the great world. A destruction shall take place of the Watchers and the impious.

The Albigensians (Albigenses), also referred to as Cathars, were the one heretical group that so threatened medieval Catholicism that an armed invasion of southern France by Catholic armies was authorized by Pope Innocent III in 1209 to suppress them. What the military forces - primarily northern French lords and their followers - began, the Inquisition finished. The Cathars called themselves the True Church of God. A Provencal manuscript, *The Vindication of the Church of God,* written around 1250, states that the Albigensians refrained from killing, theft, and swearing oaths and otherwise followed Jesus's teachings; consequently, they suffered "persecutions and tribulations and martyrdom in the name of Christ."

The Albigensians also made use of the Bogomil work, known as the Interrogatio Johannis (The questions of John) or sometimes called The Secret Supper. Brought to Italy in the late twelfth century, it describes the apostle John questioning Christ at a heavenly Last Supper about the origins of the world, the cause of evil, the rebellion of Satan, and the process of human salvation. According to this work, Satan created the world; after his rebellion against God the Father, he could find no peace in heaven, so out of pity God gave him seven days to create what he would. What follows is a version of the Genesis creation story with Satan (Enki) as creator; he commands a fallen angel Semjasa to enter a body and animate Adam and an angel of the first (lowest) heaven to animate Eve's body. Directed by the devil, the first couple "were affected by a lust for debauchery, together begetting children of the devil and of the serpent, until the consummation of the world." In other words, physical creation is the result of Satan's rebellion.

SUMMARY OF *THE BOOK OF GIANTS* by James R. Davila - NOTE: You are strongly advised to read the Book of the Watchers (*1 Enoch* 1-36) before tackling the *Book of Giants!* The story will make much better sense if you do.

I. THE MANICHEAN VERSION

Fragments of and allusions to the Manichean version of the Book of the Giants have been recovered in medieval manuscripts in various languages, including Middle Persian, Sogdian, Uygur, Coptic, Parthian, and Latin. The following is a summary of the surviving fragments and allusions, which I have attempted--extremely tentatively!--to put in sequence. The summaries are also very tentative; I have not consulted the texts in the original languages, most of which I do not read. For the sequencing I follow some of the many (mutually inconsistent) suggestions and observations by the various editors and commentators along with occasional bouts of my own gut feeling, but in many places the ordering is extremely doubtful. Readers may find it an interesting exercise to try to work out equally or more plausible arrangements. See after the summary for some notes on my rationale for the sequencing.

M1. The two hundred demons descend to earth.

M2. Their descent from heaven stirs up the other heavenly beings.

M3. They descend because of the beauty of the women they saw there (cf. *Genesis* 6:2; *1 Enoch* 6:1-2; *Jubilees* 5:1).

M4. They reveal forbidden arts and heavenly mysteries in order to seduce these women (cf. *1 Enoch* 7-8) and they bring about ruin on the earth (cf. *Genesis* 6:5, 11-12; *1 Enoch* 7; 9:8; *Jubilees* 5:2-3).

M5. Someone (Enoch) warns that the coming of the two hundred demons will lead only to "hurting speech" and "hard labor."

M6. They subjugate the human race, killing hundreds of thousands of the righteous in battle, forcibly marrying beautiful women, and enslaving the nations. The angels "veil" Enoch (cf. *Genesis* 5:24; *1 Enoch* 87:3-4, 70:3; *Jubilees* 4:21, 23).

M7. The righteous endure burning and Enoch the Sage is mentioned.

M8. Shamizad (Shemihazah, cf. *1 Enoch* 6:3; 9:7) begets two giant sons, Sa(h)m (=Ohyah) and Pat-Sam (=Nariman or Ahyah/Hahyah). The other demons and Yaksas beget the rest of the giants.

M9. The giants grow up and wreak ruin upon the earth and the human race. The lamentation of humanity reaches up to heaven.

M10. Yima (a transmogrification of the Jewish God according to Mani's cosmology) accepts the homage of humankind as they plead for help.

M11. Someone boasts that Sa(h)m and his brother will live and rule forever in their unequaled power and strength.

M12. The giant Hobabish (=Humbaba) robs someone of his wife. The giants fall out among themselves and begin killing one another and other creatures. Sa(h)m and his brother are mentioned. It appears that Sa(h)m has a dream in which a tablet was thrown in the water. It seems to have borne three signs, portending woe, flight, and destruction. Nariman has a dream about a garden full of trees in rows. Two hundred of something, perhaps trees, are mentioned.

M13. Someone recites a list of proverbs involving contrasts, usually between the lesser and the greater or the derivative from the source. Nariman tells how he saw (in the dream) some who were weeping and lamenting and many others who were sinful rulers.

M14. The giant Mahaway, son of Virogdad (=Baraq'el, cf. *1 Enoch* 6:7), hears a cautioning voice as he flies along at sunrise and he is guided to safety by Enoch "the apostle" and the heavenly voice, which warn him to descend before the sun sets his wings on fire (shades of Icarus). He lands and the voice leads him to Enoch.

M15. Enoch interprets the dream, indicating that the trees represent the "Egregoroi" (Greek for "Watchers," cf. *1 Enoch* 12:4 etc.) and also mentioning the giants who were born of women. Something (the trees) are "pulled out."

M16. Someone reports that someone ordered him not to run away but to bring the message written on two stone tablets, showing it first to Nariman. He has brought them in order to share the contents of one tablet, pertaining to the demons, with the giants. Shamizad tells him to read the writing by Enoch.

M17. Enoch the apostle gives a message of judgment to the demons and their children, telling them that they will have no peace and that they will see the destruction of their children (the giants--cf. *1 Enoch* 14:6; 16:3; *Jubilees* 4:22). He refers to someone (presumably the giants) ruling for one hundred twenty years (cf. *Genesis* 6:3). Then he predicts either an era of earthly fecundity, presumably after the Flood (cf. *1 Enoch* 10:11-22), or else the Flood itself (cf. *Genesis* 7:8-9).

M18. Sa(h)m exhorts the other giants to cheer up and eat but they are too sorrowful to eat and instead fall asleep. Mahaway goes to Atanbush (=another giant) and tells him all. When Mahaway returns, Sa(h)m has a dream in which he ascends to heaven. He sees the water of the earth consumed with heat and a demon comes out of the water. Some beings (the protecting spirits) are invisible but he sees the heavenly rulers.

M19. Sa(h)m, Shamizad, and Mahaway have a conversation. Mahaway mentions his father, Virogdad. There are obscure references to weapons and a blessing on someone who saw something but escaped death. Samizad and Mahaway search for something.

M20. Someone gives satisfactory assurance to Mahaway that he will be protected from Sa(h)m but nevertheless Sa(h)m and Mahaway fall out and begin to fight.

M21. The wicked demons are glad to see the "apostle" (Enoch) and assemble timidly before him. Apparently they promise to reform their ways and they ask for mercy (cf. 1 Enoch 13:4-6, 9).

M22. Someone (Enoch) warns a group (the demons) that they will be taken from a fire to face eternal damnation, despite their belief that they would never lose their misused power. He also addresses their "sinful misbegotten sons" (the giants--cf. Gen 6:3) and describes how the righteous will fly over the fire of damnation and gloat over the souls inside it.

M23. "They," presumably the demons, take some heavenly helpers hostage. As a result the angels descend from heaven, terrifying the two hundred demons, who take human form and hide among human beings (cf. *1 Enoch* 17:1). They, the angels separate out the human beings and set a watch over them, seize the giants from the demons, and lead "them" (the children of the giants) to safety in thirty-two distant towns prepared for them by the "Living Spirit" at Aryan Wezan (the traditional homeland of the Indo-Iranians) in the vicinity of the sacred Mount Sumeru and other mountains. These people originated the arts and crafts. The two hundred demons fight a massive and fiery battle with the four angels.

M24. Atanbush does battle, accompanied by Watchers and giants, and three of the giants are killed. An angel and others are also killed.

M25. Ohyah and Ahyah resolve to keep their promise to do battle, and they boast of their prowess.

M26. The four angels, by divine command, bind the Egregoroi with everlasting chains in a dark prison (cf. *1 Enoch* 10:11-14; Jub. 5:6, 10) and annihilate their children (cf. *1 Enoch* 10:15; 15:8-12; *Jubilees* 5:7-9, 11).

M27. Even before the rebellion of the Egregoroi, this prison had been built for them under the mountains. In addition, thirty-six towns had been prepared for the habitation of the wicked and long-lived sons of the giants before they were even born.

M28. Ohyah (or Ahyah), the primordial monster Leviathan, and the archangel Raphael engage in a great battle, "and they vanished." According to one tradition, Ohyah survived the Flood and fought this battle after it.

M29. Three thousand, two hundred and eighty years passed between the time of Enoch and the time of King Vishtasp (who ruled at the time of the prophet Zoroaster, who, along with Buddha and Christ, was an apostle who came before the final apostle Mani).

I regard the order of the following passages as nearly certain. The order of M1-4, 6 is clear, and M5 belongs in the same vicinity. M8-9 must follow these and M11-12 seem to go in the same vicinity. M15 appears to interpret the dream in M12. M16 and M18 are opposite sides of the same page, with an undetermined amount of text lost between them at the bottom of the page. M23, 26-27 belong to the same late episode, and M28-29 deal with the postdiluvian period.

I regard the order of the following passages as plausible but uncertain. M14 introduces an episode in which Enoch's interpretation is solicited while he is distant from the giants. M16 pertains to (Mahaway's) bringing back of a message from Enoch on stone tablets and M17 gives a message sent by Enoch whose content fits the context.

I regard the order of the following passages as possible but speculative. M7 could also fit with the episode in M23, 26-27. The placement of M10 here is based on Skjaervø's speculation that Yima is identified with the Jewish God. M13 fits where I have placed it but could also fit in later contexts. M19-20 seem to follow a natural progression in which Sa(h)m and Mahaway fall out after M18, but other placements for both are possible. I place M21 late in the narrative on the assumption that Enoch first sends a message to the giants but then (in a passage now lost) as the situation deteriorates he comes to see them himself. M22 fits as an Enochic response to the appeal of the demons for mercy, although it could also go with M17 (although it seems doubtful that so much text could fit between M16 and

M18). M24-25 fit well where I have put them but could conceivably also go with M9-12.

II. THE ARAMAIC VERSION FROM QUMRAN

There have been many attempts to reconstruct the sequence and content of the Aramaic Book of Giants. Here I follow Stuckenbruck's sequencing, essentially uncritically, since his is the most recent and most comprehensive attempt with all the fragments available. An effort to nuance this version is given after the summary. I do not always follow Stuckenbruck's readings or interpretations.

A1. The angelic Watchers beget the Nephilim and the giants through miscegenation with mortal women (cf. *Genesis* 6:1-4; *1 Enoch* 6; *Jubilees* 5:1). These rapacious monsters inflict bloodshed and injustice upon the earth and destruction upon the sea animals, plants, cattle, and humanity (cf. *Genesis* 6:5, 11-12; *1 Enoch* 7; 9:8; *Jubilees* 5:2).

A2. All this is reported to Enoch, the "scribe of interpretation."

A3. Enoch addresses God, praising him for his glory, knowledge, strength, and creative acts.

A4. A number of giants, including Hobabis (=Humbaba), Mahaway, [, and perhaps the Watcher Baraq'el, have a conversation in which they discuss killing, perhaps of human beings.

A5. Following hints from the Manichean version and the Midrash of Shemihazah, perhaps we should reconstruct here an episode in which the giants have a first pair of dreams predicting the great Flood. If so, the first dream seems to involve the effacing of a writing-tablet by submerging it in water. Stuckenbruck also suggests that a fragment which refers to three shoots in a garden (6Q8 2-3) belongs to the second. The first dream may have told of an angel doing the effacing as a symbol of the destruction wrought by the Flood. The second may have told of an angel descending and cutting down all but three shoots (representing the sons of Noah) in the garden.

A6. [Mahaway consults Enoch the first time. It is possible that the first tablet was introduced at this point. These episodes are entirely lost but their existence is deduced by later references in the fragments.] The giants Ohyah and Mahaway have a conversation in which Mahaway tells Ohyah something he heard while in the presence of his (Mahaway's) father, the Watcher Baraq'el. Ohyah responds that he too has heard "fou[r] marvels" and he starts to make a comparison which pertains to a woman giving birth.

A7. There is a conversation among the giants in which one of them admits that, despite his own might, he has been unable to prevail in war against some heavenly beings, presumably the archangels. Ohyah mentions an oppressive dream which has disturbed him, and someone tells the giant Gilgamesh to recount his dream as well.

A8. Ohyah says something to his brother Hahyah about the Watcher Azazel (cf. *Leviticus* 16:7-10; *1 Enoch* 8:1; 9:6, etc.), the Watchers, and the giants. In another fragment that may continue this speech, one of the giants resigns himself that there is no escape and that he and the others must die for their misdeeds. He refers to a vision that hinders him from sleeping. Someone enters the assembly of the giants. Perhaps a conversation continues in which the giants anticipate with dread their coming destruction in the Flood for their sins, in which they will be stripped of their form and reduced to being evil spirits (Cf. *1 Enoch* 15:8-12).

A9. The Watchers tell the giants that they themselves are imprisioned and perhaps that the giants are being defeated.

A10. Mahaway and the two tablets are mentioned. The second tablet is now read. It is a letter from Enoch to the Watcher Shemihazah and his companions. They are rebuked for their and their sons' (the giants) corrupt acts, which have come to the attention of the archangel Raphael (cf. *1 Enoch* 9:1?). They are warned of imminent destruction and ordered to release their hostages and to pray.

A11. Neverthless, Ohyah informs the giants of a message from Gilgamesh and Hobabis which involves the cursing of "the princes" and which cheers the giants up.

A12. The two giants Ohyah and Hahyah have dreams. Hahyah describes his in the assembly of the giants. He dreamed of gardeners watering a garden which produced great shoots. But a disaster of some sort destroyed the garden in a deluge of water and fire. The other giants are unable to interpret his dream. Hahyah proposes that they consult Enoch for an interpretation. Then his brother, Ohyah reports that he too had a dream, in which God descended to the earth, thrones were set up, and God sat enthroned amid a multitude of angels and presided over a judgment based on the opening of certain books (cf. *Daniel* 7:9-10). The giants, presumably unable to interpret this dream either, summon Mahaway and send him to Enoch, whom he has encountered before, to ask him to interpret the dreams.

A13. Mahaway takes wing and flies across the "Great Desert" until Enoch sees him and calls to him. Mahaway refers to this as his second visit and makes the request. Bits of Enoch's interpretation may survive in a fragment that mentions the violent deaths of a number of Watchers, Nephilim, and giants, and also in a small fragment that says "no peace to you."

A14. Enoch pronounces an eschatological or postdiluvian blessing of earthly prosperity.

(Presumably much of the story came after this point and is now lost. Cf. M18-28 above.)

Reconstruction of the Aramaic *Book of Giants* remains extremely subjective, but a number of objective factors limit the possible arrangments and point us in certain directions. The most important external factor is the assured sequence of fragments in some of the manuscripts based on physical joins. A9 and A10 must come in this order, since they are adjoining columns in 4Q203. Likewise, A11-13 come from an assemblage of three columns of fragments in 4Q530. Other sequences are regarded as assured by some commentators but not others.

A second factor is that some individual fragments of the Manichean version contain material parallel to more than one fragment of the Aramaic version, suggesting (assuming--optimistically--that the order of material in the Manichean version was not radically reworked) that the Aramaic fragments go together. Stuckenbruck notes the following. The fragments 2Q26 and 6Q8 are assigned together in A5 on the grounds that they parallel material in a single fragment of the Middle Persian Manichean version (M12). Another Middle Persian fragment (M 17) suggests that 1Q23 1+6+22 belong together to form A14. And the content of a third Middle Persian fragment (M19) is taken to imply that 6Q8 1 (A6) came before 4Q531 17 (A7). For my own part, I find only the first two suggestions convincing, but not the third, since the correspondences are not very close.

A third factor is the internal evidence of the fragments themselves. Stuckenbruck, building on Garc<'i>a Mart<'i>nez's comments, allows for passages that pertain to the early part of the Watchers/giants narrative when the giants are free agents (A1-4 [5-6?]) and passages after they (or better, the Watchers) have been imprisoned (A9-10). He also points to the reference to two tablets in A10, with the second tablet being read later than the first, and to Mahaway's second visit to Enoch in A13. In both cases, earlier, lost portions of the narrative are hinted at.

The biggest difference between Stuckenbruck's sequencing and those of some other commentators is that he reconstructs two pairs of two dreams. Beyer, Reeves, and Garc'ia Mart'inez group the fragments pertaining to dreams into one episode. Cook, however, does reconstruct multiple dream episodes, although not in precisely the same order as Stuckenbruck, and Puech accepts the necessity of an earlier pair of dreams, although he does not accept that the material assigned to the second dream by Stuckenbruck in A5 belongs there (he puts it, correctly in my view, in the first dream in A12). My own reconstruction of the Manichean version also supports the view that there was more than one episode of dreams.

Another major difference in reconstructions is Garc'ia Mart'inez's argument that material that Stuckenbruck places late in A1 and in A8 and A14 belongs at the very beginning of the work and constitutes a summary of the Book of the Watchers. Beyer, Cook, Reeves, and Stuckenbruck begin the work with much the same material, partially overlapping what Garc'ia Mart'inez uses, as an independent description of the birth and career of the giants.

Otherwise, there are numerous smaller differences of sequencing and interpretation. For example, Beyer puts A10 before A9 which does not seem to be physically possible, and Reeves takes A14 to describe the loading of the ark with animals. There is broad agreement that the narrative began with an account of the birth of the giants, with dreams of the giants, Mahaway's journey to Enoch, a prayer of Enoch, and conversations among the giants assigned different orders from commentator to commentator. (c) 2002.

*The Book of Giants* - Summary of a lecture by J. R. Davila on 1 March 2002 - In this lecture I wish to supplement the previously circulated handout on the Book of Giants with brief overviews of the historical backgrounds of, respectively, the Manichean and the Aramaic versions, along with some observations on the mythological contexts of each version. For reasons already indicated in earlier lectures and reading assignments I will work backwards, starting with the more recent Manichean version and concluding with the question of whether the Aramaic version is a Jewish composition. The Book of Giants has been omitted from all editions of the *Old Testament* Pseudepigrapha, no doubt because of its highly fragmentary state in highly obscure languages, as well as the unavailability of the Aramaic fragments until recently, but it has just as much right to be included as central works like *1 Enoch,* and we can only hope that future editions with find a place for it.

1. THE MANICHEAN VERSION

The founder of the Manichean religion was the apostle Mani (216-76 C.E.), who was raised in Southern Mesopotamia in a Jewish-Christian baptist sect called the *"Elkesaites."* From age twelve on, Mani began to have visions. Eventually, his visionary experiences led to his being expelled from the sect, and he then founded his own religion, sending out missions to Iran, India, Syria and Egypt. Late in his life, he fell out of royal favor and was sent to prison, where he died. He wrote detailed scriptures so that his doctrines would be preserved forever, even going so far as to invent a new script to write them in, but over time nearly all of these scriptures have been lost. This loss makes it very difficult to reconstruct his original theology. We know that he drew on other world religions to interpret himself as the culminating revelatory intermediary for Christianity, Zoroastrianism, and Buddhism. We also know that the Manichean religion taught an extremely complicated system of gnostic dualism centered around a cosmological myth about the war between the originally pristine realms of light and darkness. The physical universe was created as a trick to liberate the captive sparks of light in living beings from the realm of darkness. There were two classes of practicing Manicheans: the Elect, who lived ascetic, monastic lifestyles of celibacy, vegetarianism, etc., and the Hearers, who supported the Elect financially and otherwise in the hope of being reincarnated themselves as Elect in due course. Although most of Mani's scriptures are themselves lost, lists of the titles of these documents survive in works by both friendly and hostile writers who wrote in Coptic, Greek, Arabic, and even Chinese. Allowing for minor corruptions, all the lists mention the same seven works, usually in more or less the same order. These are: the" *Gospel*," the "*Treasure of Life*," the "*Pragmateia*" ("*Treatise*"), the "*Book of Mysteries*," the "*Book of Giants*," the "*Epistles*," and the "*Psalms*."

For our immediate purposes, the only one of interest is the *Book of Giants,* a work apparently composed in Syriac (an eastern dialect of

Aramaic). The book was entirely lost until the twentieth century, but scant references to it survived in Latin, Greek, and Arabic, indicating that it involved battles of the ancient giants. Then about a century ago many highly fragmentary Manichean works written in Central Asian languages were recovered archaeologically at Turfan, in China (and much of the find remains unpublished even at present). Among the published fragments are many badly eroded manuscripts of the *Book of Giants* in various languages. The articles by Henning, Sundermann, & Skjaervø; translate these and try to put them into some order and context. Reeves and Stuckenbruck also make use of many of them. In the previously distributed handout I have also tried to set them into a possible order, although many problems remain. It is not entirely clear, for example, whether there were two sets of dreams or only one, or whether the tablets in the dream of Sa(h)m are the same as or different from those mentioned in M16.

The Manichean versions adapted the story of the giants to fit Iranian mythology. Skjaervø discusses these adaptations at length. Three of the most striking adjustments have to to with the names of major characters. Sam or Sahm is the name of an immortal dragon slayer in later Iranian epic. His name is given to the giant Ohyah. Ohyah's brother, Hahyah, is given the name Nariman, who in Iranian epic is a figure closely connected to Sa(h)m; either identified with him or presented as one of his close relatives. The name of the father of the giant Mahaway, the demon *"Virogdad,"* means *"given by lightning"* in Persian, a loose translation of *"Baraq'el,"* which is Hebrew for *"lightning of God."* The Watcher Baraq'el seems to be the father of Mahaway in the Aramaic version of the *Book of Giants.*

2. THE ORIGINAL ARAMAIC VERSION FROM QUMRAN

In my handout I have noted numerous connections between Mani's Book of Giants and the stories of the giants related in the Enoch literature and in Jubilees. These were already good indicators of Mani's use of earlier Jewish traditions, a use confirmed by the discovery of the *Dead Sea Scrolls* in 1947.

These consisted of many hundreds of parchment and papyrus manuscripts in Hebrew and Aramaic (with a few also in Greek), most of which had rotted away into tens of thousands of fragments. Fragments survived of some of the Enoch books (in Aramaic) and also the *book of Jubilees* (in Hebrew). J. T. Milik also discovered roughly six to ten extremely poorly preserved manuscripts of an Aramaic *Book of Giants,* apparently the document used by Mani as the basis for his scriptural work. These manuscripts give no indication of being sectarian compositions. Their paleographic dates fall roughly across the first century B.C.E., so presumably the book was composed before this, although how long before remains open to question. The kernel of the same story appears in the *Bible* in *Genesis* 6:1-4 but, as with the Book of the Watchers, it remains debatable whether the traditions about the Watchers and giants are creative expansions of the *Genesis* passage or (more likely in my view) independent transmissions of stories that have been summarized and truncated in *Genesis.*

There is evidence that the Aramaic *Book of Giants* continued to be transmitted in Judaism apart from Mani's version. Hebrew manuscripts survive of the *"Midrash of Shemihazah,"* which Milik has published and translated in his edition of some of the Aramaic fragments of the *Book of Giants.* This work tells how at the time of the corrupt generation of the Flood, the angels Shemihazah and Aza'el make a bet with God that if they were to descend from heaven to earth they would be able to resist the lure of the evil inclination. But after descending they promptly lose the bet: they notice the beauty of mortal women and cannot restrain themselves from becoming sexually involved with them. Soon they find themselves revealing heavenly secrets to their mortal wives. Shemihazah begets sons named Heyya and Aheyya. The angel Metatron (another name for the deified Enoch in the Hekhalot traditions) sends them a warning of the coming Flood. Heyya and Aheyya each have a prognostic dream. In the first, an angel descends from heaven and scrapes an enormous stone tablet with writing on it, which was spread across the whole world, until only four words remain. In the second, there is a garden full of trees and gems, but an angel descends and cuts down everything but one tree with three branches. Both dreams predict the coming of the Flood and the destructions of all human beings except Noah and his three sons. The giants are then killed in the Flood, but are consoled by the fact that mortals will use their names in incantations and thus their fame will never cease. Shemihazah repents and suspends himself upside down between heaven and earth. Aza'el refuses to repent and becomes a demon who entices men to corrupt deeds and who bears the sins of Israel on the Day of Atonement (cf. *Levi* 16:7-10).

The numerous and striking parallels with the *Book of Giants* are obvious. Although there is only one pair of dreams in the Midrash of Shemihazah, Stuckenbruck argues that the original *Book of Giants* had two sets. This may well be true also of the Manichean version.

Moving now from history of transmission to background influences, we should note that the Aramaic *Book of Giants* draws on ancient Near Eastern myth rather as the Manichean version draws on Iranian myth. Two of the evil giants in the Aramaic version are named Gilgamesh and Hobabis. Gilgamesh is an epic figure in Sumerian and Akkadian literature, best known from the *Epic of Gilgamesh,* a work whose importance in ancient Mesopotamia was comparable to that of the Homeric epics in ancient Greece. According to the Epic, Gilgamesh, a huge semidivine man, has many adventures with his friend, the wild man Enkidu. One of these is the slaying of the monster Humbaba (Huwawa) in the Cedar Forest. But Enkidu dies tragically and Gilgamesh sets out to discover the secret of immortality in order to avoid his friend's fate. He meets Utnapishtim, the Babylonian version of Noah - the only man to survive the Flood. Unlike Noah, Utnapishtim was made immortal by the gods. Nevertheless, Gilgamesh fails in his quest, eventually dying and leaving only his heroic fame behind him. The giants Gilgamesh and Hobabis are reflexes of the Gilgamesh and Humbaba/Huwawa of the

Gilgamesh Epic. Likewise, a Sogdian text of the Manichean version refers to Atanbush, who is either another giant or Enoch under another name (Enoch also survived the Flood and was made immortal). Atanbush is clearly a reflex of Utnapishtim and we may assume that he appeared also in some lost passage or passages in the Aramaic *Book of Giants.*

Finally, we must ask whether the *Book of Giants* is a Jewish work. The dates of the Aramaic manuscripts rule out the possibility of it being a Christian composition, and it clearly does contain Jewish traditions. Nevertheless, it contains Babylonian mythic material as well, which opens up the possibility that it is an indigenous polytheistic (i.e., "pagan") work which borrowed Jewish traditions and in turn was borrowed by Jews. The extremely fragmentary nature of the surviving manuscripts rules out the kind of full analysis of the text we would like, but in what survives I see no obviously Jewish signature features, nor any obvious polytheistic signature features. The context of the Aramaic manuscripts in the Jewish Qumran library should be our starting point, so it makes sense to try to read it as a Jewish work in the first instance, and no obvious obstacles arise when we do so. The use of Babylonian mythic figures, one of whom is demoted from hero to wicked giant, is not too jarring and can be paralleled by the similar demonization of Indian mythic figures in Zoroastrianism or the Classical gods in early Christianity.

## Seni (Shini)

Seni or Shini, son of Canaan. Father of the Shinites. The name of this people is still to be found today in the cities of Nahr as-Sinn and Sinn addarb, which are both in close proximity to Arqa. The Phoenicians knew the Sinites as the Usnu; the Assyrians called them the Usana and Siannu; and the Ugaritic tablets refer to them as the 'sn'.

## Shem (Sem)

Shem, son of Ziu.su.dra (Noah) and Emzara (Emzarah). In the *Book of Jubilee* it states that Shem's mother was Emzarah. Father of the Semites.

## Sidon (Zidon)

Sidon, Sihon or Zidon, son of Canaan. Sidon of Jahaz, King of the Amorites, dwelled with his descendants, on the Mediterranean coast of Canaan, where his name is still preserved today in the city of Sidon. Originally known as Zidonians, his posterity were later called Phoenicians.

*Numbers* 21: 21-25 - And Israel sent messengers unto Sihon (Sidon) king of the Amorites, saying, let me pass through thy land; we will not turn into the fields, or into the vineyards; we will not drink of the waters of the well; but we will go along by the king's high way, until we be past thy borders. And Sihon would not suffer Israel to pass through his border; but Sihon gathered all his people together, and went out against (attacked) Israel into the wilderness: and he came to Jahaz, and fought against Israel. And Israel smote him with the edge of the sword, and possessed his land from Arnon unto Jabbok, even unto the children of Ammon: for the border of the children of Ammon was strong. And Israel took all these cities: and Israel dwelt in all the cities of the Amorites, in Heshbon, and in all the villages thereof.

## Solomon (Jedidiah)

Jedidiah or Solomon, son of King David (Davjd) and Bathsheba. Jedidiah changed his name to Solomon, on his accession to the throne of Israel 1015-931 BC. Advisor to the Egyptian Paraoh Shishak I. Owner of the enchanted ring. Solomon's harem had one primary wife; 300 wives; 1000 secondary wives; and 300 concubines. King Solomon's Seal was the 'Star of

David' with a circle around it. The Bible tells us that God (El Shaddai/Enlil) gave Solomon His promise that the title to the throne would pass through his descendants. *(1 Kings 9:5; 1 Chronicles 22:8-10; 2 Chronicles 7:18).*

## SOTH.IS (Sottis)

SOTH.IS by the Sumerians, son of An.ki and Anu.kis. SIRIUS by the Egyptians. SOTTIS by the Greeks.

## STEROPES (Sterpes)

STEROPES or STERPES was a Cyclope, son of Uranos (Anshar) and Gaea (Kishar). The Cyclopeans are remembered in Polynesian mythology as gods with golden skin who came long ago in flying machines and built pyramids throughout the Pacific.

## TAMIEL (Tamel)

TAMIEL, TUMMIEL, TAMEL, TEMEL, or TAMUEL a "fallen angel" who taught men "astronomy."

## TAMJELA

TAMJELA a "fallen angel" who mated with earth's human females and produced human giants.

## THEIA (Thia)

THEIA, THIA, BASILEA, EURPHAESSA, VASILEIA by the Greeks, daughter of Uranos (Anshar) and Gaea (Kishar). Theia was a NEREID or goddess of the sea. They were the patrons of sailors and fishermen, who came to the aid of men in distress, and goddesses who had in their care the sea's rich bounty. Individually they also represented various facets of the sea, from salty brine, to foam, sand, rocky shores, waves and currents, in addition to the various skills possessed by seamen. The Nereides were depicted in ancient art as beautiful young maidens, sometimes running with small dolphins or fish in their hands, or else riding on the back of dolphins, hippokampoi (fish-tailed horses) and other sea creatures.

## THEMIS (Thamis)

THEMIS, daughter of Uranos (Anshar) and Gaea (Kishar), a Titaness, Zeus's advisor and was respected by all the Olympians. She was the god of eternal law, she was the second of the consorts of Zeus. Her temple was in the citadel of Athens, and she carried a pair of scales. She was another form of the Earth Mother, personifying law and order. Her festival was near the end of September. She protected the innocent and punished the guilty. She taught Apollo the technique of prophecy. She was one of the few Titans and Titanides to be given a place of honor on Olympus. She was the goddess of the collective consciousness and social order, the Law, peace, settlement of disagreements, justice and righteousness, feasts, social gatherings, oath-swearing, wisdom and prophecy, order, childbirth, courts and judges. Inventor of the arts and magic. Themis acting as Zeus' adviser. She ordered him to clothe himself in the skin of the she-goat Amalthea, the Aegis, and to use it as a breastplate during the fight against the Giants. Sometimes she was also ascribed with having been the first to suggest the Trojan War, which according to some was caused by her, to remedy the overpopulation of the earth.

## Ti.Amat (Eva)

Ti.Amat or Eva a Cro-Magnon female, daughter of Neanderthal Man and Nin.ki (Eos). With fifty heroes an expedition to the Abzu (Abdju/Abydos in Khem/Egypt) Ninurta led, with weapons were they armed. In the forests and the steppes of the Abzu, the Earthlings (Cro-Magnon) they chased. With nets they them captured, male and female to the Edin (Poseidon) they them brought (Sounds like *Planet of the Apes*). To do all manner of chores, in the orchards and in the cities, they trained them. In the Edin, the Anunnaki the Earthlings with admiration observed: Intelligence they possessed, of commands they had understanding. They took over all manner of chores; unclothed they were the tasks performing. Males and females among them were constantly mating, quick were their proliferations.

According to Edgar Cayce, the "fall of man" was an event recorded symbolically in *Genesis* where souls from heaven first descended to the Earth plane and began incarnating as humans. The "first wave" of souls to incarnate (known in the *Bible*as "the sons of men") became entrapped in the Earth plane accidentally, through their misuse of free will. These events gave rise to legends of the "fall of the angels" and to mythical beasts of the kind described in J.R.R. Tolkien's, *The Lord of the Rings.*

Edgar Cayce continues: The second wave of incarnations (known in the *Bible*as "the sons of God") consisted of those souls led by AMILIUS - the Christ soul - who voluntarily became entrapped in order to assist the "first wave" of trapped souls. They accomplished this by steering the process of physical evolution in a way that created more appropriate physical forms for these pure souls. Cayce places Amilius on Atlantis, but says that he did not physically incarnate until the human physical form had been created, at which time the *Genesis*accounts of Adam and Eve begin. Cayce sometimes used the word "Adam" to also refer to the entire group of souls which had accompanied the Christ soul into incarnating into the Earth plane and who incarnated as the five races of humanity on five separate continents at the same time.

Adam (as the Christ soul) joined his twin soul Eve in allowing himself to be seduced by materiality himself. This is symbolized by his acceptance of "the forbidden fruit." The other sons of God followed his lead and incarnated, and as a result were moved to express their materiality by interbreeding with the "daughters of men" (*Genesis :1-2) who were the homo sapiens that evolved from Cro-Magnon man. According to the Cayce material and Christian Gnosticism, their banishment from the Garden of Eden was actually a great blessing because death and reincarnation are designed to draw our attention away from materiality and the flesh, and toward our true spiritual nature.*

## Tíras

Tiras, son of Japhet (Japheth) and Adataneses. Dwelled by the sea Jabus, by the river Cura, which flows into the river Tragan (Trajan, Trojan). Founder of the tribes of Rushash, Cushni and Ongolis. Progenator of the Tiracians (Turshans, Tarushans, Thirasians, Thracians). Merenptah of Egypt, who reigned during the thirteenth century BC, provides us with what is so far our earliest reference to the people of Tiras, recording their name as the Tursha, and referring to them as invaders from the north. The Greeks were later to know them as the Tyrsenoi, whom they feared as marauding pirates. Josephus identifies them as the tribe who were known to the Romans as Thirasians, but to the Greeks as Thracians. History attests that they were indeed a most savage race, given over to a perpetual state of 'tipsy excess'. They are also described as a 'ruddy and blue-eyed people'. Tiras himself was worshipped by his descendants as the god Mars, but under his own name of Thuras. The river Athyras was also named after him, as also does the Taunrus mountain range.

## TISIPHONE

TISIPHONE, daughter of Uranos (Anshar) and Gaea (Kishar). Known as the three FURIES or FAIRIES. The three virgin goddesses: ALLECTO,

TISIPHONE, and MEGAERA. They defended mothers and the laws of blood relationship; revenge; justice against those who broke customs or taboos, social and bloodline laws. Later identified with the fairies. The angry ones; Avengers; the kindly ones; Children of Eternal Night; Daughters of Earth and Shadow. Punishers of sins, they had serpents twined in their hair and carried torches and whips. They tracked down those who wrongly shed blood, especially a mother's blood.

## Tubal

Tubal, son of Japhet (Japheth) and Adataneses. Dwelled in the land of Tuskanah by the river Pashiah. Father of the Western Russians, the Tibareni and the Tartars. The descendants of Tubal are first seen on the inscriptions of Tiglath-pileser I, King of Assyria c.1100 BC. He refers to them as the Tabali, whose original area of settlement (Tabal) was adjacent to that of Tegarama (Togarmah). Josephus recorded the names of Tubal's descendants as the Thobelites, who later became the Iberes. Their land, in Josephus' day, was known to the Romans as Iberia, and covered what is today the state of Georgia in the old USSR. From here, having crossed the Caucasus mountain range, this people migrated due northeast, where they gave their old tribal name to the river Tobol, and hence to the modern-day city of Tobolsk.

## TURIEL (Turel)

TURIEL, TUREL, TURAEL, TURYAL or "rock of God." A "fallen angel" listed in the *Book of Enoch* who followed Semyaza in the descent from Heaven to cohabit with the daughters of men.

## Ubar-Tutu (Lamech)

Ubar-Tutu by the Sumerians, son of Matushal (Methuselah) and Ednat (Edna). Ubara-Tutu by the Akkadians. Lumach or Lamech by the Hebrews.

## ULLI.KUM.MI

ULLI.KUM.MI, son of Ku.mar.bi and Nin.mah (Metis). An appeal was made to the gods to mediate the dispute, and an Assembly of the Gods was called. It was led by an *"olden god"* named Enlil, and another *"olden god"* named Ea (Enki), who was called upon to produce *"the old tablets with the words of destiny"*-some ancient records that could apparently help settle the dispute regarding the divine succession.

When these records failed to settle the dispute, Enlil advised another battle with the challenger (Ulli-kummi), but with the help of some very ancient weapons. *"Listen, ye olden gods, ye who know the olden words,"* Enlil said to his followers: *"Open ye the ancient storehouses Of the fathers and the forefathers! Bring forth the Olden Copper lance With which Heaven was seperated from Earth; And let them sever the feet of Ulli-kummi."*

## URAKABARAMEEL (Amazarak)

URAKABARAMEEL, AMAZARAK, AMENZYARAK, AMAZAROC, or AMAZAREC one of the "fallen angels" who taught men "all the sorcerers, and dividers of roots." (see Semjasa)

## Ur-Nammu (Ur-Namma)

Ur-Nammu or "The Joy of Ur" by the Anunnaki and Sumerians, giant demi-god son of demi-god Lugal.banda and Anunnaki goddess Nin.su

(Anobret). Ur-Nammu's assignment was to steer the people "away from the evil ways" of following the wrong gods.



# UTU (Apollo)

UTU or "The Bright One" or "The Shiny One" by the Anunnaki and Sumerians, son of Nannar (Phobos) and Nin.gal (Artemis). He was called BABAR or "Shining One". SAMA and SHAMASH or "The Bright One" by the Akkadians. SHEMESH by the Phoenicians. CHEMOSH by the Assyrians and Moabites. Sun God; Protector of the Poor; Judge of the Heavens and the Earth; Sublime Judge of the Anunnaki; Lord of Judgement and Prince of Light. The Lord of Righteousness. Son of the Moon god. He rode in a chariot with Sun rays streaming from his shoulders. Shown with a scepter and ring in his right hand.

The god of the Sun and of Justice, Utu goes to the underworld at the end of every day and while there decrees the fate of the dead. When Inanna's huluppu tree is infested with unwelcome guests, he ignores her appeal for aid. He aided Dumuzi in his flight from the Galla demons by helping him to transform into different creatures. He opened the "ablal" of the Underworld for Enkidu, to allow him to escape, at the behest of Enki. Through Enki's orders, he also brings water up from the earth in order to irrigate Dilmun, the garden paradise, the place where the sun rises. He is in charge of the "Land of the Living" and, in sympathy for Gilgamesh, calls off the seven weather heroes who defend that land. He brings up water from the Earth to Dilmun. Dilmun was thus situated on a mountain top but more probably Dilmun was situated in our solar system, another planet, Mars.

He rises from the mountains with rays out of his shoulders. He enters and exits the underworld through a set of gates in the mountain, guarded by scorpion-people. He travels both on foot and in a chariot, pulled by fiery mules. He upholds truth, and justice. He is a lawgiver and informs oracles.

Nergal is a corrupt aspect of his nature. He loves Gilgamesh, hates evil and instigates Gilgamesh's quest against Humbaba, guiding him and receiving prayers from him along the way. He tries to intercede to Enlil on Enkidu's behalf, but is unsuccessful. He rebukes Enkidu for cursing the Stalker and the temple prostitute for bringing him out of the wild. In Kish, the eagle and the serpent swore an oath to him that they would not overstep his limits.

The eagle broke the oath and ate the eggs of the serpent. Utu's, 'whose net is as wide as earth', told the serpent how to serve the eagle justice. The serpent lured the eagle with a bull carcass and captured him. The eagle requested to be spared and the serpent refused, saying that Utu's punishment would fall on him if he did not carry it out. He cut the eagle's wings and left him to die in a pit. The eagle prayed to Utu for mercy, and he refused to help personally, but sent Etana to help the eagle. He agreed to help Etana's infertility problem if Etana would help the eagle.

Sippar or "Eagle City" is the fourth city of the Anunnaki and the location of their spaceport in the pre-Diluvial E.din; in time placed under the command of Utu/Shamash. According to Berossus, it was there that "every available writing was concealed" to be saved from the Deluge; it was from there that the gods lifted off in rocketships to escape the avalanche of water. Rebuilt after the Deluge precisely at the same location, it served as the 'cult center' of Utu/Shamash and the seat of Sumer's equivalent of a Supreme Court. According to a text quoted by Zecharia Sitchen, after the Deluge Utu, nicknamed SHULIM, was put in charge of Mission Control Center in Ur-Shalim (later called Jerusalem). Shalem - is a divine epithet, probably for El Elyon (Enlil), from which the early name of Jerusalem, "Ur-Shalem" or "City of Shalem" probably originated. In his old age, Utu/Shamash, retired in Sippar, was considered the "god of justice and laws".

ORZMUND, ORMUZD, ORMAZD, ORMIZD, OHRMAZD, HOURMAZD, and HORMIZD or "prince of the heavens" by the Zoroastrians. THE LORD; GREAT GOD; SUPREME GOD; Illumined

DIVINE BEING; MASTER OF HEAVEN. He gave the Asha, or universal law. SPENTA MAINYU by the Persians.

He was called the archangel URIEL, AURIEL, ORIEL by the Hebrews. Prince of Knowledge and Truth; Angel of the Presence; Flame of God; Regent of the Sun; Archangel of Salvation; Heavenly Interpreter; Divine Light. The Archangel URIEL or "Fire of God" by the Hebrews, he was originally called PHANUEL. One of the leading angels in non canonical lore, and ranked variously as a seraph, cherub, regent of the sun, flame of God, angel of the presence, presider over Tartarus, archangel of salvation in *II Esdras.* In *Enoch I,* he is the angel who "watches over thunder and terror." He is supposed to be the spirit who stood at the gate of the lost Eden with the fiery sword. He was the dark angel who wrestled with Jacob at Peniel; as the destroyer of the hosts of Sennacherib *II Kings* 19:35, *II Maccabees* 15:22; as the messenger sent by God to Noah to warn him of the impending deluge *Enoch I* 10:1-3. Uriel is said to have disclosed the mysteries of the heavenly arcana to Ezra; interpreted prophecies, and led Abraham out of Ur. Known by the Hebrews as the God of Abraham called YAHWEH, JEHOEL or JEHOVAH.

The *Magus* claims that alchemy "which is of divine origin" was brought down to earth by Uriel, and that it was Uriel who gave the Cabala to man. In apocryphal and occult works Uriel has been equated or identified with NURIEL, URYAN, JEREMIEL, VRETIL, SURIEL, PURUEL, PHANUEL, JEHOEL (JEHOVAH). Called the archangel ISRAFIL by the Arabs. He rules the Element of Earth and the North (North Wind); his color is green. Uriel is the angel of teaching, insight, stability, endurance, bringer of knowledge from God. LORD OF THE TRUMPET because he will sound the trumpet at the Day of Resurrection, thus bringing the dead back to life.

To illustrate in what high esteem Uriel was held, we find him described in the second book of the *Sibylline Oracles* as one of the "immortal angels of the undying God" who, on the day of judgement, will "break the monstrous bars framed of unyielding and unbroken adamant of the brazen gates of Hades, and cast them down straightway, and bring forth to judgement all the sorrowful forms, yea, of the ghosts of the ancient Titans and of the giants, and all whom the flood overtook . . . and all these shall he bring to the judgement seat. . .and set before God's seat."

Utu the ruler over the Fourth Region, the Spaceport at Sippar, the Mission Control Center at Nippur. It was decided by the Nibiruan Council to use a plutonium bomb to wipe out the space facilities and other critical areas. In 2024 BC this was accomplished. It was the only way to stop Marduk (Lucifer) from gaining control of these facilities and going after the control of the entire Pleiades star system. The Council chose Abraham to carry the bomb stored in Sumer to the spaceport for detenation by UTU (YAHWEH), the grandson of Enlil and a commander in charge of the spaceport.

The bomb caused the destruction of all the space facilities along with the cities, Sodom and Gomorrah. The radiation from the bomb swept in the wind to the cities of Sumer, killing the inhabitants and desolating the surrounding area.

Marduk (Lucifer), son of Enki (Satan), was now in control of Nibiru (Mardek, asteroid-belt) and the planet Earth. He set about changing many things. It was at this time that women fell in stature and were considered the lesser of the species, along with children. Marduk would begin the churches, to stamp out the Goddess and the Pleiadian way of communal life which we were given by the Founders of the Universe.

Women who were leaders in the communities were stamped out by being branded as witches and burned at the stake. This process continued through the Dark Ages, and ended in the latter part of the 18th century. This was one of the most important things Marduk would have to do to achieve absolute control of mankind. Secondly, Marduk (Lucifer) would set himself up as the God among gods. Later, this would be changed to God. He would rule through fear, and this he has done down to the present day.

HENN by the Pleiadians. HEH, NEHEB by the Egyptians. A god shown as a man squatting on the ground and wearing on his head a reed, curved at the end. God of eternity, longevity, happiness.

YAHU by the Canaanites. EL HAWA, Y-HAWEH or YAHWEH by the Hebrews. He was known as "the Cruel One" to his followers. The name JEHOVAH came from the original Hebrew stem YHWH (YOD HE VAU HE), which meant *'I am that I am'* - said to be a statement made by God to Moses on Mount Sinai. However, the early Hebrew texts only refer to 'El Shadai' (Enlil - Most High) and his opposing counterpart, 'Adon' or "Lord" (Enki - Lord of the Earth). "When the Ely-on (another name of El) apportioned the nations, when he divided humankind, he fixed the boundaries of the peoples according to the number of the gods (each god controlled one nation of people); Yahweh's own portion was his people, Jacob his allotted share."

The name JEHOVAH is a late and somewhat Anglicized transliteration of Yahweh, which is itself a form of the four-consonantal Hebrew stem YHWH. Originally, these four consonants represented the four members of the heavenly family: Y represented El (Enlil) the Father; H was Asherah (Ishtar) the Mother; W corresponded to He (Henn) the Son; and H was Anath (Anat) the Daughter. Yod He Vau He (YHVH), was an androgynous deity whose transcendental presence was the infinite Spirit and whose manifest aspect was the Holy Fire or Holy Spirit.

The Bible explains that around 600 BC Jerusalem was overthrown at Jehovah's bidding and tens of thousands of Jews were taken into Babylonian captivity because their king (a descendant of King David) had erected altars in veneration of Baal (Enki/Poseidon/Satan).

It was during the course of this captivity that the Israelites weakened and finally conceded. They decided to succumb to the 'God of Wrath', and developed a new religion out of sheer fear of his retribution. It was at this time that the name of Jehovah first appeared - and this was only 500 years before the time of Jesus.

Subsequently, the Christian Church took Jehovah on board as well, calling him simply 'God'--and all the hitherto social concepts of the Adon (Enki) were totally discarded. The two religions were henceforth both faiths of fear. Even today, their followers are classified as 'God-fearing'.

In *Psalm 82,* Jehovah (Yahweh-Utu) takes his stand at the Council of El (Enlil) to deliver judgement among the elohim. We also know from the Old Testament that Yahweh, the biblical Lord, was a bitter adversary of Baal (Enki); and as Baal's influence grew among the Isralites when their king married a Canaanite princess, the prophet Elijah arranged a contest between Baal (Enki) and Yahweh (Utu) upon Mount Carmel. When Yahweh prevailed, the three hundred priests of Baal were executed. In this adversity, it was for Yahweh that the Old Testament claimed mastery over the Crest of Zaphon (the temple at Baalbek, Lebanon). The Prophet Isaiah envisioned Baal flying south toward Egypt, "riding swiftly upon a cloud, he shall descend upon Egypt; the gods of Egypt shall quail before him." In Egypt, Ba'al (Enki) became the god Ptah (Amon/Amen/Baal/Satan) and his son Bel (Marduk/Lucifer) became the god Ra (Amen-Ra).

From the *Erra Epos* text we know that Ishum (Ninurta) "to the Mount Most Supreme set his course" in his Divine Black Bird. He raised his hand and the mount was smashed. The plain by the Mount Most Supreme he then obliterated; in its forests not a tree was left standing. According to the Sumerian texts, Ninurta tried to dissuade Nergal from distroying the "sinning cities". Text continued: Erra (Nergal), emulating Ishum (Ninurta), the cities he finished off, to desolation he upheavaled them. Sodom and Gomorrah and three other cities in "the disobedient land, he obliterated." The Bible, in virtually identical words, relates that "as the sun was risen over the Earth, from the skies were those cities upheavaled, with brimstones and fire that have come from Yahweh." These verses clearly show that the god Yahweh of the Hebrews sent the god Nergal of the Sumerians to destroy the sinning cities. "And Abraham got up early in the morining, and went to where he had stood with the Lord, and gazed toward Sodom and Gomorrah, in the direction of the place of the Plain; and lo and behold - there was steaming smoke rising from the ground like the steaming smoke of a furnace." *Genesis* 19:27-28

The idea of 'life' has been traditionally connected with the name YHWH from medieval times. Its owner is presented as a living God, as contrasted with the lifeless gods of the 'heathen' polytheists: God is presented as the source and author of life (compare *1 Kings* 18; *Isaiah* 41:26-29, 44:6-20; *Jeremiah* 10:10, 14; *Genesis* 2:7; and so forth). In the *Masoretic Text* the name YHWH is vowel pointed and pronounced YAH-HO-VAH in modern Hebrew, and Yehowah in Tiberian vocalization. Traditionally in Judaism, the name is not pronounced but read as Adonai, "my Lord" during prayer, and referred to as HaShem, "the Name" at all other times. This is done out of hesitation to pronounce the name in the absence of the Temple in Jerusalem, due to its holiness. This tradition has been cited by most scholars as evidence that the Masoretes vowel pointed YHWH as they did, to indicate to the reader they are to pronounce "Adonai" in its place. While the vowel points of Adonáy and Yehowah are very similar, they are not identical. This may indicate the Masoretic vowel pointing was done in truth and not only as a Qere-Ketiv.

Halakha requires that secondary rules be placed around the primary law, to reduce the chance that the main law will be broken. As such, it is common Jewish practice to restrict the use of the word Adonai to prayer only. In conversation, many Jewish people, even when not speaking Hebrew, will call God "HaShem", which is Hebrew for "the Name" (this appears in *Leviticus* 24:11). Many Jews extend this prohibition to some of the other names listed below, and will add additional sounds to alter the pronunciation of a name when using it outside of a liturgical context, such as replacing the "h" with a "k" in names of God such as "kel" and "elokim". While other names of God in Judaism are generally restricted to use in a liturgical context, HaShem is used in more casual circumstances. HaShem is used by Orthodox Jews so as to avoid saying Adonai outside of a ritual context. For example, when some Orthodox Jews make audio recordings of prayer services, they generally substitute HaShem for Adonai; others will say Amonai. On some occasions, similar sounds are used for authenticity, as in the movie Ushpizin, where Abonai Elokenu is used throughout.

Up until the mid-twentieth century AD, however, another convention was quite common, the use of the word, Adoshem-combining the first two syllables of the word Adonai with the last syllable of the word Hashem. This convention was discouraged by Rabbi David HaLevi Segal (known as the Taz) in his commentary to the Shulchan Aruch. However, it took a few centuries for the word to fall into almost complete disuse as a name word. The rationale behind the Taz's reasoning was that it is disrespectful to combine a Name of God with another word. Despite being obsolete in most circles, it is used occasionally in conversation in place of Adonai by Jews who do not wish to say Adonai but need to specify the substitution of that particular word. It is also used when quoting from the liturgy in a non-liturgical context. For example, Shlomo Carlebach performed his prayer "Shema Yisrael" with the words Shema Yisrael Adoshem Elokeinu Adoshem Ehad instead of Shema Yisrael Adonai Eloheinu Adonai Ehad.

Rabbinical Judaism teaches that the four-letter name of God, YHWH, is forbidden to be uttered except by the High Priest in the Holy Temple on Yom Kippur. Throughout the entire Yom Kippur service, the High Priest pronounced the name YHWH "just as it is written" in each blessing he made. When the people standing in the Temple courtyard heard the name they prostrated flat on the Temple floor. The name ceased to be pronounced in Second Temple Judaism, by the 3rd century BC Passages such as: "And, behold, Boaz came from Bethlehem, and said unto the reapers, YHWH [be] with you. And they answered him, YHWH bless thee" (*Ruth* 2:4) could be interpreted to indicate that the name was still being pronounced at the time of the redaction of the Hebrew Bible in the 6th or 5th century BC. The prohibition against verbalizing the name never applied to the forms of the name within theophoric names (the prefixes yeho-, yo-, and the suffixes -yahu, -yah) and their actual pronunciation remains to be in use. Since the Temple in Jerusalem does not exist today, this name is never said in religious rituals by Jews, and the correct pronunciation is currently disputed. The historical pronunciation of YHWH is suggested by Christian scholars to be Yahweh based on some historical and linguistic evidence. Orthodox and some Conservative Jews never pronounce YHWH for any reason, especially not Yahweh, as it is connotated with (dark-times medieval) Christendom. Some religious non-Orthodox Jews are willing to pronounce it, but for educational purposes only, and never in casual conversation or in prayer. Instead of pronouncing YHWH during prayer, Jews say Adonai.

When the Masoretes added vowel pointings to the text of the Hebrew Bible around the 8th century AD, they gave the word YHWH vowels very similar to that of Adonai. Tradition has dictated this is to remind the reader to say Adonai instead. Later medieval Christian Biblical scholars took this vowel substitution for the actual spelling of YHWH and misinterpreted the name of God as Jehovah. Its use became widespread in Christendom and eventually became the name of a millenarian restorationist Christian denomination with nontrinitarian beliefs distinct from mainstream Christianity, Jehovah's Witnesses. The Jewish Publication Society translation of 1917, in online versions does use Jehovah once at Exodus 6:3, where this footnote appears in the electronic version: The Hebrew word (four Hebrew letters: HE, VAV, HE, YOD) remained in the English text untranslated; the English word 'Jehovah' was substituted for this Hebrew word. The footnote for this Hebrew word is: "The ineffable name, read Adonai, which means the Lord."

APOLLION, APOLLON, APOLLYON and APPOLYON by the Greeks, son of Zeus (Enlil) and Leto. PHOEBUS APOLLO by the Romans. God of healing, art, oracles and light. The arrows in his quiver could bring sickness and death to mortals. In *Revelation* 9:11 Apollion is the angel of the bottomless pit. In *Revelation* 20:1 he "laid hold of the dragon, that old serpent, which is the Devil, and Satan, and bound him a thousand years."

APOLLO or "Shining"; god of solar light; greatest of the gods after Zeus. Twin brother to his sister, Artemis (Ningal), his chariot was pulled by golden horses. He used the bow and lyre with skill. His arrows brought illness or death. Pictured as extremely handsome, perfectly built with fair hair. He was bi-sexual, a possible result of his worshippers overrunning and absorbing a matriarchy, such as at Delphi. He represented lawful punishment of crimes, not revenge; justified revenge. He demanded tolerance of his followers. The laurel was sacred to him. Patron of priests, God of prophecy, poetry, music, medicine, oracles, healing, reason, inspiration, magic, the arts, divination, harmony, spiritual goals gained through use of the arts, ravens, earthquakes, woodlands, and springs.

ABBADON, ABADDON or "destroyer" by the Hebrews. APOLLYON, APOLLION, APPOLYON, or "The Destroyer" in Greek. The "angel of the bottomless pit," as in *Revelation* 9:10. In '*The Thanksgiving Hymns,*' a copy of which turned up among the recently discovered *Dead Sea Scrolls*, speaks of "the Sheol of Abaddon" and of the "torrents of Belial that burst into Abaddon." Abaddon has also been identified as the angel of death and destruction, demon of the abyss, and chief of demons of the underworld hierarchy, where he is equated with Samael (Satan). In *Revelation* 9:11 Apollion is the angel of the bottomless pit.

**Anunnaki god Utu (Yahu/Yahweh)**

## YOMYAEL (Yomiel)

YOMYAEL, YOMIEL, YOMAEL or JOMAEL a "fallen angel" who mated with earth's human females and produced human giants.

## Zarpanitu (Sarpanit)

Sarpanit by the Sumerians, daughter of Enkime (Enoch I) and Edinni (Edna). Zarpanitu by the Akkadians. Ament, Amenti and Amaunet by the Egyptians. The Westerner; hidden goddess; goddess of the land of the West or the Underworld; goddess with beautiful hair. Her emblems were the hawk and the feather. Ament was represented in human female form wearing either an ostrich feather on her head or an ostrich plume and a hawk.

## ZAVEBE (Zakebel)

ZAVEBE or ZAKEBEL a "fallen angel" who mated with earth's human females and produced human giants.

## Zimodi (Zemari)

Zimodi, Zemar or Zemari, son of Canaan. Father of the Zemarites. The descendants of Zimodi were known to the Assyrians as the Simirra, and to the Egyptians as the Sumur. The name is still preserved in the modern city of Sumra, just north of Tripoli.

## Ziu.su.dra (Noah)

Utana.pish.tim by the Sumerians, son of Utu (Apollo) and human female Ashmua. Ziu.sud.ra by the Akkadians. Noe by the Hebrons. Noah by the Hebrews. Utanapishtim-King of Sumer-reigned in Shuruppak before the flood. Bergelmir by the Nordic-Germanic tribes. Noah's real father may have been El Shaddai (Enlil), which was the god who Noah worshiped.

*The Dead Sea Scrolls* - Noah's earthly father was named Lamech, but in fact Lamech was not his physical father-you can read this for yourself in the *Dead Sea Scrolls*. It says there that one day Lamech returned home from a journey which had taken more than nine months. Once home he found a baby who did not belong to his family-it had different eyes, different hair-color and a different kind of skin. Furious, Lamech went to his wife, who swore by all that was holy that she had not slept with a stranger, let alone a soldier or a son of heaven. Worried, Lamech went off to ask his father's advice. This was no other than Methuselah. He had no light to shed on the matter, and so, in his turn, went off to ask his father, Lamech's grandfather Enoch. Enoch said to his son Methuselah that Lamech should accept the boy as his own son and not be angry with his wife's womb. They had done this so that the offspring should grow into the progenitor of a new race after the flood.

*Hebrew Myths*-The *Book of Genesis*, by Robt. Graves & Raphael Patai, cr 1983, pps. 108-109 - Zillah, one of Lamech's wives, bore him a son already circumcised: a sign of God's special grace. Lamech called him Noah, finding great consolation in him. Noah's cheeks were whiter than snow and redder than a rose; his eyes like rays of the morning sun; his hair long and curly; his face aglow with light. Lamech therefore suspected him to be a bastard fathered on Zillah by one of the Watchers, or Fallen Ones; but Zillah swore that she had been faithful. They consulted their ancestor Enoch, who had lately been caught up to Heaven. His prophecy, 'In Noah's lifetime God will do a new thing on earth!', and gave Lamech his needed reassurance.

*The Book of Enoch,* Chapter 105:1-16 - After a time, my son Mathusala took a wife for his son Lamech. She became pregnant by him, and brought forth a child, the flesh of which was as white as snow, and red as a rose; the hair of whose head was white like wool, and long; and whose eyes were beautiful. When he opened them, he illuminated all the house, like the sun; the whole house abounded with light. And when he was taken from the hand of the midwife, opening also his mouth, he spoke to the Lord of righteousness. Then Lamech his father was afraid of him; and flying away came to his own father Mathusala, and said, I have begotten a son, unlike to other children. He is not human; but, resembling the offspring of the angels of heaven, is of a different nature from ours, being altogether unlike to us. His eyes are bright as the rays of the sun; his countenance glorious, and he looks not as if he belonged to me, but to the angels. I am afraid, lest something miraculous should take place on earth in his days. And now, my father, let me entreat and request you to go to our progenitor Enoch, and to learn from him the truth; for his residence is with the angels. When Mathusala heard the words of his son, he came to me at the extremities of the earth; for he had been informed that I was there: and he cried out. I heard his voice, and went to him saying, Behold, I am here, my son; since thou art come to me. He answered and said, On account of a great event have I come to thee; and on account of a sight difficult to be comprehended have I approached thee. And now, my father, hear me; for to my son Lamech a child has been born, who resembles not him; and whose nature is not like the nature of man. His color is whiter than snow; he is redder than the rose; the hair of his head is whiter than white wool; his eyes are like the rays of the sun; and when he opened them he illuminated the whole house. When also he was taken from the hand of the midwife, he opened his mouth, and blessed the Lord of heaven. His father Lamech feared, and fled to me, believing not that the child belonged to him, but that he resembled the angels of heaven. And behold I am come to thee, that thou mightiest point out to me the truth.

Then I, Enoch, answered and said, The Lord will effect a new thing upon the earth. This have I explained, and seen in a vision. I have shown thee that in the generations of Jared my father, those who were from heaven disregarded the word of the Lord. Behold they committed crimes; laid aside their class, and intermingled with women. With them also they transgressed; married with them, and begot children, who are not like spiritual beings, but creatures of flesh.

A great destruction therefore shall come upon all the earth; a deluge, a great destruction, shall take place in one year. This child which is born to you shall survive on the earth, and his three sons shall be saved with him. When all mankind who are on earth shall die, he shall be safe.

And his posterity shall beget on the earth giants, not spiritual, but carnal. Upon the earth shall a great punishment be inflicted, and it shall be washed from all corruption. Now therefore inform thy son Lamech, that he who is born is his child in truth; and he shall call his name Noah, for he shall be to you a survivor. He and his children shall be saved from the corruption which shall take place in the world; from all the sin and from all the iniquity which shall be consummated on earth in his days. Afterwards shall greater impiety take place than that which had been before consummated on the earth; for I am acquainted with the holy mysteries, which the Lord himself has discovered and explained to me; and which I have read in the tablets of heaven.

After the flood the descendants of Noah are allotted three regions. Ninurta, Enlil's foremost son, dams the mountains and drains the rivers to make Mesopotamia habitable; Enki reclaims the Nile valley. The Sinai peninsula is retained by the Anunnaki for a post-Diluvial spaceport; a control center is established on Mount Moriah (the future Jerusalem).

*Original Chaldeo-Babylonian cuneiform tablets* found at Nineveh, and now in the British Museum. Here the narrative of the second Deluge appears as an episode in the eleventh tablet, or eleventh chant of the great epic of the town of Uruk.

"I will reveal to thee, O Izdhubar, the history of my preservation--and tell to thee the decision of the gods. The town of Shurippak, a town which thou knowest, is situated on the Euphrates--it was ancient, and in it [men did not honor] the gods. [I alone, I was] their servant, to the great gods - [The gods took counsel on the appeal of] Anu - [a deluge was proposed by] Bel - [and approved by Nabon, Nergal, and] Adar.

And the god [Ea], the immutable lord, repeated this command in a dream. I listened to the decree of fate that he announced, and he said to me: "Man of Shurippak, son of Ubaratutu--thou, build a vessel and finish it [quickly]. [By a deluge] I will destroy substance and life. Cause thou to go up into the vessel the substance of all that has life. The vessel thou shall build 600 cubits shall be the measure of its height. [Launch it] thus on the ocean, and cover it with a roof." I understood, and I said to Ea, my lord: "[The vessel] that thou commandest me to build thus [when] I shall do it, young and old [shall laugh at me.]" [Ea opened his mouth and] spoke. He said to me, his servant: "[If they laugh at thee] thou shalt say to them: [shall be punished] he who has insulted me, [for the protection of the gods] is over me. . . . like to caverns . . . - . . . I will exercise my judgement on that which is on high and that which is below . . . - . . . Close the vessel . . . - . . . At a given moment that I shall cause thee to know, enter into it, thy grains, thy furniture, thy provisions, thy riches, thy men-servants, and thy maid-servants, and thy young people - the cattle of the field, and the wild beast of the plain that I will assemble - and that I will send thee, shall be kept behind thy door." Khasisatra opened his mouth and spoke; he said to Ea, his lord: "No one has made [such a] ship. On the prow I will fix. I shall see . . . and the vessel . . . the vessel thou commandest me to build [thus] which in . . ."

"On the fifth day [the two sides of the bark] were raised, In its covering fourteen in all were its rafters fourteen in all did it count above. I placed its roof, and I covered it. I embarked in it on the sixth day; I divided its floors on the seventh; I divided the interior compartments on the eight. I stopped up the chinks through which the water entered in; I visited the chinks, and added what was wanting. I poured on the exterior three times 3600 measures of asphalt, and three times 3600 measures of asphalt within. Three times 3600 men, porters, brought on their heads the chests of provisions. I kept 3600 chests for the nourishment of my family, and the mariners divided among themselves twice 3600 chests. For [provisioning] I had oxen slain; I instituted [rations] for each day. In [anticipation of the need of] drinks, of barrels, and of wine [I collected in quantity] like to the waters of a river, [of provisions] in quanity like to the dust of the earth. [To arrange them in] the chests I set my hand to. . . . of the sun . . . the vessel was completed. . . . strong and I had carried above and below the furniture of the ship. [This lading filled the two-thirds.]"

"All that I possessed I gathered together; all I possessed of silver I gathered together; all that I possessed of gold I gathered all that I possessed of the substance of life of every kind I gathered together. I made all ascend into the vessel; my servants, male and female, the cattle of the fields, the wild beasts of the plains, and the sons of the people, I made them all ascend."

"Shamash made the moment determined, and he announced it in these terms: "In the evening I will cause it to rain abundantly from heaven; enter into the vessel and close the door." The fixed moment had arrived, which he announced in these terms: "In the evening I will cause it to rain abundantly from heaven." When the evening of that day arrived, I was afraid, I entered into the vessel and shut my door. In shutting the vessel, to Buzur-shadi-rabi, the pilot, I confided this dwelling, with all that it contained."

"Mu-sheri-ina-namari rose from the foundations of heaven in a black cloud; Ramman thundered in the midst of the cloud, and Nabon and Sharru marched before; they marched, devastating the mountain and the plain: Nergal the powerful dragged chastisements after him; Adar advanced, overthrowing before him; the archangels of the abyss brought destruction, in their terrors they agitated the earth. The inundation of Ramman swelled up to the sky, and [the earth] became with luster, was changed into a desert."

"They broke . . . of the surface of the earth like . . . ; [they destroyed] the living beings of the surface of the earth. The terrible [Deluge] on men swelled up to [heaven]. The brother no longer was his brother; men no longer knew each other. In heaven the gods became afraid of the waterspout, and sought a refuge; they mounted up to the heaven of Anu. The gods were stretched out motionless, pressing one against another like dogs. Ishtar wailed like a child, the great goddess pronounced her discourse: "Here is humanity returned into mud, and this is the misfortune that I have announced in the presence of the gods, for the evil I announced the terrible [chastisement] of men who are mine. I am the mother who gave birth to men, and like to the race of fishes, there they are filling the sea; and the gods, by reason of that which the archangels of the abyss are doing, weep with me." The gods on their seats were seated in tears, and they held their lips closed, [revolving] future things."

"Six days and as many nights passed; the wind, the waterspout, and the diluvian rain were in all their strength. At the approach of the seventh day the diluvian rain grew weaker, the terrible water-spout which had assailed after the fashion of an earthquake grew calm, the sea inclined to dry up, and the wind and the water-spout came to an end. I looked at the sea, attentively observing and the whole of humanity had returned to mud; like unto sea-weeds the corpses floated. I opened the window, and the light smote on my face. I was seized with sadness; I sat down and I wept; and my tears came over my face."

"I looked at the regions bounding the sea: toward the twelve points of the horizon; not any continent. The vessel was borne above the land of Nizir, the mountain of Nizir arrested the vessel, and did not permit it to pass over; the third and fourth day the mountain of Nizir arrested the vessel, and did not permit it to pass over; the fifth and sixth day the mountain of Nizir arrested the vessel, and did not permit it to pass over. At the approach of the seventh day, I sent out and loosed a dove. The dove went, turned, and found no place to light on, and it came back. I sent out and loosed a swallow; the swallow went, turned, and found no place to light on, and it came back. I sent out and loosed a raven; the raven went and saw the corpses on the waters; it ate, rested, turned, and came not back."

"I then sent out (what was in the vessel) toward the four winds, and I offered a sacrifice. I raised the pile of my burnt offering on the peak of the mountain; seven by seven I disposed the measured vases,--and beneath I spread rushes, cedar, and juniper-wood. The gods were seized with desire of it the gods were seized with a benevolent desire of it; and the gods assembled like flies above the master of the sacrifice. From afar, in approaching, the great goddess raised the great zones that Anu has made for their glory (the gods). These gods, luminous crystal before me, I will never leave them; in that day I prayed that I might never leave them. "Let the gods come to my sacrificial pile! but never may Bel come to my sacrificial pile! for he did not master himself, and he has made the water-spout for the Deluge, and he has numbered my men for the pit."

"From far, in drawing near, Bel saw the vessel, and Bel stopped; he was filled with anger against the gods and the celestial archangels: "No one shall come out alive! No man shall be preserved from the abyss!" Adar opened his mouth and said; he said to the warrior Bel: "What other than Ea should have formed this resolution? for Ea possesses knowledge, and [he foresees] all." Ea opened his mouth and spake; he said to the warrior Bel: "O thou, herald of the gods, warrior, as thou didst not master thyself, thou hast made the water-spout of the Deluge. Let the sinner carry the weight of his sins, the blasphemer the weight of his blasphemy. Please thyself with this good pleasure, and it shall never be infringed; faith in it never [shall be violated]. Instead of thy making a new deluge, let lions appear and reduce the number of men; instead of thy making a new deluge, let hyenas appear and reduce the number of men; instead of thy making a new deluge, let there be famine, and let the earth be [devastated]; instead of thy making a new deluge, let Dibbara appear, and let men be [mown down]. I have not revealed the decision of the great gods; it is Khasisatra who interpreted a dream and comprehended what the gods had decided."

"Then, when his resolve was arrested, Bel entered into the vessel. He took my hand and made me rise. He made my wife rise, and made her place herself at my side. He turned around us and stopped short; he approached our group. "Until now Khasisatra has made part of perishable humanity; but lo, now Khasisatra and his wife are going to be carried away to live like the gods, and Khasisatra will reside afar at the mouth of the rivers." They carried me away, and established me in a remote place at the mouth of the streams."

In the Chaldean legends the god Ea (Enki) ordered Khasisatra to inscribe the divine learning, and the principles of all sciences, on tables of terra-cotta, and bury them, before the Deluge, "in the City of the Sun at Sippara."

Berosus, in his version of the Chaldean flood, says: "The deity, Chronos (Annu), appeared to Xisuthros in a vision, and warned him that, upon the 15th day of the month Doesius, there would be a flood by which mankind would be destroyed. He therefore enjoined him to write a history of the beginning, procedure, and conclusion of all things, and to bury it in the City of the Sun at Sippara, and to build a vessel," etc.

**William Ashley Hinson was born in Plymouth, North Carolina and grew up in the Blue Ridge Mountains of Virginia and the Piedmont area**

**of North Carolina. He has lived in the Murrells Inlet area of South Carolina since 2004 with his wife and three children. William received his Bachelor's Degree from High Point University. He has taught history in the public schools for ten years. He has published numerous family history books over the years and he is the author of the non-fiction book – *Discovering Ancient Giants.***

42987837R00226

Printed in Poland
by Amazon Fulfillment
Poland Sp. z o.o., Wrocław